The Ancient Comme
on Plato and Aristotl

Ancient Philosophies

This series provides fresh and engaging new introductions to the major schools of philosophy of antiquity. Designed for students of philosophy and classics, the books offer clear and rigorous presentation of core ideas and lay the foundation for a thorough understanding of their subjects. Primary texts are handled in translation and the readers are provided with useful glossaries, chronologies and guides to the primary source material.

Published

The Ancient Commentators on Plato and Aristotle
Miira Tuominen

Ancient Scepticism
Harald Thorsrud

Cynics
William Desmond

Neoplatonism
Pauliina Remes

Presocratics
James Warren

Stoicism
John Sellars

Forthcoming

Aristotle
Vasilis Politis

Classical Islamic Philosophy
Deborah Black

Confucianism
Paul Goldin

Epicureanism
Tim O'Keefe

Indian Buddhist Philosophy
Amber Carpenter

Plato
Andrew Mason

Socrates
Mark McPherran

The Ancient Commentators
on Plato and Aristotle

Miira Tuominen

ACUMEN

First published in 2009 by Acumen

Acumen Publishing Limited
Stocksfield Hall
Stocksfield
NE43 7TN
www.acumenpublishing.co.uk

ISBN: 978-1-84465-162-7 (hardcover)
ISBN: 978-1-84465-163-4 (paperback)

British Library Cataloguing-in-Publication Data
A catalogue record for this book is available
from the British Library.

Typeset in Minion.
Printed in the UK by the MPG Books Group.

Contents

Acknowledgements

This volume was mainly written during the time in which I had the privilege of concentrating on a book like this at the Helsinki Collegium for Advanced Studies. Towards the end of this project I had already started my job at the University of Jyväskylä. I would like to thank my colleagues and superiors at both places.

When it comes to the content of the book, I would first like to express my gratitude to the anonymous readers from whom I received constructive and insightful suggestions. I am also deeply grateful to Monte Johnson, who agreed to read the whole manuscript. All these comments greatly benefited the resulting book. Individual chapters were read by Eyjólfur Emilsson, Sara Heinämaa, Simo Knuuttila and Pauliina Remes, and I would like to thank them all warmly. I would also like to express my gratitude to Richard Sorabji for encouraging my work on the commentators.

At Acumen, Steven Gerrard and Kate Williams have been most helpful and wonderfully patient to work with. I would also like to thank my language editor Robert Whiting, whose comments I enjoyed very much. Some changes have been made after he commented on the manuscript. All shortcomings in content and style are mine only.

On a more personal note, thank you Teemu for our discussions and simply for being there for me. Finally, I had just started writing this book when my father passed away. Hence it is perhaps one example of the consolation of philosophy.

Abbreviations

Agathias
    Hist. = *The Histories*

Alexander of Aphrodisias (Alex.Aphr.)
    de An. = *De anima* (in CAG Suppl. II 1)
    Fat. = *De fato* (in CAG Suppl. II.1)
    in APr. = Commentary on Aristotle's *Prior Analytics* (in CAG II 1)
    in Metaph. = Commentary on Aristotle's *Metaphysics* (in CAG I)
    in Mete. = Commentary on Aristotle's *Meteorology* (in CAG III 2)
    Quaest. = *Quaestiones* (in CAG Suppl. II 2)
    in Sens. = Commentary on Aristotle's *De sensu* (in CAG III 1)
    in Top. = Commentary on Aristotle's *Topics* (in CAG II 2)

Ammonius (Ammon.)
    in APr. = Commentary on Aristotle's *Prior Analytics* (in CAG IV 6)
    in Cat. = Commentary on Aristotle's *Categories* (in CAG IV 4)
    in Isag. = Commentary on Porphyry's *Isagoge* (in CAG IV 3)

Anonymous
    in Cat. = Commentary on Aristotle's *Categories* (in CAG XXIII 2)

Aristotle (Arist.)
    de An. = *De anima*
    APo. = *Analytica Posteriora* (*Posterior Analytics*)
    APr. = *Analytica Priora* (*Prior Analytics*)
    Cael. = *De caelo*
    Cat. = *Categoriae* (*Categories*)
    EN = *Ethica Nicomachea* (*Nicomachean Ethics*)

Metaph. = *Metaphysica* (*Metaphysics*)
Mete. = *Meteorologica* (*Meteorology*)
PA = *De partibus animalium* (*Parts of Animals*)
Ph. = *Physica* (*Physics*)
Pol. = *Politica* (*Politics*)
SE = *Sophistici elenchi* (*Sophistical Refutations*)
Sens. = *De sensu*
Top. = *Topica* (*Topics*)

Arrian (Arr.)
    Epict. = *Epicteti Dissertationes*

Asclepius (Ascl.)
    in Metaph. = Commentary on Aristotle's *Metaphysics* (in CAG VI 2)

Aspasius (Asp.)
    in EN = Commentary on Aristotle's *Nicomachean Ethics* (in CAG XIX 1)

Boethius
    in Cat. = Commentary on Aristotle's *Categories*
    in Isag. = Commentary on Porphyry's *Isagoge*

CAG = *Commentaria in Aristotelem Graeca*

Cicero (Cic.)
    Fin. = *De finibus*

CLCAG = *Corpus Latinorum commentarium in Aristotelem Graecorum*

Dexippus
    in Cat. = Commentary on Aristotle's *Categories* (in CAG IV 2)

Diogenes Laertius (D.L.)

Elias/David
    in Cat. = Commentary on Aristotle's *Categories* (in CAG XVIII 1)
    in Isag. = Commentary on Porphyry's *Isagoge* (in CAG XVIII 1)

Erastius *et al.*
    in EN = Commentary on Aristotle's *Nicomachean Ethics* (in CAG XX)

Galen
    Consuet. = Peri ethōn, *Scripta minora*, ed. Müller 1891

Libanius (Lib.)
    Ep. = *Epistulae*

Marinus (Marin.)
  Procl. = *Vita Procli*

Olympiodorus (Olymp.)
  in Cat. = Commentary on Aristotle's *Categories* (in CAG XII 1)
  in Grg. = Commentary on Plato's *Gorgias*
  in Mete. = Commentary on Aristotle's *Meteorology* (in CAG XII 2)

Philodemus (Phld.)
  Acad.Hist. = *History of the Academy*

Philoponus (Phlp.)
  in de An. = Commentary on Aristotle's *De anima* (in CAG XV)
  in APo. = Commentary on Aristotle's *Posterior Analytics* (in CAG XIII 3)
  in APr. = Commentary on Aristotle's *Prior Analytics* (in CAG XIII 2)
  in Ph. = Commentary on Aristotle's *Physics* (in CAG XVI, XVII)

Plato (Pl.)
  Tht. = *Theaetetus*
  Ti. = *Timaeus*

Plotinus (Plot.)
  Enn. = *Enneads*

Plutarch (Plu.)
  Sull. = *Sulla*
  Comm. not. = *De communibus notitiis adversus Stoicos*

Porphyry (Porph.)
  in Cat. = Commentary on Aristotle's *Categories* (in CAG IV 1)
  in Harm. = Commentary on Ptolemy's *Harmonics*, ed. Düring 1932
  Isag. = *Isagoge* (in CAG IV 1)
  Plot. = *Life of Plotinus*

Proclus (Procl.)
  in Metaph. = Commentary on Aristotle's *Metaphysics*
  in Parm. = Commentary on Plato's *Parmenides*, ed. Cousin 1864
  in Ti. = Commentary on Plato's *Timaeus*

Pseudo-Philoponus (ps.-Phlp.)
  in de An. = Commentary on Aristotle's *De anima* (in CAG XV)

Pseudo-Simplicius (ps.-Simp.)
  in de An. = Commentary on Aristotle's *De anima* (in CAG XI)

Sextus Empiricus (S.E.)
> *Math.* = *adversus Mathematicos* (*Against the Mathematicians*)
> *Pyr.* = *Purrōneioi hupotupōseis* (*Outlines of Pyrrhonism*)

Simplicius (Simp.)
> *in Cat.* = Commentary on Aristotle's *Categories* (in CAG VIII)
> *in Cael.* = Commentary on Aristotle's *De caelo* (in CAG VII)
> *in Epict.* = Commentary on Epictetus' *Handbook*, ed. Hadot 1996
> *in Ph.* = Commentary on Aristotle's *Physics* (in CAG IX & X)

Strabo (Str.)

Syrianus (Syrian.)
> *in Metaph.* = Commentary on Aristotle's *Metaphysics* (in CAG VI 1)

Themistius (Them.)
> *in APo.* = Paraphrasis on Aristotle's *Posterior Analytics* (in CAG V 1)
> *in APr.* = Paraphrasis on Aristotle's *Prior Analytics* (in CAG XXIII 3)
> *in de An.* = Paraphrasis on Aristotle's *De anima* (in CAG V 3)
> *Or.* = *Orationes*
> *in Phys.* = Paraphrasis on Aristotle's *Physics* (in CAG V 2)

Chronology

*c.*234–305	Porphyry: Plotinus' student and a commentator
*c.*240–325	Iamblichus
c.304	Iamblichus, having perhaps been a student of Porphyry, returns to Syria to found a school
*c.*320	Dexippus, follower of Iamblichus, dies
*c.*317–88	Themistius: in Constantinople
Late 300s/ early 400s	Plutarch of Athens
411–85	Proclus: born in Constantinople, studies in Alexandria
431	Proclus comes to Athens from Alexandria to study under Plutarch of Athens and Syrianus. Syrianus succeeds Plutarch of Athens as head of Plato's Academy
435/45–517/26	Ammonius, in Alexandria: his father is Hermeias
*c.*480–524/5	Boethius, in Rome, a Christian
Late 400s	Hermeias and Ammonius (his son) lead the Alexandrian school; John Philoponus (a Christian) and Simplicius study there with Ammonius
529–31	Justinian's edicts cause closure of the Athenian Platonic school
531	Simplicius continues working, first in Persia, then in an uncertain location. In Alexandria, Olympiodorus follows Ammonius as the head of the Alexandrian school
500s onwards	The first translations and commentaries are made by Syrians on Aristotle's *Categories*
700s–900s	Teaching continues in the Byzantine world, even though real universities do not yet exist. Arabic philosophy grows and after 750s begins an active translation movement of Greek works into Arabic, often via Syriac. *Aristotle's Theology*, a paraphrase of some of Plotinus' *Enneads* is influential and connected to the works of Aristotle.
*c.*730–	Byzantine commentaries on Aristotle. The only commentary on Plato from that period is George Pachymeres' supplement to Proclus on the last sections of the *Parmenides*
980–1037	Ibn Sīnā (Avicenna): writes extensive commentaries on Aristotle's works
1000s	Michael Psellos comments on and paraphrases Aristotle's *Organon*
Early 1100s	Michael of Ephesus and Eustratius of Nicaea work on a project of commenting on neglected works by Aristotle initiated by princess Anna Komnene. Michael of Ephesus writes several commentaries on Aristotle's biological works (e.g. *De partibus animalium* and *Parva naturalia*) and on the *Nicomachean Ethics*. Eustratius writes on *Posterior Analytics* Book II and the *Nicomachean Ethics*
1126–98	Ibn Rushd (Averroes): continues commenting on Aristotle, writing commentaries of three different lengths (short, intermediate, long)

ONE

Introduction

A starting-point

What is a commentary?

What distinguishes a philosophical commentary from all other philosophical treatises? Can we pinpoint a set of presuppositions that characterize a commentary? In the colloquial sense, commenting refers to presenting opinions on or reacting to something, be it something scientific or artistic, written or spoken, advanced or ordinary. If this were all there was to commenting, it would be virtually impossible to find any philosophical works that are not commentaries. Thus philosophical commenting – or perhaps all commenting in texts – requires something more than making comments in ordinary speech. Yet some conceptual link remains between the two activities. At the least, in both cases it is vital that comments are presented *about* something: commenting has an object. However, this is not a sufficient criterion for identifying commentaries. In a sense, any reasonable philosophical activity is about something, whether the object is a literary product (a written or oral text) or reality.

A closer description of a commentary can be arrived at if we require that the object of a commentary be a text, written or oral. Let us call such a text "the object text" of a commentary. Commentaries

in this sense can proceed more loosely if only parts of a text are commented on and others are not, and the commentary does not aim
at anything like a complete coverage of the text. Such works can be
distinguished from linear or formal commentaries, which follow the
object text line by line and cover most of its contents. Even though
there are interpretive works on oral texts that can be characterized
as commentaries, the more extensive linear commentaries require
that the culture in which they are produced be sufficiently literate
(see also Baltussen 2007). This is also true of the ancient commentaries (*exēgēsis, hupomnēma*).[1] Some less comprehensive and non-
linear commentaries were written quite soon after the death of Plato
(Plato's pupil Crantor apparently wrote such a commentary on the
Timaeus; Procl. *in Ti.* 1.76,1–2), but we have to wait until the first
century BCE before more extensive linear commentaries emerge.
Probably the earliest such commentary is an anonymous commentary on Plato's *Theaetetus* (ed. Bastiniani & Sedley 1995).[2] In the first
century BCE, we also find the first linear commentaries on Aristotle's
works. Before the linear philosophical commentaries that we are
concerned with in this book, there was an exegetical tradition of
interpreting religious statements such as the oracle statements (see
e.g. Betegh 2004: 46; Baltussen 2004). In philosophy too, texts closely
resembling formal commentaries are found quite early; a famous
instance is the section in Plato's *Protagoras* (339a–348c) containing
an interpretation of Simonides' poem. Even though this section has
humorous or ironical undertones, it must be noted that these can
only produce their effect if they sufficiently resemble a real instance
of such an interpretive activity.[3]

As regards commentaries in general, a typical prerequisite is that
the object – written or oral text, or an artistic piece – is important or
valuable. Further, commentaries are often written because the object
is considered difficult to understand. The implicit purpose of a commentary, then, is to convey the valuable text, oral material or artwork
to an audience who might otherwise be deprived of the information
it provides, its artistic value or the skill of expression with which the
piece has been produced, or whatever it might be that the difficult
surface of the commented object conceals. A similar idea can also

be found in the ancient commentaries. When the commentaries dominated the philosophical scene, special value was attributed to a particular set of (philosophical) texts. The most important such texts were works of Plato and Aristotle, and often other commentaries already written about them.

The supposition that the content of the object text is not accessible because of its obscurity played a role in the ancient commentators' work. With respect to Aristotle's treatises, obscurity was even used as an argument for authenticity (see e.g. Olymp. *in Mete.* 4,16–18, in Sorabji 2004: vol. 2, 46). Olympiodorus responds to those who had claimed that the *Meteorologica* could not have been written by Aristotle because of its clarity. Olympiodorus' argument is that this appearance is false: in fact there are many unclear statements in the *Meteorologica* and hence the treatise must be Aristotle's. Sometimes a definite function was attributed to the obscurity of the sources. According to Ammonius, Aristotle employs obscurity because for intelligent students it offers an opportunity to stretch their minds even further. By contrast, empty minds will feel aversion when encountering the texts and will not even attempt to understand them (Ammon. *in Cat.* 7,7–14, in Sorabji 2004: vol. 2, 54–5). Sometimes such a double function of being secretive to some and inspiring to others was also assigned to poetry and myths (Olymp. *in Grg.* 238,20–239,11, in Sorabji 2004: vol. 2, 52–3).

However, the ancient commentators did not merely aim to clarify the hidden meaning of existent texts. In this sense, we could say that they were not merely commentators. This is important to keep in mind, since describing someone as "a commentator" might suggest that the author is writing just about a text and not about how things really are at all. Sometimes this could even be taken in the sense that commentators are to be distinguished from real philosophers.[4] However, in the case of the ancient commentators, the dichotomy does not hold. The ancient commentators did not disregard the question of how things really are. They were interested in the further objective of attaining the truth through their activity of interpreting the classical masters and started from the idea – which is not a completely detrimental one – that in order to attain the truth they needed to consider how previous philosophers had answered the questions they were concerned with. To some extent, this objective can be found in Aristotle and his dialectical accounts of predecessors' theories at the beginning of treatises such as the *De anima* and the *Metaphysics*.[5] The fact that the ancient commentators started from object texts did set some limitations on their activity, but this does not mean that they were not philosophers. During the period that we are concerned with, roughly 500 years from the first to the sixth century CE, philosophy was written in the commentaries (see also Baltussen 2007).

In scholarly research in the earlier parts of the twentieth century, the late ancient commentators on Plato and Aristotle were used mainly as sources of information concerning the masters they comment on: they were read as secondary sources for Plato and Aristotle. Since the late 1980s, largely thanks to Richard Sorabji's translation project and the work done by scholars such as Ilsetraut Hadot, it has become increasingly acknowledged that the commentaries are philosophically important sources as such and that the commentators, even though they work in the Platonist–Aristotelian framework, are critical, original and innovative when it comes to this tradition. In this volume, we are concerned with the commentators as philosophers and their works as philosophical sources, not as secondary sources to uncover the "hidden meaning" in Plato or Aristotle.

The Hellenistic period

By the first century CE writing commentaries had become a well-developed and self-conscious practice. One traditional explanation of the emergence of the linear and comprehensive commentaries is related to what happened to the object texts, especially Aristotle's specialized works. In an old story related by Strabo and Plutarch (Str. 13.1.54, 13.608; Plu. *Sull.* 26), Aristotle's books disappeared soon after his death. They remained hidden in a cellar in Scepsis (being eaten by worms) until, in the first century BCE, they were restored by a man called Apellicon, whose philosophical competence the sources find dubious. Another main figure in this piece of narrative is Andronicus of Rhodes, who is reported to have produced a complete edition of Aristotle's works in the first part of the first century BCE on the basis of Apellicon's initial work (Plu. *Sull.* 26; Porph. *Plot.* 24). Doubts have been raised concerning the reliability of this story (e.g. Frede 1999: 773–6; Gottschalk 1990) and many argue that not only is Apellicon's role dubious, but also that of Andronicus has been seriously overstated (e.g. Frede 1999: 772–6; Barnes 1997; cf. Fazzo 2004).

The dramatic details of the story are fantasy, but it remains a fact that in the time between Aristotle's death (322 BCE) and the first century BCE we do not hear of explicit discussions on Aristotle's so-called esoteric works. Esoteric works are the more specialized philosophical treatises, whereas the works published for wider audiences are called "exoteric".[6] The exoteric works most probably influenced the Hellenistic schools. For example, some scholars have argued that Lucretius attacks not the Stoics but the Platonic–Aristotelian view as it is represented in Aristotle's lost exoteric treatise *On Philosophy* (Furley 1980; see also Sedley 1998a). Other important exoteric works by Aristotle are called *Eudemus*, *Protrepticus* (Exhortation to philosophy) and *On Philosophy*. The exoteric works were also known to Cicero and to his contemporaries, but they were not included in the collection attributed to Andronicus (see Moraux 1973: 63). As for Cicero, he refers to the distinction between the exoteric works (he uses this Greek term) and those works that are more specialized (*Fin.* 5.11–12). Of the more specialized works he mentions Aristotle's studies on political life, including the collections of the constitutions of city-states, which he attributes to Theophrastus, and the *Nicomachean Ethics* (which Cicero also claims was not written by Aristotle but by his son Nicomachus, to whom the treatise is dedicated). The commentators knew the exoteric works as well. Simplicius, for example, refers to them occasionally (see e.g. *in Cael.* 289,1–15 for a reference to *On Philosophy*) and Alexander of Aphrodisias quotes the *Protrepticus* in his commentary on the *Topics* (149,9–17).[7]

The legend of hidden texts and their restoration may also tell us that Aristotle's esoteric works were not easily found on the market during the period from his death to the publication of the edition attributed to Andronicus (Fazzo 2004: 4 n.11). It has been suggested that the diminished interest in Aristotle's esoteric works during this period is due to the fact that the popularity and readability of the exoteric works greatly surpasses that of the much more difficult and demanding esoteric ones containing logical analysis and complex dialectical argument strategies (Johnson n.d.). Further, as Cicero also notes (*Fin.* 5.12), the more specialized esoteric works were "in the form of a notebook", which means that their literary quality was not as polished as that of the exoteric works. Ironically, the course of history has deprived us of direct access to almost all of the exoteric works, whereas the esoteric ones come down to us in a manuscript tradition that most probably is uninterrupted from Aristotle's time, and codified or canonized in the first century BCE collections.

Further, many important philosophical trends after Aristotle's death up to the first century BCE were non-Aristotelian and non-Platonic. The Peripatetic school stagnated within a couple of generations after Aristotle. Plato's Academy remained alive until the first century BCE but turned sceptical fairly soon after Plato's death, with Arcesilaus (*c.*315–241 BCE) as head of the school.[8] The main Hellenistic philosophical schools understood the general aims of philosophy in a way that diverges from that adopted by Plato and Aristotle.[9] The Sceptics typically argued *ad hominem* in the sense that they wanted to show that if the "dogmatic" authors accepted their aims and principles, inner contradictions should lead to Scepticism rather than to Stoicism or Epicureanism. How exactly the Hellenistic approach differed from the Platonic–Aristotelian one is a complex question, and for the present only some very general differences can be pointed out.

Most importantly, during the Hellenistic period – just after Alexander the Great and Aristotle had died – a new meta-philosophical position started to dominate. According to this general outlook, endorsed in Stoicism and Epicureanism, philosophy has a therapeutic end and its task is to help us attain peace of mind. From such a point of view, discussions concerning the nature of the universe or the possibility of knowledge, for example, must be subordinated to an ethical end: they are studied to make people's lives better. Such therapeutically motivated philosophy also was much less academic than the commentary tradition that followed, and much less scientific than the philosophy in the Lyceum (Aristotle's school). The Cynics and Cyrenaics belonged to what can be called a "performative strand" of ancient ethics: rather than writing lengthy treatises or teaching in class about ethics, these philosophers took ethics into live situations and underlined their point of view by unconventional or socially unacceptable behaviour. A similar trend was important in early Stoicism but diminished later. Yet even a late Stoic, Epictetus (first to second century CE), a Greek living in Rome, expresses a dismissive attitude towards bookish philosophy. One of his discussions reported by Arrian is called "for those who study philosophers just in order to talk about them" (Arr. *Epict.* II 19). In any case, at some point what can be referred to as the Hellenistic approach to philosophy started to yield and give way to a new kind of interest in both Plato and Aristotle. This was the kind of approach that we know from the commentaries; philosophers started to write works that cover most of one treatise and proceed in a linear manner through its main contents.

In addition to its historical dubiousness, a misleading aspect of the old story about Aristotle's texts is that it probably gets the causal relations wrong. The story supposes that Aristotle's texts were discovered and that this discovery, aided by editorial activity and publication, caused a revival of Aristotelian philosophy. It is in fact much more likely that the situation was quite the opposite: some sort of "revival" of Plato and Aristotle was underway and this same development caused new interest in the *texts* of Plato and Aristotle (see also Frede 1999: 772–6). However, identifying this problem in the old story raises new questions: why did this revival take place; why did philosophers feel that they would like to investigate a different attitude towards their discipline; or, why did they feel that they wanted to go back to old philosophical texts rather than continue in the Hellenistic framework where philosophy has a pragmatic therapeutic end?

This question is parallel to the puzzle of why the philosophers working after Aristotle's death in the Stoa and Epicurus' Garden, for example, started to employ different approaches from those that were familiar from Plato's Academy and Aristotle's Lyceum. Why did they start to conceive philosophy as being therapeutic? Why did they abandon the notion of form and turn to a more materialistic worldview? There are no easy answers to these questions and it may be the case that, on the basis of the existing evidence, we cannot say anything very definite about why the commentators started to write commentaries either. But we may in any case raise the question of why it is that sometimes the attention of philosophers turns to other questions and the basic methodological and meta-philosophical assumptions change as well. Evidently it typically is *not* the case that the problems that have been engaging the attention of philosophers have found a solution.

Some attempts at establishing general patterns of the dynamics of the history of philosophy have been made, but the developments of thought seem to remain impervious to valid rational generalization. Yet it is an interesting fact about our history that the works of Plato and Aristotle have been making repeated comebacks. One example concerns Aristotle's works and how they flooded the universities of western Europe, particularly in Paris, during the first half of the thirteenth century. In the 1210s it was forbidden to teach Aristotle's works at the University of Paris; by the 1250s, they had become obligatory. As to the commentaries themselves, a parallel could be the fact already alluded to that for some two decades now there has been a "revival" of interest in the ancient commentaries on Plato and Aristotle. The edition series (*Commentaria in Aristotelem Graeca*) was published a hundred years ago. Why did no one start a project to translate it into German or English right away? Why was no one asked to write an introduction to the commentators' philosophy a hundred years ago?

Commentators as philosophers

As indicated, in this book we are concerned with the group of authors called "commentators" *as philosophers*. Even though these authors work in a tradition in which some tools of analysis (such as the notion of form) come from earlier philosophers, it is clear that our authors do not merely aim to clarify what someone wrote several centuries earlier; rather, their aim is to solve philosophical problems and often to question important notions and tenets in their tradition (perhaps the most extensive reserve of critical arguments is found in Philoponus and his attack on Aristotelian physics and cosmology). The commentators clearly are philosophers, and this book concentrates on introducing the reader to the *philosophy* of the commentators.

When talking about the philosophy of the commentators, we need to bear in mind that this does not mean that there is one philosophy that all commentators share. The commentators do share tendencies, agreements and disagreements with each other, but they do not form a coherent philosophical school, even in the sense of ancient philosophical schools that were not obsessed with orthodoxy. Rather than a set of beliefs, tenets or teaching, the commentators have common practices, and sometimes also philosophical views. Yet we can talk about the philosophy of the commentators, since they clearly do philosophy.

Do the common practices of the commentators, then, include a common methodology? Not quite. In recent scholarship on the commentators no unanimity has been reached about whether there even was a method they followed – partly because the commentators' own remarks on their methodology are sparse. Further, when reading such commentaries as Aspasius on the *Nicomachean Ethics* and Simplicius on *Physics* one cannot help but note that there are rather significant technical differences in how the authors separate the lines of the object text from what they themselves say and to what extent there is a fixed order in which the authors raise some issues of interpretation. In general, it can be said that in addition to the degree to which the commentaries are systematic in such technical procedures as outlining lemmata from the object text, the later commentators are also more outspoken when it comes to written statements about their own methodology.

One important dividing line among the group of philosophers known as "ancient commentators" is whether they are Platonists or

Aristotelians. What it means to be a Platonist and what it means to be an Aristotelian is not an altogether simple matter.[10] In the case of the commentators, however, it is relatively easy to distinguish the main members of these groups. Alexander of Aphrodisias, for example, is an official Aristotelian, both in the sense of holding an Aristotelian chair of philosophy in Athens (see below, § "Alexander of Aphrodisias") and in the sense of defending Aristotelian views against criticism from other schools, often from the Stoics. Aspasius, the earliest commentator from whom a considerable part of a commentary has been preserved, also clarifies, expands and argues for genuinely Aristotelian views. Platonists include authors such as Porphyry, Iamblichus, Simplicius and Philoponus (not to mention Proclus, who is more in the background in this book). Their Platonism is reflected, for example, in the postulation of transcendent Platonic forms in addition to the Aristotelian immanent ones. They also often defend the idea of a cosmic demiurge or a divine artificer against an Aristotelian eternal and uncreated cosmos. A more problematic case with respect to Platonism and Aristotelianism is Themistius, from whom the most typical signs of Platonism are absent but who also lacks the tendency to defend Aristotle.

However, the Platonic commentators were not hostile towards Aristotle either. Rather, they often argued that, despite the initial appearance to the contrary, Plato and Aristotle are in harmony on some basic philosophical issues. As George Karamanolis (2006) has shown, this thesis was strong in the Platonic tradition (so-called middle Platonism) already before Porphyry, even though Numenius and Atticus did not accept it, and nor did Plotinus. After Porphyry it became widespread. Some scholars have suggested that the harmony thesis is hopelessly apologetic, a "perfectly crazy position" that nonetheless proved philosophically fruitful (Sorabji 1990: 5; see also Sorabji 2004). Others have argued for a new version of the thesis that Aristotle was a Platonist (see Gerson 2005a). In this book we shall accept none of these claims as a general guiding principle; rather, we shall consider what the commentators claim and how they perceive harmonies and discrepancies between Plato and Aristotle. We shall see that even though the thesis of harmony is fairly common among

Platonic commentators, although by no means uniform,[11] they are also innovative and critical in important respects.

Sorabji has suggested (2004: vol. 1, 14–15) that one important function of the harmony thesis was that it worked as a safety measure for pagan authors against Christians: while the Christians could try to dismiss the classical masters, Plato and Aristotle, by pointing out that they cannot even agree on the very central points, the commentators could defend them (and, derivatively, themselves) by claiming that the contradictions are merely apparent and do not pertain to the doctrines themselves. Sorabji's suggestion is intriguing but does not exhaust the meaning of the harmony thesis in the commentaries. On many occasions, coherence is not just a disguise under which traditional pagan philosophy can be done in a Christian environment. Rather, it seems that the harmony thesis is needed to account for the possibility that both Plato and Aristotle *could* have expressed the truth.

All the Platonic commentators that we discuss here are writing after Plotinus, who lived in Rome, 205–70 CE. Today we do not see Plotinus as a commentator, but he himself sometimes describes himself as one. When introducing his three hierarchical levels of reality, Plotinus describes himself as a commentator on Plato (*Enn.* 5.1.8). The later commentators also include Plotinus in the group of commentators (e.g. Simp. *in Cat.* 2,3–5; *in Ph.* 706,25–8, 769,6ff., 791,27; ps.-Phlp. *in de An.* 535,8–12; see also Sorabji 2004: 4). During the eighteenth century, encyclopaedists started to call the later developments in Platonism in Plotinus and the Platonic commentaries "Neoplatonism".[12] Plotinus and his followers certainly did not see themselves as Neoplatonists but as Platonists. However, since "Platonism" is too wide a term to pick out any sufficiently limited group of philosophers, the term "Neoplatonism" will be used in this book to serve the pragmatic purpose of referring to the Platonism after Plotinus (from the third to the sixth century CE) in which the general supposition of a hierarchical reality is accepted. This kind of hierarchy did not come to Platonism only with Plotinus; there were earlier developments in that direction too (see e.g. Numenius in Karamanolis 2006: 140–44).

The levels in the hierarchical reality are called "hypostases" (Greek *hupostasis*). In Plotinus, soul and intellect are not only psychological units or capacities, but they also carry a strong metaphysical status as distinct realms of being. The activity of the highest principle, the One, has a mode of being of its own. The self-sufficient being of the One produces as external overflow the hypostasis Intellect in which being becomes diversified according to the intelligible forms that are understood in an eternal act of intellectual apprehension. The Intellect's activity also has an external by-product: the level of Soul, where forms are connected with and organize some material. The mode of being characteristic for Intellect cannot be realized on this level, since the realization of forms in a spatiotemporal frame entails restrictions as to the extent to which forms can be realized (e.g. there is no perfect beauty in the sensible world).

The doctrinal unity of late ancient Platonism after Plotinus, that is, what is called "Neoplatonism", has been challenged by authors such as Lloyd Gerson (2005b). He argues that it is not at all clear that there are doctrines that distinguish collectively those philosophers writing between the third and the sixth centuries CE from the members of the Old Academy, such as Speusippus and Xenocrates.[13] Hence "Neoplatonism" should not be taken to imply a perfect unity of doctrine or complete exclusiveness.

It is important to note that even though the harmony thesis has until now been referred to as a principle that the Platonic (or Middle Platonic) or Neoplatonic commentators used to accommodate Aristotle, this does not mean that the Aristotelians would have been hostile towards Plato or quoted him only as someone with whom to disagree. On the contrary, the Peripatetics also supposed that Plato's works must be studied. One reason was that they understood Plato to be the first Peripatetic. They also recognized that to understand Aristotle properly one needs to know Plato as well, at least to some extent. Some even supposed that Plato's and Aristotle's philosophies form one school of thought, which is opposed to other schools, particularly the Sceptics, the Cyrenaics and the Epicureans. This view was taken by Aristocles of Messene, whose dates are uncertain, but who might have lived from the late first century BCE to the early first century CE (discussed in Karamanolis 2006: 37–41). Aspasius also quite often refers to Plato as the origin of some ethical views he considers as being both Aristotelian and correct. This applies, for example, to the explanation of how virtue comes about and that virtue is a mean between two extremities (vices) (see *in EN* 53,1–5; see also Karamanolis 2006: 41). Alexander of Aphrodisias' references to Plato are not infrequent or hostile either. Typically he says something like "as Plato also has argued in such and such a work". One example is found in Alexander's arguments against Protagorean relativism (*in Metaph.* 313,6–7), where he refers to Plato's arguments against the same theory in the *Theaetetus*. (Alexander, however, uses the name *Protagoras* for the dialogue.)

For Aristotelians and Platonists alike, some works by Aristotle were particularly popular as objects of commentary. These are the *Categories*, the *Physics* and the *De anima*. *Prior Analytics* and *Posterior Analytics* were also rather widely commented on, but, for example, the biological works did not attract much attention: the very early Peripatetic Nicolaus of Damascus in the first century BCE composed a commentary on Aristotle on plants (*de Plantis*; see Drossaart-Lulofs 1965: 9ff.), Alexander and Philoponus (based on Ammonius) wrote on Aristotle's *On Generation and Corruption*;[14] and Michael of Ephesus' commentaries were completed later than 1138 CE. No full commentary was written on any of them. *Politics* was also relatively neglected, probably because the political circumstances had changed drastically from the time when Aristotle's treatise was written. No commentaries were produced on *Rhetorics* or *Poetics*, but *Rhetorics* did function as a basic reference work for theories in rhetoric.

Aristotle's ethical works had a disputed history of their own. In one catalogue (Ptolemy nos. 35–6) only the *Eudemian Ethics* in eight books and the *Magna Moralia* are mentioned, and the *Nicomachean Ethics* is omitted. However, this omission of the *Nicomachean Ethics* may not have been significant, since Arius Didymus mentions its Book 10 and Atticus (third century CE) refers to all three works on ethics. In any case, some doubts were clearly raised from very early on about which ethical treatises were by Aristotle himself and which was his main work on the topic. For example, Aspasius, whose commentary on the *Nicomachean Ethics* survives in part, mentions a debate about whether the *Eudemian Ethics* should be attributed to Eudemus (*in EN* 178,3).[15]

The Hellenistic discussion in general and the Stoics in particular are an important factor in the commentators' discussion. Sometimes the influence is on the level of terminology, but there are more important connections between Stoicism and the commentaries as well. As for the terminology, some terms that are important in the Stoic sources figure prominently in various commentaries, such as the notion of a contributory cause (*sunaition* – with Platonic antecedents too) in the commentaries on the *Physics*, "common notions" (*koinai ennoiai*) in the commentaries on the *Analytics*, notions (*ennoiai*) in Alexander's *De anima*, and so forth. In some cases the terminology does not tell us anything very specific about whether Stoic influence is involved. On the one hand, as Jonathan Barnes (1999) has argued, sometimes it is just that some philosophical terms have been taken over from Stoicism, but by the time of the commentators they have become common property without specific doctrinal significance. On the other hand, terms such as "common notion" (*koinē ennoia*) and "contributory cause" (*sunaition*) may have influenced the Stoics through Aristotle's exoteric works, especially the *Protrepticus* (Hutchinson & Johnson forthcoming). However, in some cases there are clear doctrinal issues involved, as when Alexander argues against the view that soul is a quality in his treatise on the soul or in the separate treatises against the Stoics on fate and on mixture.[16]

The aim and organization of this book

The main objective of this book is to offer a philosophically focused introduction to the ancient commentators. It is aimed at students as well as scholars. Of students, it is best suited for those who already are familiar with some aspects of ancient philosophy, Plato and Aristotle in particular. In addition to the scholars working on ancient philosophy, this book is useful for those working on later periods of the history of philosophy, especially Arabists and medievalists. However, because this book is a philosophical introduction, it is accessible to philosophers interested in the development of thought and arguments presented in the ancient framework. It offers a progression of themes in late ancient philosophy in general and complements the existing introductions to late ancient philosophy[17] because it encompasses a wider scope of authors and themes.

There is a wealth of material in the commentaries themselves but no general introduction comparable to this one exists. During the past twenty years, more and more texts by the commentators have become available to English-speaking students and scholars in the translation series led by Sorabji. Sorabji has also edited a sourcebook (2004) that contains a selection of translated texts with brief introductions. Scholars working in continental Europe (such as Hadot's group at the National Centre for Scientific Research [CNRS] in France) have produced considerable research, as well as new editions, on the commentaries. All these works make the commentaries much more accessible than they used to be. However, none of these works serves exactly as an *introduction* to the topic.

In order to introduce the commentators as philosophers, some restrictions have been necessary. Anything like a complete overview of the commentators' thought would be unimaginable. The text material is simply too large, not to mention the fact that the group that could justifiably be called "ancient commentators" would include many more than the authors studied in this volume. The selection of material concentrates on themes that have been found philosophically inspiring during most periods of the history of Western philosophy. They also are themes that were central in the commentaries themselves. Methodologically speaking, the discussions in this book start from generally recognized philosophical problems or themes (such as the nature and possibility of knowledge, explanatory principles of nature, the nature of reality, the content of a good human life and so forth) and ask how the commentators formulated questions related to these themes and how they answered them. The most important reason for choosing this approach is that it helps integrate the commentators into the continuum of thinkers who work in different historical periods, employ different methods and follow divergent meta-philosophical guidelines.

In this volume, we shall mainly be concerned with commentaries on Aristotle's texts. This choice is motivated by both philosophical and historical concerns. It is important for an introductory volume like this to have a philosophical focus. Completeness in terms of object texts would have prevented us from attaining this end and spread our attention to too many authors and themes. Such a book could only be a sightseeing tour around the commentaries and we could only take snapshots of the objects on display. The historical reason for our approach is the fact that the commentators operated with a hierarchy where Plato and Aristotle had tasks of their own. In this general hierarchy, Aristotle was conceived as being most author-itative when it comes to logic and natural philosophy, and these topics were understood to be the ones that one should study first.[18] These works were supposed to best serve the purpose of introducing a student to the topics at hand.[19]

In the general curriculum, the student was supposed to read Plato's dialogues in a specific order. The apex was to be reached in the dia-logues *Timaeus* and *Parmenides*. Consequently, such complex com-mentaries as Proclus on Plato's *Parmenides* are excluded from the scope of this book because they presuppose that the student already is well versed in Aristotle's and the commentators' logic, natural phil-osophy and metaphysics, and the more mundane works of Plato. In addition, the commentaries at the highest levels of the hierarchy require rather extensive knowledge about the Platonism of Plotinus, which can only be touched on briefly in this book, and about the other commentaries on Plato and Aristotle's works. In an introductory vol-ume like this, a discussion of the commentaries on the highest levels of the late ancient philosophical curriculum would be premature.

The arrangement of this book follows the general guidelines of the commentators' curriculum just presented. We shall begin by consid-ering the commentators' discussions on the nature and possibility of knowledge and their reactions to the question of what should be made of the fact that perceptions are often in conflict. After that we shall ask how the commentators understood the nature of knowledge:

the kind of knowledge in the strong sense that Aristotle discussed in the *Posterior Analytics*, often referred to as "scientific knowledge". Connected with this, the questions of how, according to the commentators, knowledge in general and this special kind of knowledge in particular can be achieved are addressed. We shall also outline the commentators' understanding of logic and its role in scientific enquiry. After that we shall move to the commentators' discussions of nature and its limits and how they defined and analysed natural change. In that context, some cosmological issues are raised, such as whether the universe is eternal or whether it has a beginning. For the ancient commentators, the soul as the general principle of life and psychic functions such as perception and intellectual understanding was, in general, a part of nature or an important explanatory principle in nature. In our discussion of how the soul was used to explain psychic life we shall concentrate on two important functions: perception and intellectual apprehension. Outlining the problems that were central in the discussions concerning perception helps us to understand the profound ways in which the commentators' conceptual framework and their basic supposition differ from modern philosophy of mind. Further, an analysis of perception and intellectual understanding brings to the surface important metaphysical assumptions that the commentators made and that were important in the development of the Platonic–Aristotelian tradition. From the exposition of issues in natural philosophy and psychology we shall proceed to the more abstract question concerning the nature of reality. Here we first outline the central problems of metaphysics as it was discussed in the commentaries. After that we consider the various reactions and answers that the commentators presented to these problems. The very final issue in this book concerns the commentators' discussions of virtues and happy life. We concentrate on such questions as: does virtue alone guarantee happiness; what is required of a virtuous person; and are emotions a part of a happy life?

Now we can turn to the questions about the commentators themselves: when did they live; with whom did they study; where did they work; what works did they write; and which of these have been preserved?

The earliest commentaries

The first century BCE to the second century CE

The first century BCE and the first century CE were the most decisive when it comes to the development of the commentaries. By that time the "revival" of Plato and Aristotle had started and the Aristotelian *corpus* had become available. The set of texts that was used was the one arranged by Andronicus (but cf. Barnes 1997), and it was from his circle that the commentaries emerged. Some of the earliest commentators were Andronicus' pupils: Boethus of Sidon, Nicolaus of Damascus, Alexander of Aegae, and Sotion.[20] We do not know very much about the works of these early commentators. One thing we do know is that Nicolaus had some views on the order of the books of the *Metaphysics*, which, famously, had received its name by being after the *Physics* in Andronicus' edition.

As to the other very early commentators, we know from Simplicius' commentary on the *Categories* that Boethus of Sidon wrote extensively on that treatise. Whether Boethus' writing on the *Categories* formed a complete linear commentary is not entirely clear. In any case, Simplicius' references show that Boethus took up questions that persisted in the ancient commentaries, and still do in scholarship on Aristotle. For example, Boethus asked whether substances as species (i.e. the secondary substances of *Cat.* 2a11ff.) are really substances and concluded that they are not on the basis of the definition of substance given in the *Categories*.[21] He also offered an analysis of the notion of time that diverged from the one given by Aristotle.[22] In addition, Boethus' work on the *Categories* might have formed the basis for some other early commentaries (e.g., Aristo, see Simp. *in Cat.* 201,34ff.).[23]

What is called the "revival" of Aristotelianism had gained such appeal that in the first half of the first century BCE, Aristo of Alexandria and Cratippus, who were students of the last head of Plato's Academy, Antiochus of Ascalon, turned to work on Aristotle's treatises (Phld. *Acad. Hist.* col. 35.11–16; Moraux 1973; Frede 1999: 774). Aristo of Alexandria wrote at least on the *Categories* and the *Analytics*

(Simp. *in Cat.* 159,32, 188,31, 201,34ff.).[24] Another Platonist who discussed issues that remain central for later commentators was an Alexandrian called Eudorus. One such issue is the question of what the correct order of the categories should be. According to Eudorus (see Simp. *in Cat.* 206,10–15), since all substances must have some qualities (the Greek for quality is *poiotēs*) and extension (*to poson*), the categories of quality and quantity must be listed immediately after that of substance. Further, even though time and place are not intrinsic properties or quantities of substances, all substances necessarily exist in time and place and, therefore, the category of time must be the next in the order of priority. We do not know the precise form in which Eudorus was writing, but it seems that he did not write a running commentary (see Karamanolis 2004: 101 n.21).[25]

In addition to these Platonists, the *Categories* also attracted the attention of some Stoics. Of these, Athenodorus and Cornutus wrote heavy criticisms of that work (Porph. *in Cat.* 86,22–4; Simp. *in Cat.* 62,25–9). However, the ancient commentators distinguish Athenodorus and Cornutus from commentators proper (Porph. *in Cat.* 88,22–4; cf. Simp. *in Cat.* 62,25–9; see Karamanolis 2004: 102 n.25).

As indicated, chronologically the earliest running commentary on a work by Aristotle of which significant parts survive is Aspasius' commentary on the *Nicomachean Ethics* from the second century CE (discussed in Chapter 7 below). Aspasius (*c*.100–150 CE) belongs to the second major group of commentators emerging after 100 CE, leading later to the work of Alexander of Aphrodisias. Other members of this group are Adrastus, Herminus and Sosigenes. The anonymous commentary on *Nicomachean Ethics* Books 2–5 printed in *Commentaria in Aristotelem Graeca* (CAG) XX has been connected to Adrastus, and it has been suggested that one of Alexander's ethical questions (*Ethical Problem* 11) is a reply to Adrastus (Sharples 1990: 88). Herminus and Sosigenes were teachers of Alexander of Aphrodisias.[26]

Some second century CE Platonists are also known to have attacked Aristotle, usually with respect to minor issues. These men, Atticus, Lucius and Nicostratus, are usually mentioned together. A list of

Atticus' works have been preserved by Eusebius in his *Preparatio Evangelica* (11.1.15,4–9); Nicostratus is known from Aulus Gellius' *Noctes Atticae*, and Simplicius reports him to have written a work where he criticized almost everything that is said in the *Categories* (Simp. *in Cat.* 1,18).[27] Apparently, Lucius produced a very critical treatise on the *Categories* and perhaps he inspired Nicostratus (Gottschalk 1990: 80). It is precisely their overall hostility towards Aristotelian doctrine that makes these authors not commentators in the same sense as such authors as Alexander of Aphrodisias, Porphyry or Simplicius.[28]

Alexander of Aphrodisias

Alexander of Aphrodisias, a commentator writing about three centuries after the "revival" began, is much better documented than those we have discussed until now. In terms of academic heritage, Alexander belongs to the same tradition as the commentators of the late second century CE: Herminus and Sosigenes were his teachers and Adrastus belonged to the same circle or school.

Some basic biographical details concerning Alexander have recently been confirmed by an inscription found at Aphrodisias (Chaniotis 2004: 388–9). The inscription tells us that a philosopher Alexander of Aphrodisias, whose whole name was Titus Aurelius Alexandrus, has erected a statue for his father who had carried the very same name and who had been a philosopher as well. The inscription also states that Alexander the son worked in Athens. The date of the inscription is in line with the biographical evidence found in Alexander's works, hence we can infer that he was named a director of a philosophical school in Athens and held the Aristotelian chair there. Alexander himself refers to a statue of Aristotle in Athens (*in Metaph.* 415,29–31) and mentions two possible locations for it, the Lyceum and the potters' quarters.

The dating of Alexander's period of leadership at the school is based on the fact that he dedicates his treatise on fate, a problem analogous to what was later to be called "freedom of will", to the double Emperors (Septimus) Severus and Antoninus (Caracalla), whose joint term lasted from 198 to 209. He does this to express his gratitude for his appointment as a teacher (*didaskalos*) of Aristotelian philosophy (*Fat.* 1.164,1–3). His position was one of the philosophical posts established in 176 CE by Marcus Aurelius, the philosopher-emperor. If one wonders why Alexander did not make similar dedications in his other treatises, one reason might have been that the particular appointment in Athens was such an honour that he felt a need to thank the authorities.

Of Alexander's teachers we have already mentioned Herminus (*ap.* Simp. *in Cael.* 430,32) and Sosigenes (Alex.Aphr. *in Mete.* 143,13). In addition, Alexander himself mentions a teacher named Aristotle. Some have suggested that this must be an error (Zeller 1903: 814 n.1, cited by Sharples 1987) and that the real teacher must have been Aristocles of Messene. However, others have argued that one of Alexander's teachers actually was Aristotle of Mytilene from the second century CE whom Galen also mentions (*Consuet.* 2.11,4ff.).

From what Alexander writes, we can observe that he presented himself as a follower of Aristotle. As he says in his own treatise on the *De anima*, he holds Aristotle in high esteem because he considers Aristotle's writings to be closer to the truth than those of any other philosopher (Alex.Aphr. *de An.* 2,4–9). In addition, at least in that work, which is not a commentary (Alexander's commentary on the same work has been lost), he regards his task to be one of articulating as well as possible what Aristotle has stated; Alexander's own remarks will be offered in addition to those clarifications. Alexander also defended Aristotelian views against opponents on topics about which Aristotle does not seem to have written a treatise. Such is, for example, Alexander's treatise on fate (*De fato*), which carries the dedication to the emperors, where he argues against Stoic determinism.

It should be mentioned that many later commentators regard Alexander as an exemplary figure in the practice of *exēgēsis*, commenting. For example, Themistius (fourth century CE) writes at the beginning of his paraphrase of the *Posterior Analytics* that he has chosen this literary form because it would be no use to try to surpass Alexander's (or all the earlier commentators') excellence in this art: it would be like trying to improve Pheidias' masterful statue of Athena by manipulating her shoelaces, Themistius says (*in APo.* 1,2–7). He continues that this could only be motivated by vain love of glory. Despite his outspoken respect, however, Themistius also criticizes Alexander on many points, sometimes even by name (e.g. *in de An.* 76,16–21). For the late ancient commentators, Alexander was a Commentator with a capital C (e.g. Simp. *in Ph.* 707,33; Phlp. *in APr.* 126,30). Some centuries later the Arab philosopher Averroes came to have such a role for medieval authors in the West.

Simplicius praises Alexander as a commentator on the grounds that "he understood without difficulty the doctrines of the ancient [thinkers]" (*in Cat.* 159,32–3). The context shows that Simplicius included Aristotle in these "ancient thinkers". This remark is extremely interesting because it may indicate that Simplicius, who lived some 300 years after Alexander and some 800 years after Aristotle, already felt some difficulty in understanding what Aristotle was writing *because of the historical distance*. Unfortunately, however, Simplicius does not elaborate on this remark.

Alexander wrote a vast number of commentaries on most of Aristotle's main treatises, many of which have been preserved. Alexander's commentary writing is of such a large volume that a complete list is not possible in this short introduction; we shall give the titles of the main works here. His writings fall into separate categories and they may be classified according to different criteria. If we just consider the content and format of the writings, the most obvious dividing line is between those works that are direct commentaries on Aristotle and those that are not. According to this criterion, the extant writings can be classified into commentaries and other works. Another significant demarcation line goes between the texts that have been preserved and those that have not.

Alexander's main commentaries on Aristotle include those on the *Metaphysics*, the *Prior Analytics* (of which only that on Book I survives), the *Topics*, the treatise on sense perception *De sensu*, and Aristotle's *Meteorology*. In the Greek context, "meteorology" does not mean merely weather phenomena but includes a wider range of natural events that take place in the region between the surface of the earth and the moon and happen naturally but not with perfect regularity; such phenomena include, for example, the Milky Way, comets and shooting stars, and also winds and earthquakes (cf. Arist. *Mete.* I 1).

There are three main surviving treatises by Alexander that are not commentaries. One of them is Alexander's *On the Soul* (*De anima*), which in terms of structure and content is a follower of Aristotle's treatise on the same topic without commenting on it line by line. Alexander also wrote two treatises on themes that were debated in the ancient philosophical schools but on which Aristotle apparently wrote no separate work. These are Alexander's *On Fate* (*De fato*) and *On Mixture* (*De mixtione*). In both cases, the Stoics had proposed a view that was in diametrical opposition to Aristotle's, and Alexander defended the Aristotelian position against the Stoics. With respect to fate, as already mentioned, the Stoics advocated a strong form of determinism, which Alexander opposes. As to the mixtures, Stoics had argued that there exists a mixture called *krasis* in which the mixed substances are completely merged with each other, but yet retain their own nature. The existence of such a mixture requires, for example, that when a drop of wine is poured in the ocean, the ocean will contain some wine. Alexander denied this and argued that the nature of the wine will be entirely overtaken by the water of the ocean and the wine drop will be lost. In addition to these works against Stoicism, Alexander also argued against Platonic and Epicurean views (examples in Sharples 1990: 90–91).

In addition, the tradition transmits to us some less unified works under Alexander's name. These include a supplement to the treatise on the soul, which has been named *Mantissa*, literally "makeweight", by J. Freudenthal and the name is accepted by Ivo Bruns in his edition (CAG Suppl. II 1, 1887: v).[29] In addition, there are two collections of short treatises on specific topics named "Questions" (*Quaestiones*): one on natural philosophy, another on ethics (which will be discussed in Chapter 7 under the title "*Ethical Problems*"). It has been debated whether these were written by Alexander himself. For the present, it seems that they cannot safely be attributed to him. The collections of questions derive from Alexander's circle or school but were probably not written by him.

In addition, there are certain works by Alexander that have not been preserved but about which there is information in other sources. Some of them are mentioned in other commentaries, and in most cases they were also known to the Arabs. These include a commentary on the *Categories*, another on *On Interpretation*, one on the *Physics* and one on Aristotle's *De anima*. In addition, Alexander possibly commented on Aristotle's *De memoria*, and this might have been a part of his commentary on the whole *Parva naturalia* (cf. Alex.Aphr. *de An.* 69,20; Todd 1976: 15 n.71). Apparently Alexander also worked on ethics but it is not clear whether he produced anything like a continuous commentary on Aristotle's ethical works, or whether he just wrote shorter treatises in the style of the questions.

Sometimes our sources give us more extensive quotations of the works they refer to. This is the case, for example, with Alexander's commentary on *De caelo* (cited by Simplicius in his commentary on the same work and by Philoponus in *De aeternitate mundi*) and on *De generatione et corruptione* (quoted by Philoponus in his commentary on the same work). Some fragments have also been preserved of Alexander's commentary on the *Posterior Analytics* (see Moraux 1979). One further group of such works that have not been preserved but that we have evidence of from other sources are those for which we have an Arabic translation. They include the *De principiis* (*On the Principles of Universe*), *De providentia*, on differences in separate genera (discussed in Rashed 2007), and a refutation of Galen's argument against Aristotle on the doctrine that all movements are initiated by a mover (see also Sharples 1987).

Further, there are some commentaries and treatises that the tradition attributes to Alexander but that were not written by him. These spurious works include a commentary on Aristotle's *Sophistical Refutations*, which has been attributed to Michael of Ephesus (Praechter 1906; the commentary has been edited by Ebbesen 1981). There is also one commentary on Books 6–14 of the *Metaphysics* that the tradition attributes to Alexander but that was probably written by Michael of Ephesus much later (in the twelfth century); Michael's name even appears in one manuscript (see e.g. Introduction to the translation of *in Metaph.* I: 3 n.6 by Sorabji & Sharples).[30]

Early Eastern commentaries: Themistius

This category is a small one indeed: it contains only one member, Themistius, who lived from *c*.317 to *c*.388 CE in Constantinople. He is classified into a separate category because of deviations from the other commentators both historically and geographically and because his method and commentary style are slightly different. This means, on the one hand, that he did not write commentaries, but, rather, interpretive paraphrases on Aristotle's works. On the other hand, whereas the early commentaries are Aristotelian in spirit in the sense that they are not influenced by later (Neoplatonic) trends in Platonism, in the case of Themistius' writings this is not clear. He is not an Aristotelian to the extent that Alexander is, but he is not reading Aristotle within a Neoplatonic metaphysics of hypostases either.

The extent to which the Neoplatonic doctrines had an effect on Themistius' writings is debated. To determine this in a straightforward manner is difficult for several reasons. One reason is that Themistius is not striving for unity in his accounts of various issues. Rather, he aims to clarify the point at hand, and such clarifications may contain interpretative trends that pull the resulting whole in different directions. In addition, there is a clear methodological difference between Themistius' works and that of the later Neoplatonic commentators. Most importantly, the Neoplatonic commentators have a fairly formal procedure of exposition where they lay out the commented lemma (i.e. a piece of text) of Aristotle (see Todd 1996: 6 n.34; Festugière 1963; Westerink 1990). By contrast, Themistius combines the quotations and explanations much more freely, so much so that it is sometimes difficult to extract the actual quoted lines from his text.

Themistius' life was exceptional too. He was a public figure, orator and politician in Constantinople. He wrote public speeches, epideictic praises and panegyrics to emperors. Such speeches were given at formal events and the basic idea was to praise the person that the speech was about. This genre has not been much respected in scholarly literature in general and Themistius in particular has been reproached for producing such formal addresses while claiming to be a philosopher (e.g. Alföldi 1952). His panegyrics have, accordingly, been regarded as mere flattery of those in power. It is undeniable that the adulatory speeches have the aim of praising their objects. However, some scholars have noted that in his speeches Themistius aimed at guiding the leaders to create a just society and to enhance the esteem of the traditional virtues (Vanderspoel 1995: 2–7).

In addition to his career as an orator, Themistius was a member of the senate from 357 onwards and he was also elected a leader of that administrative assembly (see Vanderspoel 1995). Despite Themistius' paganism, Emperor Constantius appreciated him, and he had the special privilege of dining at the emperor's table (Lib. *Ep.* 66.2; Them. *Or.* 31.353a). Before devoting himself to his public career, Themistius ran a school of his own *c.*345–55. His paraphrase on Aristotle's *De anima* probably dates from that period.[31]

As already indicated, Themistius did not write commentaries but paraphrases on Aristotle's works. The Greek word *paraphrasis* does not appear in Themistius' own texts (see Todd 1996: 2 n.15), but is the term that was already being used to refer to his works on Aristotle in antiquity (see Simp. *in Cael.* 188,30). Themistius was not the inventor of this genre, but apparently his role in transforming the paraphrastic method into a didactic device was considerable (cf. *in de An.* 39,33).[32] Themistius' own accounts of his method are brief (*in de An.* 1,2–5; *in APo.* 1,2–12). In his paraphrase on the *Posterior Analytics* he explains the nature of his project to be that of extracting the intentions of what is written in Aristotle's books and reporting it quickly, since this seems to him a novel and beneficial enterprise. In brief, the purpose of Themistius' works was to make Aristotle's writings more accessible to students.[33]

In this introduction to the philosophy of the commentators, we concentrate on Themistius' works on Aristotle; his speeches will be left out. There are three paraphrases that have been preserved: on the *Posterior Analytics*, the *Physics* and, the most ambitious, the *De anima*. In addition, Themistius wrote a paraphrase on the *Metaphysics*, of which his discussion of the Aristotelian god in Book XII of the *Metaphysics* has survived in Arabic and in Hebrew (Pinès 1987). In the paraphrase on *De anima*, Themistius' individual voice is clearest in his discussion on the intellect. The question of how much his account is dependent on earlier sources remains as yet unanswered. Themistius' own influence was considerable, particularly during the Renaissance, because his paraphrases were the most widely published of the ancient commentaries. Further, for us his paraphrase on *De anima* is a very important source, partly because it is the first surviving line-by-line work systematically expanding on Aristotle's *De anima*. As we saw above, even though Alexander's treatise on the soul survives, his commentary has been lost.

In his paraphrase on Aristotle's *De anima*, Themistius was influenced by Alexander, at least the *De anima* of Alexander, not necessarily the commentary (Todd 1996). As mentioned, it is controversial whether Plotinus influenced Themistius and, if he did, to what extent that influence transformed Themistius' account on the intellect.[34] John Vanderspoel, who has written a comprehensive book on Themistius, concludes that Themistius is difficult to locate in the map of Platonism and Aristotelianism, but in the field of Platonism he seems more like a late Middle Platonist than a Neoplatonist (1995: 21). When Themistius writes on Aristotle, he is more often defending than criticizing him (*ibid*.: 22). Further, he is very critical in his orations towards such developments in Neoplatonism as Iamblichus' discussion on theurgy, that is, ritual practices through which one is supposed to be in contact with the intelligent god and perhaps also aid the realization of divinity in the world (*ibid*.: 18 n.65).[35]

Themistius lived during a time when the Christian faith and church had already become important factors in Roman life. Themistius himself seemed to aim at a conciliatory position between believers and non-believers, possibly also inside particular tendencies within the church. He argued that it is natural that there is a plurality of gods and religions on the grounds that god created diversity: never do we understand things similarly (*Or*. 5.70a, quoted in Vanderspoel 1995: 24). Therefore, it is better to accommodate rather than condemn positions that diverge from one's own.

Porphyry, Iamblichus, Simplicius and Philoponus

Developments in Platonism: Plotinus, Porphyry, Iamblichus

As mentioned previously, a gradual development of Platonism culminates in Plotinus who lived in Rome, 205–70 CE. Rather than writing line-by-line commentaries on the works of Plato and Aristotle, he wrote treatises on various philosophical topics. Those treatises were edited by Plotinus' student Porphyry (c.234–305), who also named them the *Enneads* (i.e. groups of nine). The name derives from Porphyry's organization of Plotinus' writings into six groups, each of which contains nine treatises. To achieve the order, Porphyry had to cut some treatises into pieces. This occasionally results in an artificial order and groups of texts in the *Enneads*, but the general ordering principles are sufficiently clear. Group I contains writings on ethics, groups II–III on natural philosophy and cosmology, group IV concerns soul, V intellect and VI being in general and the highest principle the One. We learn the chronological ordering of the treatises from Porphyry as well, and it does not correspond to Porphyry's thematic arrangement (e.g. *Ennead* I 1 is number 53, second last, in the chronological order.)

Plotinus' philosophy grows out of the philosophy of Plato and the middle Platonists, but he also incorporates material from Aristotle and the Stoics. In addition to the metaphysical hypostases mentioned above, a significant distinguishing mark of Plotinus' philosophical project is an inward turn. With this turn, the importance of the empirical world diminishes and the supposition that knowledge and insight is to be found within oneself starts to dominate. The material world and our perceptions concerning it are located on the metaphysical level of the Soul. The material world itself is understood as a kind of living being; it is operated by a world soul. Ordinary reasoning is also grasped as a function belonging to the level of Soul. Intellect consists of an eternal intellectual agent grasping in an instantaneous act of apprehension the intelligible principles structuring the world. The structuring principles of the world according to Plotinus include the greatest kinds (*megista genē*) introduced in

Plato's late dialogues and species and genera familiar from Aristotle. On the rare occasions when we grasp general aspects of reality by understanding how several things hang together, we manage to take part in the eternal intellectual activity on the level of the universal Intellect. The highest hypostasis, the One, cannot be described directly, since it does not allow for any distinctions. However, Plotinus supposes that we human beings are capable of merging into the One and losing sense of our individuality altogether. In such peculiar experience, unity with all is gained for a moment.

This extremely brief survey of the ontological hypostases provides only the very basic outlines of Plotinus' conception of reality. It does not tell us anything about the complex ways in which Neoplatonism comes into play in the philosophy of the commentators. The question of how the commentators were influenced by Platonism in general and Plotinus in particular needs to be addressed in connection with the systematic treatment of the individual problems.

Plotinus occasionally saw himself as a commentator on Plato, but his attitude towards Aristotle was often very critical. Plotinus' criticism of Aristotle's *Categories* in *Enneads* 6.1–3 set the stage for the later debates in the commentaries, and some scholars even today find it devastating for Aristotle's philosophy (e.g. A. C. Lloyd 1990). However, most followers of Plotinus tend to try to reconcile the apparent contradictions between Plato and Aristotle. One general idea that helps coin those views of Plato and Aristotle that seem to conflict is the following division of labour found in Simplicius: Aristotle is authoritative when it comes to the sensible world, whereas Plato is authoritative on the intelligible realm (Simp. *in Cat.* 6,19–7,33). Simplicius also states that a good commentator should not suppose disagreement on the basis of the letter (*lexis*) only, but he should find the insight (*nous*) behind the words and trace the harmony there (Simp. *in Cat.* 7,23–32, quoted in Sorabji 2004: vol. 3, 38).[36]

A central figure in the transmission of the Platonic–Aristotelian tradition and Neoplatonic philosophy into the Latin West was Plotinus' student Porphyry (*c.*234–*c.*305 CE), who was born at Tyre in Phoenicia and to whom, as we have seen, we also owe the collection of Plotinus' *Enneads* and the *Life of Plotinus* that forms a preface to them. He came to Rome to study with Plotinus in 263 CE; before that he had studied with Longinus in Athens. Porphyry wrote extensively and on various philosophical topics; he was interested in more strictly philosophical subjects as well as grammar, rhetoric and geometry.

Porphyry's introduction to Aristotle's *Organon* (*Isagoge*) had an incomparable influence as a basic text in both the Arabic world and the Latin West through Boethius' translation (see e.g. de Libera 1998). The *Isagoge* is not only a logical work in the modern sense of the word but also includes a basic mapping of reality into genera, species and differentia, definitions, peculiar properties, accidents and so on. However, it does not go into deep metaphysical problems. As Porphyry himself puts the purpose of his treatise:

> to know what is a genus and what a difference and what a species and what a property and what an accident – and also for the presentation of definitions, and generally for matters concerning division and proof, the study of which is useful, – I shall attempt, in making you a concise exposition, to rehearse, briefly and as in a manner of introduction, what the older masters say, avoiding deeper inquiries and aiming suitable at the more simple.
>
> (*Isag.* 1,5–10, *Introduction* trans. Barnes 2003)

Porphyry explicitly points out that he wants to avoid questions such as in what sense the species and genera exist (1,10–15). Yet he presents the general framework to structure any exposition of the world or a science, regardless of whether this structure is itself realized in the world.

Porphyry also taught Iamblichus (*c*.240–*c*.325), who is the next important figure in the development of Platonism (and what we call "Neoplatonism"). He was born in Chalcis in today's Syria. He went to study with Porphyry in Rome but later returned to Syria to found a school of his own. After having returned to Syria, Iamblichus apparently wrote commentaries on the works of Plato and Aristotle, but only fragments of these works survive. Iamblichus has been characterized as a "reforming prophet" (Sorabji 2004: 7), and he probably moulded Plotinus' philosophy into the form that is known from the later author Proclus, who lived and worked in the 400s in Athens (see also O'Meara 1989: 2). Iamblichus is a very influential figure, much of whose work has unfortunately been lost. In his writing, he also carried further the Pythagoreanization of the Platonism he inherited from Plotinus and Porphyry, and he wrote a treatise *On Pythagoreanism* (discussed in O'Meara 1989).

One of Iamblichus' disagreements with Porphyry concentrates on a form of ritual practice called "theurgy". Iamblichus held that through engaging in this practice we promote the divine cause in the sensible world. One of Iamblichus' main treatises, *On the Mysteries of the Egyptians* (*De mysteriis Aegyptiorum*), was dedicated to this topic, and in the treatise he directly attacks Porphyry. Iamblichus is also known to have disagreed with Plotinus and Porphyry on the interpretation of Aristotle's categories. Iamblichus argued that they can be applied in the intelligible realm as well, and hence his interpretation is called "intellective" (*noera*) (see Dillon 1997). In his Pythagoreanizing programme, Iamblichus also interpreted the emanation hierarchy in Pythagorean terms, where the gods were assimilated with divine numbers, the transcendent forms with ideal numbers and the enmattered forms with physical numbers (see O'Meara 1989: 79). Iamblichus' own writing caused strong reactions and, as mentioned, he had great influence on later commentators (Proclus in particular). It has also been argued that Iamblichus' *Exhortation to Philosophy* accurately reports the contents of Aristotle's lost treatise on this topic (the so-called *Protrepticus*; see Hutchinson & Johnson 2005).

One commentary on the *Categories* has been preserved from Iamblichus' contemporary Dexippus (died *c*.320), about whose life we know little. Simplicius characterizes Dexippus as being "Iamblichean" (Simp. *in Cat.* 2,9) and it is possible that Dexippus was Iamblichus' student, but this has not been confirmed (Dexippus is not mentioned in Eunapius' list of Iamblichus' students).[37] Dexippus also was in charge of a philosophical school about which we know little more than that an otherwise unknown Seleucus was one of its best students. As Dillon notes, it is clear that Dexippus is not an amateur philosopher, but we do not know for certain where he was educated.

Schools of Alexandria and Athens

Plotinus worked in Rome, but the Neoplatonic school tradition did not persist there; it continued in Athens and in Alexandria. One of the Athenian Neoplatonists is Proclus, who lived from 411 until 485 and worked mainly in Athens, even though he was born in Constantinople and began his philosophical career in Alexandria. In Athens he was taught by Plutarch of Athens and Syrianus. Proclus himself was a teacher for many who carried the tradition further. Proclus also wrote commentaries, the main ones being on Plato's *Timaeus* and Euclid's *Elements*. He also wrote an influential treatise called *Elements of Theology*. Proclus' commentaries belong to the highest peak of the school curriculum, for students who are already well versed in Aristotle and in many of Plato's other dialogues. Proclus' commentaries do not belong to the scope of our introductory study because they would demand all the knowledge that we can give in this book, and much more, to be enjoyable.

As to the schools in Alexandria and Athens, Karl Praechter once suggested that those schools had very different approaches to philosophy. According to this suggestion, the Alexandrians were reading Aristotle for the sake of his own philosophy and they restricted themselves to "sober explanation" (Hadot 1990a: 276 n.2), whereas the Athenians proceeded from a Neoplatonic point of view (Praechter 1926: esp. 638). Praechter's suggestion is exaggerated and it has been shown to be such (Hadot 1978). In this introductory volume, our discussion is guided by the assumption that such predetermined attitudes towards the methodologies of the commentators cannot be sustained. If there are important methodological connections or differences between individual commentators, or between teachers and students, these will emerge in more detailed discussion of their works.[38]

After Proclus, the tradition was carried further by two figures in Alexandria, Hermeias and his son Ammonius. Ammonius held a position as the head of the Alexandrian school even though he had studied with Proclus in Athens. Ammonius (435/45–517/26) was an important figure and a teacher in Alexandria, whose students include the main commentators in the later ancient tradition, Simplicius and Philoponus, who are to be discussed here, and Asclepius and Olympiodorus, to whom we make occasional reference in the discussion of systematic points but whose lives will not be accounted here. About Olympiodorus, who lived and taught in Alexandria and flourished in the mid-500s, it needs to be said that he was able to continue as a school head even after the Byzantine Emperor Justinian's restrictive legislation had forced the teachers of the Platonic school in Athens to leave the city about 530 CE (see Watts 2006: 111–42). Other figures of the school of Alexandria include Eutocius, Elias, David and Stephanus, whom we shall not discuss in this book.[39]

Many of Ammonius' influential lecture series were published: those on the *Categories* and the *Prior Analytics* under his own name. In addition, some of the commentaries that come to us under Philoponus' name are from Ammonius' lectures. They are four in number: commentaries on the *Prior Analytics*, the *Posterior Analytics* (the commentary on the second book is spurious), and the *De anima* (the commentary on the third book is probably spurious) and a rare commentary on the biological work *On Generation and Corruption*. However, Philoponus was also a remarkably independent writer and did not confine himself to reporting his teacher's lectures. Our exposition of the late commentary tradition concentrates on Philoponus and Simplicius, who were writing in the sixth century CE.

The members of the Athenian Neoplatonic school saw themselves as heirs of Plato's Academy, but the school was not a direct continuation of the Academy (see e.g. Glucker 1978). The Athenian school presumably originates from a figure known as Plutarch of Athens. Plutarch of Athens is to be distinguished from another, better known Plutarch from Chaeronea, a Platonist in the late first and early second centuries CE, the author of the lives of eminent men, moral treatises and many smaller philosophical pieces, some of which were critical of Stoic philosophy. Plutarch of Athens, whom we already mentioned as Proclus' teacher, lived in the late fourth and early fifth centuries CE, and sometimes his views inspired later commentators on certain questions of interpretation (see e.g. Ch. 5, § "Perception requires rational reflexivity"), but this Plutarch will not be a major character in our story.[40]

Simplicius

We know little about the early life of Simplicius. He was probably born in Cilicia in Asia Minor and is, hence, called Simplicius the Cilician. On the basis of his own writings (e.g. *in Ph.* I 59,23, 183,18, 192,14, II 1363,8), we know that he studied both in Alexandria and in Athens. His teacher in Alexandria was Ammonius (who also taught Philoponus) but we do not have any conclusive evidence that Simplicius and Philoponus knew each other. In fact, Simplicius claims that he did not know Philoponus personally at all (*in Cael.* 26,17–24). In Athens Simplicius was taught by Damascius from Syria (*in Ph.* I 642,17, 774,28).

Simplicius also worked in Athens, but had to leave about 531. Emperor Justinian's laws had already deprived the pagan Platonic teachers of their right to teach in 529, but Edward Watts argues that only when the school was deprived of its meeting place and the teachers of their personal property, were the Athenian Platonists forced to leave the city (2006: 130–42). According to a historian called Agathias, all of the following had to go: "Damascius the Syrian, Simplicius the Cilician, Eulamius (/Eulalius) the Phrygian, Priscianus the Lydian, Hermias and Diogenes, both from Phoenicia, and Isidore of Ghaza, the most noble flower of our time" (*Hist.* 2.30.3ff.). The first location of their exile was in Persia, the court of a learned king of Persia, Chosroes (or Khusrau), at Ctesiphon in modern Iraq. The Persian court offered a haven for many of those who had difficulties with Christian authorities, among them heterodox Christians and pagan philosophers.

An important open question is where Simplicius and his companions went after the Persian exile. The report given by Agathias (*Hist.* 2.31,4) has been taken to indicate that Simplicius returned to Athens (e.g. Cameron 1969), but this suggestion has been contested (Thiel 1999). A fascinating suggestion that has been argued for in recent years is that Simplicius went to Harran (ancient Carrhae) in modern Syria, near the ancient border of Persia, for his late and presumably most productive years.[41]

Interesting clues concerning Simplicius' whereabouts come from his own works. For example, we learn that, wherever he was, four different conventions were used to define the beginning of the year: the Athenian, the Roman, the one employed in the Asian provinces, and that of Arabs and Damascenes (*in Ph.* 875,19–22; Hadot 1987a, criticized by Folkes 1992). Simplicius knows about Syrian methods of transportation by river and place names. In Harran there also were Manichees, and Simplicius attacks one in his commentary on Epictetus' *Handbook* (e.g. *in Epict.* Hadot 1996: 325/D 71,48).[42] All of these interesting facts are well in line with the hypothesis that Simplicius immigrated to Harran but, unfortunately, none of them is sufficient to conclusively establish that this was the location of his final exile (see Lameer 1997). There is a collection of Arabic narratives of how the teaching of logic and medicine travelled from the Greeks to the Arabs: "from Alexandria to Baghdad" (as the thesis has been named by Max Meyerhof 1930, cited by Gutas 1999). In these narratives, the route of the teaching goes via Antioch and Harran, but no special role is assigned to Simplicius.[43]

To put it mildly, Simplicius was a voluminous writer. What has been preserved to us consists of four commentaries, the authorship of which has not been contested. Of these four, three are on Aristotle's works and one on the *Handbook* of Epictetus. Of the Aristotelian commentaries, those on the *de Caelo*, the *Physics* and the *Categories* are indisputable. In addition, a commentary on Aristotle's *De anima* has come down to us under Simplicius' name, but its authenticity has been questioned as early as the beginning of the seventeenth century (*Francisci Piccolominei Sentensis commentaria in libros Aristotelis De caelo, ortu et interitu; adjuncta lucidissima expositione, in tres libros eiusdem de anima, nunc recens in lucem prodeunt*, Moguntiae 1608, 1001ff.). F. Bossier and Carlos Steel (1972) have argued that the author of this commentary must have been Priscianus the Lydian, who, according to Agathias, had to leave Athens with Simplicius. The arguments of Bossier and Steel have been heavily criticized by

Hadot (1978; 1996) and Henry J. Blumenthal (1982). I tend to share Bossier and Steel's feeling that it would be surprising that Simplicius, who wrote such a voluminous commentary on the *Physics*, would confine himself to such a short piece on the *De anima*. Further, both the philosophical and the linguistic style of the commentary are rather different from the ones that we know to be by Simplicius. The commentary will be discussed along with the commentaries by Simplicius under the name "Pseudo-Simplicius", because it seems unlikely that Simplicius wrote it. However, I shall not commit myself to definite claims about its authorship.

In addition to the commentaries that are extant, Simplicius apparently wrote a whole commentary on Euclid's *Elements*. Parts of it have been preserved as an Arabic translation, the date and author of which are unknown, in a commentary on the same work by a mathematician called al-Fadl ibn Hātim al-Nayrīzī (see Sabra 1969: 1). Even though the passages preserved in al-Nayrīzī's translation seem to constitute a whole, Sabra argues that there is an important omission: al-Nayrīzī does not give us Simplicius' proof of the parallel postulate. There are also some indications that Simplicius wrote a commentary on the *Metaphysics*, an epitome on Theophrastus' *Physics* and a commentary on Iamblichus' *On Pythagoreanism* (*De secta Pythagorica*), mentioned above. He might also have written on Hermogenes' *Tekhnē* (there is evidence in an eighteenth-century manuscript in Vienna), on Aristotle's *Meteorology* (evidence discussed in Hadot 1996: 6 n.20) and on syllogisms, but the text in question could be a later appendix to Simplicius' commentary on the *Categories*. In this volume, we shall concentrate on Simplicius' preserved commentaries on Aristotle's works.

One additional remark has to be made about Simplicius. His commentaries are not just sources for Simplicius' own views. More than any other ancient commentator, Simplicius quotes and paraphrases his predecessors' philosophical works. He is one of the main sources, not only about some lost commentaries of late antiquity, but also much of Presocratic philosophy, and many of Aristotle's otherwise lost works.

Philoponus

The last figure chosen as an object of closer study in this book is Philoponus or, more precisely, John Philoponus. The same man is also known as John the Grammarian or John of Alexandria. As already mentioned, this Philoponus (lover of toil) was, like Simplicius, a student of Ammonius in Alexandria, although Simplicius claims that the two never met. Unlike all the other commentators discussed here, Philoponus was a Christian. Independently of the question of how Philoponus himself understood his Christianity and its relation to his work, there is one issue where his disagreement with the old tradition becomes very clear. This is the question of whether the world is eternal or whether it has been created.

The question of the eternity of the world was of considerable significance for Philoponus himself. He wrote two separate treatises on it: *Against Proclus on the Eternity of the World* and *Against Aristotle on the Eternity of the World*. The first of these was written in 529 CE and the second some five years later. In fact, Philoponus' way of constructing his arguments is very complex, and these treatises may contain layers from different periods (Verrycken 1990: 233–74). Despite this complexity, however, one methodological choice is clear. Even though the rejection of eternity is compatible with the Christian faith and eternity is not, in his arguments against Aristotle and Proclus, Philoponus does not bring faith and biblical texts into his argument at all. Rather, he proceeds on premises or suppositions of his pagan adversaries and shows that they are contradictory.[44]

We have already seen that the years around 530 CE were a turning point when it comes to the history of Platonic–Aristotelian pagan philosophy in the West. Emperor Justinian's edicts led to the closure of the school in Athens and the main authorities teaching this tradition had to go into exile. Olympiodorus was able to continue as a school head and teacher in Alexandria (Wildberg 1990), probably because of an agreement that the Alexandrians had reached with the church authorities (see O'Meara 1989: 2). Even though for some, such as Simplicius, the exile was no personal disaster and he in fact probably wrote his most important works after the closure of the

Athenian school, the tradition itself was never again what it used to be. The discrepancies between the Christian doctrines and the old pagan tenets had surfaced, and the old tradition was to become marginal in the West.

Around 530 and the time of the closure of the Athenian school, John Philoponus experienced a personal change. Even though he was on the side of the establishment in the sense that he was a Christian, his philosophical background was in the old pagan tradition. For reasons unknown to us, Philoponus abandoned his philosophical career in the 530s and never succeeded Ammonius as the head of the Alexandrian school. Philoponus dedicated the rest of his intellectual life to theology. We do not know what caused Philoponus' "conversion" to theology, but we do know that his theological views were to be rejected by the clerical authorities. Much later (680–81) he was condemned as a heretic for defending the so-called tritheistic interpretation of the Trinity. According to the tritheistic reading, the Trinity of God, Son and Holy Spirit contains three genuinely separate divinities, not just one God with three personae. The attitude that the church authorities took toward Philoponus' theological views may explain why he did not have quite as much influence on later philosophy and science as the novelty of his ideas would have indicated.

Some of Philoponus' commentaries, as already mentioned, are based on Ammonius' lectures, and so reflect readings and tenets that were shared in the circle of Ammonius. There are four commentaries that explicitly present Ammonius' teaching: on Aristotle's *On Generation and Corruption*, *On the Soul*, *Prior Analytics* and *Posterior Analytics*. Philoponus' commentaries on *Categories*, *Physics* and *Meteorology* do not indicate such an origin. Philoponus himself is particularly original, critical and innovative in questions of natural philosophy. These arguments are discussed below in Chapter 4 (§§ "Final causation in the commentaries" and "Challenging Aristotelian dynamics").

In addition to his commentaries, which are on many occasions heavily critical of the philosophical tradition, Philoponus wrote two treatises against the eternity of the world, one against Proclus and the other against Aristotle. Philoponus devoted himself to a theological career after having written these treatises. His theological works include one on the creation of the world (*De opificio mundi*) and one on the Trinity. In this book, we shall concentrate on his commentaries.

The later commentary tradition: a note

One important figure in the transmission of Greek philosophy to the Latin West was Boethius (executed in 524/5), who also produced many well-known translations of Aristotle's works as well as Porphyry's *Introduction* (*Isagoge*; discussed e.g. in de Libera 1998), and whose translation method is rather well attested. We shall not, however, discuss Boethius in the present context. There are several reasons for this exclusion. First, it is a typical convention that, despite being an early figure, Boethius is discussed in connection with the medieval philosophy of the Latin West owing to the historical fact that Boethius had a strong influence on this philosophical tradition. Secondly, it has been a matter of dispute whether Boethius actually engaged in the commentary work. Some have argued (Shiel [1954] 1990) that Boethius did not write comments of his own but simply translated scholia: comments that were written in the margins of the Greek text he was translating. Some have contested this view and argue that even though Boethius built on existing commentaries, he may well have been combining information from several works and thus have created new interpretations (e.g. Ebbesen 1990). There is a recent monograph on Boethius by John Marenbon (2003), and the reader is advised to consult that book for further information.

   In the Byzantine world, the commentary activity continued. For example, the main surviving commentaries on Aristotle's biological works come from this later period. Michael of Ephesus (twelfth century) wrote commentaries on *De partibus animalium*, *De motu animalium* and *De incessu animalium*. He also produced a commentary on *Parva Naturalia* (CAG XXII 1) and on (at least) parts of the *Nicomachean Ethics*, of which the one on Book V has survived (CAG XXII 3). He may have written the commentary in the tradition handed over to us as that by Alexander of Aphrodisias on *Metaphysics* Books VI–XIV, but this is not known for certain. In any case, this commentary was not written by Alexander but originates from a much later period. In this introductory book, we have had to exclude the Byzantine exegetical tradition.[45]

Even though we do not know the details of how the transmission took place,[46] we know that the commentary tradition lived on in Arabic philosophy. In the early phases it was Christians in Syria who translated and commented on Aristotle's *Categories* (de Libera 2004), but later the commentary tradition spread to wider circles. In the medieval Latin West, the Commentator with a capital C was no longer Alexander of Aphrodisias but Averroes (Ibn Rushd, 1126–98). The interpretational moves made in the Arabic commentaries were influenced by Plotinus and later (Neo)Platonism, and for the Arabs the tradition transmitted some of Plotinus' works as being by Aristotle, for example, the so-called *Aristotle's Theology*, which included a paraphrase of some of Plotinus' *Enneads* (see Adamson 2002). The ancient commentators were well known by the Arabic philosophers, the most famous of whom lived in the earliest centuries of the new millennium.[47] Important translations into Arabic were also made of many commentaries, some of which are only known to us through these translations or fragments.

In the Latin West, important medieval authors such as Thomas Aquinas also engaged in commenting on the works of Aristotle, and the Renaissance saw the revival of commentaries on Plato. Throughout the period the ancient commentators continued influencing the readings and interpretations in the West through Latin translations (published in the series *Corpus Latinorum commentariorum in Aristotelem Graecorum* [CLCAG]). In fact, the commentary tradition is still thriving: modern expert commentaries are published worldwide. We can see that by better understanding the late ancient commentators we are able to better understand our own philosophical tradition.

TWO

Epistemology

Epistemology is a characteristically modern field of philosophy, one where Cartesian or post-Cartesian scepticism plays a prominent role. One might thus raise legitimate concerns about the application of this term in connection with ancient philosophical literature. Ancient philosophers in general and the commentators in particular discussed various questions related to knowledge (*epistēmē*) and some of these questions resemble issues in today's epistemology. However, much of the commentators' discussion about knowledge or *epistēmē* is more akin to what we conceive of as philosophy of science: philosophical research into questions of what are the methods, limits, objects or aims of a systematic study into the world around us. We shall address these concerns in Chapter 3.

This chapter concentrates on the following questions: if there is knowledge, is it based on some starting-points that are known without proof? Are there different kinds of knowledge? Could we find starting-points for knowledge in perception? Given that perceptual conflicts exist, can we rely on our perceptions? If the same wind appears to me to be cold and to you to be warm, is it cold or warm? Or is it both cold and warm? If an apple turns from green to red, is it green or red? And, more generally, if we have knowledge, how should it be defined? In the ancient material, we do find lively debates centring on these kinds of questions. The first major work concentrating on knowledge is Plato's *Theaetetus*. It may be misleading to say that it is an exclusively epistemological work in our sense of the word, but the dialogue does deal with many of the questions central in later epistemology – in particular the questions of how knowledge (*epistēmē*) is to be defined.

One basic intuition that is found in both Plato (*Tht*. 201eff.) and Aristotle, and that is argued for in the commentaries as well, is the following: if we are to have knowledge at all, it cannot be based on infinitely long arguments or accounts. In the opening of his study on *epistēmē*, namely the *Posterior Analytics*, Aristotle claims that all teaching and learning based on reasoning is based on pre-existent knowledge (*APo*. 71a1–2). Would this not seem to imply that all knowledge will be based on some pre-existent knowledge, and hence destroy the possibility of knowing? This conclusion is not necessary if we find types or kinds of knowledge that are not based on reasoning. What could this be? As Philoponus suggests in his commentary on those lines (*in APo*. 5,1–5), perceptual knowledge does not involve pre-established knowledge. Hence it seems like a good candidate for providing us with starting-points of knowledge. Whether we can rely on our perceptions about the world was already, by the time of Plato and Aristotle, a well-established philosophical debate. This debate can be traced back to the Presocratics. Aristotle does so (*Metaph*. IV 5), and scholars of our time have also taken note of discussions on the reliability of the senses in the Presocratics (see e.g. Baltussen 2003). Therefore, it could not be taken for granted that perceptions do provide us with knowledge. The debates concerning the reliability of the senses will be discussed in § "Arguments against perceptual relativism or subjectivism", below.

As to the question of how knowledge should be defined, we already mentioned Plato's *Theaetetus*, the main ancient treatise on the theme. Apart from this dialogue, the question remained somewhat in the background in the ancient discussions. Aristotle does make a casual remark according to which *epistēmē* is always with an account (*meta logou*; *APo*. II 19, 100b10). Here we find the expression "with an account", which is also used in the third attempted definition in the *Theaetetus* (201c–d). Therefore, it might seem that

Aristotle presents the same definition: knowledge is true belief with an account. To some extent, this impression is correct. In *Posterior Analytics* I 2, where Aristotle formulates his most developed general characterization of what *epistēmē* is, he outlines it as follows: we think we know (*epistasthai*) something in the unqualified way when we know the reason why (*aitia*) a fact holds, and we know that this reason is the reason for the fact and that the fact cannot be otherwise (71b9–12).[1] Even though the term "account" (*logos*) does not appear in this context, knowing the reason implies possessing the account: knowing the reason why involves possessing a very specific account, namely, the account of why the fact holds.

However, even though this characterization strengthens the impression that *epistēmē* for Aristotle comes with an account, it does not mean that he would subscribe to the idea that all forms of knowledge require an account. Rather, *epistēmē* is one kind or type of knowledge; it may well be one of the most desirable or highest forms of knowledge, but it is not the only one. In fact, Aristotle is not entirely consistent about the requirement of an account in the case of *epistēmē* either; elsewhere in the *Posterior Analytics* (e.g. I 3) he does allow for *epistēmē* that does not require a proof (*epistēmē anapodeiktos*). Even if he did, Aristotle's approach to knowledge deviates from modern discussions about the definition of knowledge in an important respect. As becomes clear in *Nicomachean Ethics* VI, *epistēmē* for Aristotle is one of the intellectual virtues. Therefore, rather than framing necessary and sufficient conditions for all knowledge, he is characterizing a specific cognitive or intellectual achievement: possession of *epistēmē*. This is one of the consequences of the fact that, among the discussions of modern epistemology, Aristotle's approach most resembles virtue epistemology.

Moving now to the commentators' reactions to Aristotle's characterization of knowledge in *Posterior Analytics* I 2, Themistius is explicit that there are several kinds of knowledge, and the requirements are different in each case (*in APo.* 5,5–8). Those commentators whose works on the *Posterior Analytics* have been preserved typically follow Aristotle's description of knowledge in the proper sense at the beginning of I 2 very closely.[2] Yet, as mentioned, it is often made clear that such *epistēmē* is not the only form of knowledge in the proper sense either; Themistius, for example, adds knowledge through theorizing on the definition and knowledge of the unprovable principles (Them. *in APo.* 5,13–16; cf. Phlp. *in APo.* 20,21–2).

When commenting on line 100b10, where Aristotle makes the casual reference to *epistēmē* and its connection with an account, the commentators do not elaborate on the remark at all. In a commentary that, in the *Commentaria in Aristotelem Graeca*, is printed after Philoponus' commentary on *Posterior Analytics* I, *epistēmē* is explained as a capacity of the rational soul (CAG XIII 3 *in APo.* 439,25). It is unclear whether a definition of knowledge in the modern sense should apply to states or capacities of the soul. Rather, the approach again resembles virtue epistemology: identifying the capacities through which we can come to attain knowledge. The origin of that commentary is unknown; Moraux (1979) refers to it as anonymous.

When it comes to the *Theaetetus*, the third attempted definition of knowledge, along with the previous two, is found to be problematic, hence we cannot conclude that Plato would be committed to this definition either. There is one anonymous commentary on Plato's *Theaetetus*, the dating of which is disputed. Within the confines of the present introductory volume we cannot discuss that commentary.[3]

In their discussions about knowledge, the commentators mainly follow the agenda set by Plato and Aristotle. Alexander of Aphrodisias discusses the question of perceptual relativism quite extensively in his commentary on *Metaphysics* IV 5–6, and we shall discuss his treatment below in § "Arguments against perceptual relativism or subjectivism". From Themistius, we do not have a paraphrase on *Metaphysics* IV; only the one on Book XII has been preserved as an Arabic translation. When it comes to Neoplatonic commentators, they do not concentrate on knowledge as discussed in the *Theaetetus*. Under the influence of Neoplatonism, questions of knowledge (*epistēmē*) yield to questions of intellectual apprehension (*nous*) and their discussion of perception does not focus on the debate about perceptual relativism.

This tendency is exemplified by Syrianus in his commentary on *Metaphysics* IV. Syrianus was a pupil of Plutarch of Athens and died *c.*437 CE. In the commentary, after a digression into Protagorean perceptual relativism and Aristotle's discussion concerning it, he adds a brief and rather abrupt remark on how intelligible objects are purer and more divine than perceptible ones (Syrian. *in Metaph.* 75,16–19). He also briefly comments on the Heraclitean Cratylus and says that in all perceptible things there is something changeable but also something permanent: even though Socrates' size changes from birth to death, the form of Socrates in him remains the same (76,4–6). Instead of preoccupying oneself with perceptible things, he instructs us to turn our gaze towards the skies and the divine beings unaffected by earthly things (76,9–17). It is undeniable that these remarks can be understood as reactions to epistemological problems concerning perceptions. However, not much can be extracted as to characteristically epistemological *questions*: the approach rather relates to the metaphysics of knowledge and perhaps to virtue epistemology rather than outlining general conditions for knowledge claims.

In this chapter, we need to resort to commentaries on different works. This is partly because, as noted above, epistemological discussions are not confined to one work of Aristotle. Discussions that are important for our present concerns are found in the commentaries on the *Posterior Analytics*, the *Metaphysics* and the *De anima*. Further, since what we call epistemology is also part of what the commentators would understand as belonging to logic, that is, to the instrument for philosophy (*organon*), it is also in the commentaries on the *Categories* that we find discussions relevant for this theme. In our discussion on epistemology in the commentaries, we shall mainly consult Philoponus and Themistius on *Posterior Analytics*, Alexander on *Metaphysics* IV, and Philoponus on *De anima* II. Occasional reference will be made to Simplicius' commentary on the *Categories*.

Problems with infinity

What do arguments from infinity show us?

In philosophical discussions about knowledge in various historical periods one intuition keeps re-emerging: if there is to be knowledge, the grounds or reasons for knowledge claims cannot be infinite. Even though diverse conclusions have been drawn from this intuition, the idea is widely accepted. (This applies to the ancient debates as well as to most epistemology; for example, most versions of modern foundationalism and coherentism presuppose this idea.) Further, it is often connected with the supposition that if we know something, we cannot simply claim to know it just like that; reasons, grounds, arguments or warrant of some kind are required. If, then, all forms of knowledge are based on further reasons, this seems to create a slippery slope, possibly continuing to infinity.

A sceptical reaction to the problem just outlined would be to say that infinity, or even the possibility of infinity, shows that there is no knowledge based on reasons. Further, since sceptics typically are reluctant to accept the idea that something could be known "just like that" or without reasons or proof, all forms of knowledge come to be excluded by the argument. Another way of responding to the problem would be to say that some things have to be taken for granted or known without proof. What such things could be is a matter of dispute. Philosophers' views also diverge as to whether some things are beyond doubt only relative to the context in which they are used, or whether there are some basic grounds for knowledge that can be supposed to hold without qualification and irrespective of the context.

The problem of infinity is sometimes countered by the claim that the chain of reasons need not be infinite because they may be circular. Again, circularity provokes different responses. Some claim that circularity must be avoided: arguing for knowledge claims in a circle is equivalent to merely supposing the intended conclusion, no matter how wide the circle might be and how credible the claims included in it (see e.g. Arist. *APo*. I 3). This response can be understood in a sceptical and non-sceptical manner. The sceptics would say that such circularity shows the impossibility of knowledge, non-sceptics that either the grounds for knowledge must be known without proof or that the claim of circularity must be understood in some qualified way (modern epistemological coherentism would be an example of the latter position). Others argue that human knowledge is necessarily circular in this way: it is simply impossible to have independent and immediate grounds for knowledge.

In the commentaries, we find several instances of arguments connected to the problem of infinity. One common denial of infinity that is indirectly connected with the notion of knowledge is an argument according to which a chain of predications cannot be infinite. It must terminate, on the one hand, at individual perceptible things (such as Callias and "indivisible substances" or *atomoi ousiai*) and, on the other hand, primary genera, be these the categories (substance, quality, quantity and such) or natural genera (such as animals, plants, minerals and so forth (the examples are from Alex.Aphr. *in APr.* 291,24–5, 293,18–19).[4]

When it comes to those regress arguments that are more directly related to the notion of knowledge, a widely shared supposition coming from Aristotle is the following: it is owing to the lack of education that requirements for infinite chains of reasons are made. On the one hand, it may be that someone demands an argument for all claims because he does not understand the nature of argument. Once the person learns what arguments are and that they must start from somewhere and end somewhere, he will abandon this erroneous requirement. On the other hand, if someone states that all knowledge claims must be proved, this is not simply a misunderstanding concerning the notion of argument. It pertains to the notion of knowledge as well.

Philoponus

An extensive and very interesting discussion concerning the problem of infinity and its relation to knowledge is found in Philoponus on *Posterior Analytics* I 3 (CAG XIII 3), based on Ammonius' lectures (the commentary on the second book is spurious). We shall here refer to Philoponus, the writer of the commentary, even though the origin of the arguments often is Ammonius. In the course of the argument, Philoponus actually severs the argument concerning infinity of proofs from arguments concerning knowledge (*epistēmē*). This is because, according to Philoponus, knowledge extends wider than proof (*apodeixis*) (*in APo.* 20,19–20). This move allows Philoponus to recognize a form or forms of knowledge that do not require proof (cf. Aristotle, *epistēmē anapodeiktos*, in *APo.* I 33, 88b35–7). According to Philoponus, those who suppose all knowledge to require proof are mistaken about the notion of knowledge, but he does not elaborate on this point. The focus of his discussion is on the question of whether proofs should go to infinity. Since he recognizes that some forms of knowledge are based on proofs, his discussion on this point is relevant for understanding his views about knowledge as well.

Philoponus classifies those who claim that proofs go to infinity into two groups (43,24–44,22). First, some aim at destroying proof on the basis of the argument from infinity: since the starting-points for proofs need to be proved, proofs must continue infinitely. However, because it is impossible to traverse infinity, there are no proofs. Secondly, some suppose that there are proofs and that the first premises of proofs must be proved as well. The main complaint that Philoponus makes about arguments of the first kind is that they are based on a vague conception of what a proof is. Further, since such arguments aim at establishing the non-existence of proofs, they are mistaken about the order in which the meaning of a notion (*ti sēmainei ennoian*; 42,26) and the existence of things belonging to the scope of that notion are examined. According to Philoponus, if it is the case that what a notion means is evident, then an enquiry into the existence of corresponding things precedes any scientific enquiry into the notion. His example of a clear notion is curious. Since, Philoponus argues (*in APo.* 43,3–10), it is clear to us what "hippocentaur" means – perhaps because we know what the myths about hippocentaurs tell us – an enquiry into the question of whether there are hippocentaurs precedes a more scientific (*epistēmonikōteros*) enquiry into the notion of a hippocentaur. If it turns out that there are no hippocentaurs, then this scientific enquiry will not be needed.

By contrast, in a case of a notion such as "void", where we only have an obscure impression (*amudros … phantasia*) of the meaning of the term, we first need to find out what "void" means and only then undertake a research project concerning its existence. Philoponus argues that those who wish to establish that because of the problem of infinity there are no proofs are confused about the order of enquiry (*in APo.* 42,22–6). They aim at establishing the non-existence of proofs with an unclear understanding of what a proof is. According to Philoponus, Aristotle is correct in stating that some things must be proved, others need not (44,5–7). Once this essential point about the nature of proofs is known to us, we can start enquiring into the question of whether there are proofs or not.

Philoponus illustrates the error of those aiming at a destruction of proof through the following argument scheme:

> If there are proofs, the first premises of proofs must be known through proof.
> It is impossible to know the first premises through proof.
> Therefore, there are no proofs.

According to Philoponus, the problem here is the addition "through proof" in the first premise, and it causes the argument to go astray (43,21–4).

When describing this argument, Philoponus refers to "the second hypothetical" (43,24–44,1). It is clear that this is not the second syllogistic figure of Aristotle but the second Stoic indemonstrable: if p, then q; not q; therefore, not p.[5] How, then, asks Philoponus, do we know that the first premises are not known through proof and that proofs must continue infinitely? Philoponus argues that this could only happen if the things themselves (*pragmata*) were infinite in their nature. Because it is impossible to go through infinity, there cannot be proof of the first premises (44,1–6).

There is yet another point that Philoponus adds to his arguments against those who wish to destroy proof through arguments about infinity. Philoponus claims that in fact their strategy implies a self-refutation. What would the argument that the adversaries are using to establish that there are no proofs be, if not a proof? If the argument that they produce is valid, it only serves to show that proofs exist: at least one does, namely, the one designed to show that there are no proofs!

Against those who argue that the starting-points of proofs must be known through proof (*di' apodeixeōs*), Philoponus points out that they have misunderstood the initial supposition of what a proof is (44,16–17). In addition, they make a simple logical error when arguing according to the first argument scheme. Here Philoponus is again referring to the Stoic indemonstrable argument forms articulated in what we would call "propositional logic" and using a notion similar to our implication. The first indemonstrable is similar to the inference principle called *modus ponens*: if p, then q; p; therefore q. The error that those arguing that the premises of proofs are known through proof make is, according to Philoponus, like the following fallacy: if there are human beings, there are animals; there are animals; therefore, there are human beings. Here the blunder would be to mix up the antecedent and the consequent of the implication. In order to use the argument scheme correctly, the existence claim should, of course, be "there are human beings" and the conclusion, "there are animals".

According to Philoponus, the adversaries' argument erroneously employs the first Stoic indemonstrable by incorrectly deriving a false conclusion through a hypothesis (44,19–22). The argument is as follows: if there are proofs, the first premises are known through proof; the first premises are known through proof; therefore, there are proofs. Again, this conclusion does not follow, since the first conditional inference principle functions the other way around. Instead of showing the antecedent through the consequent as Philoponus' adversaries do, it concludes the consequent through the antecedent, supposing that the antecedent is true. The analysis is somewhat puzzling, since the idea should have been to show that there are *no* proofs because the starting-points for proofs must be known through proof and hence problems of infinity follow. Rather than this, however, the conclusion of the implication argument is that *there are* proofs and the condition that the premises of proofs are known through proof.

How should we understand Philoponus' argument? One possibility is the following. The argument seems to show that there are proofs on the condition that the premises of proofs are known through proof. Therefore, it creates the illusion that in order to maintain the conclusion (there are proofs), we must accept that the premises of proofs are known through proof. However, this appearance is only illusory, because we know that even when its antecedent is false, an implication is true provided that the consequent is true. Therefore, from accepting the conclusion that there are proofs it does not follow that we must accept that premises are known through proof. This might be Philoponus' analysis, but he does not give it in detail. Be that as it may, his main aim is to show that there are proofs and that they cannot be infinite.

Alexander and Themistius

Alexander and Themistius agree that there are no infinite proofs and that the premises of proofs are known without proof. Themistius' paraphrase on the *Posterior Analytics* does not contain anything remarkable on this point. However, it is of interest that he applies the Hellenistic expression "evident" (*enargēs*; *in APo.* 9,9–10) to the first premises of proofs and that he, as well as Philoponus (44,7–9), denies that proofs could be infinite. Alexander, for his part calls the premises of proofs "axioms" (*axiōmata*, *in Metaph.* 267,6), and this is something Aristotle does not do. Alexander's commentary on *Posterior Analytics* has been lost, but he expresses the idea that proofs cannot go on forever in his commentary on *Metaphysics* IV. He briefly points out that there can be no proof without a starting-point (as, he claims, has been shown in the *Posterior Analytics*) and the starting-point of proofs must be unprovable (*anapodeiktos*). All teaching and learning involving reasoning (*dianoētikē*) starts from pre-existent knowledge and these starting-points are called axioms (*in Metaph.* 266,32–267,6). Here Alexander's wording reflects Aristotle's opening of the *Posterior Analytics*.

In his commentary on *Metaphysics* IV Alexander presents a remarkable version of the argument that not all things can be proved (*in Metaph.* 317,17–25 *ad* 1011a3–4). His example of the kind of thing that is unprovable is whether we are awake or asleep. What he says bears some resemblance to Aristotle's discussion in *Metaphysics* 1010b1–10, where Aristotle likens those who deny the principle of non-contradiction to someone who would act on the basis of a dream impression, which Aristotle presents as a counterfactual possibility. In addition to recognizing whether one is asleep or awake, Alexander mentions the principle of non-contradiction. Are axioms of this kind the only ones Alexander would acknowledge? This cannot be the case. The fragments we have from Alexander's lost commentary on the *Posterior Analytics* (collected by Moraux 1979) indicates that he followed Aristotle in positing various kinds of starting-points that we shall discuss more closely in Chapter 3. What remains to be considered here is how Alexander and the other commentators reacted to perceptual conflict. If we perceive something to be the case, do we know that it is the case?

Arguments against perceptual relativism or subjectivism

Background

Protagoras had famously claimed that "man is the measure of all things: of the things which are, that they are, and of the things which are not that they are not" (Pl. *Tht.* 152a, trans. Levett, rev. Burnyeat, ed. Cooper 1997). As Plato interprets him in the *Theaetetus*, Protagoras draws relativistic conclusions from this idea: if things are as they appear to us to be, there is no shared truth or knowledge about them. If the wind feels cold to me and warm to you, then it is cold to me and warm to you; as such it should not be thought to be either. Alexander of Aphrodisias, for his part, analyses Protagoras' claim as the statement that all perceptions are true. To talk about the truth or falsity of perceptions may strike today's reader as odd: are perceptions the kinds of entities that can be true or false? Does truth-value not apply to propositions rather than perceptions? Ancient authors do not typically refrain from ascribing truth or falsity to perceptions. For us it is more natural to speak about correctness or reliability, or to apply a derivative phrase: my perception that there is a tree over there is true if the proposition "there is a tree over there" is true, and similarly with falsity.

The habit of referring to the truth or falsity of perceptions was central in the Hellenistic debate concerning the criterion of truth. Epicurus was famous for claiming that all perceptions are true (e.g. D.L. 10.32): it is just our judgements added to them that can be false (D.L. 10.51; S.E. *Math.* 7.203).[6]

With certain qualifications it could be suggested that Platonists were inclined towards the claim that no perceptions are true. This would not mean, however, that if we taste wine as sweet we could not perceive the sweetness quite correctly; nor would it mean, for a Platonist, that the wine is never sweet if we taste it as sweet. Rather, the point would be to say that since sweetness is not a constant property of the wine – it may always be, for example, that it has turned bitter before we taste it the next time – we should not invest very much on the epistemic value of perceptions. Further, the metaphysical status of perceptible qualities in Plato's *Theaetetus* is rather weak. Sweetness, for example, does not pre-exist our perception of it, but is created simultaneously with our perception. According to such a view, perceptible qualities only exist in acts of perception (see Pl. *Tht.* 156a–c.)

The Platonic attitude towards perceptions can be contrasted with another position, put forward by a certain Cratylus, a student or follower of Heraclitus. (This Cratylus must be distinguished from the Cratylus after whom one of Plato's dialogues has been named.) According to Aristotle, Cratylus denied the Heraclitean thesis according to which it is impossible to step into the same river twice: Cratylus' claim was that it is impossible to step in it *even once*. In the end, Aristotle reports, Cratylus was just moving his finger and refused to say or claim anything (*Metaph.* IV 5, 1010a11–15).

Cratylus' position is taken up by Alexander of Aphrodisias in his commentary on the *Metaphysics*. Alexander explains it (*in Metaph.* 308,25–39) as follows: perceptual statements are never accurate, because when you present one, the world has already changed. The problem is not simply that even though a perceptual statement would be true, if we make it later it might have turned false. Rather, the point is that we can never catch the changing flow of things around us, hence it is no use making perceptual claims at all. A better way to relate to things is just to wave one's finger and point at them. This is the only way we can refer and relate to the constant flow that makes up the external world. Making perceptual claims would, so to speak, separate the things from this flow and petrify them, whereas their nature is constantly changeable. If Alexander is correct in his interpretation, Cratylus is not saying that our perceptions are completely inaccurate. Perhaps they present things to us as they were just when we noticed them. But this is the best we can do. Our perceptions are always delayed; whatever we perceive to happen is already past.

In addition to those who claim that all perceptions are true and to those who doubt the truth of any perceptions, there are others who claim that some perceptions are true and some are false. Various consequences are drawn from this basic claim. Some, such as the Aristotelians, draw a non-sceptical conclusion from this idea. They claim that even though perceptual error is possible, this does not undermine the epistemic value of perceptions. Basically, the reason why this is so is that errors are due to unnatural states, such as diseases of the organs of the perceiver, or misinterpreted but correctly received perceptions (e.g. when someone is seen to be approaching but the person is misidentified, or when sweet wine tastes bitter to a person with a temperature).

However, some ancient thinkers reacted sceptically towards the falsity or possible falsity of perceptual claims. Some supposed that the mere *possibility* of perceptual error makes it impossible for us to have knowledge since it destroys our capacity to distinguish between true and false appearances. If there are some situations where this distinction cannot be made – for example, in dreams and with respect to objects that seem to be identical but are not – we cannot trust our perceptions at all. This position was advocated by Academic Sceptics, mainly Carneades (see S.E. *Math.* 7.402–3). Pyrrhonian Sceptics, most importantly represented by Sextus Empiricus, argued that such an attitude is not in fact genuinely sceptical but dogmatic. Sextus points out (*Pyr.* 1.124–8) that we cannot universally deny that our appearances do not reveal things as they are; we simply do not know whether they do. Sextus argues that there is no way of checking the reliability of perceptions independently of perceptions themselves, and this leads to a vicious circle: to confirm whether our senses are reliable, we cannot but resort to our senses.

Aristotle tends to make rather dismissive remarks concerning arguments challenging the reliability of perceptions. In a passing remark in the first book of the *Topics* (*Top.* I 11, 105a3–7), where he examines what kinds of questions are suitable for argument, he points out that not all questions are. For example, one should not argue about whether snow is white or not and whether one should honour the gods (or one's parents) or not. Anaxagoras, famously, had argued that snow is black because water is (or seems) black. According to Aristotle, however, if one is in doubt about whether snow is white or not, one should not embark on a disputation about the question. What would be lacking in that case would not be argument but perception.[7] It is obvious that Aristotle's attitude does not serve as a defence of the reliability of perceptions. Rather, he seems to indicate that any global doubt concerning whether our senses show the world to us as it is, is misguided.

The remark in the *Topics* notwithstanding, Aristotle picks up many issues from the *Theaetetus* in *Metaphysics* IV 5. The general outlook of his discussion in the context is peculiar. Aristotle is arguing against those philosophers, whose identity is not certain, who have denied the principle of non-contradiction. In the course of that discussion, Aristotle identifies Protagoras' perceptual relativism or subjectivism with the denial of that principle. As Aristotle himself admits, it is impossible to argue against people who do not subscribe to the principle of non-contradiction, since all forms of argument presuppose that principle. However, he finds it important to *attempt* to show that the denial is absurd, and does so in arguments.

Perceptual relativism and the principle of non-contradiction

Perhaps the most extensive treatment of perceptual relativism in the commentaries discussed in this book is found in Alexander of

Aphrodisias on *Metaphysics* IV. Alexander follows Aristotle's lead and identifies Protagorean perceptual relativism with the denial of the principle of non-contradiction. According to Alexander, these two claims are logically equivalent so that the truth of one implies the truth of the other, and similarly with falsity (*in Metaph.* 301,28–39; cf. also Arist. *Metaph.* IV 5, 1009a6–10). The core of Protagorean relativism as Aristotle interprets it is the claim that things are as they appear to us to be. For example, if the wind appears to me to be cold, then it is cold. If it appears to you to be warm, it is warm. Alexander follows Aristotle in taking this to entail that the same thing, that is, the wind, carries two contradictory properties at the same time (it is both cold and warm, i.e. non-cold). He starts with the formulation according to which perceptual conflict entails that the same thing carries contradictory attributes (*x* is *F* and *x* is non-*F*) at the same time. Towards the end of his discussion, however, Alexander also treats a relativized form of Protagorean relativism: if something appears to me to be cold, then it is cold for me (*x* is *F* for *a*); if the same thing appears to you to be warm, then it is warm, that is, non-cold, for you (*x* is non-*F* for *b*). Alexander argues that this version of the claim leads to a relativistic ontology with serious problems of its own.

Alexander also follows Aristotle in dividing those who deny the principle of non-contradiction into two groups. On the one hand, some people deny it because they do not yet know it, or because they have not understood it. There are, on the other hand, those who love quarrels and arguments, and they deny the principle just for the pleasure of it. Alexander, again not unlike Aristotle, makes it clear that he does not consider it possible to really subscribe to the denial and suppose or believe (*hupolambanein; in Metaph.* 271,25) that the principle of non-contradiction does not hold. What people are more likely to do is to just say (*legein*) that they deny it (see also 298,30–32).

Those who deny the principle owing to ignorance are, according to Alexander, easy to cure, and doing this does not require force, meaning force in arguments, that is, in disputation and refutation (*agōn, elenkhos*) (303,5–7; cf. Aristotle *Metaph.* 1009a16–17). Those who deny the principle out of ignorance can be addressed on the level of their reason (*dianoia*) – as opposed to their speech (*logos*) – and they can be led to change their views when the principle is made familiar to them. By contrast, those who deny it for the sake of argument have to be addressed in argument, that is, speech and words. These people are not, according to Alexander, even convinced of what they are saying (*in Metaph.* 303,8–15). He expresses his concern about the fact that philosophers, whose main objective in life is to attain the truth, present such views as the denial of the principle of non-contradiction. If they do so, Alexander asks (307,16–22), why wonder that people are deterred from further studies in philosophy?

Since Alexander's discussion of Protagorean perceptual relativism is connected with the general argument scheme, inherited from Aristotle, of opposing those who deny the principle of non-contradiction, the overall conclusion that Alexander draws is the following: the contradiction that the adversaries wish to draw is dependent on some qualifications that they overlook or deliberately neglect (326,22–328,4). Our perceptions are not contradictory without qualification: never do we perceive that something is white and non-white or white and black at the same time. If we go by the senses, contraries *cannot* be the case at the same time, and nor can contradictories (314,20–23; cf. Arist. *Metaph.* 10101b18–19). Rather, perceptual conflict only follows with respect to different perceivers (the healthy person perceives the wine as sweet and the sick as bitter), different times (I first perceive the wine as sweet and then as bitter), different senses (sight perceives bile as sweet but taste as bitter), and so on.

Before we continue to follow Alexander's arguments, we need to pause to consider the last-mentioned example about bile being sweet to sight but bitter to taste (*in Metaph.* 320,2–3). It most probably refers to an example that Aristotle discusses in the *Sophistical Refutations* (5, 167b6–7). Aristotle mentions a fallacy of perception, where bile is supposed to be sweet when it in reality is bitter. Such a "fallacy" is probably related to Greek mothers' alleged practice at that time of first encouraging their babies to nurse by applying honey to their nipples. Then, when the mother wishes to stop breastfeeding, she replaces the honey with bile. The colour misleads the baby into taking the mother's nipple eagerly and then, because of the bitterness of the bile, developing a strong aversion towards breast milk.[8] The practice had led to proverbial sayings such as "No, but he applied some gall to the table, weaning himself like children from their mother's milk" (fragment of Diphilus, in Edmonds 1961: vol. 3A, 136–7, quoted by Schreiber 2003: 132 n.49).

What perceptual conflicts show us

Alexander's point concerning perceptual conflict turns out to be that the alleged cases do not in fact create a conflict or contradiction; they only do so with the qualification that the contradiction holds between two distinct senses. Since it is taste, not sight, that is authoritative with respect to flavours, the conflict is easily solved. It would be crazy to wonder whether flavours are such as they seem to be to sight or such that taste deems them to be.

With respect to perceptual conflict over time, Alexander claims that Aristotle has established that such conflict does not exist (*in Metaph.* 314,31–6). The point, however, is not to claim that it would be impossible for me first to taste wine as bitter and later as sweet. Rather, what is denied is that my perception of sweetness as such should change over time. If it did, what sweetness tastes to me would be different over time, but Alexander claims that this does not happen. Whatever my perception of sweetness today is caused by, sweetness as such is the same for me when I experience it next time.

According to Alexander, the conflict about whether wine is sweet or bitter should be analysed as a conflict arising in the subject of these properties, not the properties as such (315,1–2). The assumption that the relativists make is that whatever the sense undergoes is also the state of the subject (306,8–9) and this supposition is, from Alexander's point of view, misguided. When we taste wine while being ill, the bitterness comes from the tongue, not from the wine. Alexander's explanation, however, is a little strange, since it analyses the conflict as pertaining to the sense organ or part of the sense organism (the tongue), *not* the subject (wine), as he just suggested.

In general, Alexander argues that whether or not perceptions are reliable should not be treated as a majority vote (305,15–23; 317,12–15). Even though it typically may be the case that there are more healthy percipients than sick ones, it is equally possible that the number of the sick could exceed that of the healthy. If this possibility were realized and we only trusted the figures, we should judge the estimate of the sick as the correct one. Instead of figures, however, the decisive question is whether the percipient is in a natural state (*kata phusin*; 312,29). In a natural state the perceptible features are observed correctly.

As Alexander indicates, when judging between conflicting observations or appearances, we need to consider many other factors as well as the mere perceptual appearances. For example, we need to check that the percipient is not too far from the object (312,13–19), whether the lighting conditions are normal, whether the person is asleep or awake (312,23–4), whether the percipient is healthy or has an illness of perceptual organs or of the brain (312,20–21), and so on.

These qualifications and conditions seem to make the situation much more complex than the case with two conflicting senses (where someone is asking whether flavours are such as they appear to the sense of sight or to that of taste). However, Alexander takes them as rather similar, and here he follows Aristotle. As Aristotle does in the *Metaphysics*, Alexander also asks if one genuinely wonders whether flavours are such as the sick claim them to be or as the healthy do. All such suspicions are, according to Alexander, similar to wondering whether we are asleep or awake. This, he claims, is like demanding a proof for everything – and this requirement is misguided:

> [S]uch puzzles (*aporēmata*) are like being perplexed over whether we are now sleeping or awake. For even in this case it is not easy to get some piece of evidence by which to make this differentiation, if one lets go of the obvious fact and seeks some sort of argument. For everything that we do when awake, we also do in the course of sleep; in fact we even explain dreams while dreaming. He [i.e. Aristotle] says that all such puzzles (*aporiai*) have the same force, and depend

THE ANCIENT COMMENTATORS ON PLATO AND ARISTOTLE

> on the same [move]; they depend on seeking some sort of
> argument, a cause and a principle, for everything, on not
> positing any indemonstrable principle, and on saying that
> nothing is reliable and obvious immediately and of itself.
> (317,17–25 *ad* 1011a3–4, trans. Madigan 1993, modified)

This is an intriguing version of the argument that one should not
require proof for everything. However, rather than talking about
starting-points for knowledge more generally, Alexander concentrates on the one example he gives. He maintains that there is *nothing* we do while awake that we could not do in sleep; we can even
explain our dreams while sleeping. Nonetheless, he states that it is
evident whether we are asleep or awake. The context does not allow
us to decide whether Alexander supposes that there is an internal
distinguishing mark of dream experience that separates it from
waking experience or whether he denies this. If he does suppose
that there is such an internal mark, the assumption is remarkable.
Most ancient authors would rather be inclined to say that it is very
difficult to distinguish experiences in sleep and while awake. On
the other hand, if he denies the existence of an internal mark, it is
unclear why it is evident that the experiences differ. It is worth noting that when saying that everything we do awake we can also do
when asleep, Alexander deviates from Aristotle, who does not make
such a concession but points out that if someone, while in Africa,
dreams that he is in Athens, he will *not* proceed to a concert hall
(*Metaph.* 1010b1–10).

As to the principle of non-contradiction, Alexander admits that
it is difficult or impossible to refute its denial. He even mentions
(*in Metaph.* 297,8–25) that the opponents of the principle have
pointed out that any arguments about the matter beg the question,
because all arguments are implicitly based on the very principle (cf.
Arist. *Metaph.* 1008a34–5). In another context, Alexander refers
to the definition of a refutation (*elenkhos*) and notes that refutations establish something by bringing the opponent to a contradiction. If the opponent, as in the present case, is happy and willing
to accept the contradiction, or any contradiction for that matter, a

refutation will merely conclude the thesis of the opponent (*in Metaph.* 318,10–20).

Despite these qualms, Alexander does not refrain from arguing against the denial of the principle. However, his arguments do carry a didactic rather than polemic tone, well in line with the proclamation made at the beginning of the argument: it is not possible to genuinely deny the principle of non-contradiction except when ignorant about it. While it is understandable why Alexander makes a claim like this, it is by no means evident that Protagorean relativism could not be sincerely advocated. In fact, Alexander does not seem to make this point, but he attempts to show that Protagorean relativism is either based on a mistaken analysis of perceptual conflict or that it leads to unacceptable ontological commitments.

Perceptions do not support relativism

As indicated above, one of the basic ideas behind Alexander's arguments against Protagorean relativism is that it does not provide us with a correct analysis of perceptual conflicts. One problem is that relativism only follows if the conflict is understood without qualifications. However, Alexander is not willing to claim that the qualifications could altogether explain away perceptual conflicts and would make all perceptions true (*in Metaph.* 314,12–14). Those that are of a foreign sense (e.g. vision of flavours) are not always true, and nor are those of sick people. Perceptions may also be made from a distance and become distorted on the way. Therefore, perceptual conflicts only appear with some qualifications concerning the percipient or the external circumstances.

Even more significant is Alexander's conclusion that from what has been said it follows that perceptions as such do *not* support the conclusion that appearances conflict:

> For no sense indicates at the same time that the same thing is such and is not such, for example that the same thing is white and black at the same time, or sweet and bitter at the

> same time. Hence, if one must go along with the senses, contraries could not be true at the same time, nor could contradictories. (314,19–23, trans. Madigan 1993)

Erroneous analysis of perceptions is not the only problem of the Protagorean approach. Alexander argues that it also leads to a bad ontology. If perceptions or appearances are supposed to determine what there is rather than the other way around, it needs to be concluded that nothing exists over and above the perceptible objects (*ta aisthēta*; 307,35–308,1).

The alleged mistake here is that since we perceive colours, sounds, odours, flavours and tangible qualities, the world is nothing but these, and, Alexander adds, the nature of perceptibles is indeterminate (*aoristos*; 308,1). From Alexander's point of view, the world is understood incorrectly if it is supposed to be a world of indeterminate properties. Rather, the properties that we perceive are properties of things: human beings, horses, minerals, stars and so on. By contrast to the changeable and indeterminate perceptible qualities, things have a permanent and unchangeable nature: what it is for a human being to be a human being does not change, even though the perceptible qualities of individual humans do. Therefore, the correct order of priority is the exact opposite of the one behind Protagorean relativism: things come first and their perceptible qualities second, even though the qualities may be more familiar to us from perception. Another conclusion that Alexander finds mistaken is that, on the basis of perceptual conflict, some have concluded that reality consists in a continuous flux, since, they suppose, flowing reality is the only one that can make contradictories true at the same time. Heraclitus, Empedocles and Anaxagoras are mentioned as proponents of this view (cf. 307,33–308,14, 314,5–6). Just because our perceptions about things change, we need not conclude that things do. Their qualities and properties may well change but, Alexander would claim, their whole nature would not.

Alexander argues that there are other mistaken priorities in Protagoreanism as well. For example, those who claim that the world is as it appears to us to be cannot avoid claiming that it is our appearances or conceptions that are prior to things rather than vice versa. According to Alexander, this ultimately leads to claiming that an earthquake cannot take place unless we have first opined that it will (322,37–323,1).

While Alexander is mainly arguing against Protagoreans in his commentary on *Metaphysics* IV 5 (he even briefly refers [313,6–7] to Plato's discussion of the position [i.e. *Tht.* 178c–179b]) there are passages that seem to indicate that his objective is wider than that. For example, before going into the more detailed arguments, Alexander refers to some thinkers who suppose that we can at best have opinions or conceptions (*hupolēpsis*) and appearances to which we assent (Alexander employs the Stoic term *sungkatathesis* here), but we cannot obtain real knowledge. These thinkers, according to Alexander (*in Metaph.* 300,5–20), make the mistake of blaming the nature of things if human conceptions are vague, and this is incorrect. If we feel uncertain, we should attend to ourselves and to our own state of mind rather than accuse things of being unclear or indeterminate. Alexander also presents a simile: when someone is ill, he should attend to his own health rather than complain that the world is upside down.

Since Alexander frequently uses Stoic terminology and since he contrasts assenting to appearances and having certain knowledge, it is possible that the object of his argument here is Sextus Empiricus' Pyrrhonian Scepticism.[9] Whereas, according to Protagoras, things are as they seem to us to be, Sextus suspends judgement concerning how things are; he restricts himself to claims about how they seem to be. These are two distinct claims and perhaps only one of them, the position of Sextus, is genuinely sceptical. However, Alexander does not comment on the differences between these two claims in his commentary.

This is an illuminating instance of how the historical situation of a writer necessarily affects his or her way of dealing with an object text, and how it did affect the situation of the commentators in particular. Here Alexander is influenced by the Hellenistic debates but operates on a text where Aristotle opposes a Presocratic figure or figures. Alexander's approach is not historical in the sense that he would aim to analyse and distinguish the origins of various arguments and his

THE ANCIENT COMMENTATORS ON PLATO AND ARISTOTLE

own viewpoint to those arguments. Perhaps he would even hesitate to bring in an author like Sextus when so clearly starting from the concerns of Aristotle.

Are perceptions true?

Aristotle on the truth of perceptions

We have now briefly discussed problems related to the claim that all perceptions are true, understood as the claim made in Protagorean relativism. However, a puzzling fact is that Aristotle seems at times to subscribe to the claim of the truth of all perceptions. In order to consider Aristotle's claim we need to recall a distinction that he makes in the *De anima* between various kinds of perceptible objects (II 6, 418a7–24). The core of his theory consists of the so-called "proper sensibles": perceptible qualities that are perceived by one sense alone – colours for sight, sounds for hearing, flavours for taste, odours for smell and tactile qualities for touch (there are several such qualities, e.g. rough and smooth, resistant and yielding). In this respect perception of proper sensibles is said to differ from those kinds of perceptible qualities that permit cognition by several senses: movement, rest, number, figure and size. Objects of the latter kind Aristotle calls "common sensibles" (Arist. *de An.* III 1). In addition to these, Aristotle also allows the so-called accidental sensibles. To talk about accidental sensibles means that perceptual capacities in some sense makes us aware of things, even though the senses are only affected by the perceptible *qualities* of things. Accidental perception also explains how animals, which in Aristotelian theory do not have reason, can recognize, for example, human individuals.

In several passages in the *De anima* (418a11–16, 427b12–13, 428a11, 428b18–19) he makes comments to the effect that perceptions of the proper sensibles of each sense are unerring. The same point is repeated in *De sensu* (442b18–20). Perceiving the common sensibles is supposed to allow falsity to a much greater degree, and in the case of accidental properties the risk of error is highest. Is Aristotle, then, saying that we cannot be mistaken about colours, sounds, odours or flavours? Or, for our present purposes, do the commentators subscribe to this doctrine? We have identified five passages where Aristotle talks about the truth of perceptions. In three of the above-mentioned ones, two in the *De anima* (427b12–13, 428a11) and one in the *De sensu* (442b8–10), Aristotle is making the claim that perceptions about the proper sensibles are true. However, in the two remaining instances his claim is more refined.

The first remark (*de An.* II 6, 418a11–16) is not concerned with the question of whether one proper sensible could or could not be mistaken for another belonging to the scope of the same sense: for example, whether it would be possible to mistake one colour for another or one flavour for another. Rather, Aristotle is talking about another way in which the senses are unerring concerning their proper sensibles: if I perceive a colour, it is impossible for me to mix it up with a sound. This seems to be a reasonable point and does not entail the difficult claim that all perceptions of the proper sensibles should be true.

The last passage (428b18–19), for its part, states that the perception of the proper sensibles is always true *or allows for a minimal amount of error*. If Aristotle's doctrine really were that literally all perceptions are true, it would be difficult to understand why he once qualifies it by saying that they are not always true. This would mean that they are true, except for the small number of cases in which they are false. By contrast, there is no difficulty at all if Aristotle is saying that senses are *reliable* about the proper sensibles, that is, that they are true in most cases but that it is nonetheless possible for them to be mistaken. In this case Aristotle just leaves the additional specification out in two references to it. In those passages his point is to contrast perception with *phantasia*: something appearing to be the case that really is not the case. Further, he makes quite clear that even though perceptual error is possible, even with respect to the proper sensibles, such errors are not very common. The origin of perceptual error, for Aristotle, lies in three main sources. First, Aristotle affirms that the belief or appearance that is added to the perception often errs. When something appears to me to be the case, it may be that the original perception of a quality, for example, was correct, but my presentation of it was mistakenly interpreted. Secondly, Aristotle also allows that the *sense organs* can be in a defective state (e.g. when one is ill; cf. Alexander on *Metaph*. IV in § "Arguments against Perceptual Relativism or Subjectivism", above), and this can disturb the natural functioning of the perceptual system. Thirdly, there are external hindrances, such as poor lighting conditions, that sometimes prevent the sense from functioning properly.

How is Aristotle's remark interpreted in the commentaries?

Irrespective of what we take Aristotle's intended meaning to be, the commentators are unanimous that one should *not* claim that all perceptions are true *tout court*. To make this clear, they proceed to add some qualifications in almost all the instances where the claims listed above are dealt with. For example, in his commentary on the second book of Aristotle's *De anima*, Philoponus adds the qualification that proper sensibles are perceived correctly when the senses are in a natural state (*kata phusin*; *in de An.* 313,27). When explaining this idea, he mainly concentrates on discussing the distance between the observer and the observed quality (313,31–314,18). The health or sickness of the percipient, lighting conditions and the position of the object are mentioned as possible sources of distortions of the natural state (313,30, 313,35, 314,4).

The qualifications that the commentators add to refine the claim that all perceptions are true can be classified under the following categories:

1. Proper sensibles are perceived correctly when the sense is in a natural state (Phlp. *in de An.* 313,27; Them. *in de An.* 57,18).

This is perhaps a general qualification that may accommodate the following, more narrowly defined cases:

2. Perception of proper sensibles is true when there is no external obstacle (Them. *in de An.* 57,20–24) such as: (a) long distance

or (b) the position of the object (57,18–19); (c) lighting conditions and (d) place (Phlp. *in de An.* 313,35, 314,4).
3. Senses (a) allow a minimal amount of error (Phlp. *in de An.* 513,15–20; Them. *in de An.* 57,17–31, 93,8–10) or (b) are true for the most part (Them. *in de An.* 90,8–9; Alex.Aphr. *de An.* [i.e. treatise, not commentary] 66,15; cf. also Alex.Aphr. *in Metaph.* 313,20ff.).

The general idea behind these remarks is familiar to us from the above discussion of Protagorean perceptual relativism. The commentators are pointing out that our senses register the quality of an object reliably, unless the natural function of the sense has been hindered. Such hindrances may occur if, for example, the person is sick and his or her sense organs are covered by some extra material such as bitter moisture on the tongue or yellow liquid in the eyeball; even some dysfunction in the brain may cause such a hindrance (see Alexander *in Metaph.* 312,20–21). In these situations, the senses are prevented from functioning normally: they do not merely register the quality of the object, but add a quality of their own. Similar obstacles to the natural functioning of the organs also occur when the medium, the air in between the object and the percipient, is affected by the qualities we are trying to perceive, for example, if the air is coloured in an exceptional manner or if it is very noisy and we try to hear something.

One somewhat different reaction to the idea that senses are in some sense truthful or reliable is found in a commentary on the *De anima* attributed to Simplicius in the manuscript tradition, but which is most probably spurious (see Ch. 1, § "Simplicius"). In this commentary, the focus is on the question of how perception differs from reasoning, and not so much on the functioning of the senses themselves. The author of the commentary, perhaps Neoplatonically influenced, points out that perception is true or correct, but cannot state its own truth or falsity. Only reason can do this. Reason can enquire into the question of whether this or that perception or conception of mine is true or false. Even though reason may err in doing so, it should not be taken as inferior to the senses that attain their objects through contact (ps.-Simplicius *in de An.* 204,36–205,17). Note that even though the author seems to be making the blunt statement that perceptions are unerring without qualification, the text does not necessarily support this reading. One could ask why reason needs to enquire into the question of truth or falsity of perceptions and conceptions if it was absolutely impossible for them to err. Therefore, a door is left open for perceptual error even in this commentary.

***

From a more general epistemological point of view, it can be seen that neither Aristotle's nor the commentators' approach to the question of the reliability of our perception concerning the proper sensibles focuses on the question of justification. Instead of trying to prove to sceptics that the senses actually do register perceptible qualities reliably when they function normally, the commentators concentrate on *explaining* why the senses sometimes fail to perform this function. The very claim that our senses are reliable when functioning normally is not seriously questioned in the commentaries. Further, the explanations are psychological rather than epistemological.

The basic idea of the explanation is as follows. A perceptual quality, such as a colour or a sound, causes us, through our sensory system, to perceive it. Since it is the quality that causes us to perceive it, this means that our senses are receptive to the nature of the qualities. Aristotle underlines just this receptive aspect of perception: since our senses, when functioning normally, do not add anything to the perceived quality or subtract anything from it, they are able to present it to us just as it is. The possible disturbances in the process are due to the external circumstances or to the unnatural state of the organ. As we saw earlier in this chapter, Alexander, Themistius and Philoponus subscribe to this explanation (see also Ch. 5, § "Themistius and Philoponus on perception"). In the later Platonic tradition, a different approach is taken (see Ch. 5, § "Attention and reflexive awareness").

Since we opened our discussion with concerns related to infinity and identified perception (and perhaps acceptance of general logical principles such as that of non-contradiction) as a source of knowledge that does not require proof, one might be tempted to conclude that the commentators' approach resembles that of modern epistemological foundationalism. However, we have already warned against this when pointing out that the approach of Aristotle and the commentators (and to some extent Plato as well) is more akin to virtue epistemology. This point is also valid against the too hasty comparison to foundationalism.

When identifying perception as a source of knowledge that does not require proof, the commentators are not making the claim that each and every knowledge claim of ours should or could be deductively derived from perceptions. Rather, the point is to identify perception as the kind of cognitive capacity that provides us with a reliable insight into the qualities of things. Perhaps even more importantly, perception functions as a starting-point for knowledge in the more instrumental sense that it constitutes the beginning of our cognitive development. Despite some disagreements in the details of the explanation, there is wide agreement among the commentators that perceptions are needed for our reason to develop or to be activated (see Ch. 5, § "Intellect"). Therefore, perception is the most elementary cognitive capacity that is required for us to start reasoning, and to attain knowledge that is more advanced and of a higher type than mere registering of perceptual qualities.

Knowledge in the sense of *epistēmē* has a very specific logical structure, and it is for *epistēmē* that Aristotle makes his argument that there must be starting-points (*APo.* I 3). This might be taken to suggest that even if foundationalism cannot be used as a general point of comparison for the commentators' concerns with knowledge, it could be used as one for *epistēmē*. However, as we shall see in Chapter 3, even for *epistēmē* the structure is much more complex than in modern foundationalism, and the role of starting-points is quite different.

THREE

Science and logic

This chapter needs to begin with some qualifications. To start with, both nouns that appear in the title of this chapter are not unproblematic when applied to ancient philosophy. For the term "science", this is because science as a technical, systematized and institutionalized activity was not, in antiquity, distinct from philosophy. What we call "science" today is an outgrowth of ancient natural philosophy, that is, theoretical research concerning the general explanatory patterns in nature to an extent inspired by actual empirical observation. In so far as we find discussions about how such activity should be carried out, what its aims are and what its structures are like, we can talk about ancient discussions about science. On the other hand, this discussion in Greek concerns *epistēmē*, which also simply means "knowledge", and in this chapter we shall also touch on issues that pertain to knowledge rather than science.

A general supposition that the commentators tend to share is that human beings have a capacity to arrive at a comprehensive understanding or knowledge of reality. What this involves, how such knowledge or understanding is achieved, and to what extent it may be called "science" are questions that need to be addressed separately in the case of individual commentators. In this chapter, we shall address these questions through examples from Alexander, Themistius, Philoponus and Simplicius. We concentrate on the questions of what kind of knowledge *epistēmē* or science involves, how we attain such knowledge, and to what extent logic is employed in scientific or philosophical research.

The main sources for our discussions are the commentaries on the *Analytics*, both the prior and the posterior. On the *Prior Analytics*, Alexander and Philoponus' commentaries, the latter of which is based on Ammonius, have been preserved. We also have Themistius' paraphrase on the *Posterior Analytics* and Philoponus' commentary (again based on Ammonius' lectures) on its Book I.[1] We shall also consult Alexander's commentary on the *Topics*, where helpful. Alexander's commentary on the *Topics* is the only larger work on this treatise preserved from our authors. Finally, reference is also made to Porphyry's immensely influential *Introduction* (to the *Categories* and, at the same time, to the whole Platonic–Aristotelian philosophy), and Simplicius' commentary on the *Categories*.

Epistēmē

When describing science as a systematic theoretical activity aiming at achieving comprehensive knowledge about the structures and workings of *nature*, we need to note that "nature" in this context must be understood generously. It includes things that we would also call "natural": the material elements (earth, water, air, fire), plants, animals, minerals and so on, and meteorological celestial phenomena, the sun, moon, heavenly bodies and stars. However, soul as a principle of life, cognition, feeling and knowledge is, to some extent, analysed by the same general notions as natural change in general (cf. Them. *in APo.* 27,29–31). Aristotle affirmed that study of the soul does belong to natural science (*de An.* 403a28), even though not all parts of the soul belong to the scope of natural science (*PA* I 1).

One debated question concerning nature in antiquity was whether or in what sense divinity is realized in nature. Most commentators seem to suppose that nature, at least to some extent, exemplifies or reflects divinity. Opinions diverge on the point of how much natural philosophy or science is supposed to derive its explanations from divine principles; sometimes one author wavers on this point. Philoponus, for example, at times recommends that we follow very Aristotelian methods of enquiry that start from experience and proceed to a more general understanding of nature, but occasionally he refers to the idea that we should try to reach divine principles outside nature in a divine intellect (e.g. *in APo.* 47,24–48,1, deriving from Ammonius' lectures). Taken at face value, these claims seem to be, if not contradictory, at least in serious opposition to one another. Yet it seems that Philoponus would not take these methods to be contradictory or mutually exclusive. At least he does not mention any discrepancy here. (On nature and divinity, see further Chapter 4.)

When we talk about science and its methodology in this chapter, the following questions need to be separated from the very beginning. On the one hand, there are discussions *about* science as a systematic theoretical activity. Methodology in this sense pertains to the question of how to proceed in order to gain knowledge about the world. This is the sense in which we discuss methodology in this chapter. On the other hand, we can speak about the methodology of the commentators themselves. Methodology in this second sense can also refer to several things: (i) how the commentators themselves proceed in their works on physics and psychology to attain general knowledge; and (ii) how the commentators (a) proceed in their own commentaries, or (b) how they understand their task as commentators. These questions do not belong to the scope of this chapter. Chapter 4 sheds some light on question (i). Question (ii) in both its interpretations is briefly addressed in the introduction as well as in the course of our discussion when the topic so dictates.[2]

Logic

What about logic then? The term "logic" comes from the Greek adjective *logikos*. "Logikos" does appear here and there in the sources, and it is not always misleading to translate it as "logical" (except, for example, when Philoponus identifies logical sciences with mathematical ones; *in APo.* 6,12). However, it is important to note that *logikos* does not quite mean what "logical" does today. Something is logical in the sense of *logikos*, when it is related to utterances, inferences and arguments in a very broad sense. For example, when Aristotle employs the term to denote a class of problems suitable for dialectical scrutiny, his example is "whether knowledge of contraries is the same or not" (*Top.* I 14, 105b24–5). This problem is said to be *logikon*, but it is not logical in the sense that we use the term today. Therefore, when we talk about logic in this chapter, we do not determine our cases by checking how Greek *logikos* is used.

A more appropriate starting-point for our discussion about logic here is to trace sources where questions related to the validity of arguments or inferences are discussed. Logic in this sense is based on the observation made in antiquity that some arguments are, as we say today, "truth preserving". An argument is truth preserving when it satisfies the following requirement: if the premises of the argument are true, the conclusion must be true as well. In modern logic, it is no news that whether or not an argument is truth preserving is not dependent on the content but on the form of the argument. By contrast, in antiquity, something analogous to this idea had to be discovered. Validity as an abstract notion was not there to be studied right from the beginning. Rather, logical considerations grew out of an interest into argument practices in classical Athens before and during Plato and Aristotle's time. Such practices had their background in law courts where the disputing parties needed to make their case through argument. Political orators also influenced large crowds through persuasive talks and thus affected the opinion in the assemblies of the free citizens of a city-state. As is well known, Plato opposed the so-called sophists' argument techniques, which he saw as both misguided and misleading. When Aristotle writes his manuals for argument strategies, it is clear that a socially determined context for argumentation, even for argument competitions, had been developed. Such arguments are dealt with in the *Topics* for more general purposes and the *Sophistical Refutations* is a more specific critique of sophistic argument forms that are merely apparent but not really compelling, or the premises of which are merely apparently acceptable.

Behind the various argument techniques, Socrates, Plato and Aristotle found a general idea acceptable to them. Arguments succeed in persuading the interlocutor (perhaps to change his mind) when the statements that he accepts in the course of the discussion are shown to contradict the claim that he made at the beginning. As for the techniques of argumentation based on leading the adversary into a contradiction, an important observation was made in Plato's Academy and highlighted by Aristotle: true claims do not conflict with each other. If someone is telling the truth and nothing else, he or she cannot be led into a contradiction, except on the level of apparitions or conceptual misunderstandings that can be sorted out by specifications.

Aristotle's syllogisms and dialectical arguments

Aristotle highlighted this discovery in his works and took the investigation further. The *Topics* is a manual for the art of dialectical disputation that takes place between a questioner and an answerer. It starts from a thesis that the answerer accepts at the beginning. The questioner's aim is to derive either a contradiction with the answerer's thesis or a very implausible claim as a conclusion on the basis of appropriately chosen yes-or-no-questions and the thesis itself. The claims conceded by the answerer can be used as premises in deriving the conclusion.[3] In addition to the idea that truths never contradict each other, the *Topics* is based on another important finding. Some arguments are such that in them the content may vary a great deal, but they share the common feature that if the premises are true, the conclusion must be true as well.

For example, if we want to explore whether pleasure is a kind of good, Aristotle instructs us to use the following strategy: suppose that pleasure is a kind of good, that is, that good is a genus for pleasure, and then see whether a pleasure can be found that is not good.

> If, then, a genus is suggested for something that is, first take
> a look at all objects which belong to the same genus as the

thing mentioned, and see whether the genus suggested is not predicated of some of them, as in the case of accident: e.g. if good be laid down as the genus of pleasure, see whether some pleasure is not good; for, if so, clearly good is not the genus of pleasure; for the genus is predicated of all the members of the same species.

(*Top.* IV 1 120b15–20, trans. Pickard-Cambridge)

This piece of advice is based on a general principle, according to which everything that is predicated of a genus is predicated of all its species. Therefore, if we want to find out whether pleasure is a kind of good, we need to check whether there are some pleasures that are not good. If we find some that are not (excessive wine drinking, for example), we have managed to show that good is not the genus of pleasure and that pleasure is not a kind of good.

Even though Aristotle does observe regularities and similarities in different argument forms, his observations in the *Topics* are still based on the content of the claims. He structures his treatment around some general notions, the mutual dependencies of which form the basis of his analysis. These notions are the so-called predicables: definition, peculiar property, genus, differentia and accident. An example of a mutual dependency is a peculiar property; it is a property that belongs universally to the members of a certain class but does not belong to their definition. These notions had great influence for Western medieval thinking through Porphyry's *Introduction* (underlined e.g. in John Marenbon 2007) the basic textbook for philosophy used in all the main universities.

The details of the argument technique of the *Topics* must be left aside in this context. What is important about it is that the treatise gives practical advice as to how to perform one's role well in a disputation, whether one is acting as a questioner or as an answerer (see e.g. Kakkuri-Knuuttila 2005). From a logical point of view, Aristotle has already observed that arguments that succeed in forcing the answerer to accept a conclusion that he at first resisted have something in common. However, he has not detached this observation from the content of the arguments.

This project is taken further in the *Prior Analytics*, where Aristotle presents his theory of syllogistic. The technical name "syllogism" for the inferences in these figures is also a name for more flexible dialectical inferences. A syllogism (*sullogismos*), for Aristotle, "is an argument (*logos*) in which certain things having been laid down something other than those that are laid down necessarily follows on the basis of them" (*Top.* I 1, 100a25–7; see also *APr.* I 1, 24b18–22; *SE* 1, 165a1–4). A syllogism in this broad sense is a truth-preserving argument in which the conclusion is non-identical with and not reducible to any one of the premises. In the *Prior Analytics*, Aristotle outlines a more specific theory of what valid inferences are like. He claims that all valid inferences can be expressed in one of the so-called syllogistic figures, which is an exaggerated claim. The syllogistic figures contain so-called categorical syllogisms, in which there are three terms that make up two premises and a conclusion. Often the terms are labelled A, B and C, where A is the so-called major term, B the middle term and C the minor term. In the premises, the relations between two terms are fixed in such a manner that a further connection becomes necessary.

The simplest example of a categorical syllogism is the first-figure universal affirmative syllogism:

A belongs to all B (every B is A).	Every mammal has a backbone.
B belongs to all C (every C is B).	Every dolphin is mammal.
Therefore: A belongs to all C (every C is A).	Every dolphin has a backbone.

In the example, having a backbone is to be contrasted with having a fish-spine. The three syllogistic figures are as follows:

I		II		III	
	AxB		BxA		AxB
	BxC		BxC		CxB
	AxC		AxC		AxC

In these figures, the two first sentences stand for the premises, whereas the third one is the conclusion; x stands for the syllogistic relations between the terms, and the relations are as follows:

Universal affirmative (AaB): A belongs to every B.
Particular affirmative (AiB): A belongs to some B.
Universal negative (AeB): A belongs to no B.
Particular negative (AoB): A does not belong to some B.

The letters a, i, e and o were introduced in the middle ages to denote the relations between terms (coming from Latin *affirmo*, "I affirm", and *nego*, "I deny"). In English, the sentences are more naturally read as follows: "every B is A", "some B is A", "no B is A", and "some B is not A". Aristotle does not employ such a formulation, because it confuses the position of the middle term. Out of these ingredients, namely the three figures and the relations between the terms, Aristotle identifies as valid those shown in Table 1.

This is not the context to present a more extensive introduction into the syllogistic of Aristotle. However, it must be mentioned that Aristotle did not just produce a theory of the syllogistic figures with general terms, but also added to it a modal aspect, that is, analysed arguments with the notions of necessity and possibility. Aristotle's modal syllogistic is notoriously problematic. From the point of view of knowledge, the most relevant modal syllogism is the first figure affirmative syllogism with necessity added to every premise. This type of categorical syllogism was the one that he saw as most important in science and it does not belong to the problematic part of modal syllogistic.

Necessarily: every mammal has a backbone.
Necessarily: every dolphin is mammal.
Necessarily: every dolphin has a backbone.

By the time of the commentators, there were several debated logical issues. One was the question of whether Aristotelian syllogistic or Stoic propositional logic makes a better logical system. Many commentators, Philoponus among them, freely employed both (see Ch. 2, § "Problems with infinity") but did not seem to commit to the superiority of one over the other. Another point of controversy was whether the so-called fourth figure should be included into logical

Table 1.

I figure	II figure	III figure
(1) AaB, BaC; AaC A belongs to every B, B belongs to every C; A belongs to every C	(5) BeA, BaC; AeC B belongs to no A, B belongs to every C; A belongs to no C	(9) AaB, CaB; AiC A belongs to every B, C belongs to every B; A belongs to some C
(2) AeB, BaC; AeC A belongs to no B, B belongs to every C; A belongs to no C	(6) BaA, BeC; AeC B belongs to every A, B belongs to no C; A belongs to no C	(10) AeB, CaB; AoC A belongs to no B, C belongs to every B; A does not belong to some C
(3) AaB, BiC; AiC A belongs to every B, B belongs to some C; A belongs to some C	(7) BeA, BiC; AoC B belongs to no A, B belongs to some C; A does not belong to some C	(11) AaB, CiB; AiC A belongs to every B, C belongs to some C; A belongs to some C
(4) AeB, BiC; AoC A belongs to no B, B belongs to some C; A does not belong to some C	(8) BaA, BoC; AoC B belongs to every A, B does not belong to some C; A does not belong to some C	(12) AiB, CaB; AiC A belongs to some B, C belongs to every B; A belongs to some C
		(13) AoB, CaB; AoC A does not belong to some B, C belongs to every B; A does not belong to some C
		(14) AeB, CiB; AoC A belongs to no B, C belongs to some B; A does not belong to some C

analysis. From the constants that Aristotle gives, it is in principle possible to produce yet another figure. Aristotle himself did not accept it, possibly for the reason that he supposed that validity is not equally obvious in it as it is in the other figures. There is some dispute about who introduced the debate about the fourth figure, but it definitely was an issue in later antiquity.[4]

Logic as an instrument or as a part of philosophy

The commentators significantly affected the transmission of the ancient tradition on the role of logic in philosophy. The main debate was between the following two positions: logic is a tool (*organon*) for philosophy; or logic is a part of philosophy. The former is the Aristotelian and the latter the Stoic view.[5] Our discussion of Philoponus in § "Syllogistic scheme", below, for example, contains an example of the Aristotelian position: Philoponus states that logic (*logikē*) is a tool (*organon*) for philosophy (*in APr.* 305,16). In fact, he adds that it is a *proper* (*idion*) tool for it. However, to know that one of the positions is Aristotelian, and another Stoic leaves open the question of what was at stake in that debate.

The Stoics did not accept the Aristotelian categorical syllogisms but presented instead five indemonstrable argument forms (*anapodeiktoi logoi*) that employ logical notions that we would call "implication". These indemonstrables are as follows:

(a) If p, then q; p; therefore q.
(b) If p, then q; not-q; therefore not-p.
(c) Not (both p and q); p; therefore not-q.
(d) Either p or q; p; therefore not-q.
(e) Either p or q; not-q; therefore p.

(D.L. 7.76–81; S.E. *Pyr.* 2.156, *Math.* 8.223)

The Stoics, who proposed that logic is a part of philosophy, seemed to suppose that their logic of implication is better suited to express the way reality works. In particular, causal relations understood in the Stoic manner can be formulated through implications rather than categorical syllogisms.

Would the Aristotelians, then, deny that a proper logic reflects the structure of the world? Not quite. Even though the Aristotelians did not see logic as a part of philosophy, there is a sense in which their analysis of the world, structurally speaking, matches with their logic. This is because reality is supposed to consist of species and genera that are characterized by specific differences, qualities that distinguish a species from all the other species in the world. And this idea can be expressed rather well in syllogisms.

In order to see what the argument is about, we need to look what kinds of positions were taken. Alexander, for example, argues for the instrumental interpretation of logic. One key point in his argument is that even though logic is a product of philosophical analysis, this does not prevent it from being a tool. An analogy that Alexander gives is that a hammer and anvil are products of a smith's art, and this does not prevent them from being tools of the very same art (*in APr.* 1,7ff., quoted in Sorabji 2004: vol. 3, 33–4). Alexander's basic point seems clear enough: even though some art produces some things, this does not prevent that very art from using these products as tools. However, would it not also seem quite natural to suppose that the fact that the art produces these things makes them parts of that art as well?

In fact, Ammonius argues for the claim that neither the Aristotelian nor the Stoic view is correct, but that logic is both a part of and a tool for philosophy. He adds that this is the way in which Plato uses logic. According to Ammonius, when logic is used as empty schemata, that is, with symbols in the place of terms, then it is a tool, whereas when there are actual contents in an argument, logic will become a part of philosophy. According to Ammonius, an example of such an argument is the following: "the soul is a self-mover; the latter is eternally moving, the latter is immortal, therefore the soul is immortal" (*in APr.* 11,10–11, trans. Flannery in Sorabji 2004: vol. 3, 35).

Ammonius' explanation of the two positions is not entirely clear. For example, our evidence of the Stoic position strongly suggests that they allowed "empty schemata". The formulation of the indemonstrable argument forms was given in the form "if the first, then the second; the first; therefore, the second" (see e.g. D.L. 7.76). The examples, on the other hand, were given by using actual terms "if it is day, it is light; it is day; therefore it is light". But perhaps this is not a fair point against Ammonius. A more charitable reading might be to suggest that Ammonius is aware of the fact that Aristotle and the Aristotelians rarely make their arguments in a syllogistic form (*pace* Alexander, e.g. *in Top.* 64,2ff.). His point, then, might be that when validity or the form of arguments is studied on an abstract level (the syllogistic of *Prior Analytics*), that study is an instrument for philosophy. By contrast, when arguments are used to make a philosophical point (which Aristotle himself would more often do dialectically than syllogistically), then that argument is a part of philosophy.[6]

In this chapter, we shall not go deeper into this topic on an abstract level. Rather, in § "Logic in science and philosophy", below, we shall ask how Alexander, Philoponus and Simplicius themselves present the use of logic in science and philosophy.

Epistēmē: proofs and principles

The general ethos in the commentaries is that for us to achieve more systematic knowledge or understanding about things requires that we come to grasp some principles that explain or explicate the object of knowledge. On the one hand, explanatory principles express reasons or causes for what we know, and this is an aspect that is underlined in the commentators' accounts of knowledge in their work on the *Posterior Analytics*. For example, they often refer to Aristotle's characterization of knowledge in I 2 (71b10–15) with approval. According to this characterization, we think we know something in the proper sense when (i) we know the reason for that thing or fact and (ii) we know that the reason is the reason for precisely this fact and (iii) we know that it cannot be otherwise. The commentators Themistius and Philoponus, who comment on these lines, do not object to the characterization but, rather, elaborate on it; Philoponus, however, is explicit that it is Aristotle's characterization (*in APo.* 20,28).

On the other hand, principles can be found by analysing a general notion into its constituent parts. In a typical case, this means that we should, in order to know properly what a thing is, find its genus and specific differences. These notions along with that of a species, definition and peculiar property (*idion*) are called "predicables" and they had incomparable influence in the later tradition, both in late antiquity and in medieval philosophy. Aristotle introduces the notions in the *Topics* and argues (I 8) that all dialectical problems and premises concern them. In Aristotle, the role of specific difference is not completely stable: in I 8 (103b12–15) he lists it as a predicable of its own, but in I 4 (101b18) it is classified under the genus. The predicables form the main content of Porphyry's *Introduction to the* Categories (*Isagoge*) and, as Barnes (2003: ix) notes, the *Isagoge* was the basic philosophy book for students for a thousand years. It was used in medieval introductory courses in logic as a basic textbook.[7]

Later the model of analysis that Porphyry introduces there became known as the Porphyrian tree, in which some sort of family tree is made in all the ten categories for all notions or species in accordance with a transitive genus–species relation (e.g. Stump 1978: 237–41). Modern commentators find such a tree in the *Isagoge* 4,21–32 (see trans. Barnes 2003: 109 n.53 for references). The idea is that the category of substance should first be divided into corporeal and incorporeal. The former would then consists of living and non-living bodies; living bodies would include percipient and non-percipient; percipient bodies would then divide into rational and non-rational animals. Now we would have produced a definition of man by dividing the category of substance.[8]

As Barnes notes, it is problematic to take the Porphyrian tree to correspond to what Porphyry says. The context of the example that has given rise to the name is an example of how there are general and specific notions or kinds and intermediaries between these (*Isag.* 4,14–20). The metaphor of a tree is found in neither the ancient commentaries nor Boethius, even though Boethius does use the word "branch" (*in Isag.* 78,9–11, quoted in trans. Barnes 2003: 109). Porphyry himself talks about predicates being under one another: "Substance itself is a genus. Under it is body, and under body animate body, under which is animal; under animal is rational animal, under which is man; and under man are Socrates and Plato and particular men" (*Isag.* 4,22–23, trans. Barnes 2003).

In this case, animal is a genus for human being, but a species of animate body. Therefore, it is intermediate between human being and animate body. However, since animate body is not such that nothing further could be predicated of it more generally (e.g. body and substance can), it is intermediate as well. In this example, only substance and the particular human beings are not intermediaries, but the most particular and the most general items. However, the example makes no claim as to how it could be used as a mechanical method for producing definitions. In addition, the idea that a negative class should be introduced as the counterpart of the intermediate type that Porphyry mentions, for example, incorporeal to complement bodies, would not be accepted by Porphyry (*in Cat.* 106,26–7), even though it was later used as a standard example (see Barnes 2003: 110–11). Such divisions would not have been accepted by Aristotle either, one reason being his overall scepticism towards division by one predicate and its negation.

Simplicius, in his commentary on *Physics* I 1, argues that we should be able to reduce or analyse things into their simplest principles or elements. What he means by them, however, is not entirely clear, since at times he refers to material elements (*in Ph.* 16,14), but more often he speaks about the elements of a definition (16,20–24; 16,31–17,25); sometimes the principles are matter and form (20,17). It is not impossible that different principles are identified in different sciences, or in different stages of one science. Other commentators occasionally refer to the divine or heavenly principles or the Neoplatonic One (e.g. Phlp. *in APo.* 47,24–48,1). When enquiring into the commentators' discussions about principles in this second sense, the Neoplatonic influence or background becomes important. For Alexander of Aphrodisias it was not relevant. In the case of Themistius, scholars debate to what extent his paraphrases infiltrate Neoplatonic influence.[9] In any case, the general outline of his views is rather Aristotelian.

All commentators later than Themistius were influenced by Neoplatonism, that is, Platonism after Plotinus. Plotinus and his followers understand reality as a hierarchical structure produced from the top down by a process called "emanation". The levels of the hierarchy are called "hypostases" (Greek *hupostasis*). The highest principle is the One, ultimate unity, which is the reason for the whole totality of being. Whether it also in a sense comprises the whole cosmos was a debated question among the Neoplatonists (see e.g. Remes 2008). As an external aspect of the overflowing fullness and highest absolute unity, the One is differentiated into intelligible forms and principles.

These forms and principles are in the universal Intellect. On the level of this Intellect, all the forms of being are grasped in an instantaneous theoretical vision that is eternal: or, more specifically, the Intellect is above or beyond space and time.[10] As an external aspect of its eternal intellectual vision, the Intellect produces structure and organization to the level of matter. In fact, matter could not even exist as a separate principle without the Intellect, which means that the Intellect gives matter its existence and organizes it into things structured by the intelligible forms. In Plotinus, the intelligible structure of the perceptible world is actualized on a different ontological level, that is, on the level of Intellect and, hence, the principles are not found in nature. However, as indicated in Chapter 1, the commentators tend to suppose that it is compatible to hold that there are Aristotelian principles of nature in nature as well.

Human beings and human action have a special role in the process of emanation, because we have a double bond to two levels of the emanation hierarchy: we are material beings, but we also have the possibility of taking part in the eternal intellectual activity. All our reasoning does not belong to that level. Ordinary thought is a process that happens in time and is limited by language. However, occasionally we are capable of transcending the level of language and of getting glimpses of the structure of the intelligible forms in an instantaneous or atemporal intellectual act that is rich and complex but not propositional (see Emilsson 2007).

Before we go into Philoponus and Themistius, one general remark needs to be made. It was a common supposition among philosophers working in the Platonic–Aristotelian tradition that two kinds of principles must be distinguished. Aristotle in fact attributes this supposition to Plato (*EN* 1095a30–b4). One type consists of the facts or things we need to know to initiate enquiry (e.g. that lunar eclipses take place, that dolphins exist, what "void" means). Another set contains the real principles: general claims or kinds and properties that we find as a result of enquiry. On the basis of the latter, the initially known facts can be proved (lunar eclipse explained), explicated (dolphins defined) or proved to exist or not to exist (void). Even though this general idea implies that we return to our starting-point

after enquiry, we come to know those facts in a totally different manner: in a framework of other things and facts, according to relations
of priority and of explanation. What this means will become clearer
through examples as we proceed.

Themistius

Themistius' paraphrasis is historically the earliest commentary work
on the *Posterior Analytics* that has come down to us. Many examples
that we also find later in Philoponus occur in Themistius, and he
sometimes elaborates on points about which Aristotle is vague. One
such case is the question of whether the knowledge of principles,
and not just that of conclusions of proofs, is also knowledge in the
proper sense (*epistēmē kuriōs*). Aristotle is not clear at the beginning
of the treatise, but later settles for the affirmative answer. Themistius'
answer is clear from the beginning: knowledge of the principles is
knowledge in the strong sense (5,13–16).

Themistius follows Alexander in calling the principles of proofs
"axioms" (*axiōmata*), and he distinguishes between such axioms that
we must know in order to know anything at all and axioms that
involve knowing the natures of things. Here he deviates from Aristotle, who only calls the logical and basic mathematical principles
axioms (*APo.* I 10, 76b12–17). When Themistius speaks about the
kinds of axioms that are necessary for all learning, he refers to Theophrastus' definition of them. This definition implies that such axioms
are natural in us and born together with us (*homogeneis*). Themistius
does not explain whether their being *homogeneis* means that they are
innate in the strong sense that we have them when we are born or
whether we come to have them when our reason is developed. In the
latter case, the principles' being innate would be dispositional; their
birth would coincide with the development of our reason. Such axioms are illustrated by the standard example: if equals are subtracted
from equals, the remainders are equal (*in APo.* 7,4).

In addition to such axioms, starting enquiry requires that we know
what the terms used in the expressions mean. The meaning, according
to Themistius, is known to all speakers of a language. We shall return
to the question of how we attain such knowledge in § "Acquiring

rationality", below. As such, knowledge of meaning is to be distinguished from knowledge of a definition that states the essence (*ousia*) of a thing and requires expertise (3,7–11, cf. 7,22). What, then, is the relation between claims about essence and premises of proofs?

In his paraphrasis on *Posterior Analytics* II 8, Themistius repeats Aristotle's example of lunar eclipse. According to Themistius, in cases like eclipse, the reason for the fact coincides with the account (*logos*) and the essence (*to ti ēn einai*) (50,10–12). Themistius presents his point in question-and-answer form: "What is the cause of the eclipse? Screening (*antiphraxis*) by the earth. The reason (*aitia*), then, is this screening" (50,12–13, my translation). If we were to take Themistius literally here, "screening" would be a sufficient definition for lunar eclipse. However, this reading would make one feel that something is missing. We would, rather, be inclined to expect something like: lunar eclipse is [sun's] light being screened by the earth. (In his paraphrase on I 34, Themistius follows Aristotle and makes it explicit that it is the sun's light that makes the moon shine; see 41,1.) Would it, then, be that Themistius just presents how we find out about the cause of the eclipse, and this does not yet spell out the whole definition? Does he suppose that we must find some additional premises?

Themistius discusses the difference between mediated and immediate premises and illustrates the point with examples, the following of which is especially interesting. Similar arguments keep reappearing in various forms in late ancient sources.[11] According to Themistius, in physics it is possible to show that the soul is immortal because it is self-moving. However, this would not be an explanation from immediate premises; the premises are immediate if they point out that the soul is immortal because it is the principle of life (*arkhē zōēs*) and a principle of life cannot be generated (*in APo*. 27,29–31). In Alcinous, for example, the soul is supposed to be a principle of *movement* and hence not generated. Themistius' addition is somewhat difficult to interpret. He seems to say that being the principle of life would be the immediate explanation of the soul's immortality. However, he also adds a further explanation: and a principle of life cannot be generated. Even if this were the ultimate explanatory principle in Themistius, one wonders whether it shows what it was supposed to show. It could be that the principle of life is distinct in individual living beings. If this is the case, such principles only have generic immortality; in individuals, souls as such principles could be mortal.

Nor is Themistius' argument for the immortality of soul clear when it comes to the relation between proofs and definitions. The options for the definition of soul it gives are the following: (i) soul is an immortal and non-generated principle of life; (ii) soul is a non-generated principle of life; and (iii) soul is a principle of life. The question now is whether being a principle of life would be sufficient to distinguish soul from other things. This, in turn, would be easier to answer if we knew what kinds of things soul is supposed to be distinct from. In order to answer this question, however, we would need to know the genus of soul or souls. Themistius does not offer solutions to these puzzles. The most we can gather from his presentation of the example is that, for him, the order of priority seems to be the following sequence: that the soul is a principle of life is primary; from this it follows that it must be non-generated; being non-generated, then, implies immortality.

Otherwise, Themistius' paraphrase of the *Posterior Analytics* remains close to Aristotle. The overall picture one gets from the work is that, rather than being a worked-out whole, it consists of remarks on various topics and some very interesting examples, many of which remain in the commentary tradition (e.g. that a magnet attracts iron appears in Them. in *APo.* 2,28–31 and Phlp. *in APo.* 12,25). The examples might be Themistius' own, but it is also possible that he inherits them from Theophrastus (at least, he refers to Theophrastus; cf. *homogeneis* principles above). In this case, the examples might even be traces of Peripatetic scientific research.

Philoponus
In his commentary on the *Posterior Analytics* based on Ammonius' lectures, Philoponus is quite close to Aristotle in his explicit remarks. Yet he makes frequent use of mathematical examples and terminology, which he often borrows from Proclus' commentary on Euclid's *Elements* (e.g. 7,20; 8,10–25; 61,1–10), and which exceed the level of sophistication in Aristotle's mathematical examples in the *Posterior*

Analytics.[12] Aristotle might have offered more elaborate mathematical proofs collected in separate works that have been lost to us,[13] but they are not found in the *Posterior Analytics*. Whereas Aristotle's examples of mathematics in the *Posterior Analytics* are typically just examples of how the class structure of geometrical figures can be expressed in a syllogism, Philoponus' examples contain actual geometrical proofs from Euclid. Further, the Euclidean examples constitute the core of Philoponus' examples in his comments on the central parts of the first book.

Philoponus sometimes distances himself from the Aristotelian outlines of the treatise. For example, once in the middle of an argument against the infinity of proofs (on I 3), he switches to another gear: Philoponus expresses as Themistius' the opinion that the principles that form the basis of proofs are axioms that express natures of things (48,3–15). Such principles, according to a view that Philoponus attributes to Themistius, are known by the human intellect; on this point he agrees with Themistius. Then, suddenly, Philoponus presents another interpretation that "the Philosopher" has put forward, and this is very different from Themistius' interpretation that Philoponus himself just a few lines earlier appeared to accept. According to "the Philosopher", Philoponus says, the intellect that knows the principles is not our own intellect but the divine intellect above us (47,24–6). In the divine intellect there are divine forms (*eidē*) that are also called "terms" (*horoi*). His formulation points to the Neoplatonic hierarchy described above, but he does not specify the connection.

First, Philoponus states as a kind of general truth that a plurality (or a whole) always begins from unity (*monas*) and is resolved or analysed (*analuetai*) into unity. According to this general idea, the terms or limits (*horoi*) of a hundred are the tens, and the limits of a thousand are the hundreds; common to all these is one (or the One) (47,28–48,1). Then he gives another example: natural things have principles in a similar manner. However, Philoponus does not say that, for example, the limits of a species contain the genus and a specific difference, which would be the standard Aristotelian analysis schematized and promoted by Porphyry. Rather, according to Philoponus, the principles of perceptible bodies are the heavenly ones, and the principles or limits of the heavenly bodies are divine essences. The first principle (*arkhē*) is common to all (48,1–3). This presumably is the One, that is, the Neoplatonic highest principle of all being that, as mentioned, is either interpreted as an absolute unity or the totality of the cosmos understood as a unity.

Philoponus does not specify the identity of the "Philosopher" he refers to. Since the commentary is based on Ammonius' lectures, he would be one candidate, unless Philoponus himself is simply writing down what Ammonius said. If Philoponus' reference to the one means the One as the Neoplatonic highest hypostasis, the reference to the Philosopher could also be Plotinus. In any case, a crucial element in the Philosopher's interpretation is the supposition that the one is prior and a beginning or a principle (*arkhē*) for composite numbers such as a thousand. What would such priority mean? Clearly, it could not be temporal priority. Analogously, the heavenly bodies do not seem to be principles of mundane material bodies in the sense that the latter should somehow evolve or come about from the former. Rather, the priority is something that could be described as conceptual or ontological.

Conceptual priority is quite easy to grasp in the case of numbers. In order for there to be numbers at all, some sort of principle for counting needs to be given. A thousand is comprehensible as a thousand times one. This could also be characterized as priority in definition: other numbers can only be defined if one is given. Mathematical number theory refers to a follower function: one is given, its follower is a natural number and so is the follower of its follower, and so on; and this is how all the natural numbers are "given" or understood. If one is understood as the given principle of counting and the follower function as the function of counting, Philoponus' idea seems quite close to this mathematical analysis.

In the case of bodies, the point about conceptual or definitional priority seems more difficult. Is it that we understand mundane bodies because we understand the heavenly ones? This does not seem promising. Nor does the idea that all other kinds of material bodies should be defined by reference to the heavenly bodies. Rather than conceptual priority, Philoponus might refer to some sort of explanatory priority. Then his point would be that the movements of material bodies on earth are affected by the movements of the celestial bodies, and that in some sense the celestial movements explain movement on earth.

If we keep insisting on the point that there must be a clearer link between the two priorities, we can perhaps look at the situation from the following angle. The point about priority might be that material bodies on earth cannot be understood without understanding bodies in heaven. In the framework that Philoponus inherits from Ammonius, the heavenly bodies possibly do have ontological priority over mundane bodies in the sense that what is bodily in earthly bodies is somehow more purely manifested in celestial bodies. If this were the case, then being bodily would mean regular movement, since this is the way in which the heavenly bodies move. However, more often the bodily aspect of things is referred to as the source of irregularity and incontrollable change in things, and the conceptual interpretation of priority seems to fail.

Be that as it may, in addition to calling principles "terms" or "limits" (*horoi*), Philoponus also calls them "common notions" (*koinai ennoiai*). This he does in passing and without commenting on the expression. Aristotle does not use "common notion" for principles, but it is Euclid's phrase for the axioms of geometry. The expression lived on in Stoicism, but in late antiquity it was so widely applied that there need not be anything particularly Stoic in its application. Further, given the extent to which Philoponus consults Euclid through Proclus, the mathematical connotation seems more relevant than the Stoic one. In any case, it is worth noting that Philoponus is not preoccupied with explaining that he employs a term that comes from the mathematical tradition and that Aristotle does not use it.

Philoponus also gives examples from natural philosophy. One of them is familiar from Aristotle: a proof that expresses the cause of a lunar eclipse. According to Philoponus, a proof that lunar eclipses occur is as follows: the moon is shadowed [by the earth]; that which is shadowed [by the earth] is eclipsed; therefore the moon is eclipsed. Here, as Philoponus explains, the cause of the eclipse, namely (the sun's) being shadowed by the earth, occurs as a middle term, as the normal Aristotelian analysis of proofs takes it. However, to construe a corresponding syllogism with "being shadowed by the earth" as a middle term implies that Philoponus is giving the premise in reverse order than is customary. When we organize the terms in the order entailed by Philoponus' remark on the middle term, the proof becomes as follows.

Terms	*Proof*
A being eclipsed	That which is shadowed is eclipsed.
B being shadowed [by the earth]	The moon is shadowed [by the earth].
C moon	Therefore, the moon is eclipsed.

Philoponus thus seems to suppose that knowledge in the proper sense can come from several different kinds of principles. One important case consists of geometrical proofs similar to those given by Euclid. The remaining kinds of principles that Philoponus recognizes are from natural philosophy (as in the eclipse example); the one as a principle might also have Neoplatonic connotations. The latter is somewhat difficult to accommodate in a syllogistic framework, and perhaps Philoponus would suppose that it functions as an explanatory principle in a more abstract manner: we understand that the one must be there in order for there to be numbers.

In addition, Philoponus also makes it clear that we need to begin enquiry from pre-existent knowledge. In one example from Euclid, he singles out many axioms as being previously known (*proginōskein*; 13,11, 13,12).[14] However, in natural philosophy the situation is different: we do not know the real principles at the beginning; rather, we need to start with some more elementary kind of knowledge. For example, in order to start more scientific (*epistēmonikōteros; ad* I 3) research into the definition or existence of something, we need to know what a notion signifies (*sēmasia, ennoia; ad* I 3). A blurred image of a notion's meaning is not sufficient for that. For example, to enquire into the question of the existence of void, we need to be clear about what we mean by this notion. However, this is not yet the full definition, since, as

Philoponus' second example shows, coming to know a full definition presupposes knowledge of existence. If the meaning is clear, as
Philoponus claims it to be in the case of "a hippocentaur", we need
to find out whether such things exist before going into an analysis
of the corresponding notion. We shall return to this example in
§ "How to achieve *epistēmē*", below.

Knowledge through principles

We have now seen that the commentators claim that knowing something in a real sense – or, knowing something scientifically – involves
knowing it through principles, which in a sense are reasons or causes
for the thing known. However, it is not primarily the principles that
are known in the proper sense of the word (*kuriōs*). Rather, when
commenting on the characterization of knowledge Aristotle gives in
Posterior Analytics I 2, the commentators emphasize that such knowledge is about the thing or event that is known *through the principles*.
In addition, we need to know that the principles, that is, the premises
of a proof, are causes of the thing or fact expressed in the conclusion
of a proof *and* that this cannot be otherwise (Them. *in AP.* 5,5–13;
Phlp. *in APo.* 20,27–21,5). Themistius formulates a crucial condition
as follows: the premises that imply the conclusion also need to state
the cause for the fact expressed in the conclusion (5,24–5).

Why are these additional requirements needed? Would it not be
sufficient to know the thing and to know what its principles are? To
illustrate the point, let us suppose that we know or observe that a
lunar eclipse takes place. In addition, we know that the earth is sometimes interposed between the sun and the moon. If we just knew
these two facts separately, something would be missing. The missing
link would be the knowledge of the fact that the lunar eclipse occurs
because the earth is interposed between the sun and the moon *and*
that this is how a loss of light in general takes place, namely, through
the interposition of a shadowing body.

There is yet another requirement: we need to know that "it cannot be otherwise". What is it that cannot be otherwise? And why is

this requirement needed? The clause seems to refer to the idea that the fact expressed in the conclusion, for example, that the moon is eclipsed, cannot be otherwise. But this seems to be a plain falsity. Of course it can be otherwise: most of the time the moon is not eclipsed. This objection is to some extent justified. However, it does not take us to the core of the issue. The point is not to restrict knowledge to permanent, necessary and unchangeable facts. Rather, the crucial point is that knowledge in the proper sense concerns phenomena that recur according to a certain regular pattern and that always have the same cause. If the moon is shadowed by something other that the earth – for example, a cloud – this is not an eclipse. Therefore, the eclipse of the moon cannot be otherwise in the very sense that whenever it is eclipsed, it cannot be because of another cause.

These are important qualifications, since they show us what kind of knowledge is at stake. Knowledge in the sense that the commentators discuss it is not knowledge of single facts in a vacuum; rather, it is knowledge that involves knowing many things in connection with each other and it is crucial that the connections are understood in a correct manner. Therefore, it must be known that a fact is either a permanent one (e.g. the nature of a species) or one that recurs eternally in the course of nature (e.g. a lunar eclipse). In addition, it must be known that this phenomenon has a stable or necessary explanation or cause (the eclipse), or that it is a thing that has an essential nature that is necessary for it to be the kind of thing it is. Further, in order for knowledge to be the kind of knowledge required presupposes knowing how the cause explains the phenomenon or how the nature of a species explains what a member of that species is like, how it lives (if it lives) and what is its natural aim (of its movement or of its life).

How to achieve *epistēmē*

Beginning enquiry

It is important to note that although the commentators often characterize principles as self-evident (*enargeis*; Them. *in Apo.* 6,10) or

93

convincing through themselves (*autothen pistai*; *ibid.*), they typically do not suppose that the principles of things should be evident
to everyone and evident without enquiry. To be more specific, it is
true that there are principles that need to be self-evident, but not all
of them are. In general, logical principles, some factual knowledge
and knowledge of meanings is used to initiate enquiry, whereas the
causes and essences are found as results of enquiry (see e.g. *Them.
in APo.* 7,22: premises of proofs must be laid out by an expert).

To illustrate, it might seem that some principles, like the one
in Philoponus as the principle of all other numbers, must be self-
evident. However, even in the case of the one, it is not sufficient just
to be able to count to one, for example. To know the one *as a principle*
of numbers, we need to know how it produces them, for example,
through the follower function. Further, if the one as Philoponus
refers to it in that context is not just the number one, but the One
as the ultimate principle of the Neoplatonic hierarchy, it certainly
cannot be evident to us from the beginning. Within the Neoplatonic
framework, to understand the One as the principle of everything
else is one of our highest cognitive achievements. In both cases – the
one as just a number and as the highest metaphysical principle – the
main point is not to ask whether the ultimate principle can in some
sense be known already at the beginning. Rather, the point is that
there is a difference between knowing the principle in some sense
and knowing it *as the principle* of other things.

In order to see how the commentators suppose us to gain knowledge in the strong sense of *epistēmē*, we need to address two different
questions. As becomes clear from the commentaries on the *Posterior
Analytics* by Philoponus and Themistius, both of them accept Aristotle's point made at the very beginning of the treatise: all teaching
and learning that involves reasoning comes about from pre-existent
knowledge of some kind (71a1–2). However, both Themistius and
Philoponus also underline that this does not mean that all knowledge
whatsoever should arise from pre-existent knowledge (see *Them.
in APo.* 2,23–5; *Phlp. in APo.* 4,30). As we saw in Chapter 2, the
addition "that involves reasoning" makes a contrast with perceptual
knowledge. In addition to perceptual knowledge, achieved simply

by exercising the capacity of perception, Philoponus and Themistius emphasize that we need to have knowledge about the meanings of the terms that are employed when we start any more scientific (*epistēmonikōteros*; e.g. Phlp. *in APo.* 43,2–10) research into things. (We shall address knowledge acquisition through reasoning below in § "Logic in science and philosophy".)

To initiate the process through which we come to know things in a strong sense, we need both perceptual knowledge and knowledge about the meanings of the terms that are utilized (and of some logical principles of which the commentators say little in this context). Such pre-existent knowledge enables us to enquire into two main questions of science (in the sense of *epistēmē* of the *Posterior Analytics*): (i) whether something is the case or whether something exists (*ei esti, hoti esti*); (ii) why something is the case or what it is (*dia ti, ti esti*). The decision of which one of the two formulations of the main questions we choose depends on the object of enquiry. If it is a thing (e.g. god, void), we ask the first questions in both sets: whether it is (i.e. exists) and what it is (what its full definition is). If the object is a fact (e.g. lunar eclipse, thunder), we ask whether it is the case and, if it is, why it is, that is, what is the cause of eclipse or thunder.[15]

Usually, knowledge of a fact precedes knowledge of its cause, but Themistius indicates that this is not always the case. His example is that he himself understands the cause of the consonance between a higher and a lower pitch in a chord, and this he knows from mathematics, but because he lacks training in music, he does not know if two pitches are consonant (*in Apo.* 29,15–20). The example is a little odd. If someone has such detailed knowledge about the cause of consonance as Themistius claims to have, it would seem strange that the person should be unable to distinguish between consonant and dissonant chords when hearing them. Of course, this is not impossible but sounds unconvincing. Another curious detail is that even though Themistius claims to know the reason for consonance from mathematics, he does not give it (the simplicity of the ratio between the two pitches). However, the cause was common knowledge in antiquity since Pythagoreanism, and Themistius might have felt that it was not necessary to repeat it.

Themistius' example illustrates his supposition that it is possible to know the reason without knowing the fact. Perhaps this is particularly likely in mathematical sciences that express reasons for facts that belong to the scope of other sciences, such as arithmetic for harmonics and geometry for optics. The way he continues his explanation about geometry and optics (29,20–24) supports this interpretation. Yet it is not entirely clear that the science of harmonics does. If all the causes belong to arithmetic, is harmonics simply supposed to identify various consonant and dissonant intervals, as Themistius' example seems to indicate? Themistius' interpretation, according to which a cause can be known without knowing the fact, is antithetical to Aristotle (*APo.* II 1). For Aristotle, observing the dissonance or consonance is a prerequisite for any enquiry concerning their causes.

Pre-existent perceptual knowledge

The supposition according to which learning through reasoning requires pre-existent knowledge implies that the pre-existent knowledge needs to be acquired without reasoning. But does this mean that the pre-existent knowledge pre-exists in the sense of being given to us before birth? When considering the question, both Themistius and Philoponus reject Plato's solution to the problem of learning, introduced in the *Meno*, according to which we have pre-existent knowledge in this sense and, hence, do not learn new things but rediscover something already known to us. Contrary to Plato's *Meno*, Themistius and Philoponus claim that learning and having pre-existent knowledge are two different things: even when we learn something on the basis of pre-existent knowledge, what we learn and what we have pre-existent knowledge about are different (Them. *in Apo.* 4,30–32; Phlp. *in Apo.* 3,30ff.). On this point, more Platonically oriented commentators disagree heavily.

In order to account for the two processes – learning through reasoning and attaining the pre-existent knowledge required by such learning – different approaches must be taken. Learning through reasoning requires a logical or inferential method (*methodos logikē*; Them. *in Apo.* 2,23–5), whereas the acquisition of pre-existent knowledge is explained by reference to our psychological capacities. In the comments on the very first chapter of the *Posterior Analytics*, both Philoponus and Themistius point out (Them. *in Apo.* 4,28ff., cf. 2,23–5; Phlp. *in Apo.* 5,5) that a solution to the problem introduced in the *Meno* lies in the recognition of a form of knowledge that can be acquired. It is not acquired through pre-existent knowledge and reasoning but simply by utilizing our capacity of perception. Hence, perceptual knowledge forms the basis of learning through reasoning.

Both Themistius and Philoponus thus assert that we come to have knowledge through perception. Such knowledge is usually distinguished by a terminological difference from knowledge in the proper sense; knowledge through perception is often called *gnōsis*, not *epistēmē* (e.g. Them. *in Apo.* 2,23, cf. 63,8). However, this terminological practice is not entirely uniform in the commentaries. In particular, the idea of pre-existent knowledge as a requirement for learning is often expressed in terms of the verb *epistamai*, for which the corresponding noun is *epistēmē* (e.g. 2,13–15).

However, the statement that perceptual knowledge is sufficient to begin enquiry is problematic. As we saw above, the kind of knowledge we need at the beginning is already quite complex: it involves knowledge of facts such as the regular occurrence of an eclipse and some knowledge of meanings. When Philoponus, for example, accounts for knowledge of facts through perception when commenting on *Posterior Analytics* I 1, the facts are much simpler: for example, this is white (Phlp. *in Apo.* 5,1–5). If perceptual knowledge is as simple as this, it clearly cannot explain all the knowledge that we need before enquiry. It just offers us a very elementary starting-point.

Acquiring rationality

Some alleviation of this problem is obtained from the following idea. Acquiring knowledge without *any* pre-existent knowledge is possible only through perception, a natural capacity that belongs to all animals from birth. However, when we talk about knowledge of facts, such knowledge already involves another cognitive capacity of ours that does not function immediately when we are born but is developed through repeated observation of things. This is our reason (we are rational, *logikos*; Them. *in Apo.* 63,14) or intellect (*nous*; 65,2), according to Themistius' account of how we attain rationality from perceptions in his paraphrase of *An. Post.* II 19.

When we acquire reason from perception, it enables us to operate with general notions and to formulate propositional claims. In fact, Themistius gives a rather complex example of the kind of observations we need to make in order to come to have rational general knowledge. The example is that when we have seen many individual human beings purify their bile with hellebore, we come to understand that hellebore purifies the bile. In order to understand that Plato purifies his bile with hellebore and that Socrates purifies his bile with hellebore (the example is given in Them. *in Apo.* 63,14–26), we clearly need advanced conceptual skills. Understanding this is very different from perceiving simple qualities or even recognizing someone on the basis of perception. This is not a problem now, since such understanding is allowed to be rational: the case is an example of how we come to recognize facts when our reason develops from perceptual capacities. The crucial and possibly problematic claim is that our reason develops from perception and this process does not require reasoning.[16]

We do not have a parallel discussion by Philoponus because his commentary on the second book of the *Posterior Analytics* has been lost. In the *Commentaria in Aristotelem Graeca*, some comments or *scholia* on the second book have been published in the same volume as Philoponus' commentary on the first book (CAG XIII 3). The example about hellebore being purifying found in Themistius (but not in Aristotle) also occurs there.

Themistius does not give a more detailed account of how we come to have knowledge about what terms mean. Supposedly he assumes having reason involves understanding speech. Philoponus is slightly more specific when analysing the difference between knowing what a term means and knowing whether things denoted by that term exist. In some cases, according to Philoponus, it is evident (*prophanes*) what a name signifies (*in APo*. 43,3–5). In others, we have an unclear image of the meaning of a name or a notion (*amudros tēs sēmasias autou phantasia*, 42,26–43,3; "notion", *ennoia*, appears in 43,10–12). If our image of what the term refers to is unclear, it is not yet sufficient as a starting-point for research into whether the thing underlying the notion (*hupokeimenon*) exists. Therefore, Philoponus attributes a role to imagination (*phantasia*) in acquiring linguistic skills, but he makes it quite clear that mere images of things are not sufficient as the kind of knowledge we need to have about things before we study whether they exist or what their nature is.

Philoponus' examples are very interesting. They occur in a context (*ad* I 3) where he argues against those who claim that proofs do not exist on the basis of insufficient understanding of what a proof is, discussed above in Chapter 2, § "How is Aristotle's remark interpreted in the commentaries?". As mentioned there, his second example is the notion of void. Philoponus says that in this case the notion must be given or made clear (*paradidonai*; 42,21) before we can proceed to enquire whether it exists. This is a powerful example, since the very notion and existence of void were matters of heated controversy in antiquity. It shows that we are not in a position to answer the question of the existence of void if we do not know what the thing is, the existence of which we are supposed to assert or deny. The sheer idea of an empty space or language skills enabling us to understand "void" would not be sufficient. A much more detailed analysis of the notion is needed. Unfortunately, Philoponus does not explain in detail how such knowledge is acquired.

Real principles

We have now seen that, according to the commentators we have discussed so far, basic forms of intellectual activity, recognition, conceptual capacity and language skills are necessary for us to begin scientific research. However, this is not the only way in which an account of our reason or intellect (*nous*) is relevant in explaining how we come to know the principles. In fact, it is a common supposition that intellect is needed in grasping the real principles themselves, not just the facts that we need to know beforehand. These real principles express causes or natures of things or are higher principles of understanding and being such as the One in Philoponus.

As mentioned, we do not have Philoponus' commentary on the last chapter of the *Posterior Analytics*, but we know from his comments on the first book that he supposes intellect to have a decisive role in our coming to know the principles through a kind of illumination (*in APo.* 48,3–7; *ellampsis* in 48,6). However, this is not our intellect or reason in the sense in which our intellect may recognize things as individuals of a certain kind or provide us with linguistic skills. Rather, the intellect that is needed in finding the ultimate principles of reality is a higher intellect. It is an Intellect with a capital I that constitutes the realm of pure thought in which principles of intelligibility are understood eternally, a conception we discussed above. Therefore, we cannot come to know such principles just by exercising our own reason. Rather, the principles need to be illuminated to us and this illumination (*ellampsis*) is supposed to take place "there" (*ekeithen*; 48,6), that is, on the level of the Intellect. The idea of illumination coming from outside the human reason is prominent in Augustine, and some ancient sources find it in Plato's Socrates as well (Apuleius *De deo Socratis* XVII–XIX, referring to *Apology* 31d). According to Augustine, our mind needs to be enlightened by a light coming from outside, and only God can light up this lamp for us (*Confessions* 4.15,25; see also 5.6,10, 10.2,2, 10.40,65). Even though Philoponus is a Christian, he – unlike Augustine – does not refer to the Christian God, but to the Neoplatonic hypostasis of Intellect.

For Themistius, we have already identified the logical principles that we need to know beforehand and we achieve some basic knowledge of facts by exercising our reason, activated by repeated perceptions. For this activation process, he gives the following, slightly more detailed, description in his paraphrase of the *Posterior Analytics*. Perceptual knowledge is acquired through the innate capacity to perceive. Perceived cases are preserved in memory. When many similar cases have been perceived, we begin to have more general ideas about the cases, and repeated observations give rise to general notions. When our rational abilities have developed through observations, we come to be able to understand that hellebore is used for purification. These thoughts give rise for yet a further generalization: all hellebore is purifying (*in Apo.* 63,23).

Themistius does not treat the question explicitly, but we can ask whether the general claim "hellebore is purifying" is already a premise that could be used in proofs: a real principle as opposed to a starting-point for research. Themistius' account might give us the impression that it is. However, this is problematic since principles should express reasons or causes for facts (e.g. 5,16–21), but to say that all hellebore is purifying still leaves open the question why this is the case. We have found a real principle about hellebore (perhaps in medicine), when we come to know *why* it is purifying. This suggests that the generalization that all hellebore is purifying does function as a starting-point for knowledge but not as a real principle.

But how, then, do we come to grasp these final principles? Nothing in Themistius' account suggests that a more divine intellectual level should be postulated to answer this question. Rather, for Themistius the capacity to recognize the principles is the human intellect. And this is what the paraphrase of the *Posterior Analytics* strongly suggests. However, Themistius' tone and theory is somewhat different in his paraphrase of the *De anima* (see Ch. 5, § "How do we come to grasp intelligible objects?", below).

Simplicius, for his part, provides us with a good example of how the Aristotelian and Neoplatonic approaches were combined in explanations of how we come to know the principles. In Simplicius' commentary on the *Physics*, he supposes that there are principles in nature. Such principles would be, for example, the material elements and the notions of matter and form (cf. Simplicius *in Ph.* 16,7–14, 16,17–24, 20,9–11, 20,17). Both of them are realized in nature (in the sense that material things are combinations of matter and form) and they are used to explain things and facts around us. Yet, in the commentary on the *Categories*, Simplicius refers to the idea that the principles are in our soul only in an inferior form: as limited by language (13,5). In the purest form, they are in an Intellect above our soul. Our soul's origin is in the Intellect and it can turn back or up towards it (12,18–25). Only this conversion can make things known to it as such, not a translation into accounts, definitions, images or prototypes. If we manage to turn or return to the Intellect in this manner, we come to understand the real organizing principles of nature. This understanding can, then, be explained and described in words as proofs that are presented in natural philosophy.

Therefore, for Simplicius, there is no harmful contradiction between the Aristotelian and the Platonic or Neoplatonic approach to the principles. Rather, there is a kind of division of labour: the Aristotelian approach is to be employed in natural philosophy, the Neoplatonic one in the realm of the divine. An additional supposition is that, ultimately, the Neoplatonic account explains why the Aristotelian approach is possible. We can come to know something because there are principles in us that we have previously gazed on (12,25–13,1) before our descent into material bodies.

If we now return to discuss our more mundane intellect, the commentators recognize that in some people it is exceptionally quick or agile; in Greek this property is *ankhinoia* (discussed by Aristotle; *APo.* I 34). Alexander's account of *ankhinoia* is preserved in a *scholium* (Moraux 1979: 77–8) and, according to this account, *ankhinoia* is the property that makes us quickly grasp the reason (expressed in a middle term of a proof) for a fact (expressed in the conclusion of a proof). When we learn the cause through agility of intellect, we recognize something that is prior through something that is posterior. What is posterior is the conclusion, for example, the moon having its illuminated "face" towards the earth, and if our intellect is quick, we come to understand immediately the cause for this fact: the moon gets its light from the sun. Alexander's example in the *scholium* comes directly from Aristotle (*APo.* I 34) and is also repeated by Themistius (*in APo.* 41,1-2) and Philoponus (*in APo.* 333,10–12). It might not be the most illuminating example (no pun intended), but it does serve to illustrate a point: we come to recognize causes for facts, and the causes are prior to the facts because they explain them. The commentators also follow Aristotle in claiming that, if the intellect is quick, it may come to recognize the cause immediately; in this context, no specific methodological procedures are introduced to train the functioning of the intellect.

Both the *scholium* reporting Alexander and Philoponus repeat Aristotle's expression that a quick intellect recognizes the cause instantaneously (*en askeptō khronō*). Philoponus also adds that a person with a quick intellect immediately draws the (syllogistic) figure where the fact is expressed in the conclusion and its reason in the premises (Phlp. *in Apo.* 333,26–9). Contrary to his commentary on the early chapters of Book I, Philoponus' discussion of *ankhinoia* does not refer to a higher intellect. What he says about *ankhinoia* is confined to reporting and explaining Aristotle's position. Philoponus does not point at any contrast with his own position, as he often does in his commentary on the *Physics*. Typically, they appear at the end of his comments and are introduced by "but we say …" or "but I say …". Nothing like this appears in the comments on *ankhinoia*.

Themistius does not say much about *ankhinoia*. However, he makes one terminological innovation: he calls the quickness of intellect "analysis" (*analusis*; Them. *in APo.* 41,5) of the conclusion of a proof into premises and finding the middle term quickly. If a similar quickness is assumed in cases where we look for a definition of a species or thing, *ankhinoia* starts to resemble what we might call "good analytical skills".

Logic in science and philosophy

From facts to reasons

We have now seen that the commentators refer to our basic psychological capacities of perception and intellect, or to a divine Intellect, to explain how we come to have knowledge of the principles and of the facts as explained or explicated by these principles. However, they do not restrict themselves to suggesting that we should merely wait for these capacities to work and give us the causes of things. As

Themistius suggests, learning through reasoning employs inferential procedures or "logical methods" (*methodos logikē; in APo.* 2,25). Alexander and Philoponus do not use this expression, but they offer accounts of how principles can be established through inference.

The basic framework of the procedures involving reasoning is, as indicated, syllogistic logic. From a logical point of view, what is typically known at the beginning of enquiry is the conclusion of the proof. What is sought is its explanation in terms of the premises. A crucial factor is the middle term, which serves to connect the two terms occurring in the conclusion with each other. For example, when we know the fact that the moon is eclipsed, we enquire into its reason. When we learn that it is because the earth shadows the sun and hence prevents the sun's light from falling on the moon, we have understood the cause of the eclipse.[17]

Another example illustrating the way in which logical methods can be employed in establishing the principles is as follows. The real proof is:

> Those [celestial bodies] that are close to the earth do not twinkle.
> Planets are close to the earth.
> Planets do not twinkle.　　　　(Arist. *APo.* I 13, 78a39–b2)

However, as Aristotle indicates and the commentators seem to follow, it is not typically the case that we know this proof quite like that. Rather, it may be the case that we need to show the second premise through another syllogism, a syllogism of a fact (*tou hoti*, contrasted with a syllogism of reason, *tou dioti*, which is the real proof). A syllogism that shows the crucial premise is as follows:

> Being near belongs to [celestial bodies] that do not twinkle.
> Non-twinkling belongs to planets.
> Being near belongs to planets.　　　　(Arist. *APo.* I 13)

The commentators usually distinguish between the real proofs and some lower sorts of proofs: in the real proofs the cause or explanation for the fact occurring in the conclusions is expressed in the premises, whereas the lower sorts of proofs can be used to establish these premises. (In the inferior syllogisms, such a premise occurs as a conclusion. Since Aristotle's terminology assumes that the order of claims in the real proof is objective, the premise is called a premise even when it is a conclusion of the inferior syllogism.) There is no systematic name for such lesser kinds of proofs in Aristotle. Themistius does not systematize them as a separate class either, but refers to them as "proofs for us" (*in Apo.* 9,21–3). The idea is that a "proof for us" can make an explanatory fact clear through valid argument. However, it presupposes that this fact is known independently – perhaps through our intellect's function – because in order to present the lesser kind of proof, a general explanatory fact must be known: it is the major premise of such a lesser kind of proof (in the example case it is that being near belongs to [celestial bodies] that do not twinkle).

Tekmeriodic proofs

Aristotle's scanty remarks about the kinds of argument that can be used to establish the second premise of a real proof were systematized by Philoponus and Simplicius as proofs of signs (called "tekmeriodic"; see also Morrison 1997). For example, Simplicius says: "Clearly, the grasp of the principles [of physical things] is through necessary signs (*tekmēriōdēs*) rather than demonstration (*apodeiktikē*)" (*in Ph.* 18,28–9, trans. Morrison 1997, modified). The name comes from the Greek noun *tekmērion* meaning a sign or indication. Thus the tekmeriodic proofs are arguments proceeding from a sign to a cause. Standard Aristotelian examples of signs were: smoke is a sign of fire; if a woman has milk in her breasts, it is a sign that she has given birth to a baby (Arist. *APr.* II 27).[18] Philoponus identifies the tekmeriodic syllogism with the kind of syllogisms we have just discussed, that is, those that establish the second, explanatory premise of a real proof (*in APo.* 168,22–3).[19]

An example that Simplicius gives of a tekmeriodic proof is distinct from the standard examples in both the Aristotelian and the Hellenistic discussion (for the latter, see Allen 2001). The example is as follows:

The better known [premises] are taken either [i] as principles (*arkhai*) and reasons (*aitiai*) of that, which is shown,
as happens in proofs in the strict sense ... as when [one
proves] the cosmos to be beautiful (*kalos*) on the basis of
the demiurge's being good (*agathos*) ... or [ii] as following
necessarily from that, which is proved, and concluding them
[i.e. the better known premises] on the basis of that. The
better known [premises] are assumed (*paralambanetai*) this
latter way, as when [one shows] God to be good (*agathos*) on
the basis of the cosmos being beautiful (*kalos*) and ordered
(*tetagmenos*), because this is more at our disposal in perception. And [the premises] assumed for this kind of conviction
are not principles (*arkhai*) of that which is proved, for they
follow from them, but [the premises of] the former kind of
proof [i] are principles, because they are better known and
clearer and on the basis of them comes the conviction of
that which is proved.   (Simp. *in Ph.* 15,15–29, my trans.)

Here Simplicius' point is that we come to grasp rather easily that
the world around us is somehow ordered: it is not total chaos, because
there are some regularities in the occurrence of natural phenomena,
general kinds and common features between beings of the same
kind. Since, he supposes, it is better for the world to be ordered than
for it to be total chaos, this means that the demiurge that is behind
the organization of the perceptual world must be good. Here the
alleged fact that the world is organized rather than disorganized is
understood as a sign that indicates that the demiurge must be good,
and as it is in Plato's *Timaeus*. If the demiurge were bad, the world
would fall apart and be chaotic; it could not be understood at all.
In the passage, Simplicius also supposes that the ordered nature of
the cosmos is not the cause of the demiurge being good. Rather, it
is exactly the other way around: the goodness of the demiurge is the
cause of the world's being ordered.

If we look at the relation between the real proofs and the lesser
kinds of proofs (whether they are called "tekmeriodic" or not), the
process starts to seem circular. One "proof" is needed to establish

a conclusion that is needed as a premise in the other kind of proof. Even though the two kinds of syllogism are distinguished in name, Aristotle's account inherited by the commentators seems to come dangerously close to the strategy opposed in I 3: establishing p on the basis of p, just through a couple of argumentative steps. Themistius explicitly addresses this issue and argues against vicious circularity on the basis of the idea that there is an objective order of priority, which is only realized in the real proof (*in APo.* 9,21–3). He contends that there is some circularity but that it is not vicious. In some sense this manoeuvre seems to be just a terminological *trompe l'oeil.*

However, somewhat ironically the poor epistemological value of the lesser kind of proof might alleviate this impression. The crucial second premise of the real proof must be known before the lesser kind of proof can be presented. In addition to leaving open the question of how we came to know that premise, it entails that our knowledge of the second premise is not dependent on the lesser proof after all. Such knowledge perhaps comes about through our intellect's capacity to recognize general explanatory patterns in reality.

Syllogistic scheme

Another context where the commentators discuss in more detail the role of logic in science is their commentaries on *Prior Analytics* I 27–30. Alexander and Philoponus' commentaries have come down to us.[20] In those chapters, Aristotle presents a scheme according to which, he says, syllogisms can be formed for any conclusion at all. His claim is exaggerated, but it reflects Aristotle's ambitions of offering a universal method for constructing arguments. In this framework, the conclusion is in one of the categorical forms:

Universal affirmative (AaE): A belongs to every E.
Particular affirmative (AiE): A belongs to some E.
Universal negative (AeE): A belongs to no E.
Particular negative (AoE): A does not belong to some E.

Aristotle explains that the scheme can be used to investigate from what kind of premises the conclusion follows in any field of study (46a3–10). Even though he does not mention science or *epistēmē* explicitly in that passage, the term occurs some fourteen lines later (46a17). The basic idea of the "method" is to collect terms that belong to either A or E, or to which A or E belongs. When suitable terms are found, a syllogism can be formed. To do so, the following kinds of terms are collected:

For A	For E
B (XaA)	*F* (YaE)
C (AaX)	*G* (EaY)
D (XeA)	*H* (YeE)

If we need to argue for a *universal affirmative* conclusion (AaE), we need premises of the form AaX and YaE. Such predicates are listed in groups *C* and *F*, respectively. If X and Y are identical, we can establish the conclusion straightaway (AaX, YaE [Y = X ⇒ XaE]; AaE). An example would be the argument showing that all planets are non-twinkling (AaE, where E stands for "planets" and A for "non-twinkling"; cf. *APo.* I 13, 78b1–3). To conclude this, we need to find the same term in two places: among those terms that belong universally to planets (YaE) and among the terms to which non-twinkling belongs universally (AaX). If we find out – as Aristotle supposes we do – (i) that all planets are near, as contrasted with the fixed stars (YaE where Y means "being near") and (ii) that non-twinkling belongs to all the celestial bodies that are near (AaX), we can establish the conclusion that the planets do not twinkle by the following syllogism: all [celestial bodies] that are near are non-twinkling; planets are near; therefore, planets are non-twinkling.

For a *particular affirmative* conclusion (AiE) we can use two kinds of premises. It is possible to establish that, for instance, some pleasures are good (AiE where A is good and E is pleasure; the example appears in both Alexander and Philoponus). The first possibility is to find a term to which "being good" belongs universally (AaX) *and* to which being pleasant also belongs universally (EaY) – and X = Y.

Such terms can be found in the groups C and G from the table. Following Alexander's and Philoponus' example, the term could be "virtuous action". All virtuous actions are good (AaX) and all virtuous actions are pleasant (EaY, and X = Y). These premises enable us to conclude that some pleasures are good: all actions in accordance with virtue are good (AaX); all actions in accordance with virtue are pleasant (EaX); therefore, some pleasures are good. The second option is to look for a term that belongs to all good things (XaA) and to which pleasure belongs universally EaY (Y = X $\Rightarrow$ EaX). This example will be discussed below in connection with Alexander and Philoponus.

A *universal negative* conclusion (AeE) can also be established in two different ways. The first way is to look for a term that does not belong to any A (XeA) but that belongs to all E (XaE); such a syllogism can be made if the same term is found in both D and F. The second way is to find a term that belongs to all A (XaA) but that does not belong to any E. These are listed in groups B and H above. An example can be adapted from the *Parts of Animals* (664a16–17): all oviparous water-animals have a fish-spine (XaA); dolphins do not have a fish-spine (XeE); therefore, dolphins are not oviparous (AeE) (but viviparous).

Finally, for a *particular negative* conclusion (AoE) the relevant term does not belong to any A (XeA) but E belongs to all of it (EaY [Y = X $\Rightarrow$ EaX]). The example comes from Philoponus' commentary. Let A be good and E be pleasure. Now we need a term of which goodness is universally denied but to which pleasure belongs universally. Such predicates are found in the groups D and G. Philoponus lists "unnatural pleasure" as such a term: no unnatural pleasure can be good, because being unnatural is completely outside the scope of being good (XeA); because unnatural pleasures are still pleasures (EaX), we can conclude that some pleasures are not good. For those who doubt whether there are unnatural pleasures, Philoponus points out that there is at least one: scratching an itch is an unnatural pleasure.

Among the universally belonging predicates, Aristotle distinguishes between those that are essential (*en tō ti esti*), those that are peculiar properties or *propria* (*idia*), and those that belong accidentally (*hōs sumbebēkos katēgoreitai*). Within the accidental predicates we must further distinguish between those that truly belong (*kat' alētheian*) to their subjects and those that it is plausible to assume belong (*doxastikōs*). From the last distinction, we see that Aristotle presented the scheme as applicable to dialectic as well. It is the same opposition (truth versus mere plausibility) that he employs to distinguish between dialectical and scientific premises. However, there is one striking aspect of Aristotle's discussion about the scheme: his instructions concern the question of how we utilize the scheme, once we have gathered all the relevant terms. He does not say anything about how to gather all the terms. How do we know whether one suggested predicate belongs to a subject term? How do we know whether it belongs essentially or accidentally? Aristotle does not address such questions at all. Therefore, his scheme is not "a method" in the sense that we typically use the term.

Alexander

Before we proceed to consider Alexander, we need to note the somewhat surprising fact that he is confused on a very basic point of logic. This occurs in his commentary on the *Prior Analytics* where he analyses arguments in which the conclusion does *not* follow, that is, in which it is possible for the conclusion to be false while the premises are true. Instead of pointing out that in these kinds of inferences the conclusion does not follow, Alexander says that in them the conclusion *sometimes follows* and sometimes does not follow. The translators of the commentary note in their introduction that an elementary error like this does not encourage one to trust Alexander as a logician (trans. Barnes *et al.* 1991: 12–14). Irrespective of this point, Alexander clearly was not an innovative logician. However, he does provide us with illuminating evidence about the application of Aristotle's syllogistic scheme.

To illustrate the syllogistic scheme, Alexander uses the following example. The two central terms are A "good" and E "pleasure". The example is remarkable in the sense that Aristotle does not recommend that this be disputed in dialectic. He says that if someone sets out to defend the hedonistic thesis that all pleasures are good, people tend to despise that person for holding that thesis and suppose that he or she has a bad character, even though the claim were merely maintained for the sake of argument (Arist. *Top.* VIII 9, 160b20–21). Despite this fact, the example reappears in Philoponus' commentary (see below). According to Alexander, when we want to establish any conclusion involving the terms A "good" and E "pleasure", the groups of predicates shown in Table 2 are gathered.

If Alexander were constructing the syllogisms on the basis of terms that are literally identical in the two columns, he would be able to show either that all pleasures are good, or that some pleasures are. For the first conclusion (all pleasures are good), "natural" (*ta kata phusin*) would be a suitable middle term: being good belongs to all natural things; being natural belongs to every pleasure; therefore, being good belongs to every pleasure. For the second one (some pleasures are good), there would be two possibilities: (i) every good thing is desirable; every pleasure is desirable; therefore, some pleasures are good; and (ii) all activities according to virtue are good; all activities according to virtue are pleasant; therefore, some pleasures are good.

However, Alexander does not limit himself to literal identity between terms. In fact, he uses literally identical terms only in establishing the particular affirmative conclusion "some pleasures

Table 2.

A, good (*agathon*)	E, pleasure (*hēdonē*)
B (XaA = all good things are X): useful, preferable, to be striven after, appropriate, profitable, agreeable, desirable	Z (YaE = all pleasant things are Y): smooth movement, the unhindered actuality of a natural disposition, untroubled, non-violent, pleasing, effortless, painless, without fear, natural, preferable
G (AaX = all Xs are good): happiness, perfect, virtues, action in accordance with virtue, bodily goods, the external [goods], the natural [goods]	H (EaY = all Ys are pleasant): health, being lucky, good progeny, action in accordance with virtue, wealth
D (XeA = no good is X): to be avoided, hurtful, bad, useless, non-profitable, shameful, imperfect	Q (YeE = no pleasure is Y): sickness, trouble, distress, fear, difficulty/poverty

(Alex.Aphr. *in APr. ad* 43b39, 301,17–32)

are good": "All activities according to virtue are good, all activities according to virtue are pleasant; therefore, some pleasures are good" (*in APr.* 302,18–25). In addition, one of his remarks concerning the universal affirmative conclusion (302,7–13) implies that it can be established by using "natural" as a middle term. To establish that every pleasure is good, Alexander does not employ the term "natural", but goes on to identify some terms from the first column with others from the second column. For instance, he identifies "perfect" with "unhindered activity of a natural disposition". "Taking these two to be one", he says, "we make a middle term" (302,6). This move is based on a characterization of pleasure that Aristotle gives in *Nicomachean Ethics* Book VII Chapter 12 (1153a14), according to which pleasure is unhindered activity of a natural disposition. Alexander, however, does not identify unhindered activity of a natural disposition only with pleasure – which seems to be the idea of Aristotle's remark – but also with being perfect.

Alexander's argument showing the negative universal conclusion (no pleasure is good) trades on the notion of movement (*kinēsis*) and its imperfect character. From these, Alexander constructs the following syllogism: every pleasure is a smooth movement; every movement is imperfect; no good is imperfect; therefore, no pleasure is good, since it is a movement or a process. This point is also discussed in *Nicomachean Ethics* Book VII, but Alexander's account is closer to what Plato says in the *Philebus* (53c–54a): pleasures are processes and as such different from the goals of such processes (Aristotle in fact denies this).

Alexander's remarks concerning the negative particular conclusion that some pleasures are not good (*in APr.* 304,19–30) are somewhat unclear. He selects unprofitable from *D* and effortless from *H*: this is what he says even though effortless is actually in *Z*. In any case, he goes on to identify unprofitable with effortless (304,26) and argues: no unprofitable, in other words effortless, thing is good (we would say, "no pain, no gain"); every effortless thing is pleasant; therefore, there are some pleasures that are not good.

There are two important points to be noted in Alexander's discussion about the scheme. First, he allows the identifying of terms with each other even though they are not initially the same. In some cases such a procedure seems reasonable. If we have a definition for a thing in one column and its name in the other, it seems acceptable to substitute one with the other. However, Alexander identifies things with each other even without definitional identity. This adds a further complication to how we can apply the syllogistic scheme of *Prior Analytics* I 27–30. If such assimilation or identification is allowed, the scheme is no longer a mechanical tool, but requires even more tacit knowledge than we first noted. A second and more important point is that Alexander does not comment on the quality or truth of the premises at all in the discussion; he does not seem to be interested in discussing what kind of premises he gets from the lists of predicates. Alexander then goes on and says that for clarity's sake, one should say what has already been said by using letter symbols for terms (304,31) and thus indicates that the scheme is intended to be perfectly general and independent of the current example. He simply presents an example of how a conclusion of each syllogistic form can be derived according to the scheme laid out by Aristotle.

As to the last point, Alexander does say explicitly that the scheme is used in science (*epistēmē*):

> This is a procedure (*hodos*) and method (*methodos*)[21] in all the sciences (*epistēmai*) and arts (*tekhnai*) that prove something appropriate by means of syllogisms … The procedure and method is necessary for a philosopher, a doctor, an orator, a cultured person (*mousikos*)[22] and everyone alike who is establishing something through syllogism.
>
> (330,32–331,1, my trans.)

Therefore, he seems to suppose that if we manage to gather predicates that belong essentially to the relevant subjects *and* we manage to find out about the explanatory relations that are vital for real proofs, we can construct the proofs from schemes like these.

Philoponus

In Philoponus' commentary (based on Ammonius), we find the same example as in Alexander. It might have been a standard one in school practice, or it may just show that Philoponus (Ammonius) is drawing on Alexander's commentary. Philoponus' version of the scheme is similar to Alexander's, but there are some changes and terminological differences. In addition, Philoponus presents the scheme in a star-shaped map (*in APo.* 274) that was to become standard in later works on syllogistic logic. Philoponus' list of terms is shown in Table 3.

Again, Philoponus is using a wider variety of connections than would be given by strict identity between terms in different groups. He does not formulate the conditions for identifying terms, nor does he point out that the scheme works on the supposition that the same terms are found in two places. In Philoponus' list, there is only one term, "virtuous life", that is found in exactly the same form in two groups, *G* and *H*. This would entitle us to conclude a particular affirmative conclusion (some pleasures are good). "Natural" is found in both *G* and *Z*, but not in exactly the same form. Philoponus, however, takes them to be the same.

By contrast to Alexander, Philoponus comments on the quality of premises. He says (276,20–29) that it is true that movement (*kinēsis*) and being desirable (*orekton*) follow pleasure, that is, that

Table 3.

A, good (*agathon*)	E, pleasure (*hēdonē*)
B (XaA = all good is X): Useful, preferable, to be striven after, appropriate, profitable, agreeable, to be pursued	*Z* (YaE = all pleasure is Y): Movement, activity according to nature, unhindered life, untroubled, preferable, naturally desirable
G (AaX = every X is good): happiness, being perfect, virtuous life, natural, good disposition, that for the sake of which	*H* (EaY = every Y is pleasant): health, good reputation, good progeny, virtuous life, wealth, painlessness, freedom of sorrow
D (XeA = no good is X): to be avoided, hurtful, bad, inappropriate, unprofitable, damaging, imperfect	*Q* (YeE = no pleasure is Y): sickness, trouble, fear, difficulty/poverty, unnatural movement

(Phlp. *in APr. ad* 43b1, 274)

every pleasure is a movement and that every pleasure is desirable. However, according to Philoponus, it is only plausible (*kata doxan*) but not true that every pleasure would be natural, because, for example, scratching an itch is not natural. Philoponus' point is not that scratching an itch would be perverse. Rather, even though scratching is desirable *if we have an itch*, it is not desirable *tout court*. Being naturally desirable would require that the action is desirable unconditionally. Philoponus might be referring to Callicles in Plato's *Gorgias*, who is ready to concede to Socrates that the pleasure resulting from scratching an itch could be desirable in itself and make life happy (cf. *Gorgias* 494c–d). Philoponus is not willing to follow Callicles here; he denies that every pleasure is natural in the sense of being desirable as such (276,20–29).

Even though Philoponus does comment on the quality of premises at points like this, he does not present any more general guidelines with regard to the question of how we come to know whether some suggested premises are true or not. Nor is he explicit on the question whether the scheme should or could be applied in science. However, Philoponus does refer to essential (*ousiōdēs*) properties and he often employs forms connected to the verb "to prove" (*apodeiknumi*) in his discussion of the syllogistic scheme (e.g. 276,31–2, 273,10). Therefore, he seems to suppose a connection between the scheme and scientific proofs. Further, he points out that logic (*logikē*) is an important tool for philosophy (*philosophia*) and that it is used in "vulgar" (*banausos*) fields too (*in APr.* 305,12–21). He does not explain what these vulgar contexts should be, but "art" or "craft" (*tekhnē*) is mentioned. He also says that in such fields common notions (*koinai ennoiai*) are used but people are ignorant of the method (*methodos*). Hence his point seems to be that all crafts involve principles and inferences but they are used implicitly. Only in philosophy (or perhaps in sciences) are the methodological tools made explicit.

***

What, then, would the commentators say about the role of dialectic in enquiry? Can it be employed in the attempt to find and establish principles? This is related to one of the central problems in the recent scholarly literature on Aristotle's philosophy of science. On the one hand, Aristotle is presenting super-strict conditions for scientific premises in the *Posterior Analytics*. On the other hand, he himself argues in a rather freewheeling dialectical manner in his own treatises.[23] As to the commentaries that are relevant for this question, we do have Alexander's commentary on the *Topics*, and what he says in his commentary on the *Prior Analytics* confirms that he supposed that dialectic plays an important role when we look for premises that could establish a given conclusion (*in APr.* 331,17–24). In fact, he claims that the scheme that we outlined above can be used in dialectic too. In science, premises are true and primary: in dialectic they are merely plausible or reputable but not true (331,20–24).[24]

Well in line with his general interpretation, Alexander tries to formulate some of Aristotle's arguments in the *Topics* as categorical syllogisms (e.g. *in Top.* 64,2ff.), but the attempts are cumbersome and the results unconvincing. When following and defending Aristotle's line of thought, Alexander occasionally has a tendency to over-systematize to the point where his interpretation is no longer helpful; this is one such case. Dialectic, as Aristotle presents it, is difficult to rigidly systematize even according to the general notions that Aristotle himself presents as the organizing principles of dialectic: the so-called predicables (genus, definition, peculiar property, differentia and accident). It is even more difficult if the dialectical syllogisms – and even the arguments that Aristotle presents to back up his theory, as Alexander supposes (64,2ff.) – should be formulated as categorical syllogisms.

There is one crucial point that Alexander makes in his account of how dialectic is employed to attain the principles (27,7–29,16). This is when he says that dialectic cannot establish which views are true and which merely plausible but not true. However, dialectic has an indispensable role in training us to distinguish between truth and falsity in cases where there are convincing arguments on both sides. In fact, his terminology in the context points to the idea that our capacity to recognize the truth, when developed through dialectical training, is analogous to seeing. He uses the Greek *sunoran*, which is constructed from the verb "to see" (*horan*) and the preposition "with" (*sun-*). Therefore, he supposes that dialectic does not establish the premises of sciences, but, rather, enables us to develop our capacity to distinguish between truth and falsity. How we can recognize if something is understood through such a capacity is not at issue.

FOUR

Physics

After our longish journey through the commentators' views concerning the structure and acquisition of knowledge, we can now turn to discuss their more specific views concerning the world around us. We shall begin with physics. By the time of the commentators, physics was understood as a systematic study of natural things, as the name also indicates (*phusikē*; Greek *phusis* means "nature"). However, to say that the topic of the present chapter is physics as a study of natural things raises a more important question: how was nature understood? This is a question to which the commentators gave different answers, and we shall address those answers in § "Definitions of nature and natural things", below. In addition to natural things, the physics of the commentators extends to notions that we would tend to categorize into metaphysics: place and time, structure of matter, possibility of change. These notions are not natural things, but they provide the abstract preconditions or tools for analysing and explaining change in natural things. The overall outlook of Aristotelian physics that also applies to the physics of the commentators is one of a philosophical analysis of change or natural philosophy rather than that of an experimental natural science.

One crucial feature of physical things in the commentators' analysis is that they change. Based on Aristotle's distinctions, change (*kinēsis*) was understood as a general category that comprises four subtypes:

- change of substance (transformations; in particular of the elements earth, water, air and fire into each other);
- change of quantity (growth and shrinkage);
- change of quality or alteration; and
- change of place (locomotion).

Change as such was not supposed to be a sufficient condition for something being natural. Rather, natural change was understood as a more specific kind of change, be it in any of these four subtypes. A change can be caused by either an external factor or an inner principle, and it is the latter kinds of changes that are natural. Natural changes are such that they are initiated by an inner principle of change and natural things contain such an inner principle. Basically, this condition excludes artefacts from the category of natural things. However, artefacts also consist of natural elements and, consequently, have inner sources of movement as well. Simplicius illustrates the difference between the movement of natural bodies and the movement of artefacts as follows. If a bed is lifted up and then released, it is not as an artefact – that is, as a bed – that it falls down. Rather, it falls down because it is wooden, and it is natural for wood to fall down towards the centre of the earth when released. (Simpl. *in Ph.* 267,1–5). Further, it is natural for wood to fall down because it primarily consists of earth, which has a natural tendency to move downwards.

On the other hand, as Aristotle's formulation of the distinction between natural things and artefacts indicates (Arist. *Ph.* II 1, 192b13–14), things that naturally change are sometimes stable. In fact he says that natural things have an inner principle of change (*kinēsis*) and stability (*stasis*). This formulation creates a problem because it seems to entail that natural things must sometimes be at rest as well. However, many commentators were reluctant to exclude from the scope of natural things celestial bodies, which move eternally in circles. They rather wanted to consider them as natural even though they never rest (e.g. Alexander, according to Simp. *in Ph.* 264,18–22; Philoponus makes a similar point in his commentary on Book II). Therefore, an internal principle of change and stability was not a necessary condition for something to be natural. A natural movement could also be eternal.

The supposition that natural things have an internal principle or cause of change was a somewhat problematic one for Neoplatonic or Platonic authors. Nature as a whole was understood as a large ensouled thing: a living being that functions through its parts. However, it was not desirable that even nature as a whole would become too independent in the sense of containing all explanations for natural changes. Rather, in Neoplatonism all explanation or causation is supposed to originate from super-natural intellectual principles, hence nature cannot be exhaustively explained without reference to these principles. A further, more specific problem concerning nature was whether or not, or in what sense, natural things were supposed to be material or corporeal and in that sense physical. We shall touch on these questions in § "Definitions of nature and natural things" and § "Is our soul natural?", below.

In the commentaries, change was not typically taken to be an obstacle for knowability. Most commentators deviated from discussions like Plato's *Theaetetus* and *Republic*, where changing particulars were not regarded as proper objects of knowledge (*epistēmē*) but only of opinion (*doxa*). Knowability of changing things was usually accounted for by the supposition that natural changes exemplify some general patterns and that explanatory regularities behind change could be established (e.g. Alex.Aphr. *in Metaph.* 104,12ff.). For many, Philoponus among them, the crucial feature of nature's knowability was related to knowing its principles, as Aristotle also points out at the beginning of the *Physics* (I 1, 184a10). Philoponus explains that *Physics* is a study of what is common to all natural things. Those are matter, form, place, time and motion (Phlp. *in Ph.* 2,13–17). Therefore, nature can be known in so far as these principles are known.[1]

However, the idea that the principles of nature, most importantly matter and form, can be known because they are unchangeable is not universally accepted among the commentators. Simplicius, for example, when recapitulating the account of material and formal causes (*in Ph.* 320,33–5), explains the Aristotelian matter and form *as changing*. For Simplicius, when a human being comes to be, the form, coming from the father, changes because it becomes materialized. The matter, understood as the menstrual blood of the mother, changes because it is changing to form. Simplicius seems to suppose that, in order for a thing to be changed by a cause or principle (such as form or matter in this case), this principle needs to change as well. However, this inference seems suspicious. The whole idea of natural principles is based on the idea that they cause change without themselves changing.

Simplicius' point here involves curious interpretive moves concerning both Aristotle and Plato. In so far as Aristotle is concerned, to claim that matter must change only applies to the so-called proximate matter: for example, when a bed made of wood burns, the wood changes. However, within the Aristotelian framework, there is a notion of unchangeable matter: the so-called prime matter. Prime matter is the principle of materiality: an unchanging ultimate subject of all predication and change. Because prime matter as such does not have qualities and nature of its own, it can remain unchanged even when the subject having those predications that determine its own matter change. For example, wood as the proximate matter of the bed has qualities of heaviness and dryness. It changes partly into fire, which is light and hot, and partly into ashes, which are heavier and dry. However, underlying these materials and qualities, there is prime matter that remains the same throughout the process. It comes to bear different qualities, but its own nature does not include any qualities and nor can it change.

On the other hand, Simplicius implicitly follows Aristotle in interpreting Plato (trans. Fleet 1997: n.229 *ad loc*). He refers to the *Timaeus* (50b), where Plato actually talks not about matter but about the receptacle. It is true that Plato's receptacle is described in terms quite similar to the Aristotelian prime matter. However, for Plato the receptacle is not matter but a space or location where the demiurge moulds material into an organized system. It is Aristotle who interprets the receptacle as matter. Therefore, Simplicius employs his own interpretation of Aristotle and Aristotle's interpretation of Plato to create a new, layered system. In this system, we need unchangeable matter and forms (Simplicius' version of Plato's receptacle and forms) and "natural", changing matter and form: proximate matter taken from Aristotle and Simplicius' own version of Aristotelian forms.

As we saw in Chapter 3, the commentators suppose that, before proceeding into more specific theorizing, a scientist or a natural philosopher needs to secure the existence of the objects of one's science. Aristotle argues that, in the case of physics, the question of the existence of nature is easily answered and need not be argued for (*Ph.* 193a3). Simplicius illustrates this with a simile in his commentary: an attempt to prove that nature exists would be as useless as trying to explain to a blind person what colours are (*in Ph.* 272,12ff.). For someone who cannot perceive, such an account provides some information, but the real method of checking whether nature exists or not is just to perceive it. Therefore, a study in physics need not begin with arguments for the existence of its object.

Before we move on, it is appropriate to briefly consider the sources for this chapter. The most important objects of discussion are the commentaries on Aristotle's *Physics* by Philoponus and Simplicius, most importantly their commentaries on Book II, where Aristotle sets the stage of most central themes in the work. From Arabic sources we know that Alexander of Aphrodisias wrote a commentary on the *Physics*, but it has not been preserved to us. Simplicius argues against Alexander in his commentary on the *Physics*, but it is not certain what his exact source is. Further, when reporting Alexander's position, Simplicius is using him for purposes of the argument, and is not necessarily a reliable source concerning Alexander's position. Themistius also wrote a paraphrase on Aristotle's *Physics*, but we cannot concentrate on it here. Towards the end of the chapter, we shall also consider Philoponus' arguments against the eternity of the world, mainly in his *On the Creation of the World* (*de Opificio mundi*) and *Against Proclus on the Eternity of the World*.

Nature

Definitions of nature and natural things

As indicated above, the commentators' discussion concerning the definition of nature is inspired by Aristotle's distinction in *Physics* II 1 (192b13–14) between natural things and artefacts, where the former are said to contain an inner principle of change and stability, whereas the latter need to be changed from outside. The distinction leads to a definition of nature as an inner principle of change and stability (192b20–23), and this definition was repeated and elaborated in the commentaries. According to Simplicius (*in Ph.* 264,18–22), Alexander added that having an internal principle of change and stability applies to animals, plants and the elements, but not to all natural things. As we have seen, this is because Alexander supposed celestial bodies to be natural things as well, and they lack a principle of rest.

When it comes to natural things, different kinds of inner principles of motion and rest have to be distinguished. One is that of inanimate bodies that do have a natural tendency to move in some direction: a stone falls down if nothing prevents it from doing so. Another type of inner principles consists of movements in accordance with soul. Such movement is peculiar to living beings: plants and animals grow and reproduce, are generated and corrupted, consume nutrition and so forth. In addition, there is movement and change according to a presentation (*phantasia*). Within the Aristotelian framework, this is peculiar to living creatures that have cognitive functions of perception and/or reason (see e.g. Alex.Aphr. *Fat.* 183,30–34). For Aristotle, plants as natural things have another kind of soul that lacks perceptive and presentational capacities, but accounts for their change of quantity (growth and decay).

The hierarchy, where plants have a soul but do not perceive or feel, whereas animals both have soul and feel is manifested in Aristotle's theory in the *De anima*, and it was by no means universally accepted in antiquity. Plato, for example, allowed that plants could feel (*Ti.* 77a–c). Others – that is, the Stoics and Galen – did not want

to grant soul to plants, possibly because they did not want to accept
that plants could perceive or feel. They replaced the notion of soul
as an explanatory principle of movement in plants by nature (Galen
Placita 6.3.7; *On the natural faculties* 1.1.1–2).[2]

Philoponus
Philoponus makes specifications similar to Alexander's in his commentary on *Physics* II. He distinguishes between animate and inanimate natural things; for the latter the inner principle of change is
not their soul (*in Ph.* 195,25–32). For non-living natural things, he
postulates inner inclinations (*rhopē*) to move towards a certain direction (195,29; see also trans. Lacey 1993: 11 n.23). The stone has an
inner inclination to fall down, whereas fire's tendency is upwards.
They have these tendencies without having any mental ideas or
intentions. By contrast, animals move because of their senses and
desires (196,30–197,5). The senses do not move the animal directly,
as Philoponus explains, but they affect the animal's desire, and it is
the desire that then moves the animal through its natural capacities
(*phusikē dunamis*; 196,33–197,1). How these capacities do so is left
unspecified.

When commenting on Aristotle's definition of nature referring to
internal and external movers, Philoponus complains that it cannot
be a proper definition for the following reason: it does not state what
nature is but what it does and is thus a definition through activity
(*energeia*) rather than through essence (*ti esti*) (197,30–33). However, when he then proceeds to define nature, it is not merely such
rephrasing of the definition that he presents. Rather, his definition
of nature radically departs from that given by Aristotle. According
to Philoponus' definition:

[N]ature is a life (*zōē*) or a power (*dunamis*) which has
descended (*kataduein* as perfect participle *katadedukuia*)
into bodies, and which moulds and manages them, being
a source of change and rest [for that] "in which it belongs
primarily" per se and not per accidens. And that nature
manages not only animate things but also inanimate ones

is clear (for each thing has a natural power holding together [*sunektikē*] its being …).

(Phlp. *in Ph.* 197,34–198,3, trans. Lacey 1993)

This passage has a strikingly non-Aristotelian ring to it. First, even though Philoponus had accepted the Aristotelian idea that nature is an internal principle of certain kinds of things (e.g. *in Ph.* 194,16–21), he here refers to nature as an agent that in some sense must be or must have been outside natural things. This is because Philoponus argues that nature has *descended into* bodies: if it has descended into them, it must have come from somewhere else. If it has descended, it must have come from above. Secondly, nature is said to manage not only animate things but also inanimate ones. Therefore, Aristotle's idea that, for natural things, the principle of change is internal has been changed into the form that it has come into them from outside, that is, from above. This descended nature also manages and moulds natural things, and hence seems like a divine agent steering nature. Yet it is not just a divine agent outside nature, because it has descended into bodies. Therefore, in the short passage we quoted, Philoponus weaves together the idea of a divine power outside nature and nature as an inner principle of change. However, nature is also said to manage both animate and inanimate things equally, and this seems to destroy the contrast between artefacts and natural things that was an important starting-point for Aristotle's definition.

Some have tried to explain Philoponus' revision of the Aristotelian definition of nature by referring to his Christianity. However, we do not need to go as far as Christianity to find parallels to Philoponus' definition. A much closer and more likely source is found in the Neoplatonic account of how lives or souls descend from a higher ontological level and come to be realized in bodies (see also trans. Lacey 1993: 148–9 n.43). However, for Philoponus there is no Neoplatonism, and it is far from clear that he intends to combine ingredients from different schools or different thinkers – or that he is revising Aristotle's definition. At least, he does not indicate that he is doing so. In fact, Philoponus' account of nature serves as a good example of the philosophical tradition in which the commentators worked. When we look at it today, we see it as a combination of elements coming from different thinkers or schools, but this was not their perspective. Rather, the schools and strands of thought had moulded the interpretive tools that the commentators used to operate on the questions discussed in the body text, as here on the notion of nature.

Simplicius

Much of Simplicius' discussion of Aristotle's definition of nature centres on his disagreement with Alexander of Aphrodisias. Simplicius reports, perhaps not quite charitably, that Alexander had in general identified nature with soul. Simplicius does not accept this. He argues that, as Aristotle had put it in the *De anima*, soul is the first actuality of a natural body. According to Simplicius, nature cannot be the first actuality of a natural body. His examples and discussion of the distinction between natural and artificial things centres on natural things as elements, for example, earth and fire, and their natural movement downwards and upwards. His example of growth is a rock that grows (264,11–15). It has been suggested that Simplicius refers to the process of how pieces of crystal come together to form larger pieces (see trans. Fleet 1997: 165 n.35). This would mean two things. First, it may be that, for Simplicius, crystals are alive and this is why they grow. On the other hand, his reference could involve an idea similar to that we found in Philoponus: nature is an external agent that manages both animate and inanimate things alike.

For Simplicius, the crucial factor in natural change consists of the natural properties that natural elements have, such as lightness for air and fire and heaviness for earth. This is somewhat problematic since artificial things are made from natural materials, hence they derivatively come to have the very same properties even though they are not as pure. On the other hand, soul is understood as an external explanatory principle. On this point Simplicius refers to Aristotle's authority by using somewhat tendentious evidence: he refers to properties that in Aristotle only belong to the active or productive intellect (*de An.* III 5), which by no means is the whole soul: it is unmixed with body and separable from it. For us it seems that Simplicius is using Aristotle to make the essentially Platonist point that soul is separate from body and also separate from nature. However, it is not likely that this is his way of understanding the issue. Rather, he probably sees Aristotle making this very point. Simplicius does not go on to explain how plant life is to be understood within this scheme, where, on the one hand, there are natural elements (earth, water, air and fire) and their natural properties and, on the other hand, an immaterial and separate soul. In any case, the Aristotelian definition of nature as an internal principle of change has, again, drastically changed.

Natural causes

If we restrict our discussion to sublunary things for a moment, what kind of internal principles of change and stability do we find there? If these principles are natural, does it also mean that they are material? If they are immaterial, how can they explain or cause change? Before we go deeper into the discussion, we need to present the classifications of causes used by the commentators.

One ingredient in the commentators' classification of causes is the famous Aristotelian fourfold distinction: "the four modes into which cause falls" (*Ph.* II 3 195a15). According to Aristotle, the question of why something happens (*dia ti*, why?) can be answered in terms of four different kinds of causality or explanation (*to dia ti*, that because of which): (a) that for the sake of which it happens; (b) what it is for it to be; (c) that out of which the change comes about; and (d) where the source of change lies. For example, if we ask why there is a house, we can answer it in the following four ways: (a) in order for us to be sheltered from rain and coldness (or, heat for Philoponus); (b) because the carpenter has a blueprint of a house in his mind according to which he builds; (c) because there are bricks and stones out of which it is constructed; or (d) because the builder builds it (cf. Phlp. *in Ph.* 241,10–16). We usually know these causes by the names standardized in the middle ages: (a) final, (b) formal, (c) material and (d) efficient cause. These names do not reflect the variety in which Aristotle himself refers to the four modes into which causes fall. However, the systematization of the terminology had already started in the commentaries (see Johnson 2005: 42–9).

Aristotle allows that all these kinds of causation exist in nature but he points out that in nature the causes often coincide (Arist. *Ph.* II 7, 198a24–7). Philoponus specifies that, nature is "not only formal cause, but also efficient cause, and final cause" and he also attributes this view to Aristotle (Phlp. *in Ph.* 195,3–5 in Macierowski & Hassing 1988: 77). Note that not even the "cause out of which" ("material cause") needs to be material in the sense of being corporeal or physical. For example, genus is such a cause for its species and so are the parts of a whole; even premises of a syllogism are "material causes" of the conclusion in the Aristotelian analysis (195a17–20; cf. Phlp. *in Ph.* 247,5–6; see also Johnson 2005: 44–5).

In his criticism of Platonic forms, Aristotle had also argued that they are not sufficient as causes (*Metaph.* I 6, 988a7–14). However, rather than following Aristotle in criticizing Plato in this respect, the commentators extend their classification of causes with Platonic explanation types mediated through Stoicism (see Karamanolis 2006). In the *Timaeus*, Plato distinguishes between causes as paradigms (*paradeigmata*) and contributory causes (*sunaitia*) (*Ti.* 46c–d, 47e–48a, 68e–69a). When the demiurge or the divine craftsman is making the world, forms or ideas are used as paradigms guiding the process of moulding the material out of which the world is made. In this respect, the Platonic demiurge differs from a Christian creator God: the demiurge does not create matter, but matter pre-exists the demiurge's "creation" and it has properties of its own that function in this process as contributory causes. What matter is like does have an effect on what the world comes to be like, but the nature of matter is not the decisive cause in the sense of being part of the plan or the blueprint of the demiurge. Matter and its properties can be characterized as necessary conditions of the process, and being necessary in this connection has the connotation of being somewhat undesirable. A world could not be made without matter, but matter and its laws prevent the blueprint (i.e. the paradigm) from being perfectly realized. In the Neoplatonic commentaries, paradigmatic and contributory causes were added to Aristotle's fourfold distinction and a new classification of causes was obtained. Within this scheme, the forms as realized in individual material objects were treated as contributory causes.[3]

Philoponus
When applying his scheme of causes, Philoponus is drawing on Porphyry, who, for his part, works in a long tradition of conflating Platonic and Aristotelian causes (cf. Seneca *Epistle* 65.4.14; see Karamanolis 2006: 274). "Contributory cause" is treated as a heading under which three kinds of causes are placed: Aristotelian form and matter are familiar to us, but Philoponus also introduces a new, instrumental cause. According to Philoponus, Aristotle does not distinguish instrumental cause as a category of its own because in some cases – such as, for example, natural internal heat – he classifies it under material causes (*in Ph.* 241,23–7). In others, Aristotle wants to distinguish instruments or tools from efficient causes (the craftsman who uses the tool) and the finished products (a house) (*in Ph.* 241,29–242,3).

Philoponus points out that even though a thing's nature could in some sense be understood as a paradigm towards which its development naturally tends, this does not happen in a manner similar to the way the demiurge uses the Platonic separate forms. The demiurge knows these paradigms, whereas natural things tend towards perfection specific to them unknowingly (242,5–7). According to Philoponus, this is why Aristotle does not accept paradigmatic causation in nature (cf. Phlp. *in Ph.* 5,7–6,7, 244,14–245,2). Therefore, Philoponus sees that the notion of paradigm would be a misleading categorization for the Aristotelian formal causes. The form of a thing in Aristotle does provide the criteria for evaluating how well a thing of that kind succeeds in being a representative of that kind, but natural things do not aim at perfecting their forms knowingly.

To illustrate the difference between the ways in which Plato and Aristotle approach physics, he draws the following contrast. According to Philoponus, Plato in the *Timaeus* does physics theologically, whereas Aristotle's account of theology in the *Metaphysics* is physical: he derives the principles of theology from physical things (5,20–25). As a natural scientist, Philoponus says, Aristotle does not employ the notions of paradigmatic and instrumental cause. He does not employ the former, because, for Aristotle, nature does not create with regard to a paradigm. On the contrary, because nature is a kind of life, "it creates in the manner of life, rather than as a sort of knowledge in the mind" (*in Ph.* 5,20–22, trans. Osborne 2006). Therefore, Philoponus clearly recognizes that Aristotelian nature is not the kind of agentive cause, as an artificer, that consciously aims at fulfilling some ends or paradigms. Rather, natural processes are teleological, that is, goal-directed, and have their own mechanisms for producing developments and activities in living things. Here Philoponus contrasts natural and internal principles of change with knowingly executed steering or moulding, and underlines that in natural things it is the former that creates change. However, we saw above that in his own definition of nature he seemed to combine these two ideas. Philoponus himself does not discuss these interpretive moves he makes; he does not seem to perceive tension between them.

The notion of instrumental cause is unnecessary in Aristotelian physics for reasons similar to paradigmatic cause. For Aristotle, the natural properties of elements and things are not instruments through which either nature as a whole or a divine craftsman should carry out a plan. According to Philoponus, Aristotle wants to explain natural phenomena by reference to themselves alone. For example, he wants to explain natural temperaments by reference to the four elements, rather than through a reference to nature as a whole (*in Ph.* 5,29–6,3).

Philoponus himself does not take sides here. He lays out the classification of causes by Plato and Aristotle: the classification that he gets from Porphyry (according to Simp. *in Ph.* 10,25–11,17). Philoponus' description of the divergent approaches of these two philosophers is concise and hits its mark. He does not aim at harmonization, nor does he attempt to explain away a clear disagreement between the two authors.

Simplicius
Simplicius makes full use of all the six causes, that is, Aristotle's causes augmented with Neoplatonic paradigmatic and instrumental causes. However, he does not keep them entirely separate. In his account of the formal cause (*in Ph.* 310,20–314,24), Simplicius shifts from the Aristotelian formal cause to the Platonic forms as paradigms. However, he points out here and there that, for Aristotle, forms are those forms that are enmattered, and nature does not use them as paradigms in the sense that it would know them. He also specifies this to be Alexander's view (312,1–3, 313,28–314,1). Nonetheless, immediately after the last-mentioned passage he glides from the Aristotelian natural forms into a position that natural causes require knowledge and are transmitted to the sublunary world only through the movements of the heavens (314,3–14). Therefore, he makes the Aristotelian forms dependent on higher, paradigmatic forms. It remains somewhat unclear whether those paradigms require a Platonic demiurge or whether they are internal to a Neoplatonic Intellect from which nature comes about through a process of descending emanation. However, Simplicius does make it very clear that formal causation in nature is possible only because there is a knowing agent from whom all causation originates.

In so far as Simplicius' method is concerned, he initially allows a disagreement between Plato and Aristotle about forms (310,22–24), but he does not comment at all on his move from the Aristotelian account of formal causation to the Platonic or Neoplatonic one. Later, when recapitulating the Platonic and Aristotelian classifications of causes, he explicitly points out that in fact the ultimate principle of change needs to be an unmoved mover. His term is an Aristotelian one but it is interpreted Neoplatonically. For Simplicius, the unmoved mover is a greatly praised Intellect (*polutimētos nous*) in a Neoplatonic ontological hierarchy; beneath it is the level of soul, that is, nature as a whole. Again, he does not mention the fact that this is a Neoplatonic rather than Aristotelian position.

Instrumental cause is analysed in a similar framework by Simplicius (316,5–13). He briefly distinguishes health as the final cause of medicine from intermediary steps, such as purging and the scalpel, towards achieving that end. Simplicius points out that, in these cases, purging and the scalpel in fact are instrumental causes rather than anything in the Aristotelian fourfold scheme. The implicit conclusion perhaps is that there is instrumental causation in nature as well, and it is subordinated to nature as a whole, again subordinated to the Intellect.

Whereas Aristotle seems to subordinate his natural causes to the unmoved mover, Simplicius' account subordinates them to a cosmic Intellect. The Intellect uses forms as paradigms and operates in nature through instruments (understood, for example, as the natural properties of the elements). The guiding supposition seems to be that there can be no goal-directedness in nature without a cosmic intelligence or a planner.

***

Before we move on to our next topic, it is appropriate to pause for a moment to consider a problem in the scope and content of the *Physics* and commentaries on it. According to Aristotle's definition of nature, artefacts are excluded from the class of natural things. However, much of the discussion in *Physics* II and in the commentaries on it focuses on changes in artefacts. This seems problematic: natural change that is contrasted to changes in artefacts is explained by reference to changes in artefacts. On the other hand, given that those natural things that have soul are discussed in the *De anima*, would we not expect that the *Physics* is restricted to a study of those beings that do not have soul? This is not at all the case. What does this tell us?

As to the first problem, Simplicius argues that the causes of change are the same whether a thing is natural or artificial (*in Ph.* 318,33–35); in both cases the material, efficient, formal and final causes are needed. The only difference is whether the principle of change is internal to the thing or not. As we saw, even though Simplicius in his pronounced statements on the definition of nature sticks to this idea, he moves freely to causes that are external to nature – a divine craftsman or a creative Intellect – and seems to understand these as primary.

As to the second problem, Philoponus characterizes the scope of the *Physics* as what is common to all natural things. Then he proceeds to separate such works as *De caelo* and *De generatione et corruptione* from natural philosophy in so far as the former deals with eternal things, the latter with those that are generated and corrupted. In the *Meteorologica*, the discussion concentrates primarily on lifeless things and, in particular those phenomena that take place in the atmosphere. Philoponus also mentions a treatise on plants, without naming it, and refers to several works on animal life: for example, *Historia animalium, De partibus animalium* and the *Parva naturalia*. Aristotle's treatise on the soul (*De anima*) is grouped together with these treatises (Phlp. *in Ph.* 1,22–2,21). Philoponus' classification suggests that the crucial point about natural philosophy is its generality. All the other treatises he lists may or may not concern natural things, but even if they do, they do not consider them from the most general perspective possible but always exclude some classes of objects, for example, temporary, living, lifeless and so on.

On the other hand, even though natural things are contrasted to artefacts, there is a specific reason to choose artefacts rather than, say, atomic motion understood in terms of chance and necessity. This is because, from the Aristotelian perspective, there is something *in common* in natural things and artefacts. This is that both of them call for final (i.e. teleological, from Greek *telos*, "end" or "aim") causation or explanation. In both cases, "the relationship between cause and effect is the same" (Arist. *Ph.* 199a15). Natural teleology and the commentators' reactions to it will be discussed in more detail in § "Teleology: background", below.

Is our soul natural?

There is one particularly intriguing question related to natural causes of change: whether the commentators supposed the human soul (or mind, if we wish) to be natural. A concise response to this question is provided by Pseudo-Simplicius. He claims that "the study of the soul is neither simply physical (*phusikos*), nor metaphysical (*ta meta ta phusika*), but belongs to both" (ps.-Simp. *in de An.* 3,4–6, trans. Lautner in Sorabji 2004: vol. 2, 54). This is because, on the one hand, soul as a principle of change in animals and human beings alike is something belonging to the scope of physics (3,9–12). By contrast, intellect should rather be studied first in philosophy (*prōtē philosophia*; 2,33), that is, outside physics. Pseudo-Simplicius attributes this view to Aristotle as well (3,25–8).

Even though Pseudo-Simplicius is positive that the limits of nature are too narrow for soul or mind in its entirety, he recommends that a natural scientist focus on soul rather than on the matter of living things. This is because, he says, when attempting to understand nature, we must study soul, because "their matter is their nature because of soul rather than the reverse" (2,16–17, trans. Urmson 1995). Therefore, for ensouled material things, it is the soul that is the cause of what kind of a body they have rather than the other way around. Consequently, a natural scientist is not aiming at a naturalization of phenomena in the sense of explaining away the notion of soul (or avoiding the notion of soul in explanations). Rather, soul is a central explanatory principle in studies on nature.

The source we just discussed is a commentary that has, in the manuscript tradition, been attributed to Simplicius but was not written by the historical Simplicius (see Ch. 1, § "Simplicius"). Let us now consider Simplicius in the authentic commentary on the *De caelo*. In this commentary, he reports that Alexander had assimilated nature and soul in heavenly bodies (*in Cael.* 380,29–381,2). Simplicius does not accept this assimilation, but argues that for the heavenly bodies soul and nature must be distinguished (*in Cael.* 387,12–19). In his arguments against Alexander, he makes some important remarks with respect to nature and soul. The arguments are based on the distinction between mover and moved. For Simplicius, nature is a power of being moved rather than a capacity of moving something (cf. Arist. *Ph.* VIII 4, 255b30–31; II 1, 192b13). Soul, by contrast, must be understood as an agent that causes movement and is something external to that which is moved (cf. Pl. *Ti.* 34b4, 36e3). Therefore, Simplicius argues, in the heavenly bodies it is the soul that moves them and their nature is such as to be moved by the soul. One reason for Simplicius – or anyone working in the broadly speaking Aristotelian tradition – to have difficulty with the identification of soul with nature is the following: Aristotle did not want to accept the idea that soul is moved in a proper sense (*Ph.* VIII 5, 258a7; *de An.* I 3, 406a3, 408b5–18; II 5, 417a31–b16). Therefore, if soul is identified with nature in the heavenly bodies, it seems that it has to be moved as well. This qualm is not restricted to the heavenly bodies but applies generally.

As mentioned above, in his polemic against Alexander's interpretation of Aristotle's definition of nature, Simplicius detached soul from nature. According to Simplicius, our soul has activities that are separable from body (*in Ph.* 269,1–4) and thus the soul's essence must also be separable from body (269,4). Therefore, soul cannot be natural.

Simplicius saddles Alexander with the suggestion that the soul moves the body in the way that the helmsman moves the ship (Simp. *in Ph.* 268,12–14; cf. Aristotle *de An.* II 1, 3).[4] According to Simplicius, this comparison is unsatisfactory for two reasons. First, it gives us an erroneous picture of the relation between soul and body. Whereas a ship remains a ship even without a helmsman, a living being is not one if soul is removed. Therefore, soul belongs *per se* to a living body. Secondly, whereas the helmsman moves the ship through intermediaries such as the ship's rudder, this is not how soul moves the body. Any local movement, if allowed at all, must be accidental to a rational soul. The soul moves the living being through desires and thoughts, and moving through desire must be distinguished from any local movement (268,18–24). Simplicius gives no further explanation of how our thoughts and desires move us. He here opposes the position that soul moves us through local movement, and perhaps he wants to make the following kind of contrast. If we suppose that our thoughts and desires move us through local movement, then we must understand a thought or desire (e.g. the desire to eat a cake) to be similar to a turn of the helm. This, then, could be mediated to our limbs through intermediaries, as the turns of the helm are mediated through levers and wheels to the rudder, and make us extend our hand towards the cake. Simplicius' point is that our desire is not a local movement like the turn of the wheel.

THE ANCIENT COMMENTATORS ON PLATO AND ARISTOTLE

However, he does not explain what the exact difference is and how body mechanics and desires are related.

Change explained

Teleology: background

When discussing final causation in nature, Simplicius refers to the account of causes (*aitiai*) given in Plato's *Phaedo*. In the passage, Socrates is sitting in prison and waiting for his death. Socrates tells how as a young man he was fascinated by the natural philosophy of the time and wished to find answers to his questions: are living creatures nurtured when heat and cold produce a kind of putrefaction? Do we think with our blood? Does the brain provide our senses? Having studied those philosophers, he had noticed that he had no aptitude for studies of this kind. Then, he heard someone reading Anaxagoras' book, where mind (*nous*) was said to govern and organize things in the way that is best, and to be the cause of everything in nature. Socrates became hopeful that he would find answers from Anaxagoras. However, it turned out that Anaxagoras, in his book, made no use of mind, gave it no responsibility for the arrangement of things and reduced natural causes to air, ether, water "and many strange things" (96a–98c, trans. Grube, in ed. Cooper 1997).

According to Socrates:

> That seemed to me much like saying that Socrates' actions are all due to his mind, and then in trying to tell the causes of everything I do, to say that the reason that I am sitting here [in prison] is because my body consists of bones and sinews, because the sinews are hard and separated by joints.   (98c)

For him, such an explanation would not be worth much: "For, by the dog, I think these sinews and bones could long ago have been in Megara or among the Boeotians, ... if I had not thought it more right to honourably endure whatever penalty the city ordered rather than escape and run away" (98e–99a). The crucial point in Socrates' disappointment with all natural philosophers is that their explanations do not refer to anything good. By contrast, throughout his consideration concerning causes, Socrates stresses that genuine explanatory force can only derive from a reference to something good.

As we saw, Aristotle did not put the point quite like this; he distinguished several types of explanations and his final causation is not strictly speaking an explanation referring to good but to *an end*. In Greek, end is *telos*, from which the name "teleology" was derived in the eighteenth century. Ends are good in Aristotle as well, but in Plato's later dialogues, in Aristotle and the Neoplatonists, the analysis of causes becomes more variegated than the one found in the *Phaedo*.

Irrespective of any other possible differences in their analyses of causes, the commentators are unanimous that final causation exists in nature. In fact, some of them identify nature as form with final cause (e.g. Phlp. *in Ph.* 317,17, where he speaks about "natural form", *phusikon eidos*). Aristotle argues for final causation in nature in *Physics* II 8–9, where it is distinguished from what happens through luck without ends on the one hand and from what is necessary on the other. Notice that Aristotle's point is not to argue that necessity and luck or chance could not exist in nature *at all*. Rather, his point is to say, first, that what is natural and what is explained by nature is not a lucky coincidence: it is not through luck that we have broad teeth in the back and sharp ones up front, but because the former are more suitable for grinding and the latter for chopping. Secondly, in nature necessities are subordinated to ends. For Aristotle, ends in nature allow exceptions and determine the material necessities.

Final causation in the commentaries

The crucial point in the commentators' arguments for the existence of final causation in nature is a dichotomy that Simplicius articulates in his comments on *Physics* II 8: either nature works by chance or for the sake of some end. This dichotomy is understood as exhaustive and mutually exclusive. Therefore, to argue that there is final causation in nature, one needs to argue against nature working at random. These arguments, in turn, are based on the idea that what happens by chance does not and cannot happen regularly. As Simplicius points out (*in Ph.* 372,30ff.), in nature a man regularly begets man rather than a horse, and this shows that it cannot be a lucky coincidence.

Natural reproduction sometimes fails: the growth of an embryo is obstructed; a seed does not grow to be a tree. The commentators follow Aristotle in arguing that this does not testify that nature should not work for the sake of an end. The existence of failure or deformity does not refute the existence of ends. Rather, the commentators argue, similar failures also take place in arts and no one questions the existence of ends in art. A scribe may spell a name incorrectly, but this does not prove that the scribe was not acting for the sake of an end, namely, to write the name correctly.[5] As to why such failures happen in arts or in nature, Philoponus offers a solution: it is matter and its irregular character that explain failures and deformities. He says that the scribe makes a mistake because there is some unevenness in the material that he is writing on. Surely, this is not the only reason for failure in arts: we can err, for example, because of thinking about another name and starting to pen that in the middle of the name that we were originally supposed to write. However, Philoponus does not mention cases like this.

Rather than being counter-examples to ends in nature, failures and deformities testify to their existence. Failure comes to be understood precisely in contrast to a certain end: a description of a failure presupposes that there was an end that did not come about. This more general point is made effectively by Simplicius. According to Simplicius, we understand all terms by reference to successful representatives. We do not understand the word "drachma" as a false drachma but as a genuine one; nor do we understand a human being as a dead one, but one that lives (Simp. *in Ph. ad* II 8). To specify, the relevant success is always related to some end. We understand it only through some evaluation criteria, and it is exactly such criteria that natural ends offer. To provide another analogy: to understand what a toaster is, it is not useful to say that it smells bad and lets smoke out. Further, it is not very informative to explain its function mechanism either, for example, as an electric appliance with two vertical slots in the top. A full and most informative description of a toaster is given by reference to its end: it is a kitchen appliance that is used to toast bread.

This kind of reasoning is based on how we understand the world. The point about understanding may or may not support the idea that ends really *exist* in nature. The claim that they do is a metaphysical point, whereas the point about understanding is an epistemological one. However, as we already saw, the commentators do make the metaphysical point as well: they argue for the existence of ends in nature, not just for the claim that we understand the world through descriptions of ends or ideals.

After the commentators' arguments for the existence of natural teleology, it may appear that they have not addressed a position that, for the modern reader, seems to be a more difficult challenge than the ones they do discuss. This is the view according to which nature is a kind of mechanism that works according to material necessity but does not include ends. Aristotle does begin his arguments for final causation in nature by opposing the position according to which nature functions, like rainfall, through basic properties of the elements (earth, water, air and fire). The commentators see such a view as some sort of misunderstanding: physical properties as such do not necessitate the outcomes (animals and their body parts). It is the other way round: the outcome (an animal) necessitates the kind of body parts and elements that are needed to produce such an animal.

As to the question of mechanism, the commentators bring in a comparison to marionettes. What kinds of marionettes they mean is not explained in detail, but the outline becomes clear. These are not the kind of puppets that an operator constantly moves from strings. Rather, the movement is just initiated by loosening a string and, after that initial impulse, the dolls start to move each other. In his notes to the translation of Simplicius' commentary on *Physics* II, D. B. Fleet suggests that the dolls move via a kind of domino effect, but one might expect the mechanism to be slightly more spectacular than dolls falling down in a row. According to Simplicius, Alexander had used this analogy to illustrate how things come to be in nature. Matter receives form that determines what is to come to be out of that matter, and changes start to come about:

> This process continues up to an end, the attainment of the natural form ... just as in the case of marionettes; when the operator starts the movement in the first doll this becomes the cause of movement to the next, and this to the one after it, until the movement passes through them all ... not according to any reason or choice in themselves when the one before moves the one after.
>
> (Simp. *in Ph.* 311,7–12, quoting Alexander, trans. Fleet 1997)

Therefore, for Alexander, there is no conflict between mechanism and teleology. Rather, the point is that the marionette mechanism functions according to certain necessities but does not exclude final causation. Rather, the whole mechanism has an end by reference to which we can understand its function: to make the dolls move in a certain way.

Aristotle had also used the comparison with puppets. Rather than the whole of nature, which is the point of comparison in the commentaries, Aristotle used it to illustrate animal motion. According to Aristotle: "Animals have parts of a similar kind, their organs, the sinewy tendons to wit and the bones; the bones are like the pegs and the iron; the tendons are like the strings; for when these are slackened or released movement begins" (*De motu animalium* 7, trans. Johnson 2007). It is important to note that Aristotle's point is not to turn animals into a god's puppets. The point is that the animals' own "imaginations and sensations" move it through a mechanism such as the one just described. However, he does not explain in detail how this happens.

Coming back to Alexander, his reported position here is well in line with Philoponus' and Simplicius' arguments against the idea that material necessities are fundamental explanatory principles in nature. They argue that such a position does not get its priorities right: it would mean that ends and functions could come out of matter without ends, for example, the capacity to perceive could come about from having certain kinds of organs. Simplicius and Philoponus argue that in reality it is the other way round: an animal with certain capacities needs definite kinds of organs, and the material constitution of the animal is such that those capacities can be realized. Therefore, the point is not to exclude material necessity from nature altogether; it just needs to be understood as subordinated to ends.

When arguing against the priority of material necessity in nature, Philoponus presents an analogy. Material conditions are conditionally or hypothetically necessary in a manner similar to the way that a conclusion in a valid argument is conditionally necessary depending on the premises. It is possible for the conclusion to be true or false when the premises are false; however, when the premises are true, the conclusion must be true as well. Therefore, the necessity by which the conclusion follows is dependent on a condition: that the premises are true. Similarly, material constitution is dependent on the existence of ends (Phlp. *in Ph.* 327,14ff.).

Aristotle uses rainfall as an example to illustrate the difference between explanation through material necessity and through final cause. The same example appears in Philoponus and Themistius. Both of them deny that rain should be explained through final cause such that it rains in order to make crops grow, let alone in order to make *my* crops grow (quoted in Sorabji 2004: vol. 2, 86). However, they deny that this should exclude final causation for rain altogether. Rather, Philoponus points out, it rains in order for the natural elements – earth, water, air and fire – to change into one another in a natural cycle. The material necessity with which the elements change is subordinated to this end: completing the natural cycle. Here we need to note that Philoponus is not explaining his own position; rather, he articulates Aristotle's argument. Yet he does bring in the notion of cosmic providence (*in Ph.* 312,26ff.), which is not used by Aristotle. Therefore, it seems that, for Philoponus himself, the circulation of natural elements is not a sufficient end as such, but nature as a whole includes providential ends such as to preserve the balance of that whole.

If, then, there are ends in nature, does this imply that there has to be a divine craftsman or a cosmic designer? Is it necessary that natural ends have been imposed by a divine artificer? We know that Plato postulated such a cosmic designer but Aristotle denied it. Given that Alexander and Simplicius employ the metaphors of marionettes, it would seem that they must suppose that cosmic design exists. However, Alexander as quoted by Simplicius is quite clear that this is not a necessary requirement. For him, the marionettes work without reason or choice. But would there need to be an operator or designer of the marionettes themselves? Even here, at least in this context, Alexander's answer is negative. In Simplicius' report, Alexander says: "'For the sake of something' is not the term applied only to coming-to-be based on reason and choice" (Simp. *in Ph.* 311,22–4, trans. Fleet 1997). Further:

> This is the case whether there is choice and reason or whether there is no reason, as we say is the case with nature. For even if natural things are through material necessities, … one should not represent nature for this reason as not acting for the sake of something. The form, then, is a model in that nature has nodded in its direction not through choice, but more like a marionette.   (311,26–30, trans. Fleet 1997)

Alexander's analogy where nature nods towards a paradigm as a marionette is a fascinating one, even though its exact meaning is difficult to articulate. It is perhaps futile to attempt to exhaust the comparison. However, it captures an important aspect of nature understood in the Aristotelian manner: there are both mechanism and ends in nature, but the existence of ends does not necessitate the existence of a cosmic designer.

When Simplicius himself employs the same comparison, he differs from Alexander in exactly this respect: he refers to the operator of the marionettes. For Simplicius, the crux of the metaphor is the following. The marionettes start to move, once the operator (*tekhnitēs*) has initiated their movement *and* given them an impulse (*hormē*) towards completing it (*in Ph.* 313,23–6). For Simplicius, the order and production of determined ends in nature requires that things owe their existence to an agent that knows them entirely. The identity and properties of this agent are somewhat unclear in Simplicius' account. He uses language that, on the one hand, points to a Platonic demiurge, but, on the other hand, he uses attributes and expressions that usually apply to a Neoplatonic divine Intelligence: for Simplicius, an agent that knows nature through and through shines forth (*ellampsis*; 314,13) and imposes forms on matter in so far as the recipient matter is capable of realizing them. It is the shining forth that is Neoplatonic here.

In another context in his commentary on the *Physics* (15,15–29), Simplicius argues not just that nature's order testifies to the *existence* of a divine artificer. Rather, the point is that from the universe being ordered (*tetagmenos*; Greek *taxis*, "order", is behind this verb) and beautiful (*kalos*) we can infer that the demiurge is *good*. However, Simplicius points out, it is not because the cosmos is well ordered that the demiurge is good. The explanatory relation is the opposite: the goodness of the demiurge is the cause for the cosmos to be ordered. The order in nature is better known to us and from this alleged fact we can infer the less well-known alleged fact that nature must have been organized by a good demiurge.

For the Christian Philoponus, the question of cosmic design is obviously of importance and a source for potential disagreement with the Pagan tradition. Philoponus' famous position on creation will be discussed in § "Eternity versus creation", below. Here, we shall see how Philoponus explains the inner logic of nature. As we saw above in connection with natural causes, Philoponus distinguishes Platonic and Aristotelian paradigm causation and concludes that, according to Aristotle, there is no paradigm causation in nature. Nature does not produce effects knowingly, but has the principles (*logos*) of the things that are to become unknowingly (*mē ginōskousa*; *in Ph.* 244,17). Here Philoponus combines his Neoplatonic or Platonic supposition of the whole nature as an agent with Aristotelian denial of the idea that nature should be mastered by a purposeful agent. Rather, nature as a whole does master things but does so unknowingly, that is, not with reference to knowing a model that it would then impose on natural things. Here we have a sophisticated example of Philoponus' method: he makes a complex mixture from Aristotelian and (Neo)Platonic ingredients by accepting some aspects but rejecting others.

Challenging Aristotelian dynamics

For Aristotle and the commentators, as we have seen, the crucial property of natural things is that they have their source of movement within. However, this does not mean that natural things move *only* according to their inner principle of movement. They can move naturally and artificially. The basic elementary nature of a thing (e.g. whether it is dominated by earth or water) affects both its natural and artificial movement. In addition, natural movement involves the idea of a natural place. The basic elements – earth, water, air and fire – each have an intrinsic tendency to move towards their natural place and they do so if nothing prevents them from doing so. Earth has its natural place at the centre of the earth; the natural places of water and air form two successive layers on the top of it; fire has its place yet higher up, just below the heavens. When reaching their natural place, the simple elements stop and stay where they are if not forcibly drawn out of their places. Pure elements are rare in nature around us; all ordinary bodies are mixed, but the movement of mixed bodies is regulated by the properties of natural elements. For example, a stone, which is mainly made of earth, moves towards the ground and stays there if not artificially lifted up.

Natural things are also subject to substantial change. For instance, when someone makes a fire, wood, which is earthy stuff, changes partly into fire. Perhaps there is not very much pure fire coming into existence there, but there is something that is light and hence moves upwards. This fiery stuff moves upwards because fire has its natural place high up just below the heavens. Now, if the fiery stuff rises up, why or how would it ever come down again? Would it be sufficient that some comets or suchlike could bring the fire back? Or, is it rather that, when moving upwards to the sky, the fiery material cools down?

If this is what happens, it will not continue to rise but changes into something, first air and then water perhaps, that is heavier and tends to come down. This is how the natural cycle of earth, air and water is explained. Water on earth is warmed by the sun, changes into air and rises up. Then the air cools down and forms clouds, perhaps continues to cool down, changes into water and becomes heavier, and finally falls down as rain again.

As mentioned, natural things are also moved artificially. To do so, they require an external mover. For example, when I lift a stone from the ground, I move the stone artificially, and the stone becomes moved by an external mover. When I let it fall, it becomes free to manifest its natural tendency to move down and falls back to the ground if nothing hinders it. However, because I do not push the stone to the ground, I am just an accidental cause of its motion. The internal nature of the stone explains why it falls down when my hand lets it fall. Aristotle perhaps needs the notion of an accidental mover to explain why things move continuously in the world around us. If it were the case that there is only natural movement, the elements would probably become separated from the mixtures they are realized in, go to their natural places and stay there.

In his arguments for the existence of the unmoved mover in *Physics* VIII 4, Aristotle makes an important interpretive move concerning the Platonic principle according to which everything that moves is moved by something. According to Aristotle, it needs to be moved by something *external*. This means that, for things that have an inner source of motion, one part of them is moving the rest. In living self-movers (animals), this means that the soul is the mover and the material undergoes the movement. Later Neoplatonic commentators challenged this idea and introduced impressed inner forces as movers.

As opposed to an internal natural tendency that moves only in one direction (e.g. the tendency of fire to move upwards), the impressed internal force or impulse can move the thing in any direction. This idea becomes important in the later ancient discussion about projectile motion. Aristotle makes a brief and rather careless remark on this issue, and the remark is not the most successful aspect of his dynamics. Philoponus seizes on the remark and ridicules it at great length. As Sorabji has shown, Philoponus' discussion on Aristotle's remark radically challenges the Aristotelian explanation of motion and in important ways anticipates later discussion of an impressed moving force called *impetus* (see Sorabji 1987, 1988, 2004: vol. 2, 327–56).

The stock example is a javelin that is thrown by an athlete. A wooden javelin has earth as the dominant element and tends to move downwards. Yet it can be made to fly for a while. An intuitive way of explaining this motion would be to say that the athlete's hand moves it. However, this is not quite what Aristotle says. Rather, he supposes that the hand can only move the javelin until it is dispatched, because the mover and moved need to be in physical contact. Since flying is unnatural for the javelin, it has to be moved all along its way. To explain the artificial flight of the javelin in the air, Aristotle introduces the idea that there are pockets of air that push the javelin forwards. Apparently, their capacity to do so is diminished on the way, because finally the javelin becomes free to exercise its natural motion downwards. Among other problems, this idea has the undesirable implication that air has two conflicting effects on movement. Aristotle recognized that in some cases it resists motion (*Phys.* IV 8, 215a24–216a11), whereas here it acts as a mover (Sorabji 1987, 1988).

Philoponus' discussion about this unhappy brief passage is a delightful read.[6] For example, Philoponus argues that if it were the case that the air moves the javelin, it would follow that soldiers need not touch their javelins at all but make the air move and let it push the javelins forwards. The main point of Philoponus' argument is this: it is not the air that moves the javelin, but the hand imposes an internal moving force (*kinētikē dunamis*; *in Ph.* 642,4) on it, and this force moves it forwards. The force can be lesser or greater, and the greater it is, the further away the javelin is carried.

The notion of impressed internal force is a significant change with respect to the Aristotelian dynamics. As mentioned above, the Aristotelian internal nature moves things only in one direction, whereas artificial motion caused by *external* movers can move the thing in all possible directions. For Aristotle, the effect of an external mover is limited by the condition that the mover has to be in physical contact with the moved. By introducing impressed internal forces, Philoponus abandons this supposition: an external mover can impress a moving force in the thing and that force continues to move it even when the external mover is not in contact with the moved object.[7]

Philoponus utilizes the notion of impressed internal forces on a cosmic scale and makes impressed force into a central explanatory notion in all of dynamics: God imposes impressed forces to natural things at the time of creation. By the time of Galileo, Newton and Descartes, the assumption that a body needs a force to *continue* its movement is replaced by the idea that the body *will* continue its movement unless some other forces affect it.[8] In Newton, of course, the Aristotelian natural inclinations or tendencies to fall, for example, have been replaced by forces too.

Sorabji has highlighted the idea of God putting internal impressed forces into things in creation as an achievement by Philoponus in particular (Sorabji 1987, 1988). However, when employing the metaphor of the marionettes we quoted above (§ "Final causation in the commentaries"), Simplicius comes very close to this idea. Nature is compared to a marionette machine, and a role is given to the operator of the machine. Simplicius specifies the action of the operator as follows: the operator initiates the movement of the marionettes, but this is not all he does; the operator also gives the marionettes an impulse (*hormē*) to complete the movement that the operator has initiated. Simplicius is slightly vague about whether those impulses are given to the individual dolls or the machine as a whole. In any case, Simplicius' account again suggests that ideas similar to those found in Philoponus were circulating among the Neoplatonic students of Ammonius in Alexandria. Further, again we have parallel developments in a pagan and a Christian commentator.[9]

Challenging Aristotelian notions of place and prime matter

In addition to the challenges for dynamics, Philoponus gives a new understanding of two central notions of Aristotelian physics, namely place and matter, and again there are parallel developments in Simplicius. For Aristotle, place is not an abstract spot or area in the three-dimensional coordinates of the universe. Place in this more abstract sense would be something that exists whether or not there are bodies in it. By contrast, for Aristotle, space is a place that begins from the outlines of bodies and hence is not coextensive with a body but *surrounds* it (*periekhein*; *Ph.* 212a5–6). Hence the existence of place is, for Aristotle, dependent on the existence of bodies. He argues against the atomist position according to which void (i.e. empty space) exists.

Philoponus argues against the idea that place should be the outer limit of the immediately surrounding body or material. He also challenges the idea that space is *only* the surrounding environment. For Philoponus, space is a three-dimensional extension, and there is space everywhere whether or not there are bodies in those places. Bodies move in space and when they stop the space is not just around them but coextensive with them as well.[10]

Similar developments took place with respect to the notion of matter, and the notion of prime matter more specifically. Whether or not Aristotle himself had the notion of prime matter is a disputed point (see Haas 1997: xii n.2), but the commentators supposed that he did. As mentioned above, prime matter is an abstract and unqualified something: a subject (*hupokeimenon*) from which everything is (potentially) predicated but which itself is not predicated from anything else. This makes it not just any subject but a subject in a primary sense (*to hupokeimenon prōton*) (*Metaph.* VII 3, 1028b36–1029a2) In itself, prime matter has neither qualities nor quantities. It is nothing in actuality. Prime matter is that which remains when all attributes have been stripped off (cf. also *Metaph.* VII 3, 1029a9–20 and *Ph.* IV 2, 209b6–11). It cannot exist in separation, since everything that exists is something, that is, is characterized by some properties, and even the natural elements (earth, water, air and fire) have a form and properties determined by that form, such as heaviness of earth and lightness of fire.

Alexander makes a similar point in his treatise *De anima*. He argues that matter in the purest sense is something that underlies all actual matter. All bodies have some shape, form or configuration, whereas the nature that underlies matter does not have any of these (Alex.Aphr. *de An.* 3,21–4,4). Further, since the notion of prime matter resembles Plato's receptacle in the *Timaeus*, this understanding was powerful in the later ancient tradition dominated by Platonists.

Simplicius and Philoponus do not accept the notion of prime matter as a substrate, that is, as an unqualified abstract principle, something to which properties belong, understood without any properties. According to Simplicius, Aristotle himself had intended matter to be indefinite extension (*aoristos diastasis*), which receives its definite magnitude from the form it receives (*in Ph.* 229,5–7). Prime matter in this sense differs from ordinary actual bodies in that all actual bodies have some extension, whereas prime matter has extension but not any particular extension. Therefore, for Simplicius, prime matter is not entirely devoid of properties but has one: it must be extended. Whether or not prime matter understood in this manner exists for Simplicius is not quite clear. It is, rather, on the threshold of being: "everywhere slackened and split, and flows from all sides away from being into non-being" (*in Ph.* 230,25–6, trans. in Haas 1997: 121). Prime matter is so close to non-being that it *almost* flows out of existence. From a methodological point of view, it is important to note that Simplicius is not presenting the new notion of prime matter to criticize Aristotle; rather, he claims that Aristotle *intended* to understand prime matter as indefinite extension. Simplicius' interpretation is a significant move and can be seen to anticipate Descartes' definition of matter as *res extensa*, extended thing.

Philoponus presents a similar kind of definition, even though his motivation was very different from that of Simplicius (Haas 1997). Similarly to Simplicius, Philoponus denies that prime matter should lack all determination, but claims that it lacks *definite* determination. However, Philoponus specifies that even though there is no definite determination for prime matter, there is a condition that limits what kind of determination is at issue: the limiting condition is that of three-dimensionality. Again, no specific three-dimensional property is required from prime matter, but being three-dimensional is not accidental to prime matter: it is its essential quantity and its specific difference. For Philoponus, who was educated in the Alexandrian Neoplatonic school, specific differences were understood as substances (Phlp. *Contra Proclum* XI 5–7; Haas 1997: ch. 4.)

A question now emerges: If Philoponus supposes prime matter to be both an essential quantity *and* a substance, does this not destroy the Aristotelian scheme of categories?[11] Perhaps this is not quite the case, since Philoponus points to the difference between existence and subsistence (*hupostēnai*). Whereas an ordinary substance, a real definite body, is capable of existing independently and in its own right, prime matter cannot do so: it only subsists. This means that even though prime matter is not a definite thing with independent existence, it has some continuity and persistence: as soon as it is destroyed in one form it takes on another (*in Ph.* 579,2–14). Therefore, Philoponus' new definition is similar to the traditional one in the sense that it does not postulate independent existence for prime matter. Its most significant new aspect is the same as in Simplicius: the stress on extension specified by Philoponus as three-dimensionality. Therefore, for Philoponus and Simplicius prime matter in a sense has a nature, namely that of being extended in space. The parallel developments with respect to space and prime matter in Philoponus and Simplicius suggest that it was not just his Christianity that made Philoponus reconsider Aristotelian physics. The process of reconsideration was underway in the Neoplatonic tradition more broadly.

Cosmological questions

The movement of the heavens

In Aristotelian dynamics, the movement of the heavens was explained psychologically. Rather than heaviness, for example, the explanatory principle of movement for heavenly bodies was their desire or love. As we saw above, Simplicius reports Alexander to have argued that the soul of the heavenly bodies is in some sense identical with their nature and it should be compared to the heaviness in earth. The exact motivation for this idea is not easy to extract, but it could be to exclude a possibility of conflict between movement originating from soul and movement originating from nature. (My desire to fly and my natural heaviness would imply such a conflict.) Simplicius argued against Alexander by pointing out that, in general, soul is that which moves and nature that which is moved, and in a sense the soul is an external mover for bodies. This is why it cannot be identical with nature.

The idea that heavenly movement should be explained psychologically sounds odd to us. Why were the heavenly bodies supposed to have souls in the first place? Could they not have been understood to move owing to their natural heaviness in a way analogous to the way a stone falls towards the centre of the earth? It is true that Anaxagoras had been accused of impiety because he claimed that the sun is just a large piece of stone. However, it would seem unlikely that mere piety should have kept the idea of ensouled heavenly bodies alive for such a long time.

One rationale for supposing that the heavenly bodies are living rather than just bodily but not living is the assumption that reality is hierarchical: to be alive is supposed to be better than not to be alive, and the heavenly bodies are assumed to be beings of a higher kind than we are. Alexander, or someone from his circle who wrote the *Questions*, puts this point as follows: "that which moves with the first among all movements is also animate; for the best of bodies is animate" (*Quaest.* 1.1, 3,10–14, trans. Sharples 1992, 1994). If there is life already in sublunary nature, there must be life in the heavens as well, which is a higher sphere of being than nature. In the Neoplatonic framework, a similar supposition is found in the following form. Heavenly bodies are not higher beings than the mundane ones just because they are further removed from the centre of the earth. Rather, they are further removed from the centre of the earth because they are higher beings in another sense: they are higher in the ontological hierarchy of things. Because of their extraordinary position in the ontological hierarchy, they act as intermediaries of cosmic causation or emanation from the Intellect to embodied nature. It is not clear why this supposition was made. In any case, it was not universally accepted in antiquity. Presocratics, for example, rather tended to suppose that those things are metaphysically prior that are located closer to the centre of the earth.

For Neoplatonists, the heavenly bodies are located between the intellectual sphere, which is "above" nature and hence beyond the limits of the universe.[12] In order for them to be in contact with both spheres, they need to have something in common with both. Being bodies, they share the property of being embodied with natural things. Being intellectual, they are similar to the Intellect. It is commonly supposed, however, that the heavenly bodies do not have senses like us human beings; they just have reason or intellect (e.g. Alexander *on the Cosmos* 11, 13).

Alexander follows Aristotle in supposing that the unmoved mover, a divine Intellect, moves the heavenly bodies not as an efficient but as a final cause, or, as Aristotle puts it "as a beloved" (*Metaph.* XII 7, 1072b3). In *Metaphysics* XII 8, the heavens are presented as a unified system of rotating, transparent, homocentric spheres carrying the heavenly bodies (see also Sorabji 2004: vol. 2, 337–8). For Aristotle, there were as many as fifty-five spheres, partly because diversities of planetary motion as well as the motion of the sun had to be accounted for. Alexander had reduced the number of spheres to eight – one for the fixed stars, seven for the sun, moon and five known planets (*Quaest.* 1.25, 40,23–30) – but his view met some criticism later.[13] One question that the followers of Aristotle such as Alexander faced was whether the sphere or its soul (the sphere was also supposed to have a soul) moves the planet, or whether it was the soul of the planet that moves it. One reason for supposing that the sphere moves the planet was to avoid assuming that the soul of the heavenly body should move naturally: if it is the sphere that moves it, then it moves only accidentally.

In his treatise on the cosmos, Alexander explains that the desires of the heavenly beings must be distinguished from the ordinary bodily desires that human beings and other animals have. Their desire or will consists of loving the good (*On the Cosmos* 11, in Sorabji 2004: vol. 2, 338). This was at least supposed to apply to the outermost sphere, if not to all the heavenly bodies or spheres. But why does their love of the good move the heavenly bodies in circles in the way it is supposed to? This is because movement in a circle "alone of all movements is eternal and continuous and even one" (quoted in Sorabji 2004: vol. 2, 339). Further, its desire for the good is not a desire to *become* the unmoved mover; perhaps the intelligent spheres or heavenly bodies understand that this is impossible. Rather, they want to emulate or become similar (*homoiousthai*), and this similarity is their even, eternal and uniform circular movement (*Quaest.* 1.25, 40,8–23).

Plotinus explains the circularity of the heavenly movement in a different yet still psychological manner. He says that because of having a higher kind of soul, the heavenly bodies desire to move upwards towards the outskirts of the universe and beyond. They want to leave behind material earth and its limitations and the whole universe: they want to enter the intelligible realm outside or beyond ordinary space. When they try to fulfil this desire, they move upwards in rectilinear motion, but are prevented from leaving the universe, because there is no more space. This is how their movement becomes bent and ends up being circular.[14]

For the Aristotelians, we saw that the idea that the soul of the sphere rather than that of the planet moves the planets had the advantage of making the movement of the planet's soul accidental. However, one of its drawbacks was that the number of the spheres remained high but still left some celestial motions unexplained. The high number of spheres caused debate about whether each sphere is moved by the same unmoved mover, or whether there have to be distinct movers that are moved by distinct spheres. Alexander's *On the Cosmos* 94 involves distinct movers for distinct spheres, whereas in *Questions* 1.25 (*Quaest.* 1.25, 40,23–30), there is only "some mover" for all of them. Of the unexplained phenomena, the most central one was that some planets approach and retreat from the earth annually, and this cannot be explained by reference to concentric spheres. Simplicius (*in Cael.* 504,17–506,3) attributes this observation to Sosigenes (second century CE).

To explain the movements that the concentric model left unexplained, some authors tried to modify the Aristotelian system by adding either eccentric spheres (circles with a different centre) or epicycles (cycles that rotate on other cycles). For example, Adrastus, who belonged to the same circle or school as Alexander of Aphrodisias, did so. He tried to update Aristotle's view of the heavens in the face of new astronomical evidence (see Moraux 1984: 305–13). However, he also added that if the planets are in fact intellectual agents, they can choose their path, and hence the approaches and retreats of the planets need not be exceptions; rather, they can be explained by decisions the planetary agents make. Even though Alexander had followed Aristotle in explaining celestial motion by reference to the desires of the heavenly agents, he had not made the same move as Adrastus had. Rather, the moving cause for him was the sphere, and this did not allow these movements.

Now, if we suppose that each planet moves across the heavens as it wills, we need to ask whether it is possible to predict celestial motion or explain it in any more detail than just saying that it is dependent on the decisions that the intelligent heavenly bodies happen to make. Further, the supposition that the celestial agents love the unmoved mover and desire to emulate it was meant to explain why they move in uniform eternal circles. Such uniform circularity was assumed to provide regularity and made understandable the complex movement of the heavens. To put it briefly, the Aristotelian explanation of celestial motion was in crisis.

Proclus (the fifth-century Neoplatonist) doubts the metaphysical status and explanatory force of the epicycles and eccentric spheres. He objects that they are just thought constructs but not the real causes of the heavenly motion (*Hypotheses* 7.50–58, 236,10–238,27, in Sorabji 2004: vol. 2, 379–80). For Proclus, the motion of the heavens is a mean between uniformity and order on the one hand and non-uniformity and disorder on the other (Procl. *in Ti.* 3.95,34–96,32, in Sorabji 2004: vol. 2, 381). He concludes that for those who wished to make celestial motion entirely uniform by reference to mechanizing it by epicycles and eccentrics, "the idea was lovely and suitable for logical minds, but it fell far short of the nature of the universe, which only Plato grasped" (*ibid.*, trans. Mueller, in Sorabji 2004: vol. 2, 381).

In objecting to the idea of epicycles, Proclus seems to be making two distinct points. On the one hand, he opposes the idea that some astronomers (e.g. Eudoxus) who postulated epicycles endorsed; namely, that we need not consider whether the epicycles are real entities or not. Rather, it is sufficient that scientific objects save the phenomena as calculating devices. In other words, Proclus is objecting to a position similar to instrumentalism in philosophy of science. On the other hand, Proclus is saying that, if heavenly bodies did move in concentric circles, the explanation would be too simple and it could be understood through very simple logic. Rather, he suggests that celestial motion is more complex and in order to understand it, one must be more creative than just master elementary logic.

Eternity versus creation

Perhaps the most famous debate in the commentary tradition is the dispute about whether the cosmos is eternal or created. Plato had suggested that there is a demiurge, a divine artificer, who has made the universe as it is. However, for Plato, this creation is not *ex nihilo*. Matter is there already and the demiurge arranges it into a cosmos where some order can be seen to be manifested, albeit imperfectly. In *De caelo*, Aristotle criticizes Plato's view and argues that the universe is eternal and non-created: it has always been and will ever be and remain, in its general structure, the same.

As a Christian, Philoponus does not accept either of these cosmologies, but the main focus of his polemic is on the Aristotelian claim of eternity. Philoponus develops his arguments in several treatises: against Proclus and against Aristotle on eternity and in a later work *On the Creation of the World* (*de Opificio mundi*).[15] Even though Philoponus' position is Christian in the sense of requiring creation and a creative agent, his arguments in the treatises against Proclus and Aristotle do not resort to scripture directly. Rather, his argumentative strategy is to start from Aristotelian positions themselves and show them to be intrinsically contradictory.[16]

One such argument is that the following two Aristotelian suppositions are contradictory:

(1) The universe is eternal.
(2) Infinity does not exist in actuality but only potentially.

If (1) our universe is eternal, it must have gone through an infinite number of years, that is, the number of years is actually infinite. However, (2) infinity does not exist in actuality. Since these two claims are an explicit contradiction, they cannot both be true. Philoponus is not willing to reject (2), but sees supposition (1) as the problematic one. Therefore, he concludes, the universe cannot be eternal.

Philoponus' argument is simple and elegant. It opposes the Aristotelian idea of infinity as expandable finitude. Infinity as expandable finitude means that if there already is a large number, we can always have a number larger than that, without the latter ever becoming actually infinite. Perhaps Aristotle had supposed that the years that have passed so far are infinite in the sense of expandable finitude: we can always count backwards from the present. Philoponus' argument, however, supposes that this is not sufficient. The eternal existence of the cosmos necessitates an *actually infinite* amount of years. Even though these years do not exist actually all at once, the universe has had to traverse an actually infinite number of years, Philoponus argues (*contra Proclum* 9,14–11,17, in Sorabji 2004: vol. 2, 176–7).

Philoponus also adds arguments in which the infinity of some individuals is increased. For example, in an eternal universe the number of human beings who have existed must be infinite as well. If we then add the number of horses the infinity of individuals is doubled, and if we add dogs it is tripled, and this is even more absurd since it supposes something greater than infinity (*ibid.*). This argument is perhaps supposed to be an *a fortiori* argument of the following kind. If it is impossible to have an actually infinite number of anything, it must be *even more impossible* to have double or triple that amount. It is often pointed out that these arguments were difficult for the Greeks, because they did not understand – as it later came to be understood by some Arabic mathematicians in the 900s and much later by George Cantor – that such infinities are of equal cardinality. There is no difference in the numerable infinity of years that have already passed and the numerable infinity of years that will have passed next year. Or, to multiply an infinite number of human beings by two will give numerable infinity, that is, infinity of the same cardinality, because there is a one-to-one correspondence between natural numbers and even natural numbers.

However, even though Philoponus' arguments referring to double or triple infinity certainly are problematic because they seem to suppose different cardinalities for those infinities, it is not quite clear how the arguments become easier if we resort to the idea of equal cardinality. If we suppose that the universe is eternal and has gone through a numerably infinite number of years (i.e. the number of years is of the same cardinality as that of the natural numbers 1, 2, 3, …), then it means that the number of years last year is of the same cardinality as the number of years this year. What does this tell us? Does it show us that the number of years this year and last year are equally great because they are of the same cardinality? From a mathematical point of view, the whole comparison is pointless, because infinities are not numbers.

We can approach and dissolve these problems through mathematical notions and tools, but they continue to puzzle us. It still sounds paradoxical to us that there is a one-to-one correspondence between natural numbers and even natural numbers. Further, it makes sense to say that, even if our universe were eternal, the number of days it has been there is greater today than it was yesterday. The lure of the arguments is still there, and Philoponus still has a point, even though his mathematics is outdated.

FIVE

Psychology: perception and intellect

Background for commentators on perception

"Psychology" means a study of soul (Greek *psukhē*, soul, and *logos*, account, theory). Today we understand psychology not in terms of soul but in terms of mind. The ancient commentators do speak about soul, and part of their studies concerning soul overlap with those that we understand as belonging to psychology. Yet the notion of soul is by no means the same as the modern notion of mind. On the one hand, soul extends more widely. For example, plant life is explained by reference to soul – be it a specific kind of soul (vegetative soul), or the world-soul, that is, nature as a whole, that also regulates the life of plants. On the other hand, for some authors, in particular those influenced by Plotinus, the notion of soul is narrower than what we would classify as mind. According to Plotinus, intellect is not a functional part of our soul but, rather, it is a separate metaphysical level or hypostasis (see also Ch. 3, § "*Epistēmē*: proofs and principles"). However, in so far as human beings can take part in the eternal intellectual activity, the Intellect can be seen to belong to the scope of psychology, as we understand the notion. Plotinus sometimes refers to this idea by applying the notion of soul up to the Intellect (e.g. *Enn.* 5.3.3).

In the Plotinian scheme, the human soul is capable of ordinary conceptual reasoning (*dianoein*), but this is to be separated from the kind of comprehensive understanding that takes place on the level of Intellect. Intellection proper involves understanding a complex theoretical whole as a whole: at a single glance, as it were. Such understanding is not conceptual; it is complex but non-propositional. It is also much richer than any propositional account that can be given of it. Intellection proper could be compared to seeing a complex and beautiful scene; such a scene can never be captured in all its mutual interrelations and aspects in a propositional description.[1] In their discussions of the soul and intellect, many commentators were influenced by Neoplatonism, and we shall point to such influence when it is relevant for our discussion. Sometimes, as is the case with Philoponus and Simplicius, questions of authenticity also complicate the treatment of these issues.

This chapter focuses on the questions of how the most important cognitive functions of perception (*aisthēsis*) and intellectual apprehension (*noein, noēsis*) were explained in the psychology of the commentators. We shall not only ask how the explanations the commentators gave differ from each other, but also consider what kind of problems motivated the theories, that is, what the *explanandum* was. Even though we concentrate on perception and intellectual apprehension, this should not be taken to entail that these topics exhaust the commentators' theories of the soul. In addition to these, *phantasia*, or imagination, is discussed in the commentaries on *De anima* III 3, and this capacity becomes increasingly important in the Neoplatonic tradition in explaining our mental life. In the confines of the present volume, we shall only be able to give a very brief overview (§ "*Phantasia*, a note") of the functions ascribed to *phantasia*.

Our main sources here are commentaries on Aristotle's treatise *On the Soul* (*De anima*). Themistius' paraphrase (CAG V 3; it is his most independent work) has been preserved as a whole. We know from other sources that Alexander of Aphrodisias wrote a commentary on Aristotle's *De anima*, but it has been lost. However, we do have Alexander's own treatise on the matter (Alex.Aphr. *de An.*), based on Aristotle's theory. This treatise also has an appendix, traditionally called *Mantissa* (a makeweight). The authenticity of the *Mantissa* is debated. The problem of authenticity cannot be solved in the present context. I tend to think that it is not by Alexander. To me the *Mantissa* sounds like a fairly dogmatic easy reader's version of Alexander. It lacks the complexity of Alexander's argumentation, as well as that of his language and style. More detailed arguments about this must be left aside for now.[2]

From Philoponus, we have only his commentary on Books I–II of Aristotle's *De anima*. There is a commentary on Book III printed after Philoponus on Books I–II in *Commentaria in Aristotelem Graeca* XV, but scholars find it spurious.[3] As the translator William Charlton (1991) points out, the style and content in the commentary on Book III is very different from Philoponus on Books I–II, and we shall in this chapter take it as spurious and refer to its author as Pseudo-Philoponus. In addition, we have a Latin translation made in 1268 by William of Moerbeke, probably for Thomas Aquinas, of a commentary on the intellect (*de An.* II 4–8) attributed to Philoponus. Scholars tend to think that the translation is perhaps made on the basis of an authentic commentary (e.g. trans. Charlton 1991: 4).[4]

We also have a commentary on the *De anima* that the manuscript tradition attributes to Simplicius (printed in CAG XI). The authenticity of this work has been doubted for a long time (see Ch.1, § "Simplicius"), and also more recently (Bossier & Steel 1972).[5] As mentioned above in Chapter 1, I share the feeling that the commentary is not written by the same hand as those we know to be by Simplicius. The discussions are much shorter and the commentary lacks the extensive historical material that is of central importance in Simplicius. The language also deviates from that used by Simplicius,[6] and there are doctrinal differences.[7] I refer to the author of the commentary on the *De anima* in *Commentaria in Aristotelem Graeca* XI as "Pseudo-Simplicius", as is customary.

Themistius and Philoponus especially follow the outline of the *De anima* and use the notions of actuality and potentiality to analyse psychic change, notions that were employed to account for change in general (cf. Ch 4). These notions already appear in Plato's discussion of perception in the *Theaetetus*, where perception is explained as an interaction between two powers (*dunameis*), one of which is active (*to poioun*) and the other passive (*to paskhon*): the active power is in the object and the passive one in the recipient. In Plato's account, both the object of perception – such as a sound or a colour – and the perception itself are born in the same "twin birth" where the act of perception comes to be (*Tht.* 156a–c). Aristotle accepts the basic idea of this analysis, namely that perception takes place through an interaction between powers. However, he challenges the claim according to which a sound or a colour should be "born" in the act of perception; he attributes this claim to earlier "natural philosophers" (*phusiologoi*; *de An.* 426a20), not to Plato. Aristotle's point in this discussion seems to be the following. The position of the natural philosophers supposes that a quality, such as whiteness, does not exist except for when it is perceived. By contrast, Aristotle affirms that it does exist as the quality of an external object, for example, whiteness that also is a potentiality to be perceived. When such a potentiality to be perceived comes to be actually perceived, it is the same whiteness but has a different mode of being: whiteness as perceived (see *de An.* III 2, 426a15–25; II 5, 417b16–26.)

An important idea in Aristotle' theory of perception is that the very same quality as there is in the external object has another mode of being in our perceptual soul when we perceive it. In the former mode, the quality exists in matter, whereas our soul receives it without matter. In the case of the intelligible objects, there is not even this much difference. Since the intelligible object (e.g. horse as conceived by the intellect, that is, what it is for a horse to be a horse) is immaterial, it is actualized in the external thing (e.g. horse) and our intellect as exactly identical. The latter supposition also fits Plotinus' conceptions about intellectual understanding and the idea is influential in the commentaries. To say that when grasping intelligible objects our intellect (or the universal Intellect) needs to be identical with its objects might sound strange. Yet, as we shall see below, none of the authors we discuss here contest this assumption. It is typical for more strictly Aristotelian commentators (Alexander and Themistius) in the form that our intellect *becomes* identical in form with the objects, whereas those who follow Plotinus rather assume that there is no becoming involved: the intelligible objects are eternally active in the universal Intellect and we are occasionally capable of taking part in its activity.

We might ask why these authors entertain this fairly odd idea in such a uniform manner. One important reason is the following. It is assumed that if our intellect were not identical with the objects or did not contain them, it could not grasp them *as they are*. We could merely understand something that functions as a stand-in or represents the objects, and this would not be acceptable for the authors discussed here. Intellectual understanding is supposed to possess the highest degree of cognitive intimacy: no gap or proxies are allowed between our intellectual apprehension and its objects.

As to the more general framework of the commentators' discussion of soul, different kinds of soul need be distinguished. According to Aristotle, human soul is divided into three functional parts: the vegetative soul, the animal soul and the rational soul. The first one is taken to explain basic life functions: nutrition, growth and reproduction. These functions belong to plants and non-human animals as well. The animal soul accounts for self-movement and perception, whereas we human beings also have a rational part by virtue of which we are capable of grasping things on a universal level.[8] This capacity is manifested as a power to operate with general notions, to use language and to make inferences. In this framework, perception is basically a function of the animal soul. As such, human perception does not differ from animal perception. However, human perception gives rise to thoughts and interpretations that take place on a rational (or conceptual) level.

In the *De anima*, Aristotle does not ascribe genuine conceptual abilities to non-human animals, but some form of perceptual generalization and something analogous to inference is attributed to them. Aristotle's view of the cognitive capacities of non-human animals varies to some extent from one work to another; in the zoological treatises he underlines the cleverness of animals, whereas the *De anima* is more schematic and animals are stated to lack reason because their souls are not able to actualize intelligible objects in it. Platonists often explain animal cognitive functions by reference to reason and attribute rationality to non-human animals.[9]

Some commentators, especially those working in the Platonic or Neoplatonic tradition, challenge the Aristotelian analysis of perception. They argue that human perception requires awareness of our perceptions. Aristotle does suggest that some elementary form of awareness of perceptions belongs to the animal soul: when we see or hear, we perceive that we see or hear (*De anima* III 2, 425b12–25; *De somno* 2, 455a12–23; cf. Plato, *Charmides* 167c–d). However, later commentators, such as Pseudo-Simplicius, argue that even such a very elementary form of reflexive awareness could not be a function of the perceptual soul.[10] Some also postulate a separate, attentive capacity that accounts for the fact that we are aware of our perceptions. We shall discuss these theories in § "Attention and reflexive awareness", below.

In so far as plants are concerned, the commentators are also influenced by Plato's remark (*Ti.* 77a–c) that plants have feelings and they, supposedly, perceive their environment.[11] On the other hand, in Platonism and Neoplatonism, one central supposition is that the whole of nature must be understood as one ensouled being that functions or lives through its parts, such as plants and animals.[12] From this perspective, the life of plants is regulated by the whole nature or the world-soul, not so much the individual plant soul in plants themselves (cf. Ch. 4, § "Is our soul natural?"). To make the notion of a world-soul more accessible, we could compare it to the so-called Gaia hypothesis in modern ecology (introduced by James Lovelock in the 1960s). According to this hypothesis the biosphere of the earth is a complex interacting system in which what happens in one part of the system (e.g. extinction of one species) affects another part of the same system (e.g. overproduction of another species).

The Aristotelian background

As we have seen, Aristotle's theory of perception, building on Plato and the notions of active and passive powers, provides the general framework in which the commentators operate. Aristotle's theory has deep and widely debated problems of its own, but in the present context we shall not address them. However, in order to be able to follow the commentators' discussion of perception, we need to identify some philosophically important suppositions made in this theory.

An important assumption in Aristotle is that the objects of perception are external (*de An*. II 5, 417b18–22). This means that perceptual objects are not inner mental items. For example, in Aristotle, what it is to be a visible quality, colour, means to be capable of affecting a suitably situated percipient through what is called the "medium", namely illuminated air or water. Colour is that which is seen in light (*de An*. II 7, 419a7–8), and a colour affects the transparent medium, that is, illuminated air or water, so that this medium then affects the percipient (*de An*. II 7, 419a9–11). Aristotle also often talks about colours as certain kinds of mixtures or ratios of the transparent and the opaque on the surface of external bodies. Therefore, according to Aristotle, sense objects are not sense data; they are objective properties of external bodies that have the power to affect percipients.

What, then, does it mean to say that perceptible properties, such as colours, sounds, odours, tastes and tactile qualities, are properties of objects with a power to affect us? The most important upshot of this idea is that an act of perception requires that the object and the percipient interact in a certain way. In this act the percipient changes from non-perceiving to perceiving. The object does not, properly speaking, change, but it comes to be actualized in another manner: as opposed to being a colour that has the potentiality to be perceived, it becomes a colour that is actually perceived. As to the other end of the chain, there is the percipient. A percipient needs to be capable of perceiving and thus must have senses. Having a sense (*aisthēsis*) means to be receptive (*to dektikon*) of perceptible forms without matter (*de An*. II 12, 424a17–19). Therefore, perception presupposes two "components", the effective and the receptive, and both of these have to have certain determined powers.

What we have said so far focuses on the interaction between the object and the percipient. But surely, for Aristotle and the commentators, perception is happening in our mind or soul. This expectation is certainly correct: when we perceive, our soul changes from not perceiving to perceiving something, and we would say that this is a change in our mind. However, it is not equally clear whether

Aristotle or the commentators concentrate on questions that would interest a modern reader. What is the relation between the causal description of form reception and the change in the mind? Are the two descriptions of the same process from a different point of view? Or, are they two distinct processes? Is the physical transmission the cause of the psychological change? If so, how is it that a supposedly physical change causes a change in the mind?

We shall not consider how Aristotle should be interpreted but focus on the commentators' accounts of perception. A discussion of their views is complicated by several factors. First, the interpretation of Aristotle's theory of perception is a matter of heated controversy in today's scholarship (Sorabji 1974; Burnyeat 1992, 2001; Johansen 1998; cf. Caston 2005). Sharp demarcation lines are drawn and polemical positions formulated. This controversy to some extent affects the treatment of the commentators' positions. Secondly, Greek terminology of perception is often ambiguous, and this ambiguity carries over to any interpretation of the central passages. The most important such ambiguity is that the term *aisthēsis*, like the English "sense", can mean several things: (i) a capacity of perception, (ii) an activity of this capacity, (iii) a sense organ. Now when we want to know, for example, how a certain author explains the changes that constitute or are required by perception, we need to know in what sense *aisthēsis* is used in the central passages. Themistius and Alexander retain some of the ambiguities of *aisthēsis* in this respect. Philoponus warns against the ambiguity and once points out that Aristotle is in a particular passage using "sense" (*aisthēsis*) to mean "sense organ" (*to aisthētērion*) (Phlp. *in de An.* 435,25 *ad* 424a4–6).

Commentators on the metaphysical status of perceptible objects

We mentioned above that, within the Aristotelian framework, perceptible objects are external things. Alexander, Themistius and Philoponus confirm that they endorse this supposition as well. Themistius, for example, distinguishes between perception (*aisthēsis*) and knowledge (*epistēmē*) exactly on the basis of whether the objects are external or not. Perception, he says, needs to be activated by objects that are outside (*exōthen*), like visible, audible and tangible objects, but this is not the case with knowledge: its objects (*ta epistēta*) are internal (*oikothen*). In this respect, the intelligible objects or thoughts (*ta noēmata*) resemble objects of knowledge. We gather and store them up in our soul and, having gathered them, we are capable of using them whenever we wish. Their being internal does not mean that they would be subjective in any interesting sense of the word. Rather, as Themistius points out, it is supposed that the objects of knowledge are the same in all individuals (*in de An.* 104,7–11; see § "How do we come to grasp intelligible objects?", below).

The main contrast between being external and being internal seems to be whether an activity needs to be initiated by an object. As Themistius puts it, the objects of perception cannot be activated by the soul; it is nature that does so. (Them. *in de An.* 56,17–25). Therefore, even a toothache, which is not external in the same sense as the qualities of bodies (colours, sounds and so on) are, would be external in this sense: we do not feel toothache if we do not have one (at least if we are mentally sane). Aristotle also supposes that we perceive that we perceive. Here the object of perception seems to be something non-external, a point that was made in the later commentaries (see § "Perception requires rational reflexivity", below). However, even in this case, there needs to be an external activator of the process: we do not perceive that we perceive unless we perceive, and our perception is about an external object in the sense employed here. Alexander points out in his commentary on the *De sensu* that when we perceive that we perceive, the object of this perception is primarily the ordinary object of perception (colour, sound, odour, flavour, tactile property) and only accidentally the perception itself. As opposed to perceptible objects, the intelligible ones are internal in the sense that once we have obtained them, we can think whatever we wish.

Further, perceptible objects are taken to be independent of the percipient in an important way. Alexander and Philoponus are clear on this point. They both distinguish between (i) what it is for a quality to be what it is and (ii) what it is for it to be perceived. For example, Alexander says quite clearly that colours can exist without being seen, but they cannot exist *as seen* apart from perception (Alex.Aphr. *in Sens.* 42,7-10). Alexander's main point is to deny the position according to which perceptible qualities such as colours and sounds come to be in the same birth as the perception of them. According to Alexander, a colour does exist independently of being seen but comes to be *a colour that is actually seen* only when someone sees it. When no one sees a colour, it is a quality on the surface of an external body (*in Sens.* 44,22-23). Alexander also gives a fairly detailed account of what kind of physical constitution colours have (*in Sens.* 53,12–55,9). The discussion follows Aristotle: a colour of a body (or its surface) is understood as being a certain mixture of what is transparent and what is not. A very high proportion of the transparent makes a body white; the absence of the transparent makes it black. The exact nature of what is transparent remains slightly unclear, but the discussion shows that Alexander wants to account for colour in physical terms.

Philoponus puts a similar point in a different manner. He says that what it is for a colour to be a colour must be distinguished from what it is for it to be visible. The essence (*ousia*) of a colour involves being the limit of the transparent as transparent; this limit lies at the intersection of a body and air. To be visible is accidental to being such a limit (Phlp. *in de An.* 444,30–32).[13] Therefore, if there were no sensitive beings or no senses in the world, there would still be colours, flavours and so on (438,18–23). However, it would make no sense to say that in this situation a colour would be visible: its visibility only exists relative to perceivers that are capable of actualizing its visibility in acts of vision. This, on the other hand, is not merely a way of speaking, but a fact about reality: if there are no sensitive beings, there are colours, but these colours are not visible since there is no one to see them. Therefore, perceptible qualities are both objective (as being the qualities of physical bodies, see 350,36ff.) and have certain regular potentialities in relation to percipients.

Themistius also mentions the contrast between colour as a quality of a surface of a body and as a visible quality and points out that they are different in definition (*in de An.* 58,27). Unlike Philoponus, he does *not* say that this should be because a surface or a colour is visible only accidentally. On the contrary, according to Themistius, every surface is visible in itself, because it is impossible to perceive or even imagine a surface without a colour. Yet Themistius wants to retain a distinction between this claim and definitional identity: visibility is defined in relation to seeing, whereas colour is defined in itself. Even though every surface is, according to Themistius, visible in itself, the existence of a colour is not dependent on an act of vision. A colour exists even when it is not seen (Them. *in de An.* 58,27–59,5). He also asserts that colour is to be defined as the capacity to cause movement in what is actually transparent, that is, illuminated air or water (61,34–37, 62,7–8), and this definition is not dependent on vision.

A problem of causation

We have now seen that for Alexander, Themistius and Philoponus perception is about external objects or qualities that exists in bodies outside us. In addition, they follow Aristotle in supposing that: (i) we cannot perceive them as we wish, but the objects must affect us; (ii) in order for them to affect us, we need to be in physical interaction with them, since efficient causation from a distance is not possible; and (iii) some sense objects (visible, audible, olfactory) are at a distance from our sense organs. These three suppositions taken together create a problem. Either the general ideas about causation are contradicted by ordinary cases of perception, or such perception needs to occur without causal interaction. The commentators that we focus on find these conclusions undesirable and they expend much effort in solving this discrepancy. Plotinus, in fact, had denied supposition (ii) and claimed that disjunct parts of the universe can affect one another without physical contact through a form of co-affection (*sumpatheia*) (see Emilsson 1988). The commentators that we discuss here generally retained (ii).

The general outlines of the solution that the commentators give to the problem are close to Aristotle: to deny the atomist theory according to which perception is caused by some atomic effluence coming from the objects to our sense organs. The causal interaction must be accounted for in less corporeal terms. The move that makes such an account possible in the case of senses that do not need to be in direct contact with their objects (i.e. vision, hearing and smell) is the introduction of the notion of a medium. Instead of physical effluences coming from the objects, the objects affect us through mediated causation; they affect air or water, and the air or water affects us. However, in the case of sight, there is a further problem: the air must be affected by colours in an invisible manner. We do not see colours flying in the air, and two percipients standing face to face can see something crosswise. For the latter, imagine that we stand face to face: you are looking behind my left shoulder and I am looking behind your left shoulder. If our seeing were due to atomic effluence, this situation would imply a collision of those effluences in air – and such a collision would supposedly make seeing, if not impossible, at least difficult.[14]

Another reason why sight is different from hearing and smell is that seeing only takes place when the intermittent air is illuminated. As Aristotle puts it and the commentators follow, the medium can be in an actual and a potential state; it is an actual medium when there is light and the medium is illuminated, and as actual it transmits the effects of colours to the eye. In fact, the medium is taken to be necessary for sight: if the objects were placed directly in contact with our eyeball, we would not see them (Arist. *de An.* II 7, 419a13–20; Them. *in de An.* 62,7–12; Phlp. *in de An.* 349,34–352,2).

What has been said about sight and the medium suggests that the causal transmission in vision is a case of its own. To some extent this expectation turns out to be correct when reading the commentaries. Yet it is a general fact that the discussion of the senses focuses on the external conditions; this is not a peculiar feature of sight. Much less is said about the psychological side of perception. Further, the commentators strive to unify the account of the several senses. Philoponus, whose commentary on senses is extensive and particularly interesting, ends his discussion (when commenting on II 12) on a careful account of what the senses do and what they do not have in common. According to Philoponus, it is not necessary to account for every sense in exactly the same way. However, he finds general principles that remain the same in the analysis of all the senses. Themistius strives for unification as well, even more so than Philoponus.

Themistius and Philoponus on perception

Themistius

Themistius is explicit that there is something that all senses have in common, namely the medium. It is the medium that is affected by the object and that changes (*kinein*) the sense organ (*aisthētērion*) (*in de An.* 62,20–22). Never does the object touch (*haptesthai*) the sense organ (*organon*) directly. Therefore, in Themistius, even the objects of touch and taste do not touch the sense organs: the flesh, skin or tongue that is touched is not the actual organ of those senses (e.g. 75,10–27). What differentiates sight, hearing and smell from touch and taste is, according to Themistius, not the existence of the medium, but the nature of the change that takes place in the medium. To be more specific, in the case of sight, hearing and smell the medium is *not* altered (*alloiousthai*) by the objects of these senses (75,12–13), whereas tactile and gustatory qualities do alter the medium. Within the Aristotelian theory of change, alteration is a change of quality, for example, from rough to smooth. In his account of the senses, Themistius is careful to point out the differences in the ways in which the medium is affected. He is much less explicit on the question of what happens in our sense organs and how they cause the psychic change from not perceiving to perceiving. When he clarifies that the medium is *not* altered, he states that the medium is still capable of changing the sense organ (75,12–13). But what is the change that takes place in the organ?

Themistius points out repeatedly that the *senses* (*aisthēseis*) are not whitened (*leukainesthai*) or blackened (*melainesthai*) (78,7–8), but this does not yet tell us anything about the sense organs. Even though he denies that the sense should be whitened or blackened, he still allows some affection (*paskhein*) in the senses. This effect is very different from how soulless things such as stones are affected (77,34–5). As opposed to ordinary material bodies that can be whitened or blackened by colours, the sense is affected in the following manner: its disposition (*hexis*) is perfected and reinforced (57,9–10). As Aristotle had done, Themistius compares the change that takes place in the sense to how wax receives the form of the golden seal without the gold: it takes on the forms (*eidē*) and ratios/principles (*logous*) of the perceptible objects (57,3–5).[15]

We mentioned above that the Greek *aisthēsis* also means "sense organ" (e.g. Phlp. *in de An.* 435,25). Could it, then, be the case that when Themistius denies whitening or blackening, he is talking about sense organs rather than senses? This is how Robert Todd interprets the passage in his translation (1996: 79) and it would be welcome to the debate concerning the interpretation of Aristotle's theory of perception in the commentaries, in which one central question is whether the sense *organ* literally is changed to be like the object of perception, that is, whether something in the core of our eye turns white when we see white.[16] Unfortunately, however, Themistius' account does not allow us to say anything about how he understood the change in the *organs*; for such conclusions his account is too unspecific. To interpret the passage we just discussed as pertaining to a debate about what happens in the sense organs, we should allow that the sense organs have dispositions (*hexeis*) that are reinforced by repeated perceptions and that the sense *organs* grasp (*antilambanein*) perceptible objects. Neither of these ideas is appealing unless we suppose that Themistius' formulations are extremely vague. Therefore, we cannot conclude anything certain concerning sense organs from the present passage.

Instead of focusing on the question of whether or not the sense organs are literally changed, Themistius does specify that the organs transmit (*parapempein*) something to the senses (*in de An.* 65,4–7). For example, the liquid of the eyeball and the internal air in the ear transmit imprints and sounds to sight (*opsis*) and hearing (*akoē*) respectively. Themistius emphasizes that this transmission does not require any matter or material to come inside our sensory system from the objects: it is the forms of the objects that affect (*kinein*) our organs (*aisthētērion*) but the matter remains outside (77,37–38). Therefore, what is crucial for Themistius is not whether or not the sense organs literally take on the qualities that we perceive, but that the sense organs *transmit* the qualities to our senses.

One might now ask: how is this account supposed to explain that we become aware of perceptible objects? Does it not just account for the transmission of the object to our sensory system? In a sense this is exactly what is does. To our modern eyes an account of this kind seems to have a huge gap. It does not explain how we perceive the changes in our sensory systems, and it leaves open the relation between the "physical" and the psychological account. However, rather than observing this as a gap or a lack, it is more fruitful to look at the situation from another angle. The nature of the explanation shows what the authors (Themistius in this case) supposed to be an answer to the most central problem in perception; namely, the problem of how distant objects affect our senses and activate our natural capacity to perceive. For authors like Aristotle and Themistius, there was not such a big gap to be bridged between our organs and our soul. Rather, our soul and our sensory organism are parts of the same thing: we humans as living beings. Even though our natural capacity to perceive is immaterial, it is in a sense located in our sensory system. Therefore, to explain how the capacity is activated, it needs to be explained how the quality comes to be in our sensory system. And this is the account given by Aristotle and the commentators.

We have seen that, according to Themistius, perception requires that the qualities of the external objects affect the medium between the object and the percipient either literally (taste and touch) or non-literally (sight, hearing and smell). Further, once the medium has affected our sense organs in a non-specified manner, these organs transmit the qualities further to our senses. When the effect is transmitted to the senses in this way, our natural capacity to perceive becomes activated.

Philoponus

Philoponus discusses sense perception extensively. His commentary on Aristotle's *De anima* II 7–12 comprises 125 pages of *Commentaria in Aristotelem Graeca* (trans. Charlton 2005), and a large portion of the commentary is concerned with questions that pertain to the external or physical aspects of perception. The general outlook of his discussion shows Philoponus as a scientifically well-informed and philosophically sensitive writer whose methodology is guided by problems or difficulties (*aporiai*), which are then to be solved with a view to saving the phenomena (*ta phainomena sōzesthai*; *in de An.* 331,27, 331,32–3). Philoponus' account of sounds, hearing and voice, including an excursus about echo, is particularly interesting and gives a very good picture of Philoponus' attitude towards the topic at hand.[17] Philoponus also briefly addresses questions that are of primary importance in the philosophy of mind. He provides an account of how he takes soul and body to be related to one another in perception. Further, he takes up the issue of how the reception of forms is related to perception proper. We shall address these questions below in due course.

Philoponus is particularly interested in various properties of the medium and how it functions in various cases, for example, how sounds are produced and what kinds of materials are suited for the production of sound. He also deals with issues such as the difference between high and low pitch, and makes very interesting remarks about this. In his account, we can find traces of both Plato (*Ti.* 67a–c) and Aristotle (*de An.* II 8, 420a26–b4), and he might have been influenced by Porphyry's treatise on Ptolemy's *Harmonics* (*in Harm.* 29ff.; discussed in Karamanolis 2006: 257–66). Philoponus follows Aristotle in saying that high pitch and low pitch are analogous to tactile sharpness and flatness. He also associates audible pitch very clearly with speed (cf. Pl. *Ti.* 67a–c). According to Philoponus, once a string or a chord is struck, a high pitch travels to our ears very quickly, whereas a low pitch reaches us slowly (*in de An.* 373,14–374,13). To illustrate the issue, Philoponus also presents an analogy: producing sounds with an instrument is like an archer shooting arrows; the more the string is tightened, the quicker is the speed of the arrow, and vice versa.

Anatomical evidence is much more important in Philoponus than it is in Themistius. The anatomical findings allow him to identify various "nerves" (*neura*), and he supposes that they transmit *pneuma* into our brain. What Philoponus knew about were not nerves but some tendons or sinews or other connective tissues that are larger and more visible. He supposes these "nerves" to be empty channels in which *pneuma* flows. Philoponus also locates the perceptual centre in the brain rather than heart (which is the usual Aristotelian location). The more scientific outlook of Philoponus' theory – if this is the right word for it – also manifests itself in his references to geometrical optics (Phlp. *in de An.* 339–40). Philoponus is informed about the geometrical optics of Galen (129–216 CE) but is reluctant to accept the idea of visual rays. For example, Galen had explained our vision of the objects' distance by reference to some sight streams or rays that are emitted from our eyes towards the objects.[18] We perceive the distance by calculating the angles at which these rays meet the object ahead of us (Galen, *de Usupartium* X). Philoponus wants to save the phenomenon – that is, seeing different distances, – without introducing visual rays. According to Philoponus, this is possible when we realize that the "activities" (*energeia*) that travel from the visible objects to our eyes are weakened on their way (Philoponus uses "form" and "activity" to denote what is transmitted from the object by the medium). Perhaps he supposes that we also become aware of this weakening and hence can count how distant the object is.

Perceptible qualities are defined in a rather typical manner by Philoponus: as capacities to change the medium or something analogous (e.g. colour in *in de An.* 349,29–31). Sound is defined as an activity in the air that perfects the air's capacity to transmit sound (361,25). This capacity of the air has received the technical name *to diēkhes*.[19] However, sometimes the definitions are modified to suit the question at hand. For example, when echoes are discussed, sound is defined as an activity that can travel in space analogously to bodies such as balls that rebound from soft surfaces (371,1–3).[20] Philoponus also presents a similar ranking as Aristotle often does among the several senses: sight is the highest or most perfect sense, hearing is next; smell is in the middle, and taste and touch constitute the least perfect senses (352,23–9).

As to the notion of the medium and its role in perception, Philoponus deviates from Themistius in his pronounced statements. Whereas Themistius is clear that for all senses a medium is required, Philoponus denies this. According to Philoponus, there is no medium for touch and taste (394,5–6). Themistius had followed Aristotle (*de An.* 432b22–26) and made flesh the medium for touch. Philoponus wants to deny this (e.g. *in de An.* 417,14–15), but he has great difficulty in disagreeing with the Philosopher. This makes his discussion longwinded and somewhat difficult to follow. Furthermore, he mitigates his disagreement by concluding that flesh is not just the organ of touch but its medium as well (433,36–434,1).

Is this disagreement between Aristotle and Themistius on the one hand and Philoponus on the other only of antiquarian interest? Or, is there a more important philosophical point behind it? When introducing the notion of *pneuma*, a material thinner than air that runs in the hollow channels that connect the brain with the sense organs such as eyes, ears and flesh (364,16–20), Philoponus points out several times that *pneuma*, not eyes, ears and so forth, are the proper organs of sensation. This may be so in two different ways. When discussing flesh, Philoponus is able to connect Aristotle's idea that flesh is a medium by identifying the proper organ of touch as the primary *pneuma* (*prōton pneuma*; 418,18–19), which is also supposed to host the so-called common sense (*koinē aisthēsis*; 433,35, 438,25–7) that explains more complex perceptual functions. However, for other senses, such as sight and hearing, it is not the primary *pneuma* that is identified as the proper organ, but the *pneuma* peculiar to those senses, optic or acoustic *pneuma* that runs in the channels connecting eyes and ears with the brain (optic *pneuma*, 336,33–337,3, 364,37–365,1; acoustic *pneuma*, 364,14–15). Whichever of these two is his considered view on the matter, his discussion shows how he attempts to unify the perceptual system physically as well as conceptually on the basis of the anatomical evidence at his disposal: it is the *pneuma* in the channels (the "nerves") that connects the brain with the remote sense organs that is crucial for the physics of perception. The unclarity about whether the *pneuma* is common or peculiar to each sense does not jeopardize the importance of this conclusion.

What, then, is Philoponus' analysis of how the objects affect our sense organs? Further, what is the role of this effect in perception? Our examples will be on the two ends of the hierarchy of the senses, sight and touch. Philoponus makes it clear that the objects of perception affect all of the following three: (i) the senses (*aisthēseis*); (ii) the sense organs (*aisthētēria*); and (iii) our body in general (438,16–17). However, he points out that the effects that take place in the sense and in the organs are of a different kind (*ibid.*).

(i) A sense is affected by the form of the object in a cognitive way (*gnōstikōs*). If qualities affect a person in a cognitive manner, he or she grasps (*antilambanetai*) and cognizes (*ginōskei*) those objects (432,38–433,4). This is to be distinguished from the effect in the sense organs and in the body in general. (ii) The effect in the organ is also characterized as being cognitive (432,36–433,4). Specifically, the change in the organ is cognitive in so far as the organ is affected *as a sense organ*. All sense organs are also parts of our body in general and hence the third kind of effect takes place in them as well. (iii) Our body in general is changed by the objects so that it comes to be the substrate (*hupokeimenon*) for the qualities: it is heated or cooled, moistened or dried (438,14, 433,4). In fact, Philoponus makes the classification slightly more complex: he allows that our flesh – even as the organ of touch – is heated or cooled, moistened or dried. However, other tactile qualities from the range light/heavy, rough/smooth only affect flesh in the cognitive manner (432,36–433,1). Therefore, when making this specification, Philoponus explicitly attributes cognitive change to our flesh. The notion of a cognitively changing flesh is a peculiar one indeed. His account also raises the question of how the cognitive change in the organ differs from the cognitive change that takes place in the senses. We shall shortly return to these issues.

As for the organ of sight, Philoponus analyses the change in the medium as something that "activities" (*energeiai*; e.g. 329,14–16) coming from objects induce on air. He is explicit that the activities do not change the colour of air, and air is not affected in the literal sense by them (335,26–30). Philoponus deviates from Aristotle in claiming that the visible objects travel (*khōrousai*; 335,26) from the objects to the eyes through the effect that their activities cause on air. Therefore, even in the case of sight the transmission of the activities of objects takes time, although the movement of light is swift (413,6–7, 327,7–12, 327,16ff.).[21] From the medium, the activities imprint (*entupousi*) colour and shape on the sense organ (which is a solid body), and because the sense organ is affected in this way (*tou aisthētēriou pathontos*), the discernment of the objects is transmitted to the sense (*aisthēsis*) (335,16–20). Here Philoponus seems to be saying that the eye takes on the qualities themselves, that is, colours and shapes. His considered view of the issue is presented later: the activities that are transmitted by the medium affect the eye so that the eye is either contracted or relaxed (439,16–18).

We have now seen that Philoponus is careful to distinguish between the effect (i) that takes or may take place in the sense organ (e.g. heating or cooling) through an agency of an object and (ii) the change that happens in the sense organ in so far as it is a sense organ (flesh changing cognitively). Further, he is quite clear that it is not sufficient for perception to occur that a sense organ is changed by an object, even though this seems to be necessary for perception (see e.g. 350,12–13). The organ needs to transmit the effect to the primary sense organ that is common to all senses constituted by *pneuma* (433,35, 438,29–31).

Is this transmission, then, a sufficient account of perception for Philoponus? Not quite. Philoponus is clear that, no matter how refined the physical explanation, reception of forms without matter is not sufficient for perception to occur. What is needed to account for perception is a psychic capacity (*psukhikē dunamis* 444,18–19) of distinguishing (*krinein*) different kinds of objects (444,23–4). For example, mirrors receive forms without matter but they do not see (437,23–4). However, we do not differ from mirrors just because of having the relevant sort of *pneuma*, because our psychic capacity is not caused by the kind of *pneuma* we have. The priority goes the other way round: it is our psychic qualities that are the productive (*poiētikos*) causes of our material constitution or mixture (*sōmatikē krasis*).[22] The movements of our soul (*psukhika kinēmata*; 388,25) coexist and are disposed together with the physical mixtures that make up our body, but the movements of our soul are not generated (*gignesthai*) by those mixtures (388,24–6). This means that the psychic movements cannot exist without the mixtures being of a certain kind (388,26–7). In any case, the primary cause for our having a certain kind of physical constitution lies in our psychic capacities.

Despite the differences between the organs of the various senses, Philoponus finds something that is common to all senses: they all receive an effect from the object in a cognitive way through becoming like the object (437,5–11). If the essential point about perception for Philoponus is the cognitive change, does this mean that for him perception is an entirely dematerialized process? Sorabji (1991, 1004: vol. 2) suggests that it is. Here we have to be extremely careful. In one sense, the answer seems to be affirmative: for Philoponus it is the cognitive change that is crucial for perception to occur and psychic capacities determine the bodily constitution in which those capacities can be realized. However, when Philoponus explains the cognitive change, he always – even in the case of sight that is the "least corporeal" of the senses – points to a *physical* change in the sense organ. For sight, this is the contraction or relaxation occurring in the eye when the "activity" arrives there (439,16–18). Further, the cognitive change is not entirely dematerialized for him, because he allows that flesh can be the subject of such change. To say that flesh can be cognitive entails that it can function as a sense organ, that is, through a change in flesh we can come to exercise our psychic capacity of perception. Further, the ways in which Philoponus uses the notion of *pneuma* is not captured by a simplistic distinction between physical and mental.

In general, the Cartesian dualistic framework, where mind as an ontological principle is distinct from body and these are two opposing metaphysical factors, is misleading in analysing the commentators' theories of sense perception. When discussing Themistius above we identified one central cause for this: there is no sharp demarcation line between our sensory system as a physical complex and as involving the psychic capacity of perception. In addition, we have found no reason to suppose that in the commentaries physical causation would be something easily explained, whereas psychic causation would be something mysterious. In fact, the situation seems to be the opposite. Philoponus, for example, explains how sun warms air by referring to how soul warms and vitalizes a living body. In a similar manner, he says, sun spreads vital activity through air, and this activity changes the inborn (*emphutos*) warmth of air, making the air warm through and through. Therefore, the way in which soul functions as a causal principle is supposed to be more familiar to us than the "physical" causality through which the sun warms the air.

Attention and reflexive awareness

Perception requires rational reflexivity

Let us now move on to consider two other commentaries in which perception is approached from a somewhat different angle. The central texts we shall discuss in this subsection are of uncertain authorship: one is the commentary on the *De anima* (CAG XI) that the manuscript tradition attributes to Simplicius and the other one is a spurious commentary attributed to Philoponus. As previously, we shall refer to these authors as Pseudo-Simplicius and Pseudo-Philoponus respectively.

Irrespective of the difficulties related to the problems concerning authenticity, the direction that the theories of perception were taking in late antiquity is clear in these commentaries: the focus shifts towards reflexive awareness and attention (see also Hadot 1997; Lautner 2000, 2004). This means that animal and human perception come to be distinguished from each other; Pseudo-Simplicius, for example, analyses human perception as a rational function (*logikē oun hēmōn hē aisthēsis*; ps.-Simp. *in de An.* 187,35–6). Referring to Iamblichus, he explains that animal perception and human perception are the same only homonymously (187,36–7). This does not mean, however, that Pseudo-Simplicius would be willing to abandon entirely the Aristotelian account of perception as reception of forms; that part of the story remains largely intact (e.g. 188,3, 190,6–10; see also Lautner 2004: 170). Rather, the point is that Pseudo-Simplicius supposes that for us to be aware of things in the external world it is essential that we have reflexive awareness of our perceptions. Further, following Neoplatonic intuitions, only what is rational and entirely immaterial can turn to itself (*epistrephein*; 187,32). According to Pseudo-Simplicius, animal perception is not reflexive in a similar manner (187,28–9).

The supposition that we are aware of our perceptions is one that the authors we discuss in this section share with Aristotle (e.g. Arist. *de An.* III 2, 425b12–13). However, as we have seen, for Aristotle such elementary reflexive awareness is common to human beings and other animals, whereas in some later Neoplatonic commentaries this supposition is denied. In these commentaries, several arguments are presented for the conclusion that it is impossible for perception to be aware of itself, unless perception is understood as a rational function. One of the arguments for this conclusion is that it is not possible for us to have perception about our own perceptions, because otherwise the perceptions themselves should be perceptible bodily objects. Since acts of perception are not perceptible bodily objects, they cannot be perceived (see e.g. ps.-Phlp. *in de An.* 464,31–465,32, quoted below in § "Attentive capacity").[23] Another argument is based on the idea we mentioned above: only things or entities that are entirely immaterial can turn to themselves. Since perception is realized in matter, it cannot do so. Therefore, reason alone as an entirely immaterial capacity is capable of accounting for reflexive awareness.

Some authors,such as Pseudo-Simplicius, also have other reasons for being unhappy with the Aristotelian theory of perception. One of them is a different understanding of what it means to be able to distinguish (*krinein*) between things. As we saw, for Philoponus perception requires a psychological capacity of distinguishing between different objects, but there is no indication that such a capacity could not exist in other animals as well. Rather, the context suggests that animal and human perceptions are alike. Aristotle, for his part, confirms that a capacity of discernment is innate in all animals (*APo.* II 19, 99b35). By contrast, as Plato had done, the authors discussed in this section deny that any discernment could be non-rational. The Greek *krinein* that is used by Aristotle and Philoponus to refer to the capacity of distinguishing also means the capacity of making judgements, and it is precisely this capacity that is crucial in perception for Plato as well as for Pseudo-Simplicius and Pseudo-Philoponus. Making judgements (e.g. this is white, this is sweet) is a rational capacity; for Pseudo-Simplicius it is an activity of the soul itself, not of the body (*in de An.* 196,17). In fact, Aristotle agrees that whereas discernment is or can be non-rational, judgement needs to be rational. Pseudo-Simplicius and Pseudo-Philoponus emphasize the role of judgement in human perception and hence distinguish it from perception in non-rational animals.

One further reason for the divergence of opinions in the analysis of perception is as follows. Our authors complain that the Aristotelian analysis makes perception a passive function. This is contrary to the intuition that we are also active in perceiving (e.g. perceptual judgement needs to be active; ps.-Simp. *in de An.* 200,14–15). Our awareness of perceptions, for example, needs to be an activity, something that we actively perform. If, then, perception were understood merely as a receptive capacity, the requirement of activity would not be fulfilled. In the Neoplatonic framework, being active is characteristic of reason, and passivity and potentiality are associated with matter; reason alone, being immaterial, is a truly active principle. The idea of activity is also related to a general principle accepted by Plotinus with respect to our soul's capacities. According to this principle, the capacities that are understood as being lower cannot strictly speaking affect those that are supposed to be higher. To put this in a simple manner: an immaterial capacity (such as reason) must be unaffected (*apathēs*) by a lower bodily capacity. If our perception were not active, it would seem that it must be affected by something lower.[24]

The active nature of perception becomes particularly clear in Pseudo-Simplicius' account of our awareness of perceptions. As

Peter Lautner (2004) has shown, Pseudo-Simplicius introduces a new interpretation of the Aristotelian notion of the common sense or unified perceptual faculty as the centre of a circle from which its radii (corresponding to the several senses) start (e.g. Alex.Aphr. *de An.* 63,6–12). Contrary to Alexander, for whom the focal point is something *to which* all the radii converge, for Pseudo-Simplicius it is something *from which* the sensitive soul attends to the effects taking place in the several senses: from there the soul discerns the portions or principles (*logoi*; *in de An.* 200,35) that are received by the sense organs from the external objects (200,25–36).

What has been just said about Pseudo-Simplicius' analysis of perception brings forward another important tendency in the later Neoplatonic commentaries: the sensitive soul interpreted as being rational in human being *directs its attention* to what is being received from outside. However, it is not just that it should observe these effects. The situation is more complex: the rational centre of perception puts forward (*proballein*) presentations to itself that are somehow congruous with the effects taking place in the sense organs and the principles or ratios received by the senses (192,12–21, 193,1ff.). Pseudo-Simplicius does not explain how it can be guaranteed that the ratios or principles and the presentations have an adequate relation to each other.

Attentive capacity

The development of emphasizing the activity of the mind in directing its attention culminates in Pseudo-Philoponus, who introduces a separate attentive (*prosektikon*) capacity or part of the rational soul. In his commentary, this attentive capacity is said to explain all awareness of our soul's functions from growth to understanding:

> But more recent interpreters neither tremble at Alexander's frown nor pay heed to Plutarch, but pushing Aristotle himself to one side they have devised a newer interpretation. They say that it belongs to the attentive part (*to prosektikon*

meros) of the soul to lay hold of the activities of the senses. For the rational soul, according to them, does not have only five powers, intellect, thought, opinion, rational wish and choice; they add another sixth power to the rational soul, which they call "attentive". This attentive part … stands over … all the powers, the rational, the non-rational and the vegetable. If, they say, the attentive power is to range over all, let it go over senses too and say "I saw" … Both [Plutarch and Alexander] are convicted of speaking wrongly, since they say that the common sense lays hold of the activities of each sense. For the common sense lays hold of nothing that is not a sense-object. Every sense-object is in a body, but the activity is not in a body. Hence it is not a sense-object. And if it is not a sense-object it does not fall under the common sense.

(ps.-Phlp. *in de An.* 464,31–465,32, trans. Charlton 2000)

Pseudo-Philoponus might be building on Proclus, who postulates a rational capacity of attention in his commentary on the *Parmenides* (957,29–958,8, discussed in Lautner 2004: 166). However, there is a difference between the positions of Pseudo-Philoponus and Proclus on the one hand and that of Pseudo-Simplicius on the other: for Pseudo-Philoponus and Proclus, attention is a distinct rational capacity, and it is directed to all functions of the soul alike. It is a unified centre of all kinds of self-awareness whether bodily or psychic. For Pseudo-Simplicius, the sensitive soul – understood as being rational – has a reflexive capacity of its own, and its awareness only explains perceptual self-awareness; it is not extended to other activities of the soul.

Despite this difference, there is an important aspect that is common to these views. From an analysis of how external objects affect us, the emphasis has moved to the question of how the effects in our sensory system come to be noticed. This is an important development and involves new research questions. The flipside of the coin is that the account of perception comes to be more dualistic than it is in the more Aristotelian writers. Whereas for Aristotle, Themistius and Philoponus, the account of perception does not involve a sharp demarcation between the physical and the psychic, something analogous to such a distinction comes in when the ratios in the sense organs come to be separated from the psychic activities.

Phantasia, a note

What we have said so far pertains to one portion of the commentators' accounts of human capacities related to perception and perceptual awareness. We have focused on the question of how we come to perceive and grasp external objects. Let us now briefly consider how the commentators explain our capacity of processing, combining and developing what we grasp in perception. First of all, in order for us to be able to process information from the senses at all, it needs to be recorded in our mind. Aristotle wrote a whole treatise on memory, but for one reason or another it did not inspire the commentators. Alexander apparently wrote a commentary on it, but it has been lost. Porphyry also presents an Aristotelian account of soul in *On the faculties of soul* (in *Fragments*, ed. Smith 1993: 255).

The general idea of a psychic capacity for producing images or presentations (*phantasia*) was a common one in antiquity, and various cognitive tasks from misperception (e.g. Aristotle) to dreams and mathematical imagination were assigned to it.[25] Our capacity of *phantasia* also explains how we are able to combine memory images or presentations in our imagination into wholes that do not correspond to anything in reality. The commentators' discussion on *phantasia* is an intriguing and vast topic, and in the present context, we can refer just to some important functions that were assigned to this versatile capacity.

For Aristotle, as well as for Themistius and Philoponus, *phantasia* in general is a capacity that we share with other animals. The capacity to retain memory images in the soul and to present them to oneself was taken to explain how animals are capable of more complex cognitive functions than merely perceiving what is around them. Themistius and Philoponus advance the explanations of animal mental life in terms of *phantasia*. One example is particularly intriguing: the role of *phantasia* for the distinction between voice (*phōnē*) and mere sound or noise (*psophos*) (cf. Arist. *de An.* 420b5ff.). In order to be able to have a voice, a creature needs to have suitable organs (windpipe and lungs).[26] However, the mere possession of suitable organs is not sufficient for the production of voice: when we cough, we are not using our voice. What is essential is that the sound is produced with the right kind of impulse (*hormē*) or image (*phantasia*).

What distinguishes the kind of image or impulse that is needed to produce voice instead of mere sound is that such an image is significant or semantic (*sēmantikos*). Because, Themistius and Philoponus argue, animals have such significant or semantic images (*phantasia sēmantikē*; e.g. Phlp. *in de An.* 375,19–20; Them. *in de An.* 67,8–10), they can express pleasure and pain (and also use their voice in looking for a mate; Phlp. *in de An.* 379,9–16). Themistius calls the signification characteristic of animal communication "natural", as opposed to human communication that is synthetic (*sunthēkē*; *in de An.* 67,9–11). Philoponus also claims that human language has a synthetic aspect (*sunthēkē*, which musical instruments also imitate; 375,35–376,5), but animal communication is based on natural semantic images. In Philoponus, the synthetic nature of human language refers to the idea that the words have been formed through combinations of sounds. In his comments concerning the combination, Philoponus underlines rhythm and melody that occur in phrasing (375,25ff.). He points out that in some sense melody and rhythm also occur in the voices of animals, for example, in jays or parrots, but that it only appears through imitation and resemblance (377,5–11), not because of systematic synthetic activity.[27]

In Aristotle, *phantasia* is not strictly speaking used to explain perceptions, which means that he does not analyse perception by the notion of perceptual appearance. Further, "appearance" (*phantasia*) for him has the connotation – as it does in Greek – that something merely appears to be the case but is not. By contrast, the notion of appearance had already become central in the analysis of perception for the Stoics, and they claimed that there are appearances that guarantee their own truth. Later Platonic or Neoplatonic authors also broadened the notion of *phantasia* to cover all perceptual presentation. One of the reasons for this perhaps was that they were more interested in the fact that our perceptual experience forms a unified whole and does not consist of isolated perceptions of single qualities. Aristotle also acknowledged this. He explained the fact by reference to what came to be called "common sense" (*koinē aisthēsis*, a term that Aristotle introduces but does not systematize).[28] However, in the later Neoplatonic commentaries, more stress was laid on the idea that our soul actively processes the material we get in perception into a continuous whole. Another reason might be related to the supposition mentioned above that the lower bodily functions cannot affect the higher ones. This means that when we perceive, our soul must produce an image (*phantasia*) of its own for it to perceive. The exact relation between such an image and the changes in the sensory system is not explained.[29]

✳✳✳

It is appropriate now to pause briefly and reflect on the accounts of perception discussed above. Given that the psychological theories today attribute a central explanatory role to attention in human cognition and awareness and to the constructive work our mind needs to do on the sketchy material we receive through the senses, it might seem that the theory that reception has a central role in perception is misguided. But is it as straightforward as this?

To consider this issue, we need to pose a further question: is the *explanandum* in the Aristotelian and (Neo)Platonic theories the same? Both speak about human perception, but the approach differs. For the Aristotelians, perception *as such* is not the crucial problem: we know what perceptions are, since we have them all the time. The main problem is to explain how we come to have perceptions in the first place – given that perceptions require that the objects affect us and that they are detached from our sense organs. A further rationale for the idea of receptivity is that if we deny receptivity and suppose our senses or reason to contribute in perception, we must ask how we can know whether we come to perceive the external objects as they are, rather than just something that is significantly manipulated by our cognitive system.

By contrast, the Neoplatonic authors inherit the theory that perception involves reception of forms as developed by several generations of authors. This is already a given for them. From this basis they focused on a further question. Granted that we all know that perceptions require reception of forms without matter, a new problem emerges: what is perception from the soul's point of view? It is to answer this question that the notions of projecting images, attention and rational perception are introduced. When we say that these questions come in focus in the later Platonic authors, it is not meant to deny that Aristotle raises similar ones. In a sense he does, but his views are not very systematic and he does not suppose that such functions require rationality. Rather, he takes them to belong to the perceptive soul.

Intellect

Aspects of intellect

Let us now leave the problems of perception and move to consider our reason. In general, the commentators suppose that there are two functions that our reason as reason performs. On the one hand, we need concepts to account for the capacities of thought and inference. On the other hand, there is a form of intellectual understanding that involves a truthful grasp of things as they are in their intelligibility. The distinction has various forms in different authors. In Neoplatonism, it means that the universal Intellect is separated from our soul. On the level of soul, there is ordinary conceptual thought and reasoning and this is limited by language, whereas intellection proper grasps its objects atemporally and in an entirely immediate manner. Alexander of Aphrodisias also distinguishes having concepts and having proper intellection, but his distinction is different from the one just outlined. According to Alexander, we come to have concepts (*noēmata*) naturally from perceptions, whereas a more advanced perfection of our intellect, consisting of comprehensive theoretical knowledge (*epistēmē*), requires that we educate and train ourselves (*de An.* 81,25–82,6). For Alexander the distinction is one between having isolated concepts and having more comprehensive theoretical understanding about a matter (e.g. having a concept of a dolphin and to be a zoologist specializing in dolphins; we shall return to this distinction below).

In so far as concepts are concerned, it is a common assumption in the commentaries that they are the same in us. If it were the case that our concepts were different, we could not understand each other and teaching would be impossible (Them. *in de An.* 103,38–104,11). Alexander has another perspective on the alleged fact that the concepts are the same. He grounds it on the idea that the acquisition process of concepts is natural: nature operates so that we all come to have certain concepts (*noēmata*) or notions (*ennoiai*) from perceptions. Alexander does not intend any significant distinction between concepts and notions here. He speaks of a theoretical vision (*theōrētikē opsis*) concerning the universal and mentions that it is called either "concept" (*noēma*) or "notion" (*ennoia*) (*de An.* 85,20–25). The former is used by Aristotle and the latter by the Stoics, but by the time of Alexander the terms have become common property and do not entail any specific doctrinal differences here. Alexander makes clear that concepts are acquired from perception, but he does not give much in the way of concrete examples. Here he only mentions the concept of white, but perhaps concepts of natural species and genera, such as human beings and horses, animals and heavenly bodies, would also belong here.

In the introductory section to this chapter, we considered one important assumption that figures in the commentators' discussion on the intellect. Aristotle's theory, on which the commentators and Plotinus to some extent build, involves the idea that, when we grasp intelligible objects, our intellect becomes the same in form with the object, and this idea implies the uniformity of intellects. The human intellect is said to be completely without a nature of its own, a pure potential for actualizing the intelligible forms (*noēta*).

It grasps things in their intelligibility by becoming identical in form with them. When I grasp a human being, the form of a human being (often explained as what it is to be a human being) is actualized in my intellect. This means that there is nothing specifically individual in my intellect: when I grasp a human being and you grasp a human being, we are identical in so far as our intellects are concerned, even though our intellects can be numerically distinct. Aristotle seems to suppose that our intellects are numerically distinct in this way: I have an intellect of my own and you have one as well, but when the same object is actualized in both, then our intellects are the same in content. One logical development from this situation is the move made by Plotinus. He separates the universal Intellect from our individuality, and denies the numerical distinctness between intellects.

In Aristotle and Alexander, the rationale for supposing that our intellect does not have a nature of its own is as follows. In order for our intellect to realize the forms as they are, it must not add anything to or subtract anything from them. Now, if our intellect had a form X, it could not become entirely identical in form with its object Y; it could only become $X + Y$ (for the argument in Alexander, see his *de An.* 26,23–38). If our intellect were something other than the object, this something would shadow our understanding of the object. Further, if our intellect contributed when grasping things, this contribution would change the thing we were supposed to grasp. In neither case would we be able to grasp things as they are. Since this is what was to be explained (how we can understand things as they are), we need to suppose that our intellect lacks a nature. When discussing this point, Alexander also presents a specified version of Aristotle's comparison between our intellect and an empty writing tablet. According to Alexander's specification, our intellect should not be compared to the writing tablet itself. Rather, our intellect is like a specific quality or potentiality of the tablet; namely, its suitability (*epitēdeiotēs*) for receiving writing on it (*de An.* 84,24–30). For Alexander our intellect is not an odd kind of thing without a nature. It is not a separate thing to begin with. Hence we should not compare the intellect to the writing tablet, which is an actual thing,

189

but understand that the intellect is a *potentiality* we have, in the same way that the tablet has the potentiality to be written on.

Another peculiarity comes to the commentaries from Aristotle's theory of intellect: intellect is supposed to have different aspects, or there are different kinds of intellects. This is not the straightforward claim that each individual human being has an intellect of his or her own. Rather, it means that to analyse the functions of intellect, we need to distinguish between potentialities and actualities. For example, human intellect as we just described it is a potentiality of receiving the forms of external things. This potential intellect (*ho dunamei nous, nous en dunamei*) is one aspect of intellect, and it is also referred to by names like "passive intellect" (*pathētikos nous*). Some commentators, such as Proclus (according to Phlp. *in de An.* 6,1–2), suggest that the passive intellect is a capacity of imagination (*phantasia*); others argue against this suggestion (Latin Philoponus *in de An.* III 4–8). In addition to this potential or passive aspect of the intellect, there is an active or productive one (*nous en energeia, nous poiētikos*).

The expression "active intellect" (*nous poiētikos*) does not explicitly occur in Aristotle's notoriously problematic fifteen lines of *De anima* III 5 (it is implied by a demonstrative pronoun), and *pathētikos nous* appears only once in that chapter (430a24–5). Yet the distinction between these two aspects of intellect (and later complex elaborations of it) becomes central in the commentaries. One of the debated questions is whether the distinction entails a difference between aspects of the human intellect or whether we must postulate different kinds of intellect, where the active one comes to be associated with a divine intelligence.

The debate about active and passive aspects (or actual and potential) aspects of the intellect is a complex one indeed. Since the commentators operate with these notions, we must touch on the controversy in our discussion. To put it simplistically, the background for the distinction is as follows. Aristotle understands intellectual apprehension as being analogous to sense perception (*de An.* III 4, 429a13–17; cf. III 7, 431b6–8): there is an object that has the potency to be grasped and we have the potency to grasp intelligible

PSYCHOLOGY: PERCEPTION AND INTELLECT

objects. However, Aristotle seems to suppose that it is not sufficient that an object and an intellect alone could explain how we come to grasp objects.

Why is this so? One reason could be that otherwise it would be difficult to explain why we do not start grasping as soon as we are born and acquire the whole intelligible structure of the world in our intellect before we go to school. In addition, the intelligible aspect of an external thing cannot, in Aristotle's theory, affect us directly (or through the medium of water or air) as perceptible objects do. Rather, the immaterial intelligibility of an object (the intelligibility of a horse, for example) needs to become separated (or abstracted) from the actual horses that we encounter in perception. Apparently this separation is so active in character that the mere potentiality to grasp, that is, our potential intellect, could not explain it. Our potential intellect is a capacity of receiving the intelligible forms, but it seems that if the intelligibility needs to become separated from material objects, they cannot be received in the manner that the perceptible objects are received. Something more active is needed.

We have now seen why an active intellect seems to be needed, but we do not know what it is and where it is. Is it a separate capacity that our soul has? If we have an active intellect in us, why do we not understand everything right from the beginning of our lives? Should we then rather understand the active intellect as a divine intelligence that contains abstract intelligible forms in it and eternally understands all objects (e.g. what being a horse is, what beauty is)? If this is the right interpretation, how does the divine intelligence affect our passive intellects? Could the active intellect be a teacher's intelligence? If my teacher already knows more about the theoretical structure of the world, perhaps he or she can activate my passive intellectual capacities. But do we not also learn theoretical things without being taught? How could this be explained in terms of the last answer?

Since the commentators took over the distinctions between different aspects of the intellect, they encountered problems like these. The topic is a complex one, and it does not seem likely that a totally unproblematic solution could be found. In our discussion below, we shall concentrate on the question of how central aspects of human thought and understanding were explained in the commentaries. In particular, we shall ask how we come to grasp intelligible objects in the first place.

How do we come to grasp intelligible objects?

Alexander of Aphrodisias

When discussing the human intellect, Alexander not only distinguishes between potential and active intellects, but also postulates a dispositional intellect (*nous en hexei*). He also labels our potential intellect as "material intellect" (*hulikos nous*; Alex.Aphr. *de An.* 81,22–5). When referring to our intellect as being material, Alexander does not mean that it should be corporeal or physical. Rather, he specifies that the point about calling our intellect material is a special, *receptive* character of our intellect. According to Alexander, everything that receives something is in some sense matter for that something that it receives (81,22–5; see Arist. *de An.* 429a13–17). This, of course, raises the question of what our intellect is supposed to receive and how. One suggestion in the general framework of actualities and potentialities would be that the active intellect somehow intervenes in the process, for example, that our material intellect receives intelligible objects from the active intellect. However, the active intellect for Alexander is God or the unmoved mover (*prōton aition*; Alex.Aphr. *de An.* 89,9), and his account leaves it somewhat unclear what its exact role is in human cognitive development. He just says that the active intellect is the reason (*aitios*) for us to have the intellectual disposition (88,23–4).

Alexander argues that we come to have general concepts (*noēmata*) and notions (*ennoiai*) from sense perception. These concepts and notions allow us to make basic statements or judgements about what we perceive, such as "this is white". This already involves some vague conception, or something analogous to "theoretical vision" (*opsin tina theōrētikēn*; 85,20–25), of the universal. This means that having the concept of whiteness involves dealing with white on a general level, not just perceiving singular instances of a colour. When explaining how we come to have general notions such as that of white, Alexander points out that this part of our cognitive development happens to us naturally, as naturally as we learn to walk. He specifies this by saying that we human beings are rational because we actualize our intellectual potential up to a point (*mekhri tinos*; 82,2). Our rationality is not just a potentiality of becoming rational; for all who are not disabled, Alexander says, this potentiality is to some extent actualized (82,5–10). He calls such a level of rationality "common intellect" (*koinos nous*) and distinguishes it from a more advanced perfection of the same capacity.

Now we have seen that, according to Alexander, we human beings come to have universal concepts from perception just because we are rational creatures with intellectual potentialities that, to some extent, come to be realized through natural learning processes. Yet his description of such processes is not very detailed. In addition to what we have already said (basically that such realization of our intellectual potentiality happens naturally through perception), the only more specific detail Alexander gives is the following. Our development from not merely perceiving "this particular something" (*tode te kai kathekaston*; 83,7) to grasping something "of this kind and universal" (*toionde kai katholou*; 83,8), happens owing to experience (*di' empeirias*; 83,8), that is through repeated observation. However, Alexander is not an empiricist in the sense that he would claim that our perceptual capacities alone would be sufficient to explain having universal concepts. Rather, he says that it is possible for us to grasp something of this kind and universal, because we have intellect. It is already a function of our intellect to put together objects that are similar (*hē ... tōn homoiōn sunthesis ergon ēdē nou*; 83,12–13). For Alexander, the natural function of intellect is to select and join together similar objects in perception and hence form genuinely universal notions. Perception can be about similar things, but it can never understand that certain things are similar and analyse in what respect they are similar and in what respect dissimilar.

Even though Alexander takes concept formation to be an intellectual function, he distinguishes it from having a proper intellectual disposition (*nous en hexei*). The most central criterion for the distinction is the diversity and manifoldness of our concepts (85,20–25). Further, to have some general concepts (i.e. to have the common intellect) comes to us naturally. To have the proper intellectual disposition does not; it requires education and training. Even with education, not all are capable of perfecting their intellect, but only those whose nature is well-suited for perfecting it (81,25–7). As mentioned, Alexander also characterizes the proper intellectual disposition as theoretical knowledge (*epistēmē*). What, then, is the difference?

Let us consider the following analogy to illustrate the point. If I have not had any intellectual training and see a horse, I cannot say very much about it. Surely, I can employ the notion of horse, recognize it as an animal and perhaps as a vegetarian animal, but it may well be that my knowledge ends here. Perhaps I can give some further details about horses on the basis of the memory images I have about horses, but this will not be an intellectual achievement. If I am left on my own in an empty room and someone asks me to write down my thoughts about horses nothing much comes to my mind (perhaps mainly images and memories, or some suspicious theoretical speculation). By contrast, someone who has learned more about horses and is habituated to use her knowledge can tell much more on the basis of her theoretical knowledge alone (what kind of an animal it is, how it lives and so forth). Or, if that other person is a trained rider, she can also give a fairly comprehensive account of how horses behave. If a person of the latter kind is left in a room to write down her thoughts about horses, it is likely that she can produce a lengthy essay. This example shows us why it is important for our notions to be "diversified and manifold" in order for us to be able to really think and grasp things about horses. To understand things requires both breadth and depth to our conceptual system.

To sum up, according to Alexander, human beings come to have general concepts from perception naturally. Mere concept possession must be distinguished from a more advanced intellectual achievement, namely theoretical understanding. Such understanding is the proper disposition of our intellect: what it really means to have an intellect is to be able to grasp complex theoretical wholes, not just to have isolated concepts. On the basis of our discussion, we can also see why the idea of receptivity is important for Alexander: to account for the alleged fact that we come to acquire naturally accurate general notions and hence some knowledge on a universal level (e.g. horses are animals). To say that we have a receptive intellect can be used to explain why and how we come to have a conceptual system that is uniform with the structure of reality. When we understand that horses are animals, this is not just a conceptual truth. It is true because horses really are animals, and our understanding reflects reality because we can receive its general structure.

Themistius

Despite the rather limited role that the active intellect as God has in Alexander's account, Themistius seizes on the point and asks: how can Alexander identify the active intellect with the first God (i.e. the unmoved mover), given that Aristotle says in the very same passage that it should be in our soul (*in de An.* 102,30–103,4)?[30] For Themistius the active intellect needs to be in the human soul. But what is its role in our cognitive development? Is it needed already in the abstraction of the very basic concepts?

In his paraphrase of the *Posterior Analytics* and its last chapter, Themistius' account suggests that we come to have general notions from experience and that perception for us already involves judgements such as "this is purifying hellebore" (Them. *in APo.* 63,2–26). Experience can also give us the generalization that hellebore is purifying. It is just for the truly universal generalization "all hellebore is purifying" that intellect is needed. All the other types of judgement and generalization take place through experience alone. However, the context of the *Posterior Analytics* is devoid of any reference to the active intellect, and we need to turn to Themistius' paraphrase of the *De anima* to see how the different aspects of intellect function in our cognitive development.

Before discussing the role of the active intellect (or intellect in actuality, *nous en energeia*) in Themistius, let us consider his arguments for the uniformity of the intellects of different human individuals. Themistius points out that in some sense there needs to be one intellect that we all share. If this were not the case, he argues, we could not understand each other at all. If all or some of us were uniquely affected by things, those people could not communicate their affections and thoughts to other people (*in de An.* 103,38–104,6). Similarly, Themistius argues, if a teacher and a student do not have the same concepts (*noēmata*), teaching and learning become impossible. Further: "if, [that concept] is the same – as it is necessary for it to be – then the intellect of the teacher will be identical with the intellect of the student because in the case of the intellect its essence is the same as its activity" (*in de An.* 104,7–11, my trans.). The question of whether or not Themistius postulates a universal hypostasis Intellect by remarks like these is a difficult one.[31] On the basis of what he says here, such a conclusion is not necessary. What his argument amounts to is a defence of the idea that the contents of the intellect need to be uniform. For this it is not necessary that there is numerically one Intellect that we all share.

But how does the active intellect come into the picture? As mentioned, Themistius argues against Alexander placing it outside the human soul. According to Themistius, the active intellect is in us, but we do not have it right from birth. In us the potential intellect is prior in time (99,30–31), but without the active or productive intellect, our potential intellect is just a storehouse for concepts (*thēsauros noēmatōn*). Only when we have the active intellect do we become capable of making combinations of and distinctions between our concepts, piling them up into thoughts and inferences, and moving from one thought to another. Therefore, as such, our potential intellect is merely a collection of concepts, and we need to come to possess the productive intellect (*poiētikos nous*) in order to be capable of thought and reasoning. The question of how we come to possess this productive intellect is not answered; it is just said to "come to us" (*epelthein*; 99,5–10).

Philoponus
As mentioned at the beginning of this chapter, with Philoponus and *De anima* III questions of authenticity become pressing once again. We must bear in mind that the Greek commentary printed after

Philoponus on *De anima* I and II in the *Commentaria in Aristotelem Graeca* XV is spurious and we shall not discuss the work here. However, the Latin translation of Philoponus on Aristotle's *De anima* III 4–8 (known as Philoponus' "*On the Intellect*") is probably authentic and we shall concentrate on that commentary.

In the Latin translation of the commentary on *De anima* III 4–8, Philoponus brings in a new interpretation of the active intellect, perhaps to some extent anticipated by Themistius. According to Philoponus, the active intellect is definitely in the human soul, but it is not the soul of the same individual who is learning. The active intellect is the intellect of a teacher who advances the student's potential intellect into a state where it is receptive of all (Phlp. *in de An.* 51,95–9, 48,32–3, 45,53–9). However, this does not mean that the teacher teaches the student genuinely new things. Rather, Philoponus defends a Platonizing interpretation of Aristotle, where learning is understood as recollection.

The intuition motivating the denial of the claim that we can learn new things is the same that motivates Plato's discussion in the *Phaedo* (74a–75a). Since nothing in the perceptible world really is large or small, we could not acquire the notion of largeness or smallness, or what it is to be large or small from perception. It must already be there in our soul and comes to be recollected in a process of learning. Or, as in the late dialogues, our soul must contain general notions such as sameness and difference that we employ to form concepts and to judge that some things in the world are the same as or different from each other. The Platonizing interpretations were not rare in later commentaries. One remarkable version of the criticism of Aristotle's theory is found in Proclus' commentary on the *Metaphysics* (discussed in Helmig 2008). There he argues against the possibility of a "later born" (*husterogenēs*) intellect, that is, one that is not there when we are born but acquired in our carnal life.

To balance the picture, it must be pointed out that even though Aristotle, Alexander and Themistius did not accept the doctrine of recollection, they were not strict empiricists either. As we have seen, they describe our potential intellect as something that is specifically capable of reception. Such potentiality is not indiscriminate. Given

197

that it is receptive to what it is for something to be the thing it is, this means that its receptive capacity is receptive of essential rather than accidental properties. Even though the potential intellect is a receptive tool and lacks form, it is a strictly qualified one. It is tuned to receive some properties but not others.

When defending his interpretation of Aristotle, Philoponus also attempts to explain away the analogy to an empty writing tablet. He writes:

> [E]ven if he here likens it [i.e. intellect] to an uninscribed thing we write on he does not mean that it has forms in potentiality in the first sense … [in the sense that we can acquire them]. But a certain latitude must be recognised in both meanings of "potentiality" … so intellect which is in actuality perfects intellect which is in potentiality and brings it to actuality not by putting into it forms that are not there, but by bringing into light forms which are non-evident and hidden because of the state of swoon which is the effect of birth. And it is this he calls "potentiality" in the first sense … The intellect which enters the world of becoming is like a person asleep or delirious.
>
> (*On the Intellect* 38,99–40,43, trans. Charlton 1991)

Therefore, for Philoponus, there are latent or hidden contents in our intellect already when we are born and nothing new is acquired when we learn. Further, senses do not have any positive role in the process in which such hidden contents of our intellect are made known. Rather, they are needed to remove an obstacle; namely, some false conceptions we come to have owing to the capacity of *phantasia* (116,75–80, 33,80–85). According to a comparison Philoponus makes here, the teacher brings into light those latent contents that there are in our intellect in a way similar to natural reproduction. This analogy only functions up to a certain point: since the contents are already there in the intellect of the student, no new intellect is born. However, Philoponus perhaps wants to point to another common feature between the two processes; namely, being continuous.

The intellect is continuous not because of being eternally actualized in the same individual but because of being actualized in a similar manner in different individuals over time. Philoponus' interpretation obviously contradicts Aristotle's account of how we come to activate our intellect given in *Posterior Analytics* II 19. In that context Aristotle points out that it would be absurd to suppose that we could have all the knowledge inside us without noticing that we do. Apparently Philoponus needs the supposition of the "swoon" caused by birth into a body to explain why we do not have any idea about how much we already know.

In the last section of this chapter, we have discussed how the human intellect can receive intelligible contents in it. In our discussion, we have repeatedly met some metaphysical suppositions behind the theory, the most important being the one that reality itself is intelligible. Let us now turn to consider how the commentators understood the structure of reality.

SIX
Metaphysics

The very term "metaphysics" comes from the early phases of the commentary tradition. In the edition of Aristotle's works made around 60 BCE or slightly before, the work that we know as the *Metaphysics* receives the Greek name *ta meta ta phusika*, "those writings that come after physics".[1] Aristotle himself had talked about "first philosophy" (*prōtē philosophia*), the study of being as being, in the middle books of the *Metaphysics*, which he also refers to as "theology". Whereas physics studies what is common to all natural things *as natural things*, first philosophy studies what is common to things in so far *as they are*. This, Aristotle indicates, is the highest and most general point of view from which we can consider things. The formulation "being as being" (*to on hē on*) immediately raises the question of whether this means being as existence, or being as being something. This question is addressed below in our discussion (e.g. § "What do the forms do?").

We have the following commentaries on the *Metaphysics*: (i) Alexander of Aphrodisias on the first five books; (ii) Syrianus on Books III, IV, XIII and XIV (CAG VI 1), (iii) Asclepius, from the lectures of Ammonius,[2] on Books I–VII (CAG VI 2); and (iv) an unidentified commentary on Books VI–XIV, which has come down to us appended to Alexander's commentary on Books I–V. The authorship of the last mentioned work is disputed; many scholars date it as late as the twelfth century and attribute it to Michael of Ephesus (e.g. Menn 1995; cf. Sorabji 2004: vol. 3, 125).

Rather than the commentaries on the *Metaphysics*, metaphysical debates centred on the *Categories*. The most probable reason for this is that, with the exception of Themistius, all the commentators after Alexander were Platonists of some sort. For a late ancient Platonist the *Metaphysics* was not problematic. The work analyses substances through the notions of matter and form, and the (Neo)Platonic commentators tended to agree: this is how sensible substances should be analysed. However, from their perspective, Aristotle's *Metaphysics* does not offer a sufficient account of being, since sensible beings are not the only beings there are. In addition to the sensibles, there are the transcendent intelligible forms that need to be added to Aristotle's analysis. Not only is it that the transcendent forms need to be added – the Platonists suppose that the transcendent forms are *prior* to the Aristotelian immanent ones. Aristotle's *Metaphysics* offers an analysis of the sensible but this needs to be subordinated to the Platonic scheme. By contrast, in the *Categories* (Chapter 5), Aristotle affirms that within the category of substance, the particulars are prior to the species. Since this claim seems to be in diametrical opposition to Platonic metaphysics, the commentators had work to do to explain how this treatise in fact was not incompatible with the Platonic assumption that sensible particulars are secondary to transcendent universal forms.

As mentioned in Chapter 1, the *Categories* was the most popular object of commentary. Six commentaries have been preserved, and Simplicius gives an account of many that have not come down to us. Simplicius also offers us the most extensive discussion about how authors before him had understood the application of the categories (Simp. *in Cat.* 9,5–13,26). The preserved commentaries are by: Porphyry (CAG IV 1), Dexippus (CAG IV 2), Ammonius (CAG IV 4), Simplicius (CAG VIII), Philoponus (based on Ammonius' lectures; CAG XIII 1) and Elias (CAG XVIII 1). In addition to these, there is an anonymous paraphrase of the work (CAG XXIII 2). Porphyry in fact wrote two separate commentaries on the *Categories*. A longer commentary addressed to Gedalius has been lost, but we do have his short commentary, which was written in question-and-answer form (CAG IV 1, trans. Strange 1992). Consequently, the references in this chapter are to the short commentary. In addition to the works written in Greek, the commentary tradition on the *Categories* continued almost uninterrupted until the sixth century in the Latin West, when Boethius wrote his commentary. In the East, there were Christians in Syria who translated the *Categories* into their own language, and those translations and commentaries contributed to the preservation and later flourishing of classical philosophy in the Arabic world (see de Libera 2004: 53ff.).

The categories

The commentators played a decisive role in the transmission of Aristotelian metaphysical notions into Western philosophy, and the main vehicle in this transmission was the commentaries on the *Categories*. Some works written on the *Categories* were critical in tone, but, somewhat ironically, even they reinforced the general feeling that everyone had to have a view on the work and its content. One decisive point in the development was when Plotinus criticized Aristotle's list of categories and Porphyry, the student and editor of Plotinus, responded to this criticism.

In the *Categories*, Aristotle lists ten items that are signified by non-combined expressions (*legomenon*, "that which is said"). He says that all non-combined expressions signify: substance, quantity, quality, relative, place, time, position, having, acting or being acted upon (1b25–27). When he begins to discuss them, he slightly deviates from this order, and settles for the following list: (i) *ousia*, substance; (ii) *to poson*, quantity; (iii) *pros ti*, relative; (iv) *to poion*, quality; (v) *poiein*, acting upon; (vi) *paskhein*, being acted upon; (vii) *keisthai*, position; (viii) *to pote*, when; (ix) *to pou*, where; (x) *to ekhein*, having. Of these, we have more extensive treatment only of the first four: substance, quantity, relative and quality. Thereafter Aristotle begins a similar discussion of acting upon and being acted upon, but there is a break in the text right after that. A short and dismissive remark about the rest of the categories has been put into Aristotle's mouth at this point (*Cat.* 11b10–16). It has perhaps been interpolated to give an impression, and a superficial one at that, of completeness.

Aristotle's terminology has been very influential and we use the notion of a category in our daily talk. In philosophy, we also often use "predication", which is the Latin translation for Aristotle's term *katēgoria*. Yet, the term *katēgoria* is not frequent in the *Categories* (it occurs at 3a35, 3a37 and 10b19), and it received its special philosophical meaning only in Aristotle (see Frede 1987).[3] This is important, because we might rather easily say things like "Aristotle lists ten categories" or "Aristotle lists ten kinds of things that can be predicated". To put it in one of these ways would imply that Aristotle was operating with an already existing philosophical notion of predication, to which he then gave the content he wanted. However, rather than using an existing notion, Aristotle was creating or establishing one, and we need to ask what kinds of questions motivated it.

One rather helpful way of looking at this question is to see what kind of linguistic expressions are included in Aristotle's list. There are many interrogatives nominalized by adding a definite article: quantity is literally "the how much", quality is "the what [is *x*] like"; other similar names are "the when" and "the where". Many of the names already appear in Plato (*Tht.* 182a), for example, the names for substance (*ousia*), relative (*pros ti*) and quality (*to poion*). Aristotle explains "substance" as "a this-something" (*tode ti*), where a definite and an indefinite pronoun occur in succession. Acting upon (*poiein*), being acted upon (*paskhein*), position (*keisthai*) and having (*ekhein*) are verbs in the infinitive, and the first two most probably derive from Plato.[4]

One might wonder how Aristotle had arrived at the list, which seems rather heterogeneous. One suggestion is as follows: the list derives from questions we can pose about things. If we think of any subject *x*, there are things that we might like to know about it. We would perhaps want to know what it is, what it is like, how large it is, where it is, when it is and so on. And it is from exactly these kinds of questions that Aristotle starts. These things can be asked and hence also said about something. What is common to the items that are grouped in the same category is that they answer the same type of question. In the category of quality, we find items that can be given as answers to the question "What is it like?", in the category of substance those that can be used to answer the question "What is it?" and so on (see also Ackrill 1963: 78–9).

On the other hand, one may think of Aristotle's categories as answering what-is-it questions about different kinds of entities (see *ibid.*: 79). If we ask, for example, "What is Callias?", we can answer: a human being, an animal and so on, and, finally, an individual thing, a this-something. By contrast, if we ask the same about courage (or whiteness), for example, we do not arrive at the answer that courage should be an individual thing like Callias as a human being is. Rather, we come to understand courage as a kind of quality. This is not the point that "courage" (*andreia*) should be linguistically different from "a human being": both are substantives; "whiteness" is a nominalized adjective (*to leukon*). Rather, Aristotle insists that the list of categories is a list of items that are signified by certain expressions, not a list of linguistic expressions as such. From this angle, it becomes clearer that courage is a kind of thing or entity different from a human being: the former is a quality or property of something, the latter a thing bearing properties.

Nonetheless, Aristotle's list is closely related to language in general and the Greek language in particular, and it is no wonder that one of the most central debated points about the *Categories* in the commentary tradition was whether it is a treatise about words. However, as we saw, Aristotle himself describes his list as those items that can be *signified* by simple or non-combined expressions (*Cat.* 1b25). Therefore, he indicates that it is not just a work on language. Given that it is a work on items signified by expressions, we need to ask: what do these simple expressions signify?

What are the categories categories of?

The stage for the later discussion of Aristotle's *Categories* is set by Plotinus' attack (*Enn.* 6.1–3). The most important point concerns the application or reference of the categories. Plotinus starts with the idea that the theory of categories is supposed to be a classification of beings (*ta onta*) into ten (6.1.1–2). He soon goes on to specify that the relevant question in this connection is whether or not the categories apply in the intelligible and sensible realm equally. He argues against this alternative on the following grounds. For example, if we assume that substance should mean the same with reference to sensible substances on the one hand and to intelligible substances on the other, we would be making the supposition that individual things such as human beings and horses and the forms of individual things are substances in the same sense. This would entail that there are relations of priority within the genus of substance. According to Plotinus, intelligible substances (*ta noēta*) are prior to sensible ones. In Aristotle's *Categories* it is individual substances that are primary; he does not even talk about intelligible objects (*ta noēta*) in that context. Plotinus now brings in a further premise from Aristotle. Aristotle himself excludes the possibility that priorities could exist within a single genus (no animal is prior to another *as an animal*; all are animals to an equal degree). Therefore, Plotinus concludes, Aristotle's categories cannot retain the status of a genus, and one needs another classification that applies to the intelligibles (*Enn.* 6.1.12,51–3, 6.3.1,3–6). For this purpose, he prefers "being" from Plato's greatest kinds (*megista genē*; *Sophist* 254b–255d), namely being, sameness, difference, movement and rest.

However, the important point in Plotinus' attack is not to accuse Aristotle of inconsistency. Rather, he acknowledges that Aristotle did not include intelligible beings in his categories. From Plotinus' perspective, this is the most serious defect in Aristotle's theory.[5] It is not just that Plotinus wants a classification of intelligible rather than sensible beings. His point is that a categorization of sensibles is impossible without the intelligibles: one cannot account for the sensibles without reference to the intelligibles.

Plotinus' requirement that a classification of beings pertain to the intelligible is diametrically opposed to Aristotle's starting-point in the *Categories*: Aristotle describes the list of categories as capturing what "each of those that are said without any combination signify" (*tōn kata mēdemian sumplokēn legomenōn hekaston … sēmainei*; *Cat.* 1b25). Therefore, he wants to find the ways in which we can talk about *things*: what can be said about them through non-combined simple expressions. For Plotinus, the term "substance" strictly speaking applies to the intelligibles and only homonymously to the sensible ones. However, since for Plotinus the Intellect and its activity is non-linguistic, we could ask how a categorization arising from linguistic expressions and our communication concerning things even could, and why it should, apply to the intelligible. In Plotinus, expressions and concepts limit discursive thought, but discursive thought cannot capture the intelligibles.

Porphyry, Plotinus' student, responds to Plotinus' criticism on similar grounds. He argues that the supposition that the categories should be a classification of being in the sense Plotinus suggests is mistaken: rather than being a classification of intelligibles, the *Categories* is a study of how words relate to the things they signify. However, Porphyry argues that the work is not *merely* a linguistic treatise, but it pertains to things to which the expressions apply. To make this point, he introduces a formulation that came to be much employed in the later commentaries. According to Porphyry, the categories apply to "simple significant words insofar as they signify things" (Porph. *in Cat.* 58,5–6, trans. Strange in Sorabji 2004: vol. 3, 61).

According to Porphyry, when a general term such as "animal" is predicated of something (e.g. Socrates), it means Socrates' essence: the immanent form that cannot be separated from the individual Socrates. Up to this point he accommodates Aristotle's claim that particulars are prior to universals: the essence means an essence of an individual. However, he does not accept the claim according to which a particular instance of a species (e.g. Socrates as a human being) should be prior to the class of all human beings. Rather, he interprets Aristotle's claim of the priority of particulars as the claim that this class is prior to the universal substance (*in Cat.* 90,29–91,2; see also 80,24–5). Further, things that are primarily signified are not the intelligibles but the sensibles (91,7–8). Porphyry's point is that linguistic expressions primarily apply to the sensibles, since they are the ones that we first encounter in perception (91,8–9). He adds that in nature the intelligibles are prior to sensibles, but contends that Aristotle must prioritize particulars since he is concerned with significant expressions (Haas 2001; see Karamanolis 2006: 313–18, esp. 317).

Simplicius, relying on Porphyry, continues on these lines. According to Simplicius, Plotinus supposes Aristotle's work to be about the genera of being (Simp. *in Cat.* 16,16–17), whereas, for Simplicius, "the concern is not with beings but with the words that signify them [i.e. beings] as significant" (16,19–21, trans. Chase in Sorabji 2004: vol. 3, 69). As such, the *Categories* must be distinguished from the *Metaphysics*, which is concerned with being as being (9,28–30). For Simplicius, the *Categories* is not a metaphysical work in the sense of discussing being as being. Rather, its subject matter is being as significant, that is, being as it is communicated in language. It is important to note that even though at first sight Simplicius' formulation seems a lot like the one given by Porphyry, the emphasis is different. Whereas for Porphyry the subject matter is *words* in so far as they signify things, for Simplicius, the *Categories* is about *things* in so far as they can be signified by words. In the general scheme of Aristotle's works, Simplicius locates the *Categories* in the logical and hence instrumental works (20,8–12).

To discuss the argument we have already sketched above according to which the Neoplatonic intelligible is not captured through language, we need to consider three figures in the Platonic commentary tradition: Iamblichus, Dexippus and Olympiodorus (see also Ch. 1, § "Porphyry, Iamblichus, Simplicius and Philoponus"). Iamblichus famously disagreed with Porphyry about the interpretation of the categories and advocated an "intellective" (*noera*) reading. In Dexippus, Simplicius does not see much originality. He claims that Dexippus added virtually nothing to what Porphyry and Iamblichus had already said (2,25–9).

In his commentary on the *Categories*, Dexippus presents the argument, coming from Porphyry, that we mentioned above against Plotinus' supposition that the categories should pertain to the intelligible. The point is that we need not expect the notion of substance, for example, to apply in the same sense to sensible and intelligible objects. This is because intelligible reality cannot be expressed in words. Strictly speaking the name "substance" applies to sensible things, and to intelligibles it can only apply metaphorically or by analogy (Dexippus *in cat.* 41,18–19).

As to the application of the categories, there is one further specification that needs to be mentioned here. We know about this through Olympiodorus, who attributes it to Iamblichus too. When Porphyry formulates the categories as being about words in so far as they signify things, Iamblichus is reported to have made the qualification of how signification works: it works through concepts (*noēmata*) (Olymp. *in Cat.* 28,25–8). However, in the context Olympiodorus does not seem to ascribe to Iamblichus the additional suggestion that the *Categories* should primarily be a work about concepts.

When it comes to Plotinus' critical questions about whether the categories are supposed to apply to the intelligible realm, Simplicius reports Iamblichus to have given a more "Pythagorean" response to this critical point (Simp. *in Cat.* 116,25–33, in Sorabji 2004: vol. 3, 71–2). On the one hand, we found above in Dexippus the argument that the categories of Aristotle primarily apply to sensible things whereas they refer to the intelligibles metaphorically. On the other hand, Simplicius reports, Iamblichus argues that the greatest kinds that Plotinus does accept as genera of intelligible substances also pertain to sensible things. However, there is a difference in how they apply in these two realms of being. In the intelligible, Iamblichus suggests, they apply simultaneously, whereas in the sensible realm, which is spatiotemporal, contrarieties such as movement and rest can only apply consecutively. Furthermore, Iamblichus also extends the scope of the Aristotelian categories, for example, the category of "where" to the intelligible realm (Simp. *in Cat.* 362,16–363,3, in Sorabji 2004: vol. 3, 75–6). We shall discuss his position briefly in § "Other categories: examples", below.

Unity of substance

Plotinus' argument, according to which the categories do not satisfy Aristotle's own demands of what being a genus requires, come in the form of criticism of the individual categories. The category of substance is perhaps the most important instance of such criticism. As we saw above, Plotinus argues against the idea that the categories could be genera of being by referring to Aristotle's own supposition that there is no priority and posteriority among one genus: a horse is no more nor less an animal than a cow. Another argument he presents with respect to the category of substance is that it cannot form a genus, since the same definition does not apply to all substances.

In Aristotle, Plotinus argues, all of the following should be fitted into the same category of substance: intelligible substance, matter, form and the composition of matter and form. According to Plotinus, it is clear that not all of these can have the same definition. To say that they form a single category would, according to Plotinus, be as good as calling the family of Heraclids (i.e. descendants of Heracles) "a single thing not as something common to all but as deriving from a single ancestor" (*Enn.* 6.1.3,1–7, trans. Haas in Sorabji 2004: vol. 3, 69). For Plotinus, the unity among the intelligible substance, matter, form and the combination of matter and form is based on the supposition that intelligible substance is the primary one and functions as an origin or source from which matter, form and the combination of these in the sensible realm are derived. If this kind of unity is considered to be sufficient to constitute a category, then there is a danger that everything collapses into the category of substance. This is because, as Aristotle supposes, everything else is dependent on substance: qualities, quantities and relations, for example, exist only as qualities, quantities and relations *of substances* (6.1.3,1–7).

We saw above that Dexippus appeals to the idea that intelligible substance is substance only metaphorically. However, he also offers another argument. The crux of the argument is that the *Categories* does not even intend to discuss the intelligible substance because it is a treatise written for young people, who can only follow simpler discussions, not advanced theories of what is fully real, that is, intelligible. Therefore, Dexippus concludes that Plotinus is not correct in expecting that the work will pertain to real questions of ontology, that is, classification of intelligible being (*in Cat.* 40,19–25; cf. Porph. *in Cat.* 56,28–9, 59,31–3, 57,6–12).

Here we see an interesting example of how the commentators understood the categories as a primary or preliminary classification of lower kinds of beings, subordinated to a superior hierarchy or structure of the intelligible realm. Porphyry notes (*in Cat.* 59,17–33) that this interpretation relies on a long tradition within the Peripatetic school itself (he mentions Boethus, Herminus and Alexander as proponents of such a reading). The move, which in the Peripatetic tradition was of course not intended to harmonize between Plato and Aristotle, allowed the commentators to do so.

If we ask what the possible merits and shortcomings of such a reading are, we encounter a fundamental difference in understanding reality. If we suppose, as Aristotle did in his criticism against Plato, that the structure of being must be the structure of sensible reality, it becomes difficult to see why we would need an additional higher hierarchy. Aristotle himself makes a distinction between the intelligibles and sensibles in the *De anima*, but this does not mean that we would need to separate between two classes of things, one for sensibles and another for intelligibles. Rather, there is only one class of things, which can be perceived or grasped intellectually. When perceived, their sensible aspect is cognized. When grasped, it is the intelligibility of the same things that comes to be actualized in our soul. Therefore, the commentators' tendency to understand Aristotle's philosophy as analysing sensible reality seems reasonable, even though Aristotle would not take it as being secondary to a higher intelligible realm.

Let us now return to Plotinus' argument against the unity of the category of substance. If intelligible substance, matter, form and the combination of matter and form are all lumped together, Plotinus argues, the only unity this group can have is that they all derive from the same origin, the intelligible substance. This argument is based on a characteristically Plotinian understanding of ontological priority, where the intelligible realm is primary with respect to the sensible one in the sense that the latter somehow originates or emanates from the former. This does not mean a temporal sequence, but that the sensible realm is a by-product or result of the Intellect's internal activity.

Given that Plotinus' argument is based on his own understanding of the priority relations within the items he classifies as substances, we can ask whether the argument would function in a similar manner in Aristotle. It is true that for Aristotle as well the category of substance is primary. However, the threat that all the other categories should collapse into that of substance is perhaps not a threat or concern in Aristotle. Even though he would certainly concede that qualities exist only in so far as they are qualities of some substance (there is no whiteness without a thing that is white), this does not mean that all qualities should collapse into substances: it is another thing to be a horse than to be white, and this is the main point of the whole distinction between different categories.

When it comes to matter and form, these two notions do not appear in the *Categories* as specifying the notion of substance. We could say that whereas in the *Categories* the question "What is it?" terminates when we arrive at individual beings determined by their species (this human being, this horse), in the *Metaphysics* Aristotle takes his analysis beyond this point. He starts to ask, for example, what it is that makes these individual beings the kinds of things they are. Individual beings are in Aristotle's logical works characterized by the condition that they can be subjects of predication (Socrates is a human being) but not predicates (except in the accidental sense when it is said that this approaching thing is Socrates – which is not a case of genuine predication). In *Metaphysics* Book VII (1028a26ff.), Aristotle pushes his questions further and asks what ultimately is a subject (*hupokeimenon*): what is it that underlies all predication? Through these new questions he arrives at the notions of matter and form. Form is what makes the thing the thing it is, and matter is the ultimate subject of predication. The individual substances of the *Categories* are thus analysed into more specific metaphysical components.

Therefore, in so far as these are the criteria on the basis of which Aristotle comes to analyse form and matter as being candidates for substance in the *Metaphysics*, Plotinus is correct in suspecting that the two have distinct definitions (cf. *Enn.* 6.1.3,1–7, 6.3.8,19–37).[6] However, the mere existence of different definitions does not show difference in genus: human beings and horses have distinct definitions and yet belong to the same genus, since both of them have a common part in their definition. The possibility thus remains that the criteria according to which form and matter are substances in Aristotle have something in common.

Other categories: examples

In addition to his specific criticism of the category of substance, Plotinus attacks some non-substantial categories by the following more general complaints. Either some categories are distinguished without justification, or a category is reducible to another. One such case is Aristotle's classification of time and place into the category of quantity on the one hand (*Cat.* 4b22–5) and his postulating distinct categories for "when" and "where" on the other. The question of whether this move of Aristotle's is justified was widely debated in antiquity.

Plotinus was not content with the overall scheme that Aristotle applied to spatiotemporal notions, and he presented various arguments against it on different levels of generality. One of his main qualms was the following: time and place should not be classified into the category of quantity, because quantity is something that can be assigned to time and place when they are measured, but the measures do not belong to time and place intrinsically (*Enn.* 6.1.33,6–10). Further, time and place are not sufficiently distinct from "when" and "where", hence these should not be separated into another category: the unity among discrete and continuous quantities is already too weak for Plotinus (6.1.4).

To start from the category of where, Plotinus argues that the correct classification for it should be along with relatives: things the being of which consists of being related to another thing. According to Plotinus, "if we say that this man is here, we are generating a certain relationship of this man in this and of what receives to what is received" (6.1.14,8–24, trans. Sorabji in Sorabji 2004: vol. 3, 96). This would mean that to say that this man is here creates a new relation between the man and this place. Therefore, Plotinus argues, "where" can only be understood as a relative and it cannot be a category of its own.

Simplicius replies to Plotinus on the basis of Aristotle's definition of relatives (Simp. *in Cat.* 360,7–20) by referring to a condition of reciprocity that Aristotle uses to define relatives (Arist. *Cat.* 6b28–35). Relatives are such things, the being of which consists in being related to something else, *and* this relatedness reciprocates (*Cat.* 8a31–2). Being a slave is relative, since (i) slaves can only exist with respect to masters, and (ii) masters only exist in relation to slaves and hence the condition of reciprocity is fulfilled. If we now apply this condition of relatives to Plotinus' suggestion that "where" is a relative, it should, according to Simplicius, entail that there is a reciprocal relation between the man and where he is, and hence also between the place where the man is and the man (Simp. *in Cat.* 360,13–16).

Simplicius allows that, in some cases, accounts of where something is can be relative in this sense: for example, if a thing x is on the upper side of some y, then y is relative to x in the sense of being on the underside of x (360,15–21). However, this reciprocity only applies to cases in which where something is is given in inherently relative terms; such relativity is not a universal property of locations. We might agree with Plotinus, as Simplicius does (349,16–17), that in some sense "here" can be said to be a place for the man who is here now and hence there is some reciprocity between a man and where he is. However, if we apply Aristotle's second definition of relatives (*Cat.* 8a31–2), being relative means a stronger dependence between the relative and what it is related to: the being of a relative must consist of being related to another thing. It seems clear that a place (here) is not dependent in this sense on the man being at that place (here), at least not in the same way as being a master is dependent on being a master of a slave, or something being underneath is dependent on something else being above it.

Even if we agreed with Simplicius about this argument, we might still be curious to know why time and place and "when" and "where" are separated into distinct categories. Why are the former quantities and the latter two independent categories? One suggestion might be the one rejected by Plotinus: time and place can be measured, whereas when and where cannot. Porphyry, in his surviving short commentary on the *Categories* in question-and-answer form, offers exactly this solution. He is explicit on the point with respect to time: "Time is a quantity because it is conceived as having extension, and because it is measured by a number of a certain amount, for example a number of hours, days, months, years" (Porph. *in Cat.* 103,30–32, trans. Strange 1992).[7] We can illustrate the point with the idea that categories are related to questions we can ask about things. It would make sense to ask about the measure of time and place: "How much time?" is a sensible question. "How much place?" is not, but it might translate to one if we take it in the sense "How much room?" By contrast, "How much where?" and "How much when?" are nonsensical.

By contrast, if we apply the second alternative according to which Aristotle's categories can be arrived at, namely to ask "What is it?" about distinct kinds of things, the difference between time and place on the one hand and "when" and "where" on the other becomes difficult. Even though it is a distinct question to ask when or where something is and to ask about time and place, the answers to the questions "When?" and "Where?" ultimately seem to lead to time and place. If we ask where he is, we can answer "in the Lyceum". However, if we keep asking what this in-the-Lyceum is, we end up with the answer: place or, at best, location.[8] The answer "location" will not delay the game for long, since if we ask "What is a location?" we must answer that it is a kind of place. Therefore, our attempt to keep the category of "where" separate from place in the category of quantity, from this second point of view, seems to fail.

If we now ask about the status of "when" and "where" as categories, Porphyry notes that Aristotle had nothing to say about them (Porph. *in Cat.* 142,6–8; there is a lacuna in Aristotle at that point). Ironically, when explaining the point, Porphyry's text breaks off as well (142,14). Simplicius (*in Cat.* 297,28ff.) and Boethius (262D–263A) report the contents in some detail, but already the few lines that have been preserved from Porphyry give us an outline. Porphyry's interlocutor (a student) denies that the categories of "when" and "where" should be categories of independently existing things; this much seems obvious, since only substances can exist independently. However, Porphyry questions their independence *as categories* and makes them parasitic on quantity, that is, time and place in that category. Therefore, Porphyry makes the sensible observation that it is difficult to see the justification for classifying "when" and "where" as independent categories. He says that the same applies to the category of having something.

One very different reaction to the problem of spatiotemporal categories is Iamblichus' so-called intellective interpretation. At first sight, it would seem that the spatiotemporal categories are particularly ill suited to organize the intelligible realm, since the intelligible is beyond time and space. However, Iamblichus, as reported by Simplicius, is not discouraged by such initial appearances and proceeds to argue that in fact the category of "where" can be applied in the intelligible realm as well. However, to do so requires that we also understand ordinary place from a more comprehensive point of view.

According to Iamblichus, place as understood in the ordinary manner belongs to the wider genus of containment (Simp. *in Cat.* 362,16–363,3), and ordinary place is not the only way in which something can be contained. Further, even though we might initially tend to think that containment is just pure spatial extension, this idea is misleading. Even the dimensions of the universe are not inactive (*argon*), but *actively sustain* everything that is in them by a certain power that Iamblichus characterizes as uplifting (*anegeirein*). When we understand place as a subspecies of containment with active uplifting power, we can, according to Iamblichus, also grasp why the intellectual soul is said to be a place for rational principles (*logoi*): it contains them and maintains them by an active power. Therefore, Iamblichus interprets the expression according to which the intellect is a place for intelligibles (also discussed by Aristotle *de An.* III 4, 429a26–9) non-metaphorically: the intellect contains within itself the principles (*logoi*) and this containment is in an important respect the same as the containment peculiar to a thing's spatial place. Iamblichus' interpretation of place as active containment also involves the supposition that place is living (*zōtikos*; 363,2) and rational (*logikos*), and it contains the rational principles, not as one thing can contain a different thing, but as something that is the same.[9]

Finally, we need to mention one common argument against Aristotle's categories, namely that the number of the categories is arbitrary. According to Simplicius, there are three basic kinds of such arguments. One is that the number of the categories is excessive, another that it is deficient and a third that some genera have been introduced in the place of others (*in Cat.* 62,30–33, trans. Chase in Sorabji 2004: vol. 3, 62). We have discussed the last of these points above. As to the criticism related to the number of categories, the accusation that there are too many is more common than that there are too few. Often those who introduce additional ones only do so for the sake of argument: to show the absurdity of postulating as many categories as Aristotle had done (e.g. Plot. *Enn.* 6.1.14,20–24). Of those who wanted to reduce the number of categories Plotinus was ready to accept five in the realm of sensible beings: four of Aristotle's ten, namely, substance, quantity, quality and relative, and a category of his own, change (*Enn.* 6.3). As a result, the number of his categories of the sensible came to match the number of five great kinds (being, sameness, difference, motion and rest) in the intelligible realm.

In fact, Aristotle himself seems to have initiated the project of cutting down the number of the categories, without highlighting it with critical arguments. The full list of ten appears only once outside the *Categories*, in *Topics* I 9. The only difference from the *Categories* is that in the *Topics* the name for the category of substance is in its interrogative form "What is it?" (*ti esti*). In works other than these, Aristotle explicitly lists those of substance, quantity and quality, and the remainder are given the vague title "and the rest of those that are said in each of the other categories" (e.g. *Met.* VII 1, 1028a2–3). This does not mean that he would have entirely forgotten about the rest of the categories, but it illustrates Aristotle's tendency to concentrate on those of substance, quantity and quality.

***

Let us now briefly conclude our discussion about the *Categories*. For Aristotle, one important metaphysical upshot of the *Categories* is the following: what a substance most fully is and what exists independently is an individual being of a certain kind (a this-something, *tode ti*, such as an individual human being or an individual horse). In a secondary sense, the category of substances also contains species (e.g. human being and horse), which cannot exist independently of their instances. By contrast, this is not at all the conclusion we could draw from the commentaries. Rather, the commentators writing after Plotinus tend to suppose that the categories deal with sensible things (individual beings), because they are the ones that primarily function as points of reference for language. Metaphysics is about being as being, whereas the *Categories* is about beings in so far as they are signified by simple non-combined expressions. Therefore, the commentators writing on the *Categories* rather supposed that what is most fully real is only found in the intelligible realm, not in individual sensible beings.

Form, universal, substance

Questions of universals, questions of forms

In today's handbooks of metaphysics, one often finds introductions where the stage is set for Plato and Aristotle in terms of universals. According to this common picture, Plato was a Platonist about universals and supposed properties such as largeness to be primary to their individual instances and to exist independently of them. Aristotle is presented as challenging Plato's view and denying that universals should exist independently of individual instances. It is undoubtedly the case that Aristotle criticized Plato's view; Plato had already done so himself in the *Parmenides*. Further, something important is grasped if the divergence of opinion is described in terms of universals and particulars and their mutual relation of priority. However, to say that the debate between Plato and Aristotle was about universals and particulars *and nothing more*, would be misleading. In any case, "universal" (*to katholou*) was not the crucial technical notion around which the debate centred; it was the notion of form (*eidos, idea*).[10]

In the middle dialogues (e.g. *Phaedo* 77a–79e) Plato introduces forms to respond to several distinct questions. One of them is to explain why individual things such as sticks and stones that we perceive can be large even though nothing in our perceptual environment is really large as such. Everything we consider as being large is large only in relation to something, whereas in relation to something else it is small. Plato can be large when compared to Theaetetus but small when compared to an athlete. If it were for these perceptual instances alone, we could not even form the notion of largeness and understand what largeness is, because nothing we perceive is large in the sense of not being small in relation to anything. It is correct to say that when introducing the forms (e.g. the form of largeness) to answer these queries, Plato is introducing universals as existent: the form of largeness exists and it is common to all perceptible large things in so far as they partake in the same form of largeness. However, Plato's main concern is not just to ask whether largeness as a universal *exists* apart from the particulars. He is asking what *explains* the imperfect largeness in perceptible things and how we can come to understand largeness even though we do not perceive it as such.

The link between forms on the one hand and cause and explanation on the other is strong in the *Phaedo*, where Socrates embarks on a separate excursus on this topic (*Phaedo* 96a–99e, discussed in Ch. 4, § "Teleology: background"). In this excursus, the forms are identified as causes: perceptible things can be said to be beautiful to the extent that they take part in the form of beauty. In Aristotle, forms have an important constitutive role in making things the kinds of things they are. The view is preserved in Alexander.[11] In short, both in Plato and Aristotle, forms function as causes. The forms also are objects of knowledge (see e.g. Fine 1993) and they are intelligible. Their intelligibility does not mean that we create forms when considering reality from an abstract point of view. Rather, intelligibility is seen as an intrinsic property of reality: reality as such is intelligible, because its general structure is constituted by forms that can be understood. Therefore, even if we formulated the question of universals as concerning essential sortal terms, this would give an overtly weak insight into the functions that forms have in the ancient discussion. The constitutive and causative role of the forms does not become clear if we claim that forms are universals and nothing more. Therefore, rather than asking how the commentators answered the question of universals, we shall ask how they answered the question of what forms are.

In fact, for Aristotle, the central metaphysical question (or the central question for first philosophy) is not even the question of forms. Rather, according to Aristotle (*Met.* VII 1, 1028b3–4), the question is one that has exercised the minds of both old thinkers and those of his time, namely, "what is being (*to on*) and, more specifically, what is substance (*ousia*)?" It is true that one of the initial responses to this question Aristotle mentions in *Metaphysics* VII 3 is "the universal" (*to katholou*), but he denies that it could be correct (*Met.* VII 13). Therefore, for Aristotle the crucial question of metaphysics is not the question of universals but the question of what being or substance is, and to say that universals are substances would not be a correct answer to this question. Even though Aristotle denies that substance should be identical with universals, this does not yet entail that he would deny that forms can be universal in the sense of being species forms rather than forms of individuals. But even species forms could not be reduced to modern universals. To make the point once more, for some authors today the question of universals boils down to Peirce's distinction between types and tokens. If we say that Plato's and Aristotle's claim that there are forms would be in an important way similar to the distinction between types and tokens with the confirmation that types are real (in some interpretation of the word "real"), we shall seriously understate or underestimate the role that forms play in the ancient metaphysical debates.

From the point of view of the Aristotelian categories, universals are most naturally connected with properties. By contrast, as we saw above, the crucial metaphysical question for Aristotle, the central puzzle in his first philosophy, is the question of what being (i.e. substance) is. This means that properties are from non-substantial categories (qualitative and quantitative properties, for example) and hence cannot answer the question of substance. There were some commentators, such as the early Boethus of Sidon, Andronicus' student from the first century BCE, who argued that form is a quality, but this interpretation was by no means dominant in the later commentaries.[12]

There is an additional aspect that distinguishes the question of forms from the question of universals. If we supposed that the two questions are identical, then we should also accept that if these questions were answered in the affirmative essentially the same point would be made. According to a standard account, the question of universals is a question of whether universals exist or not. However, answering the question of whether the forms exist or not in the affirmative is not simply the claim that universals exist, because the forms have much more active functions in the ancient metaphysics than the universals of our time do. But this is not the only reason. In the ancient commentaries, the question about forms is not simply a question of their existence. There is broad acceptance that forms exist. The point is, rather, to articulate what this claim amounts to.

Universals in the commentaries

Even though the question of forms is not identical with the question of universals, this does not mean that Plato, Aristotle and the commentators would not have addressed the question of universals. They all surely did. Aristotle had characterized a universal in *On Interpretation* as follows: "By 'universal' (*katholou*) I mean what is of a nature to be predicated of several things and by 'particular' (*kath' hekaston*) what is not" (17a39–40, trans. Sorabji in Sorabji 2004: vol. 3, 130). Aristotle's formulation leaves open the possibility that a universal actually need not be predicated from many things; it just has to be of such a nature that it *could* be predicated of many things. This qualification was important for Alexander, whose overall interpretation of universals has been characterized as being deflationary, that is, as diminishing the importance of universals (Sorabji 2004: vol. 3, 129). In the *Questions* originating from Alexander's school it is said, for example, that "the universal is not a thing in itself" (*Quaest.* 1.11, 23,25–6, trans. Sharples in Sorabji 2004: vol. 3, 154). However, as we saw above, what is a universal (*to katholou*) or what is common (*koinon*) is not identical with the form, and hence Alexander's deflationary statements about universals do not necessarily imply a deflationary reading of forms or essences. For Alexander, a form or nature is actualized in individual instances and does not exist as separate from them, except as a universal concept in thought abstracted from the particulars (Alex.Aphr. *de An.* 90,6–7). Those universal notions or concepts are dependent on thought for their existence in the sense that they are not (existent) when they are not thought of.[13]

Therefore, for Alexander there are natures and forms of things and those natures or forms can be common to several individuals, or even several species (as genera are, see Alex.Aphr. *in Top.* 355,18–24), but it is not necessary for such natures to be universal, because there are natures with one single instance, for example, the sun, the moon or the universe (Alexander, according to Simp. *in Cat.* 85,13–17, in Sorabji 2004: vol. 3, 154–5). However, this does not mean that, for Alexander, forms should be individual either: for example, that I as the author of this book and you as its reader should have different natures.[14] The natures may or may not be shared by several individuals, and hence cannot be defined by reference to universality or individuality but to their role in constituting a thing's essence. Even though Alexander affirms that natures of things are real, he by no means wishes to claim that the natures should exist as separate from their instances. He denies that they could. The form of a human being, even though being universal or general in the sense of being a form of a species and belonging to several individuals, is existent in the sense of being realized *only* in individual human beings. It is not individual in the sense of being different as a form (e.g. form of me or you) in these instances; it is only different numerically. But it is dependent on the instances in the sense of being incapable of independent or separate existence.

When discussing the question of whether individual instances of a species are prior to the species (as Aristotle suggests in the *Categories*, chapter 5) or the other way round, Simplicius introduces an interpretation he attributes to Iamblichus. The interpretation is based on Aristotle's distinction between what is prior in nature and what is prior to us (cf. Chapter 3). According to Iamblichus, individual instances are prior to us, that is, we come to know them first in perception, but this does not mean that they should be prior in nature. Rather, it is the species that are prior in nature (Iamblichus according to Simp. *in Cat.* 82,16–22). As opposed to Iamblichus, Simplicius notes, Alexander had suggested that the individual instance is prior both in nature and to us. Simplicius does not specify what this means, but most probably the idea is to claim that an instance is prior in existence, that is, that species could not exist without their instances, and that they are prior to us in the sense that we come to know them first in perception. Simplicius' comment on Alexander's suggestion is that this supposition is mere obstinacy on Alexander's part: he does not prove that this is so but just assumes this to be the case (82,22–6).

An influential distinction concerning the ways in which something can be universal was made by Porphyry, and the distinction was later endorsed by Ammonius, Simplicius' teacher (Ammonius *On Porphyry's Introduction* [*in Isag.*] 41,10–42) and Elias (*in Isag.* 48,15–49,23) (see also Karamanolis 2006: 315; Lloyd 1990: 67–8). Porphyry emphasizes that the *Categories* is concerned with words in so far as they signify things. A general term, such as "animal", can either be predicated or not be predicated of something. When predicated of something, for example, in the statement "Socrates is an animal", it means the essence of Socrates as an animal. This essence only exists in the instances of that essence, that is, in individual beings; they do not have independent existence as such. In thought essences can exist as abstracted (*in Cat.* 91,2–7; *in Harm.* 14,1–14), but this does not amount to independent existence. In his treatise on Ptolemy's *Harmonics* (Porph. *in Harm.* 11,31–3), Porphyry argues that the predicate "animal" as an essence means immanent forms in both Plato and Aristotle.[15] Outside predication, "animal" refers to animality as a transcendent Platonic form. This form of animality is prior in existence to individual animals and accounts for their existence. Therefore, Porphyry distinguishes between (a) animality as the transcendent form, (b) "animal" as an abstracted universal concept, and (c) the immanent form or essence of an animal realized in particular animals. It seems that, for Porphyry, (a) is not a universal in the sense Aristotle defines universality (i.e. in the sense of being predicated of many particulars), but is rather to be understood as the common cause for the existence of all animal species and their individual instances.

Simplicius presents a rather similar classification when he considers what is meant when something is said to be common (*koinon*) to several individuals (*in Cat.* 82,35–83,20). As Porphyry had done, Simplicius also points out that being common can be understood in three distinct ways. According to Simplicius, something is common when: (i) it transcends the individuals in the sense of being the cause of their common nature (*koinotēs*) such as animal-itself; (ii) it is a common cause of each animal species, which resides in the animals; and (iii) it is a common feature established in thought through abstraction. The first kind of universal (i) corresponds to Porphyry's (a), the second (ii) to Porphyry's (c) and (iii) to Porphyry's (b). However, by contrast to what we found in Porphyry, when describing (ii) in this connection, Simplicius does not speak about immanent forms.

The first common cause in Simplicius' list is not common as opposed to individual instances: it is common as opposed to species. The second one is a cause for the instances of the same species to be the kinds of things they are and this cause, according to Simplicius, resides in the instances. The last mentioned is, supposedly as compared to the first two common causes, later generated (*husterogenēs*). Simplicius attributes to Alexander the view that such a common feature only exists – in so far as it can even be said to exist – in thought as posterior to the individuals from which it is abstracted. However, Simplicius is not representing Alexander's view accurately. As we saw above, Alexander did not deny animal species forms (Simplicius' class (ii)); he just emphasized that species natures only exist in the individual instances. Further, he denied that it would be necessary for natures *to be common*, but he did not deny that some natures are common in the sense of being species natures.

The important point in Simplicius' classification is that he identifies the first two kinds of common features as common causes. Therefore, here what is common to several individuals, or to several individual species, is not just a property that they happen to share; rather, they have common causes as species and as genera. Here again we see the general supposition that the discussion of universals is related to a discussion of explaining why some individuals are the same in kind or have similar properties.

Another interpretation of universals (i.e. what is common) is found in Proclus (*in Parm.* 880,3–11). Proclus is searching for an answer to the question of what is common to the Platonically interpreted form and the many instances that are referred to by the same name (e.g. large things and the form of largeness). Proclus denies that sharing the same name could provide sufficient grounds for the unity of these two. Some common element must be found in them. However, when going on to identify the common element, he is no longer concerned with what is common to the instances *and* the form. Rather the question has become what is common to the many instances. This common element is that they are derived from the same source or focused towards some one thing (*aph' henos, pros hen*).

As to the question of the existence of universals, Porphyry mentions it in his *Introduction* to the *Categories* (*Isagoge*), but he says that he is not willing to go deeper into it in an introductory work. Even there, he is not exactly talking about universals or common things (*ta katholou, ta koina*) but about species and genera that are central organizing concepts in the whole work. The questions concerning species and genera that he leaves out of the discussion are whether (a) they subsist (*huphistēmi*), or (b) depend on thoughts. Further questions that the first alternative raises are, if they subsist, whether the species and genera are corporeal or incorporeal and whether they are separable from the instances or not. These questions Porphyry formulates but leaves unanswered. (*Isag.* 1,9–16; see trans. Barnes 2003).

In his commentary on the *Categories*, Porphyry makes a similar rejection, now explicitly with respect to the notion of universals (*ta katholou*; *in Cat.* 75,24). However, he does return to the topic later on in the treatise (90,12–91,3) in relation to the question of priority between primary and secondary substances, that is, individual instances of a species and the species itself. The criterion by which priority is determined in the context is the following:

> *a* is prior to *b* if and only if the elimination of *a* entails the elimination of *b*.

For example, animal is prior to human being because the elimination of all animals entails the elimination of human beings as well. Now the problem is that, in the framework of the *Categories*, the primary substances – that is, individual instances such as human beings – are supposed to be prior to species: the existence of a species depends on there being instances of that species. This seems to create a contradiction between the criterion of priority by elimination and the statement that individual instances are prior to the species and genera to which they belong. If Socrates is eliminated, the human species will not be eliminated, because other members of the species (e.g. Plato) can still exist. How, then, can individuals be supposed to be prior to the species?

The crux of Porphyry's response to the problem is the following. To say that individual instances are prior to the species in the sense in which the individual instances are meant to be prior to the species in the *Categories* is not meant as the claim that the elimination of any individual instance *alone* would eliminate the whole species. Rather, the claim is that if there are no instances *at all*, the species will be eliminated as well. That is, for example, that if no individual instances of the human species existed, the species would not exist either. Therefore, according to Porphyry, species are dependent on the existence of individual instances, but they are not dependent on the existence of all and every individual instance separately. This is a reasonable point to make regarding the fact that human individuals are mortal: a death of an individual does not mean extinction of the species – only the death of all individuals.

225

Iamblichus, who studied with Porphyry, refused to follow his teacher on this interpretation (Simp. *in Cat.* 82,1–83,29; trans. Strange 1992: 81 n.176). When discussing Alexander's position above, we saw that Iamblichus brought in the distinction between priority to us and priority in nature. Whereas Iamblichus concedes that individual instances are prior to us (i.e. in the sense that we first come to know them through perception), the species are prior in nature, because the individuals are organized under universals (Iamblichus, as reported by Simp. *in Cat.* 82,18–19). Simplicius himself also denies Alexander's order of priority; for Simplicius universals (*koina*), species and genera (*eidē, genē*) are prior in nature to individuals (85,1–9).

Despite the divergences of opinion concerning the relations of priority between what is universal and what is particular, there was one formulation of the types of universals that was widely accepted in the commentaries and it was influential in the transmission of classical philosophy into the Latin West. The formulation is found in Ammonius and it seems to have been standard in his school in Alexandria. According to the distinction, there are three kinds of universals: (1) before the many (*pro tōn pollōn*); (2) in the many (*en tois pollois*); and (3) after the many (*epi tois pollois*) (Ammon. *in Isag.* 41,17–20, in Sorabji 2004: vol. 3, 137). The distinction is also found in Proclus, who chronologically precedes Ammonius. Type (1), a universal before the many, corresponds to the transcendent forms, for example, animality-itself (Porphyry's (a) above): such universals are prior to all the particulars because they pre-exist them. The demiurge uses the transcendent forms in creating the world. Type (2) is the animality realized in particular instances (cf. Porphyry's (c) and Simplicius' (ii) above). Type (3) represents the universals that are "after the many", when the notion of animality is formed in our minds after we have perceived the many particular animals. They correspond to Porphyry's (b) and Simplicius' (iii) above.

The important point in the threefold distinction just quoted is that it accommodates both the Platonic transcendent universals and Aristotelian universals in matter as well as later-generated (*husterogenēs*; in Ammon. *in Isag.* 41,17–20)[16] notions in the mind. Therefore, rather than opting for either a Platonic or Aristotelian alternative or downgrading universals into mere notions in the mind, the distinction allowed the writers to accept all three kinds.

What do the forms do?

When we now move to consider what kinds of questions motivated the postulation of forms, we need to distinguish between Alexander's Aristotelian approach and the later commentators for whom Platonic and Neoplatonic influence is significant. For Alexander, the starting-point is in concrete individual things of which it must be asked what makes them the things they are. To this question the answer is: their enmattered form that guides and regulates what happens to things of that kind. The constitutive activity characteristic of form has to take place somewhere and to structure something, and this is how the notion of matter comes in. Form and the determinations it implies cannot have concrete being, unless they are determinations *of something*, that is, matter. Whereas form is the constitutive and defining principle, matter provides the concrete setting in which the form can be realized. In addition to being enmattered, the form has yet another mode of being, namely when it comes to be understood by someone; then the form becomes actualized in a human intellect without the matter. For the Neoplatonic authors, these questions are not sufficient. They take the enquiry further and ask how and why it was that the things came into being in the first place. Transcendent forms and forms as understood by the demiurge answer this question: the transcendent forms function as models for the divine artificer, whereas the divine artificer's understanding of them gives them creative force.

For Alexander, as we have seen, the forms are in individual things. These forms need not be shared by several individuals, but, in the case that there are several individuals, they have the same form, which is only numerically different in them. So far we know that in an individual thing x there is the form of x (e.g. of a human being). But what does the form do there? We have seen above that it is not merely instantiated; that would be too weak. To understand the function of form, it is useful to contrast it with another metaphysical component of the thing, its matter. These two basic metaphysical notions are of course familiar to us from Aristotle's *Metaphysics* VII.

For Alexander, the respective functions of form and matter seem quite clear. Form is the formative or constitutive principle of a thing that determines its essential properties. An essence, in turn, is what it is for a thing to be the thing it is, that is, what it is for a human being to be a human being. A definition of a human being, "a terrestrial biped rational animal", for example, is in accordance with the essence or nature of a human being (cf. *Quaest.* 1.3, 8,12–17, in Sorabji 2004: vol. 3, 153). If this is a correct definition for a human being, then a human being's nature is to be a terrestrial biped rational animal (cf. Alex.Aphr. *in Top.* 46,6–14; Rashed 2007). The form determines the nature of a thing and matter individuates it into particular individuals (Alex.Aphr. *de An.* 85,15–20).

On the one hand, form for Alexander can be understood as a series of essential properties or determinations that can come to be expressed in a definition (terrestrial, biped, rational and so on). These determinations make it possible for a compound of matter to come into being since all things need to have properties and qualifications; matter without these cannot exist. On the other hand, the form is an efficient principle that moulds and informs matter so that it comes to be individualized into comprehensible units existing in time and space.[17]

One might wonder how it is possible that the form performs such a central role in the individuation of things when Alexander also advocates what has later come to be called the traditional interpretation of Aristotle: that matter is the individuating principle of things (Alex.Aphr. *in Metaph.* 215,15–18). This latter declaration indicates that the form as a species form (e.g. of a human being) cannot constitute an individual human being as an individual, since it only provides the species characteristics. To the extent that the species forms and the essential properties of the species are concerned, Plato and Socrates cannot be distinguished from each other; they are both rational animals. To distinguish between Plato and Socrates, Alexander seems to be saying, two separate chunks of matter are needed in order for these properties to be actualized in a thing that consists of matter and form.

Even though Alexander indicates that matter individuates composite things, form is doing important work here as well. This is because matter cannot even exist as separate individual chunks *without a form*, that is, all identifiable and individuated chunks of matter already contain some form. Therefore, for a piece of matter to be singled out as an individual, it needs to come to be singled out as an individual *of a certain kind*. This holds not only for more complicated material individuals such as animals, but also for very simple material things such as stones. Individuality requires matter, but in order to exist matter must be determined by a form.[18] A similar problem is raised with respect to Aristotle's *Metaphysics* VII. Michael Frede and Günther Patzig (1988) challenge the traditional interpretation and argue that Aristotle advocates a theory of individual forms in *Metaphysics* VII.[19]

In an individual enmattered being, the form is the cause for the thing being the kind of thing it is. It is a metaphysical element in the compound of matter and form that determines what kind of material is needed in order for that kind of a thing to be. This means that those kinds of things cannot exist without their forms. This supposition originates from the basic Aristotelian conviction according to which existence is always existence of some definite things, not just existence without any specification. Further, the form regulates the material interaction in the body and the way in which an individual being of that kind exists. For example, a human being grows from a foetus and, having been born, continues its growth into maturity. In this process, the way in which the body utilizes nutrition to make the organism grow and, possibly, to produce like offspring is all determined by form. This means that the form explains how a thing of a certain kind is a thing of that particular kind, that is, how a human being is a human being and not something else. To some extent, the enmattered form for Aristotelians such as Alexander can be compared to how the DNA functions in living organisms understood in modern terms (analogy from Quarantotto 2005). However, if we take the supposition that a form is a species form strictly, as Alexander seems to do, then the form deviates from the DNA because DNA also contains elements that are specific only in some human families, for example.

Aristotle did develop theories of inheritance (in his *Generation of Animals* Book IV) in his biological works, where he also paid heed to the fact that children often resemble their grandparents. This means that he tried to explain certain more specific aspects of what kind of regularities there are in human reproduction that surpass the effects of a species form. However, for some reason Aristotle's biological works were not frequently commented on. We only have a late commentary on the *Parts of Animals* by Michael of Ephesus, but none of our main figures in this volume produced a commentary on the *Generation of Animals*. Therefore, we need to refrain from developing the analogy between form and DNA in the commentaries any further. In any case, it can be noted that there is a rather basic difference between the notions of form and DNA, since forms are abstract and immaterial metaphysical factors, whereas DNA is a specific material structure within living organisms. Nonetheless, if we generalize and take the point of reference to be not the material DNA helix itself but the information content of that helix, then it is not equally clear how easy a distinction we can draw between the two notions of DNA and enmattered form.

Alexander's account of forms is in contrast with those found in the late Neoplatonic commentaries. The Neoplatonic commentators have a tendency to postulate a greater variety of forms to perform the explanatory functions required of forms. One type of form that many of them accept is roughly correspondent to the forms as understood by Alexander: enmattered forms in individuals – the immanent forms we mentioned above. The important difference seems to be the one already discussed: whereas Simplicius (e.g. *in Cael.* 275,2–8, in Sorabji 2004: vol. 3, 155), for example, supposes forms in matter to be necessarily universal common natures (i.e. to be shared by several individuals), we saw that Alexander did not require this (e.g. the sun has a unique nature determined by an enmattered form).

However, the Neoplatonic authors did not consider immanent forms as sufficient for fulfilling the requirements that were set on forms. As noted above, the immanent forms were not even considered to be the primary forms there are. Rather, the existence of individual things with their immanent forms requires that the forms pre-exist in time or at least have a primary mode of being. Such pre-existence or priority can be understood in several ways. One way to do so is to relate the pre-existence of forms to cosmology, following Plato's *Timaeus*. Another influential framework is Plotinus' hierarchy of being involving emanation on different hypostases (briefly presented in Ch. 3, § "*Epistēmē*: proofs and principles"). On all hypostases, the internal activity of a particular hypostasis creates another level of reality through its external activity. For example, the universal Intellect's eternal intellectual activity produces the intelligible structure of the sensible world in this way.

For Alexander the central metaphysical question that is answered by the notion of form is what it is that makes things the kinds of things they are. By contrast, the Neoplatonic commentators did not pose just this question. Rather, as mentioned above, they wanted to know how and why it is that the concrete world comes to be at all. In this process an important role was given to a divine artificer or a demiurge. The demiurge, for most Platonists, differs from a creator God in two important respects. The demiurge does not create the forms or models for being out of nothing. Nor does he create matter. Rather, the demiurge works on pre-existing material and has a model in accordance with which the world is made. The model is constituted by transcendent forms, for example, beauty as such, equality as such, sameness and difference.

In order to mould material according to this model, the divine artificer needs to grasp the transcendent models. This latter type of forms had already been introduced in middle Platonism (e.g. Alcinous in his handbook of Platonism, *Didaskalikos*). Forms of this type were not postulated merely to explain the demiurge's grasp of the transcendent models; rather, they were postulated because forms need to have creative power in order to structure a concrete world. Were it just for transcendent forms, these forms might seem to be too inert for the world to come to be.[20]

Even though it might, to our modern eyes, seem rather odd to postulate these two distinct kinds of forms, there is a familiar rationale behind the point. As we saw above in § "Questions of universals, questions of forms", universals as merely existing common properties (largeness as such, human being as a universal, equality as such) could not function efficiently enough to perform their constitutive and formative activity on matter. To illustrate, if we ask why there are large or beautiful things and then answer "because universal largeness or beauty exists", we might feel that an insufficient response has been given. We could then specify: yes but we meant why they *come to be* in the first place, or what causes those things to be. If this question is answered "because universals exist", this sounds unsatisfactory. Simplicius seems to follow a similar intuition when he reformulates the point about transcendent universals. He starts to prefer to talk about common causes rather than nominalized properties, such as largeness itself (*in Cat*. 83,10–12).[21]

But why do we need to postulate two distinct kinds of forms to explain all this? Would it not be sufficient if we just supposed that there are transcendent forms and that it is these *same* forms that the demiurge understands and imposes on matter? One reason why the same forms would not have been sufficient is the one referred to above. In so far as the forms are understood as being transcendent, they do not seem to have creative power (this argument occurs in Alcinous, *Didaskalikos*, and Proclus *in Parm*.).

In addition to functioning as causes, an important function attributed to forms in Plato and Aristotle was to explain how we come to grasp things. Plato was particularly concerned about this, since he supposed that the forms such as largeness are not perfectly realized in the perceptible world: nothing we perceive is large without being small (in comparison to something else). This is why he introduced the theory according to which forms such as that of largeness need to be pre-programmed or pre-existent in our soul. Aristotle argued that the forms cannot exist as pre-existent in our soul, but we come to receive them from external things because of our receptive intellectual capacity and, when we grasp things, our intellect becomes identical with the form.

Let us now turn to Ammonius and the following passage in order to see what kinds of forms he distinguishes from each other.

When we recognise that the individual human beings all possess the same form of human being, … we replicate it for ourselves in our mind, and this is called after-the-many or subsequent-on-the-many and later-generated. These are separate from bodies – for they do not exist in a body, but in a soul. But they are separate without qualification, because they cannot be apprehended in themselves as Plato supposes the Forms before-the-many can be. For he does not want them to be mere thoughts of the Demiurge, but in all respects intelligible substances at which the Demiurge gazes as archetypes as he creates their images down here.   (Porph. *Isag.* 42,10–19, trans. Haas in Sorabji 2004: vol. 3, 137)

It seems that Ammonius in fact accepts the Aristotelian supposition according to which the form of the individuals comes to be actualized as identical in our intellect. Ammonius mentions that it is "replicated" in our mind, but nothing indicates that it should differ from the forms of particulars except numerically. This is puzzling, since if he accepts the claim that the form in the soul is a replica of the form in the thing, he seems to deny the distinction he himself makes between immanent forms in particulars and those in the soul that are abstracted from the particulars (see his kinds of universals (2) and (3), above; from Ammonius *in Isag.* 41,17–20).

However, after introducing the replica theory Ammonius goes on to point out that, in addition to forms of individuals and the later-generated forms in our minds, there must be two other types of forms: Platonic transcendent forms that function as archetypes for the demiurge's creation work and forms in the mind of the demiurge. Therefore, he distinguishes between transcendent forms and forms in the mind of the demiurge. If he does make such a distinction, this would suggest that he also needs to suppose that there is a distinction between the forms in things and abstracted forms in the human soul. Therefore, he seems to mean that being a replica involves being of a different kind; the forms as replicas in our soul are different from the immanent form (forms in-the-many), since they are after-the-many or later-generated, as he says (corresponding to (3), above). All in all, this leaves us the impression that the important point about distinguishing between immanent forms and the later-generated forms in the soul is not that they should be completely different in kind (because Ammonius also says that they are replicated); rather, the difference seems to be in the mode of existence – whether they are realized in things or in the soul.

Substance, quality, differentia

We have now seen that for all the commentators the essence as being immanent in particular things was an important tool for metaphysical analysis, whether subordinated to transcendent forms or not. Essential properties, or specific differences, are what differentiate a species from other species of the same genus (being rational was the most common example of an essential property for human beings), and hence they seem to be important in constituting the specific essence for things. This seems reasonable, but the idea creates a problem when we consider the categories. The essential properties, even though closely related to the notion of substance, are in the wrong category: they typically are qualities or perhaps quantities, but not substances. Independently of whether the interpretation according to which the essential properties constitute a form is a correct interpretation of Aristotle, this problem was central in the commentaries. Alexander in fact seems to have interpreted Aristotle so that the essential properties do constitute the form (Rashed 2007).[22]

The problem is also found in Plotinus, who solves it within his ontological hierarchy. According to Plotinus, the essential properties are activities of the intelligible forms (called *logoi*) existing in the realm of the Intellect. In this world, the *logoi* are the essential properties of things (texts in Sorabji 2004: vol. 3, 73). Plotinus introduces a new expression when taking the essential properties as completing (*sumplēroun*) the substances (*Enn.* 6.3.8,23–30). By contrast, there are accidental properties of things, for example, being white for Socrates or having a broad chest for Plato. Both Plato and Socrates could well exist without exactly these properties, but they could not exist without being human beings. The accidental properties, for Plotinus, would be even dimmer shadows of the forms: they would have their origins of existence in the intelligible, but they would not even be activities of forms, but just shadows.

Porphyry followed this suggestion and claimed that anything that completes a substance must be classified into the category of substance (*in Cat.* 95,22–35). He also introduced a new name, substantial quality (*ousiōdēs poiotēs*), for the essential properties (see e.g. 95,10–22).[23] Iamblichus, Porphyry's student, wanted to mediate between this position and the one taking the essential properties as qualities. He suggested that the essential properties should be understood as being in between substances and qualities (reported by Dexippus *in Cat.* 49,4–6 and Simp. *in Cat.* 99,3–9, quoted in Sorabji 2004: vol. 3, 115–16). In Ammonius' school in Alexandria, where Philoponus and Simplicius studied, this solution was not met with approval. Rather, it was argued that this could not be right, because it would create an additional, eleventh category for essential properties. The standard solution in Ammonius' school was that the specific differences should be considered substances.

As mentioned, specific differences are properties that distinguish between the species belonging to the same genus. For example, as opposed to horses that have four feet, human beings have only two. As opposed to sharks that live in water, both human beings and horses live on land. In these cases, the specific differences would include "living in water", "living on land", "being four-footed" and "being two-footed". To say that these should be classified under substance sounds rather surprising. Would we rather not suppose that these are qualities, perhaps involving quantities as in the case of being two-footed or four-footed?

One direction in which we could look for clarification in this matter is Plato. In Plato's middle dialogues most examples of forms are qualities. Authors whom we have discussed here often tended to accept Plato rather than Aristotle as the ultimate authority. Perhaps they did not see such a severe problem in supposing to be substance something that appears to be quality. Perhaps this suggestion goes some way towards explaining the classification of specific differences as qualities, but it does not seem to solve it in its entirety. The *Categories* was very widely read and commented on, and the distinction between substances and qualities was never contested. In this context, however, we cannot go more deeply into this puzzle but must now move to our final topic, ethics.

SEVEN

Ethics

When we turn to ethics in the commentaries, we find ourselves in a new situation: none of the main figures discussed in this book wrote a commentary on Aristotle's *Nicomachean Ethics* that has been preserved to us. Of these authors, we have *Ethical Problems* attributed to Alexander of Aphrodisias (in CAG Suppl. II 2); it is a discussion of ethical issues based on Aristotle but by no means a commentary on the *Nicomachean Ethics*. The work contains responses to questions and problems deriving from Alexander's school. It most probably was not penned by Alexander himself but rather by his close associates or students on the basis of debates involving Alexander (see e.g. "Introduction", *Ethical Problems*, trans. Sharples 1990). It is unclear whether Alexander himself wrote a commentary on the *Nicomachean Ethics* (Sharples 1987, 1990).

The only more extensive continuous commentary on the *Ethics* is from the Aristotelian Aspasius, whose main activity can be dated to the first half of the second century CE.[1] From him, we have a commentary on Books I–IV and VII–VIII, of which the commentary on Book VII is only partial. Aspasius refers to a debate about the authorship of Book VII and the claim that it was not written by Aristotle but by a certain Eudemus, Aristotle's pupil, from the Peripatetic school (Asp. *in EN* 151,21–25; Barnes 1999: 20; Natali 2007). Aspasius' commentary has the special interest of being the earliest extant commentary on any work of Aristotle. It has the overall appearance of being a course on ethics based on Aristotle (Barnes 1999). When it comes to content, the work contains many philosophically interesting discussions, and in them Aspasius' voice is unique. He is markedly Aristotelian but does not aim to defend Aristotle with the same vigour as Alexander later did.

In addition, we have a composite commentary edited by Gustav Heylbut from various sources containing scholia on the *Nicomachean Ethics* and Eustratius' commentary on *Nicomachean Ethics* Books I and VI. Eustratius' commentary dates from the Byzantine period (eleventh and twelfth centuries). We shall not be concerned with these works in this book.

Aristotle's ethics concentrates on human life in a city-state very much like Athens in the fourth century BCE, and the change of political circumstances might have diminished the interest in his *Ethics* and *Politics*. But this historical contingent is not a sufficient explanation for why the *Ethics* was not widely commented on. Surely, the political situation of our own time is very different from life in the Athens of Aristotle, but this does not entail that Aristotle's ethics would not attract attention today. Quite the contrary: Aristotelian ethics has made something of a revival recently (e.g. Hursthouse 1999; MacIntyre [1981] 2007). Further, Aspasius, for example, explains how some of Aristotle's remarks can be translated into new political conditions (Asp. *in EN* 113,19–23, discussed in Barnes 1999: 28). Some of Aristotle's ethical and political works did belong to the Neoplatonic curriculum (O'Meara 2003), but clearly it was Plato who was dominant in ethics. In fact, in a sense the whole of Plato's philosophy can be seen as being ethical, and it could be said that the commentators did not need Aristotle in ethics as much as they did in natural philosophy, for example.

Because of the paucity of commentaries on the *Nicomachean Ethics*, this chapter does not centre on that work. Even with the addition of the *Ethical Problems* from Alexander's school, this would give us a one-sided picture of how the commentators discussed ethics. To reflect the variety of issues and the practices of teaching ethics in the Neoplatonic schools, we shall include two works, one a commentary and another a separate treatise on ethically relevant questions, by two of our central figures: Porphyry and Simplicius. From Porphyry, we have *On Abstinence from Killing Animals* (*De abstinentia*), in which he argues that it is wrong for us to kill and feed on animals. Another work by Porphyry that will be referred to is *Starting-points Leading to the Intelligibles*, which is often called *Sentences* on the basis of the Latin title, *Sententiae ad intelligibilia ducentes*. There is evidence that Porphyry wrote on Aristotle's ethics too but not in the form of a commentary (see Karamanolis 2006: 303ff.). In addition, Simplicius wrote a commentary on the Stoic philosopher Epictetus' *Handbook* (*Encheiridion*) (see Hadot 1996: 51–151).[2]

Aspasius' commentary, the *Ethical Problems* from Alexander's school and Simplicius' commentary on Epictetus' *Handbook* are directly connected with the teaching given in the Aristotelian and Neoplatonic schools. As mentioned, Aspasius' commentary seems to be designed to form the frame and material for a course on ethics. It is based on, and comments on, Aristotle's *Nicomachean Ethics* because teaching ethics for Aspasius most probably was teaching Aristotelian ethics. The *Ethical Problems*, as we have seen, reflect the debates and arguments presented in favour of Aristotelian ethics against rival theses and views in Alexander's school (Sharples 1990).

One might wonder why ethics in a Neoplatonic school was taught with the aid of a Stoic handbook. Simplicius' commentary is not a unique case or a strange exception in this respect but exemplifies a common practice (see trans. Brennan & Brittain 2002: 4–10). The target audience were novices, and Simplicius points out some qualities that make the work suitable for teaching such an audience: "The speeches are very effective and stirring, so that anyone not totally deadened would be goaded by them, become aware of his own afflictions, and be roused to correct them" (Hadot 1996: 193/D 1,29–33, trans. Brennan & Brittain 2002).

Starting from a Stoic framework, Simplicius formulates the objective of the work in explicitly Platonic terms. For example, the effect of ethical education is "to make our soul free, as the Demiurge and Father, its maker and generator, intended it to be" (Hadot 1996:

193/D 1,20–25, trans. Brennan & Brittain 2002). Further, human beings, the subjects of moral development, are described as "having their essence in accordance with a rational soul and using the body as an instrument" (Hadot 1996: 193/D 1,35, trans. Brennan & Brittain 2002). The formulation according to which the soul uses the body as an instrument derives from Plato's *Alcibiades* I, and the idea plays an important role in the commentary.

To some extent, the variety of works that we shall discuss here would seem to diminish the systematic unity that can be achieved: because the objects of the commentaries vary, the themes and questions must vary as well. However, the ethical treatises are slightly more homogenous than these considerations would *prima facie* suggest. Further, there is additional unity to the discussion that derives from the influence of and adversity towards Stoic philosophy. For example, Aspasius embarks on an excursus on the classification of emotions with an anti-Stoic aim in his commentary on the *Nicomachean Ethics*, and the *Ethical Problems* are mainly formulated in Hellenistic rather than Aristotelian terms. However, the latter fact does not necessarily entail that the arguments or problems that the author of the *Ethical Problems* is addressing should be Stoic or Epicurean arguments or positions; it is the terminology that is (Sharples 1990: 2). Simplicius, by contrast, does not concentrate on refuting Stoic positions. Rather, he builds on Epictetus to such a great extent that he might even be taken to harmonize not only Plato and Aristotle but also Plato and the Stoics (trans. Brennan & Brittain 2002: 1). For the most part he switches smoothly from a Stoic to a Platonic or Neoplatonic formulation of a certain point. Even when the point changes, Simplicius is not eager to underline the change (e.g. when non-rational desire and appetite are brought in; see Hadot 1996: 199/D 4,40–50).

The commentators operate in the context of ancient ethics, where considerations of virtue or excellence (*aretē*) and happiness or flourishing (*eudaimonia*) dominate. More specific divergences aside, there is an agreement among the authors we shall be concerned with on the point that it is important for us to be virtuous or excellent. An excellent or virtuous person is also better equipped to attain happiness than a non-virtuous one (see § "Does virtue entail happiness?", below). For Porphyry and Simplicius, moral development is also a programme of purification. Here they build on Plotinus, who builds on Plato's *Phaedo*. In addition to its Platonic origins, the idea of purification bears some resemblance to the Stoic programme of getting rid of emotions. The Aristotelian virtues of character exercised in a city-state in a social and political setting have only minor importance in their discussions. In addition to the common framework of virtue and happiness, it was widely held that self-governance or self-discipline is typical of a virtuous person. What exactly this means and, for example, to what extent one should control one's emotions is debated, and we shall concentrate on the debate in § "Emotions", below.

Virtue, function, happiness

Virtue and excellence

As we have seen, the ethics of the commentators is situated in the general framework of ancient virtue ethics. For Aristotle, the focus is on happiness (*eudaimonia*) and virtue is a candidate for a way of life that leads to happiness. When determining what human virtue is, Aristotle presents the important argument that it consists in an excellent performance of the human function (*ergon*) (*EN* I 7, 1097b24ff.). In the course of his argument, Aristotle compares the human function to functions that, like those of a flute player or a sculptor, can be performed in an excellent manner. When we look at this argument it might seem to confuse two distinct forms of excellence. We might object that virtues have ethical significance that is not present in excellent flute playing.

In a sense, Aristotle does attribute ethical significance to virtues: human excellence is ethical virtue (*aretē ēthikē*) for him. However, we need to be cautious with the word "ethical" here. When we speak about "ethical virtue" (*aretē ēthikē*), we easily interpret it as meaning the same as "moral" and to be opposed to the goodness involved in excellent flute playing, for example. However, to suppose that "ethical virtue" means only and precisely what we mean by "moral" would not be correct, particularly if we also assume that there is an entirely distinct meaning of goodness that is not moral. The Greek substantive *ēthos*, related to the adjective *ēthikos* (ethical), means character, and, therefore, ethical virtues in Aristotle are virtues of character. These are such stable and desirable character traits or dispositions (*hexis*) to behaviour as courage and justice. One has virtue of character when one is courageous or just, and having these character traits means that one also acts accordingly: a just person does just deeds. Even though virtues of character are more important traits in one's personality than are professional excellences, they are not different in kind. Rather, they both exemplify common teleological structure, where good consists of attaining one's end.[3]

On the other hand, virtues of character can be contrasted with what Aristotle calls "natural virtues" (*aretai phusikai*), which children have (*EN* VI 13). For example, one child may have natural courage, another natural justice, but neither of them can be just or courageous in the proper sense of having these virtues as virtues of character, unless they continue and persist in doing just or courageous deeds. When one has stabilized one's "natural virtue" (tendency towards real courage or justice) through habituation and action, one can be said to be a just person. The acts of that kind of person are constantly in accordance with virtue. Hence virtues of character are also good in a sense similar to what we would call "ethical" or "moral". However, as already noted, their goodness is not different in kind from the excellence in performing tasks, such as that of a flute player.

This is an important point that, to some extent, distinguishes Aristotelian ethics from many variants of modern ethics. Aspasius and the author of the *Ethical Problems* follow Aristotle in specifying virtues of character by first laying out what is good in several fields (such as flute playing and sculpture) and abstracting what is common to all of them (Asp. *in EN* 15,15–21; *Ethical Problems* 25.148,12–33). In addition to arts where the end is rather clear, the *Ethical Problems* also mentions animals such as dogs and horses and their functions. Guarding and hunting are mentioned as possible functions of a dog, running for a horse (148,16–20). Such an anthropocentric conception of animal functions would be antithetical to Aristotle (see Johnson 2005: 204–10).

The relation between human good and ethical virtue on the one hand and the goodness involved in the performance of functions on the other implies some problems of translation. Traditionally, *aretē* has been translated as "virtue", and this term will also be utilized here. It has been argued that this traditional translation should be replaced by "excellence", since the human good is connected with excellent performance of functions. If someone is a skilled flute player, we will not call him a virtuous flute player but an excellent one. (On the other hand, we could call him "a virtuoso".) In this chapter, the general strategy is to talk about "virtue" when such desirable and valued character traits as courage, wisdom, temperance or justice are at stake and of "excellence" when the reference is to an outstanding performance of a skill ("Introduction", *Ethical Problems*, trans. Sharples 1990: 8–9).

Function, good and end

As the opening lines of the *Nicomachean Ethics* state, the good is an end. This means, on the one hand, that human beings in their action aim at some good. However, to motivate their action the end must *appear* to them to be good. This entails a possible divergence between an apparent good and a real good: something can appear to be good even though it really is not good. On the other hand, real ends are good in the sense that they provide standards by reference to which actions related to a particular end can be evaluated. As within arts, one is excellent to the extent to which one has succeeded in reaching the end of a particular art. In a similar way, a human being is good in so far as he or she succeeds in attaining the end that is peculiar to the human function. For a virtuous person, the goods that appear to him to be good are really good.

One way of coming to understand what the end or goal of human life is starts from the following intuitions. An end is something for the sake of which other things are done. In human life, Aristotle supposes, ends can be such external goods as pleasure or honour. To have pleasure as an end of an action, for example, means that I eat a cake because I find it pleasant. If I enjoy eating that cake and it feels pleasant, I can choose eating it for the sake of an end, the pleasure involved. Similarly, it is possible to act for the sake of honour: donating money to finance a public project or fight courageously in a war. However, Aristotle affirms that in fact pleasure and honour are something else as well as being ends; they also are means to a further end. If we suppose that the goal of our life is honour or pleasure, we are mistaken about it and do not understand that in fact pleasure and honour are done for the sake of yet a higher end.

An ultimate end is such that other things are chosen for its sake, but it is not chosen for the sake of anything else. For Aristotle, happiness or flourishing (*eudaimonia*) is such an end. It is the only thing that satisfies both these conditions. This means that, even though it is sufficient in a particular situation to act for an end such as pleasure or honour, our whole life will not be happy if all our actions aim at these kinds of intermediate goals. By contrast, this is not the case with happiness: if all our actions throughout a complete life aim at happiness, our whole life will be happy. Happiness, for Aristotle, is a property of a complete life and cannot be momentary ("one swallow does not make spring, neither does one day"; *EN* 1098a19–20, my translation). Yet, because there are intermediate ends such as pleasure and happiness, we do not arrive at the absurd conclusion that, in particular situations, I cannot make a decision if I do not know how it affects the happiness of my whole life. Rather, I can well choose to eat a cake just for the pleasure of it, provided that this is not my sole model for action. A complete life consisting of eating cakes will not be happy because it is not in accordance with my nature. In fact, it would not even *feel* pleasant anymore. According to Aristotle, human nature involves other capacities and needs that must be attended to in order for our lives to be happy.

For Aristotle, our character is manifested in all choices we make. In every situation, be it about cakes or about life and death, what I do is an expression of my character. It is precisely for this reason that I need to improve my character in order to act well. Only if my character is good will I be able to act well throughout a complete life. Virtues, for Aristotle, are means between two extremes. For example, courage is a mean between cowardice and rashness. It involves a right kind of fearlessness in a fearful situation. A coward is not courageous because he is too afraid: a rash person is not courageous, because he is not afraid at all. When it comes to cakes, Aristotle instructs that we need to steer clear between two extremes: gluttony and asceticism.

Another viewpoint from which we can consider the human goal is from the point of view of functions. We have seen that Aristotelian ethics supposes that a human function exists, but we have not yet identified what it is. To do so, we shall move to Aspasius. "What, then, is the function of human beings as human beings?" asks Aspasius (*in EN* 17,29, my translation). Is it life? No, it is not life, because life also belongs to animals. Even though the function is not life as such (as growth, nutrition and reproduction), our function is *a certain kind of life*. Is it a life of perception? No, it is not a life of perception, because perceptive life can be lived by any other animal. What is distinctive of human beings, that is, what we can do in our lives but plants and other animals cannot, is to be active and rational (*praktikē kai logikē*; 18,1).

We can act, as opposed to mere reaction, because we are deliberative beings. We make choices that are in accordance with our character. Further, as Aspasius points out, rationality is characteristic for the human function, because only human beings have a rational part in their soul. Therefore, our function in this world is to employ those capacities that are in accordance with our own distinctive nature: act on the basis of deliberate decisions and exercise our rationality.

Aspasius seems to suppose that the human function needs to be distinct from that of plants and animals because human beings are distinct from plants and animals in an important respect: their souls have a rational part, and in this part "resides what is specific to a human being" (18,3, trans. Konstan 2006). This is not a surprising answer. A more interesting move is the one Aspasius makes when blocking the idea that life, pure and simple, would be the human function (17,30–31). In addition to the point that life is not distinctive because it belongs even to plants, Aspasius adds that it cannot be the human function because it belongs to us by nature. This is a rather surprising thing to say, since it would also seem that the human function must be something that belongs to us by our nature *as human beings*. Perhaps Aspasius' idea is to say that life as growth, consumption of nutrition and reproduction are functions that we just perform without actively being engaged in them. Hence this kind of life must be distinguished from the human function, which must be something we actively and deliberately do. Unfortunately, Aspasius does not elaborate on this point.

One of the most central questions in the scholarship of Aristotle's ethics in recent years has been whether the human good consists in exemplifying all virtues of character (e.g. justice, courage and so forth) or whether a contemplative life (*theōria*) alone constitutes the goal and happiness: or how one can combine the two. Aristotle himself does not discuss this question explicitly when introducing the function argument in the first book (I 7). The question is related to the *Nicomachean Ethics* as a whole: the middle books (II–V) concentrate on virtues of character that are manifested in everyday life within a society, whereas Book X states that there is a highest form of human activity, contemplation, the exercise of which is the ultimate goal for human beings.[4]

We can already see this contrast between a life of action and a life of contemplation in Aspasius' formulation of the human function. In defining the human function, he distinguishes between action and rationality. Further, the notion of contemplation (*theōrein*) figures prominently throughout his discussion concerning the human function (*ad* I 7 15,12–14; cf. 23,25ff., 29,22). He asks whether happiness is a sufficient description of the end or if something (e.g. contemplating, *theōrein*), should be added. This reference can mean several things (that can also be true at the same time). For example, it may simply show that Aspasius read Aristotle's reference of the possibility that there is one highest end as a reference to the contemplative life described in Book X. It can also indicate that the interpretation of Aristotle's ethics and the human good was already a disputed issue. Be that as it may, one thing is quite clear on the basis of Aspasius' reference. Aspasius did see an important distinction between a life of action and a life of contemplation (15,12–14). However, he included them both in his description of the human function: we need to exercise these two sides in us in order to be fully human.

Does virtue entail happiness?

The Stoics had defended the tempting claim that virtue is sufficient for human happiness (on which Plato, in the *Republic*, seems to agree): tempting because it leads one to expect that virtue should guarantee protection against misfortune in life. It suggests that no matter how many drawbacks one encounters, they do not destroy one's happiness. This view is based on a characteristically Stoic understanding of virtue and happiness. Happiness follows when we realize that it is not the things that happen to us that are bad; only our beliefs and convictions about the badness of external things are really bad. To become virtuous, we need to revise our belief system and disengage value from external things. From a Stoic point of view, virtue consists in wisdom. Wisdom understood in the Stoic manner requires not omniscience but knowledge of the nature of the true good, virtue. A wise person, the Stoics maintain, never attaches value to external things such as health and wealth. He or she also understands that external misfortunes are part of the cosmic order in which things happen for the good of the whole. For an individual human being they are neutral with respect to moral value. The decisive factor in human life is one's conception about it: if we understand what is truly good (virtue) and what is the only bad thing in life (vice), we shall never fail to gain what is good and avoid what is bad.[5]

In the commentaries, the question is discussed in the following form: do we need external things (such as health and wealth) to become happy? The flipside of the question is whether our happiness can be destroyed by external conditions (e.g. war, illness, loss of children).

The question of the significance of external things for our happiness is discussed in terms of whether happiness can be increased by externals. In the history of this debate, an important figure is Antiochus of Ascalon, who lived *c*.130–68 BCE and was a student of Philo of Larissa in the Platonic Academy. Antiochus departed from the sceptical tendencies of the Academy exemplified in the work of Arcesilaus and Carneades, and reformed his Platonism considerably by incorporating Peripatetic and, even more importantly, Stoic influence (see Annas 1993). Antiochus had argued that even though the Stoics were correct in supposing that virtue is sufficient to make life happy, external goods make it *even happier* (Cic. *Fin*. 4.59, 5.71; Sharples 1999: 88). Therefore, if we compare life consisting of virtue to life consisting of virtue *and external goods*, the latter is happier.

Aristotle was not, of course, reacting to these arguments presented after his death. However, a similar theme appears in the *Nicomachean Ethics* I 7 (1097b14–19), where Aristotle states that "happiness is most choice-worthy but it is not reckoned in" (17,13–14, trans. Konstan 2006). It is not entirely clear what Aristotle means by this. The following three options are the most natural readings of his claim.

First, Aristotle might mean that were other goods added to happiness, happiness could become excessive, which seems absurd. If we take the argument this way, then Aristotle is making a counterfactual claim concerning the point whether happiness can be reckoned together with other goods: it cannot, because what is sufficient becomes excessive through addition (for the principle, see Cic. *Fin*. 5.81). According to the second option, Aristotle is saying that happiness itself provides us with a basic level: "it is the most choice-worthy *even if* not counted in with other goods" (Sharples 1999: 89).[6] If we take this position as being similar to what Antiochus suggests (as Sharples 1999 does), then it means that even though happiness is sufficient as a basic level without the external goods, it can be made *even greater* with the addition of the externals. A third option deviates from the second in understanding Aristotle's claim to be that happiness is perfect even without external goods, not just a basic level. In this case, to try to add some external goods to happiness would not affect the sum total. It would be like trying to add one digit to infinity: the sum remains the same. The third option diverges from the first in not allowing happiness to become excessive: the addition of external goods just does not affect the sum total at all.

Aspasius

Aspasius takes up this point in his commentary (*in EN* 16,32–17,17) and argues in a manner similar to our third option just sketched. According to Aspasius, Aristotle means that "happiness is the most choiceworthy of all, but it is not reckoned in" (16,33–34, trans. Konstan 2006). Therefore, it cannot be compared to the other goods and is hence not increased by the addition of external goods. He argues that the case of happiness is similar to any situation in which ends and things contributing to those ends are at issue: healthy things and health cannot be compared; health is equally choice-worthy whether or not it is taken together with those things that contribute to health (e.g. diet or medication). For Aspasius, happiness is perfect and an addition to what is perfect is useless; it does not add to its value. If someone is perfectly healthy, it does not add to his or her health to take medication and to follow a special diet. Aspasius concludes: "[W]ealth and health and the rest together with happiness are not more choiceworthy than happiness alone. For if we have happiness, we have everything" (17,6–8, trans. Konstan 2006).

We have now seen how Aspasius analyses the relation between happiness and external goods: happiness is self-sufficient in the sense that it is not increased by the addition of external goods. We shall now move on to the second aspect of our main question, that is, whether happiness can be destroyed by the loss of externals. In fact, Aspasius argues in quite clear words that it can. If a person witnesses "great sufferings on the part of his wife, children, parents and country, his life would still not be self-sufficient", or happy (16,17–18, trans. Konstan 2006).[7]

When claiming that happiness needs external goods, Aspasius does not suggest that they would be necessary as *constituents* of a happy life. To say that they are would amount to the claim that happiness is a collection of external goods throughout a complete life. Rather, Aspasius' claim is that external goods are necessary for a happy life *as instruments* (24,3–5). For example, one needs friends in order to overthrow tyranny (24,9–11; cf. Arist. *EN* 1099a33–4). If I am alone and have no friends to conspire with, I have no chance to succeed in bringing about a regime change. Further, external goods such as political power are necessary for acting virtuously. If one does not have political power within a community, it is impossible to do noble deeds. Without such power, one is condemned to live a private life and keep still (*in EN* 24,16–19). Aspasius' examples of great actions with political power are about powerful people indeed: law-givers Lycurgus in Sparta, Solon in Athens and Zaleucus in Locris (24,21–3). Therefore, for Aspasius, external goods are means and instruments to an end, happiness. As in the case of any other end, so it is with happiness: it cannot be attained without certain means, and those means include external goods, including political power or status.

As to the question of how virtue contributes to facing misfortunes, Aspasius repeats a line from Simonides (fr. 37 *Poetae Melici Graeci*) also quoted by Plato in *Protagoras* 339b and Aristotle (*EN* 1100b21–2). The poetic expression used to characterize a virtuous person is that such a person is "four-square without blame" (*tetragōnos aneu psogou*; Asp. *in EN* 29,29). Aspasius explains this metaphor as follows. To say that a virtuous person is four-square refers to the fact that when a four-square stone falls down, it will always land on one side and stay that way (30,2–3). Here the geometrical shape of the stone is compared to the property of virtuous people that they "stand upright against every fortune" (30,3, trans. Konstan 2006). However, according to Aspasius, people can be four-square in different ways. The blameful way of being four-square is to be a chameleon in character. To be such a chameleon involves changing impressions according to company: with dissolute people they seem dissolute, with temperate ones temperate. By contrast, those who are four-square without blame nobly bear their fortunes. They are neither "cast down by misfortune nor elated by good fortune" (30,2, trans. Konstan 2006).

It is noteworthy that, following Aristotle, Aspasius underlines that both good and bad fortune may jeopardize one's happiness:

> For it is difficult to bear not only misfortune but also good fortune, and great mishaps befall those who cannot bear

> prosperity ... [G]reat strokes of good fortune produce a turn
> of the scale so as sometimes to shake a happy person out of
> his happiness, but small ones do not. For there must occur
> many and very great misfortunes to dislodge a person from
> his happiness.   (30,3–8, trans. Konstan 2006)

Aspasius does not explain in more detail why it should be the case
that great strokes of good fortune also challenge one's happiness;
he puts this forward in a manner of a commonplace truth. One
obvious reason could be that one is often prevented from excess in
food and drink and consumption of money by limitations in one's
economic situation. If, for example, one wins a lottery or receives a
great inheritance, these limitations are removed and self-discipline
needs to be applied in new circumstances in order not to consume
supplies excessively. Further, in the framework of Aristotelian ethics, virtuous use of money is seen as a challenge in general. It is not
obvious that one knows how to do it in a proper manner, for example,
how much to pay to finance a tragedy choir. Therefore, this is an area
where one needs to exercise good judgement in general, and not only
when one's situation changes.

Even though virtuous people are, according to Aspasius, more
resistant to smaller boons and blows of fortune, they are not untouchable. Many and very great misfortunes dislodge even the virtuous
person from happiness. However, even in these cases, virtue "shines
forth" (*dialampei*; 30,11; Arist. *EN* 1100b30–31). As Aspasius specifies, this means that someone bears misfortunes calmly, not because
of insensibility (*analgēsia*) but because of greatness of soul (*megalop-
sukhia*). In the opposite situation, namely when a virtuous person
encounters "great strokes of good fortune", these adorn or embellish the happiness of that person. Aspasius compares it to the way
in which beautiful bodies can be adorned: the adornments do not
constitute – or perhaps they do not even contribute to – the beauty
of those bodies; they just embellish something already beautiful (*in
EN* 30,14–18).

Simplicius

For Aspasius, adversities can destroy one's happiness if they are significant and great. Simplicius denies this possibility and takes the Stoic point of view, which is also found in Plato. When commenting on Epictetus' *Handbook*, Simplicius writes:

> He says, then, that the things which are thought to be terrible when they happen to us, and hence disturb us on the grounds that something terrible is happening to us, are neither terrible themselves, nor in reality the causes of our disturbance; rather, it is our belief about these things (the belief that they are terrible) which disturbs us.
>
> (Hadot 1996: 242/D 28,1–10,
> trans. Brennan & Brittain 2002)

This point is explicitly put in the mouth of Epictetus, but Simplicius' subsequent discussion shows no willingness to deny it. Quite the contrary, when illustrating the point he merely adds Neoplatonic flavour to the argument. Simplicius' example is Socrates who, in the face of what is "most terrible of all", namely premature death at the hands of human beings, "endured it undisturbed", and did so, even though he could have escaped (Hadot 1996: 242–3/D 28,10–20). Instead of fleeing, Socrates spent his last day "revealing the truth about soul to his friends and teaching the nature of the cathartic life of philosophers" (*ibid*.). It is in the idea of purification (cathartic life) that the specifically Neoplatonic aspect comes in. According to Plotinus, being pure (*katharos*) and free of emotions is an ideal intellectual virtue; intellectual virtues were even called "purifications" (*katharseis*; Plot. *Enn.* 1.2.5–6). Therefore, Simplicius continues Epictetus' point with the example of Socrates interpreted in Plotinian terms: no external thing can destroy my happiness if I am pure and do not believe that it does.

Simplicius follows Epictetus in pointing out that people who acquire the highest level of moral development will not blame anything or anyone. If a person has not undergone such development at all, he or she will constantly blame external circumstances for his or her own unhappiness (Hadot 1996: 248/D 30,50ff.). Those who have started moral education have improved so much as to be able to identify the main source of the misery: themselves. Thus they blame themselves, rather than external circumstances, for the miseries (e.g. Hadot 1996: 249/D 31,30–40). However, blaming oneself is not the aim of moral education. Rather, when we come to understand the true nature of virtue and happiness and have become capable of acting accordingly, we no longer accuse anyone. This is not just because we endure hardship. Rather, this state has been acquired by a complete revision of our belief system: the difficulties are not even considered bad any more. If a person is free from error, there is no need to make accusations, because nothing bad can happen to that person. As Simplicius puts it, those who are perfectly free from error "never get into any situation that is bad for them ..., either through their own doing or through others – *because they do not locate their bad in external things*" (Simp. *in Epict.*; Hadot 1996: 249/D 31,23–6, trans. Brennan & Brittain 2002; emphasis added).

Even though such a transformation is essentially based on reconsidering and reshaping one's beliefs about external things, Simplicius emphasizes that adopting correct beliefs and manoeuvring a superficial change of desires is not sufficient: "we must also exhibit deeds that are consonant with our correct beliefs" (Hadot 1996: 253/D 33,25). Therefore, for Simplicius, moral development is a thoroughgoing change.

Simplicius argues that if our moral development is already secure, we can *use* external things. If we grasp the main objective of our journey – Simplicius praises Epictetus' maritime imagery (Hadot 1996: 254ff./D 34,9ff.) – and keep this firmly in mind, we may pick those things that incidentally fall in our way, that is, external goods. When considering how one correctly employs external things, Simplicius presents the idea that difficulties in life serve a teleological purpose. It is given in the Neoplatonic metaphysical framework, where human souls descend from a higher life to a body to live there and, ideally, to return to their intellectual origin. The descent of souls, that is, separate immaterial rational souls coming to be embodied, is a plan of God (demiurge). God sent rational souls here in the realm of generation and, according to Plotinus, human action is a part of the chain of emanation through which the material world comes into existence and comes to be organized and hence perfected.[8] Simplicius points out that the souls descended equipped with powers not to be harmed by external misfortune.

Even though the misfortunes cannot harm the core of our being, our true self as rational beings, they have a purpose in our moral development. If there were no "snares and distractions", our souls might "grow slack and lose intensity" (Hadot 1996: 266/D 39,35, 40,40). The problems and misfortunes thus serve as exercises or contests in which our souls can be trained or tried. As there is no courage without fear, there is no excellence of character without serious hardship: it is only in extreme difficulties that a character is truly tested. Simplicius illustrates the point by referring to such figures as Heracles, Theseus, Diogenes and Socrates, who:

> would not have become such as they were, had God not challenged the first two to struggle against the most fearsome of the beasts and wrong-doers among men, or propelled the second two to the extremes of simplicity and the natural life.   (Hadot 1996: 266/D 40,40–50, trans. Brennan & Brittain 2002)

In fact, it is not just that a virtuous person can endure misfortune: those difficulties allow one to become truly virtuous. If one lived a life sitting in an armchair, meditating on theoretical questions and bathing in warm water, and constantly had an appropriate amount of food to consume, one would not grow truly courageous and resistant, or at least it could not be assured that one would. If virtue has not been tested, it cannot be guaranteed to have solidity.

This example of Simplicius' understanding of virtues brings forth a similarity between him and the Stoics and dissimilarity from Aristotle. Whereas flourishing or happiness (*eudaimonia*) for Aristotle (in the middle books of the *Ethics*) involves action in a society with certain specific social roles and excellent performance of those roles, with good progenitors and good progeny, for the Stoics happiness consists in freedom from disturbances (*ataraxia*). When Simplicius refers to endurance and the idea that it is just our beliefs about things that are terrible to us, not the things themselves, his discussion shows a much closer affinity to happiness as freedom from disturbances than as the life of an Aristotelian citizen. From the Stoic point of view, which Simplicius here endorses, virtue offers protection from external hardship: it guarantees freedom from disturbance on the condition that the true source of disturbance (one's own beliefs) has been identified and the beliefs revised to the extent that a radical change in our view of life and action has been brought about.

We are now in a position to see why it is important for Simplicius to underline that we should understand our true nature as rational souls. If our soul did not do so, it might identify too much with the body and even lose its rationality. This would be the case if we supposed that the body is a part of our soul: our soul would then take the desires of spirit and appetite *to be its own desires* and appetites, and it would also grieve when not attaining the objects of those appetites. However, Simplicius claims that when we conceive in a profound manner our identity as rational beings as separate from body, no bodily damage can be transmitted to the soul. Some activities of the soul are carried out through the body and bodily damage does extend to them. By contrast, our soul as separate, when it is *conceived as being separate*, will be protected against all external difficulties (Hadot 1996: 261–2/D 38,8–31). Further, true understanding of external things shows us that we cannot lose them. This is because they never were and never will be ours (Hadot 1996: 278–9/D 47,15–30). Simplicius instructs us to follow Epictetus here: rather than saying that we have lost something external, we should say that we have given it back (D 48,14).

Emotions

Are emotions a part of a happy life?

In the introduction to this chapter we saw that many ancient schools shared an ideal of self-discipline. From a Platonic–Aristotelian point of view, it is important to distinguish between the self-control that an encratic or controlled (*encratēs*) person has and the compelling attractiveness of the good that a virtuous person experiences. Even if a controlled person believes that he must aim at the good and that the good is an end, he does not experience it as desirable to a sufficient degree. This is why, for Aristotle as well as for Plato in the *Republic*, a controlled person cannot be fully virtuous and fully happy: he has to fight against his own desires all the time and hence does not experience virtuous action as entirely satisfactory. By contrast, the virtuous person feels the attraction of the good with the dynamic lower layers of his soul, so he wants to act to attain the good in all circumstances and will derive full satisfaction from acting accordingly. For Aristotle and Plato, discipline is needed for emotions not to get out of hand. A virtuous person will experience emotions, but to a moderate degree. The moderate ideal of emotions in a happy life (*metriopatheia*) is well expressed in the *Ethical Problems*: "It is like this in the case of the emotions and of actions concerned with them. So excesses and deficiencies of pleasures and distresses destroy the goodness in these things, while due measures create and preserve it" (*Ethical Problems* 25.149,27–30, trans. Sharples 1990, modified).

The idea that one should not experience excessive emotion is not in conflict with the possibility that sometimes a strong emotional reaction might be needed. In the quoted passage, this idea is reflected in the fact that *deficiencies* as well as excesses of pleasure and distress are said to destroy one's happiness. We could, for example, imagine a situation where it is necessary that a virtuous person must experience very intense emotion: if there is a great injustice at hand and it needs to be prevented, to be very angry might help to provide energy. Or, if one loses a close relative, it is appropriate to become very sad. However, the crucial point is that the emotional response needs to correspond to the quality of the situation. No explicit numerical instructions can be given: good judgement is needed. (Getting furious about a lost penny would not be virtuous.)

The ideal of moderating the emotions is in contrast with the Stoic ideal of *apatheia*: liberation from emotions. The Stoics understand emotions as beliefs concerning the value of external things. They divide emotions into four kinds according to the content of the belief involved:

Desire: belief of a future good	Fear: belief of a future bad
Pleasure: belief of a present good	Distress: belief of a present bad

These beliefs are accompanied by strong physical reactions: elation (desire and pleasure) and a sinking feeling (fear and distress) in one's chest. These reactions promote the acceptance of such beliefs and are increased by it.

The Stoic ideal, according to which one should get rid of all emotions and of beliefs that goodness and badness belong to external things, is based on the supposition that all beliefs that attribute value to external things are false: external things are not genuinely valuable. A virtuous person will experience, not emotions or passions, but proper feelings (*eupatheiai*) that involve true attributions of value and no excessive physiological reactions such as growing pale connected with fear. Whereas emotions involve false beliefs attributing value to external things, the proper feelings of a virtuous person concern his or her virtue. The proper feelings can be classified as follows:

Wish towards a future good (wishing one's virtue to continue)	Caution towards future bad (a virtuous person is cautious about vice, even though knowing that virtue cannot be lost).
Joy of a present good (enjoying one's own virtue)	–

Note that belief of a present bad is non-existent, because virtue does not allow any vice. This raises the question of why caution is needed. If virtue cannot be lost, why be cautious about losing it in the future? Or, if caution is needed, should we not need something analogous to distress when we actually are in a situation where virtue is lost? No, because the wise person can never lose virtue. Despite this response, the asymmetry of the virtuous responses is somewhat puzzling.

These proper reactions differ from real emotions, because none of them contain a false attribution of moral value. In addition, the bodily effect felt together with these beliefs is milder than the agitation accompanying false emotional beliefs.

Before asking how Porphyry and Simplicius understood the role of emotions in human life, we shall briefly consider Plotinus' reconciliation between the two ideals: emotionless life (*apatheia*) and moderately emotional life (*metriopatheia*). His position is based on a heavily dualist distinction (also found in Simplicius) between rational soul and body, where the person is identified with the rational soul. Following again the metaphor from *Alcibiades* I, the rational soul is said to use the body as an instrument. This dualism implies two different stages of virtue (*Enn.* 1.2.6,20–28, 1.2.5,4–12, 2.1); for our purposes, the most important division is into the intellectual and the political. For Plotinus, total purification of emotions is possible only on the level of rational soul: the purified or cathartic intellectual virtues of the rational soul are emotionless and aim at a complete detachment from, or transcending, the body. Moderate emotions belong to the compound of soul and body, and they are needed to exemplify political virtue (see also trans. Brennan & Brittain 2002: 15).

In accordance with the relation between soul and body, Plotinus understands political virtues as instruments of the rational soul. In the Plotinian hierarchy of the world, the Intellect is, in addition to its internal activity, externally organizing and structuring the material world. A similar twofold action is also taking place with respect to virtues. Through political virtues, the rational soul is acting in order to make the human environment more rationally organized. It is necessary that emotions are regulated and controlled, because otherwise the ordering process would be disturbed and the gradual detachment from the body could not make any progress. From Plotinus' point of view, emotions tie us more closely to the bodily aspect of our being and hence hinder the ascent towards pure rational life.

Purification and instruments: Porphyry and Simplicius

Porphyry

Following his teacher Plotinus (*Enn.* 1.2), Porphyry also distinguishes different kinds of virtue. In Porphyry, the distinction contains the following four groups: civic or political (*politikai*), purificatory (*kathartikai*), theoretical (*theōrētikai*) and paradigmatic (*paradeigmatikai*) virtues (*Starting Points to the Intelligible* or *Sentences* § 32). In general, Neoplatonic ethics aims at harmonizing and systematizing Plato's various discussions on virtue: the one on four cardinal virtues (justice, temperance, courage and wisdom) in the *Republic*; virtue as purification of the bodily in the *Phaedo*; and, finally, virtue as attaining similarity with god (*Tht.* 176a–b). This general objective can also be seen in Porphyry. However, unlike Plotinus, Porphyry does not consider Aristotle's ethics as being flawed or in serious opposition with this ideal. Rather, he seems to suppose that Aristotle argued, in *Nicomachean Ethics* Book X, that attaining similarity with god is the human ideal, an ideal also advocated by Plotinus.[9]

Porphyry's crucial move that allows him to accommodate Aristotle's ethics and in which he deviates from Plotinus is to see civic virtues as not only having a specific realm of application but also a distinct kind or degree of happiness (Karamanolis 2006). The happiness related to the exercise of civic virtues is not identical to the more perfect or greater happiness related to the higher virtues (purificatory, theoretical and paradigmatic), but it can nonetheless be understood as happiness. This idea allows Porphyry to harmonize Aristotle's ethics with the various statements of Plato's ethics, and to see the whole of the *Nicomachean Ethics* as structured around a similar idea. The theoretical ideal discussed in Book X comes to be understood as the highest expression of human nature and virtue, whereas the earlier books complement the picture with the less-perfect virtues belonging to civic life.

When virtues are discussed on a level not bound to social life, new interpretations need to be given to them. As a paradigmatic virtue, for example, courage can no longer be defined as suitably fearless action in a fearful situation. Porphyry takes up the task of reinterpretation in his *Sentences* (§ 32 24,9–25,6, 27,7–29,7, trans. Lamberz in Sorabji 2004: vol. 1, 338–40).

Civic or political virtue is described in terms of moderate emotions that we should experience in the field of action. However, Porphyry also adds a qualification according to which our actions need to be performed with regard to community (*koinōnia*) and this means avoiding doing harm to those who do not harm us (see further § "Human community", below). On the level of purificatory virtue, this viewpoint is no longer present. Practical wisdom (*phronēsis*) must be understood as not sharing any opinions with the body. The formulation is curious: how could the body have opinions? Perhaps the point is to refer to the idea that our body has desires and hence in a sense some views – supposedly mostly false ones – about what is good (cf. Plato's *Phaedo*). Supposedly Simplicius' idea that we should not share opinions with the body is to underline that we should not take such desires or opinions to be ours. This means that we should avoid mixing our rational conceptions with the lower desires and appetites. Temperance is described as the result of not sharing the experiences of the body, courage means not being afraid of departing from the body, and justice is the result of reason and intellect leading the soul and nothing opposing them.

Having acquired purificatory virtue, one can stop worrying about the body. On the level of theoretical virtue, theoretical and practical wisdom consist in contemplating the contents of the intellect. Justice involves doing one's own share (as it does in society; cf. Plato *Republic* 434c8), but it is not easy to see what this means on the level of intellect. Porphyry speaks about following after intellect while directing the activity towards intellect. Perhaps he refers to a distinction between the metaphysical Intellect as such and individual intellects within it. Against this background, he might mean that, when engaged in intellectual activity, we should attempt to follow the universal Intellect. Temperance is described as turning inwards towards the intellect, and courage consists of freedom from emotion. The description of courage is slightly unclear, since emotions proper belong to the body and theoretical virtues seem not to be concerned with the body at all. Perhaps Porphyry wants to insist on the difficulty of constantly being detached from the body.

Finally, we arrive at a description of paradigmatic virtues that, according to Porphyry, consist mainly in the intellect's understanding of itself and its own superiority. Such virtues could perhaps be characterized as self-reflective:

> At this level, intellect is that in which the paradigms enjoy existence together, practical wisdom (*phronēsis*) is scientific understanding (*epistēmē*), theoretical wisdom is intellect in that act of knowing, temperance is direction to oneself, sticking to one's own job [i.e. justice] is one's own job, and courage is self-sameness and remaining one's own in purity through superabundance of power.
>
> (Porph. *Sentences* § 32, from 27,7–29,7,
> trans. Sorabji in Sorabji 2004: vol. 1, 340)

Emotions are absent. Potentially fearful situations where courage was once exemplified are far away. These paradigmatic virtues are fully and solely intellectual, determined and actualized in the intellect's eternal self-sameness. They do not require correct action according to a virtuous character in a social setting. The only kind of action they involve is self-contained intellectual contemplation completely detached from social life. Further, on the level of paradigmatic virtue, practical reasoning collapses into the theoretical. As Porphyry's own formulation shows, once practical wisdom has become theoretical scientific knowledge, it has been entirely detached from human action within a civic society and the particularities involved therein.

Porphyry's meaning when he explains the highest paradigmatic virtues is not entirely transparent. For example, justice is described simply as "one's own job". It is not entirely clear how this differs from theoretical justice that distinguishes between the universal Intellect and our intellectual activity. One possibility might be that, on the level of paradigmatic virtue, the distinction between different aspects of intellect is not necessary, but a person who has acquired paradigmatic virtue has become merged with the higher layers of reality. We shall return to Porphyry's conception of virtues in § "Porphyry: Ascetic ideal and animal ethics", below.

Simplicius

Simplicius also supposes that the main objective of our ethical development is to become detached from the bodily world around us and to return to the Intellect, our origin, as Plotinus taught. In order to begin the journey back to this origin, we need to understand how we arrived at our present predicament. From Simplicius' perspective (cf. Proclus), an important moment in the process through which we became embodied is a pre-bodily decision made by rational souls: they *decided* to descend into bodies. This is a free decision, where a lesser good is chosen instead of a greater good (Simp. *in Epict.* Hadot 1996: 336/D 77,53; trans. Brennan & Brittain 2002: 17).[10]

Why did the rational souls choose to descend to bodies in the first place? Would it not have been better for them to remain undescended, pure and untouchable? To some extent this reaction is correct: it is better to be pure and untouchable and not mixed with the body. However, even the descent has an explanation, which makes it desirable from the perspective of cosmic perfection. Apparently, the Intellect cannot mould and improve the lowest material levels directly, because it is not in proper contact with those levels. If it were, its essence could not be entirely pure. By contrast, human beings are embodied and our soul is in "intimate interaction" with the body (trans. Brennan & Brittain 2002: 18). Because of this connection, cosmic improvement and beautification of matter and its shadowy existence are possible through human activity. The rational souls descend to bodies to rationally organize and improve the material world. Notice that even though this point is made in a characteristically Neoplatonic framework, it is not completely alien to the Stoic view of cosmic rationality. The Stoic cosmos is also a rational being that functions in and through human rationality.

Simplicius describes the double role of human beings as follows:

> Human souls, however, are given their form of existence
> so that they can be a bond between the things that always
> remain above [i.e. the intelligibles], and the things that always
> remain below [i.e. material bodies]; and this is why it is in
> their nature to turn both towards the higher and towards
> the lower. When they incline their whole selves towards the
> higher things, their desires are simple and unconflicted.
> But sometimes they are incapable of this upward turning,
> because they wish to activate their turning towards the things
> below.   (Simp. *in Epict*. Hadot 1996: 202/D 6,41–8,
>   trans. Brennan & Brittain 2002; my insertions)

Following the lead of Plotinus, Simplicius claims that the soul
can use emotions along with the body as instruments (Hadot 1996:
194/D 2,1–10). However, doing so requires careful control, since
there are irrational motivational forces in us, too. This means that, as
opposed to the Stoics, for whom desires are beliefs formed by reason
and hence rational (even though not rational in the further sense
of being true), Simplicius allows desires that come from the two
lower parts of the soul introduced in Plato's *Republic* Book IV: spirited desire (*thumos*) and appetite (*epithumia*). These lower desires
are, according to Simplicius, to a large extent moved externally, so
that we do not have full control over them. Even though the lower
desires are moved externally and hence cannot control themselves,
the rational soul retains a freedom and responsibility as to how to
react to the lower desires:

> But as for the rational soul, when it surrenders itself to bod-
> ies and to irrational and bodily movements, it too is pulled
> about like a marionette and shoved, and it no longer has its
> motions really up to it. Whereas when it acts in accordance
> with its own nature and nobility, it is moved internally from
> itself, freely and self-determinately.   (Hadot 1996: 199/
>   D 4,40–52, trans. Brennan & Brittain 2002)

Here we encounter an important distinction formulated at the very beginning of Epictetus' *Handbook* between things that are up to us (*eph' hēmin*) and things that are not up to us. Simplicius understands the distinction in the way that even though there are different sources of motivational energy in our soul, we have full responsibility for and control over only those things that are in accordance with reason. Therefore, if we follow our lower desires, we are outsourcing our decisions, so to speak. And if we do so, we do not exercise our responsibility in an optimal manner or in a maximal degree. Simplicius illustrates the situation with the powerful metaphor of a marionette. A marionette moves because of external pushes and pulls. A human being should not do so. If we did, we would reject an important and noble force in us: to make decisions and to act in accordance with them. As we saw in Chapter 4, Simplicius also uses the marionette metaphor to describe cosmic teleology. In that context, the operator of the marionette device has a prominent role. In the same spirit, Simplicius here seems to imply that, because of our rational soul, we can become sovereign operators of our own inner movements, that is, emotions.

For Simplicius, moderate emotions in social life are useful to the extent that they allow us to try to impose rational organization and beautiful order on external matter and irrational desires. However, one needs to be extremely careful when utilizing emotions as instruments. We can illustrate this point by reference to how Simplicius instructs one to act with respect to marriage. He recommends that one postpone marriage to a stage of life when moral education has already gained a solid foundation (Hadot 1996: 254/D 34,2–9). Marriage and child-rearing can be chosen if one is able to handle them well. This is why postponing marriage is recommended. On the other hand, the older one becomes, the more one needs to become detached from earthly things, and hence marriage is not beneficial to old age either:

> [I]f you are an old man, and are already near the end, then do not bind yourself with any of these bonds, but instead direct your whole self to your return and separation from here.

> Otherwise, when the moment for the departure impends and you are called, you will be found a dawdler, someone dragged down by your own bonds and lamenting your newly-wedded wife and infant children.
>
> (Hadot 1996: 255–6/D 34,50–35,5, trans. Brennan & Brittain 2002)

Therefore, even though emotions carry some instrumental value for Simplicius, the improvement of material conditions "down here" is not our ultimate task. Our real objective is to ascend and detach ourselves: get ready for departure or, to be more specific, return to the Intellect and our noble origin. This ideal belongs to those who want to be genuine human beings, those who are "eager to regain the nobility of [their] ancestry" (Hadot 1996: 195/D 2,49–50), that is, the divine Intellect. In this context, Simplicius makes the somewhat surprising claim that even in this detachment process, ethical and political virtues involving moderate emotions are useful. It is only with the ultimate goal in mind that one is able to use the earthly instruments in a correct manner, but using them in an appropriate manner further promotes the ascent towards our true origin. When formulated in this way, the claim perhaps becomes less surprising. It serves to underline the point that, in all human activity, the crucial task is to understand our ultimate goal: the return to the Intellect.

The psychology of emotions: do they require belief?

Ancient discussion of self-discipline is based on theories concerning the psychology of emotions and, as recent scholarship has shown, significant analytical achievements were made in this discussion.[11] One of the central questions was whether or not emotions require beliefs or even are beliefs. As we saw above, the Stoics advocated the position that they are. Emotions are promoted by physiological reactions or pre-passions (*propatheiai*) such as growing pale or experiencing sinking or expansive feelings in one's chest. These reactions are not emotions unless followed by assent to an appearance that something good or bad is at hand or can be expected to be gained or encountered in the future.

We can simplify the Stoic analysis of emotion by using examples as follows. If one is in a ship at sea and a storm breaks out, one might at first grow pale, because this is how the body reacts to such a situation. One also gets the impression that something bad (death or injury) is approaching. Neither the reaction nor the appearance are emotions; they only become such if one *assents* to the appearance and accepts the belief that something bad actually is at hand. The exact nature of the beliefs that Stoics suppose to be necessary for emotions is disputed among scholars,[12] and even different Stoic philosophers proposed slightly different analyses. However, they agreed that emotions are beliefs. This analysis has an implication concerning emotional control: controlling one's beliefs will be sufficient to control one's emotions, because a genuine emotion never arises without assent to an appearance of value.

Aspasius

When discussing Aristotle's point (*EN* 1104b8–9) that ethical virtue is in a crucial way connected with handling pleasure and pain, Aspasius embarks on an excursus concerning emotions. A large part of his discussion is devoted to the classification of emotions where Aspasius' categorization deviates from Aristotle and the Stoics. Aspasius argues that all emotions can be classified under the two most generic ones: pleasure (*hēdonē*) and distress (*lupē*). He refers to Plato (*Laws* 636d) for the claim that these are the two most generic emotions. The same also appeared in Epicurus' list of the two *pathē* (D.L. 10.34), but it is not clear whether this statement amounts to the same claim as Aspasius makes.[13] Even more interesting than Aspasius' classification is his take on the question of whether beliefs are necessary for emotions. He argues firmly that they are not. This is not to say that emotions would, for Aspasius, be devoid of cognitive content. By contrast, Aspasius underlines the role of an appearance or *phantasia* in emotion. His point is that a mere appearance can be sufficient for causing an emotion in us.

Aspasius argues against some earlier Aristotelians, in particular Andronicus (of Rhodes) and Boethus (of Sidon), who belong to the very earliest phases of the commentary tradition in the first century BCE. According to Aspasius, Andronicus had defined emotion as "non-rational motion of the soul because of a supposition of evil or good" (*in EN* 44,21–2, trans. Konstan 2006). The crucial word here is "supposition" (*hupolēpsis*). Of the kinds of supposition Aristotle distinguishes in the *De anima* (427b25) – knowledge (*epistēmē*), practical reason (*phronēsis*) and belief (*doxa*) – it is the last one that is relevant here. The question is whether or not an emotion requires that we suppose something good or bad to be at hand in the present or future.[14]

Aspasius' argument against Andronicus is charming: perhaps Andronicus *did not know* that there are some emotions that arise in us without belief (*in EN* 45,1–10). Aspasius argues that sometimes desire or appetite arises on the mere perception of something beautiful; it is not necessary to believe that it is good (or that it would be good) to acquire the beautiful object for us to desire it. Aspasius is in fact making two separate points here, which he aims at Andronicus but that could equally well be directed at the Stoics: (i) belief is not necessary for emotion but it can arise on a mere perception or appearance; (ii) we need not evaluate something *as good* (or bad) in order to desire it (or dislike it). It is the mere appearance of something as pleasant or painful that is sufficient to trigger an emotion.

The latter point serves Aspasius' general argument in the context: to argue that the most generic emotions are pleasure and pain. He draws exactly this conclusion from his analysis of the psychology of emotion (45,15–16). However, he is careful to point out that this is not to deny that sometimes emotion does involve the supposition that something is good or bad. However, even in these cases he finds the appearance of pleasure or pain; the supposition of good or bad is made because what is good is pleasing and what is bad is painful (45,10–13).

Another objective for Aspasius is to argue against Andronicus about the definition of emotion. Whereas, according to Aspasius, Andronicus had defined it as "non-rational motion of the soul because of a supposition of evil or good" (44,21–2, trans. Konstan 2006), for Aspasius it becomes: "a motion of the non-rational part of the soul by what is pleasing or painful" (45,13–14, trans. Konstan 2006).

In addition to the point concerning suppositions, Aspasius' definition shows that his understanding of the soul is characteristically Platonic–Aristotelian. Whereas for the Stoics movements of the soul in adult human beings are movements of reason, Andronicus allows non-rational movement (*alogos kinēsis*; 44,22). However, Aspasius is even more explicit and defines emotion as a movement of the non-rational *part* of the soul (*kinēsis tou alogou tēs psuchēs*; 45,13). Therefore, Aspasius is more outspokenly Aristotelian than Andronicus was. Andronicus was very much under the spell of Stoicism. Whereas Andronicus speaks about non-rational movements in the soul, Aspasius expressly refers to a non-rational part of the soul. One of his examples is even based on the idea that the non-rational part can be moved without rational assent: this is when witty speech moves the non-rational part. In this case, Aspasius specifies, the appearance is *not* that something good is at hand, but that "we are moved by what is pleasing" (45,9–10, trans. Konstan 2006).

Aspasius' point that belief is not necessary for emotion does have intuitive appeal. It seems perfectly plausible to suggest that ideas or fantasies can produce emotions in us without belief. For example, a mere idea or image of one's beloved in another's arms may be sufficient to cause pain without the belief that this bad thing is at hand (or to be expected in the future). Or, the idea of getting a top grade for one's essay can already induce pleasure. In neither case, it seems, is it decisive whether the person having these ideas or images actually believes in them. The mere *possibility* of either of these alternatives being true seems to be sufficient to trigger an emotional reaction.

Simplicius
In his commentary on Epictetus' *Handbook*, Simplicius discusses the question of desires and aversions within the framework of Epictetus' distinction between what is up to us and what is not up to us.

Simplicius follows Epictetus in asserting that judgements are up to us. The object of a choice we make when assenting to or dissenting from an appearance is external; the act of assent or dissent itself is fully internal and fully up to us. Therefore, it is fully in our own power whether or not to believe that wealth or death, for example, is good or bad for us, even though wealth and death are external things (Hadot 1996: 197–8/D 4,1–12). When dealing with this point, Simplicius lays great stress on the priority of belief:

> It is clear that what comes first is belief (*hupolēpsis*), which is a sort of rational cognition (*logikē tis ousa gnōsis*), and fitting for human beings. And whenever the belief concerns our own good or bad, whether real or apparent, then either aversion or desire is always set in motion, and impulse follows them. (Hadot 1996: 198/D 4,30–35, trans. Brennan & Brittain 2002, modified)

This passage strongly suggests that all desires and appetites are based on a belief concerning good or bad and that Simplicius in this respect follows the Stoics. However, soon after making this claim, Simplicius goes on to add that there are irrational desires, of spirit (*thumos*) and appetite (*epithumia*), corresponding to the lower parts of a Platonically understood tripartite soul. Simplicius affirms that, as opposed to rational choice and judgement based on an act of assent or dissent, the spirited or appetitive desires are moved by external things (Hadot 1996: 199/D 4,40–50). This is because they are contiguous to the body and spring up from the composition of bodies; they are not strictly speaking up to us.

Even though Simplicius allows irrational desires and appetites, for which belief is not necessary, he is confident that even such desires can be tamed and brought under reason's control by acts of reason. As pointed out, if the rational soul identifies too much with the body, the lower desires may start to dominate so that the person's agentive power and control over his or her feelings diminishes. By contrast, a thorough understanding and stable conception of oneself as the rational soul separate from the body does entail control over the irrational desires as well. In sum, Simplicius does not fully agree with the Stoics that belief is necessary for all desire; he does allow irrational spirited and appetitive desires. However, even though all desires do not require beliefs, beliefs have a key role when it comes to controlling emotions – given that those beliefs are deeply experienced as truths concerning one's true nature.

Virtue and environment

Human community

Up to now, we have been discussing virtue and happiness from the point of view of the person to whom the virtues and happiness possibly belong. From this perspective, it might seem that ancient ethics was hopelessly egocentric or anthropocentric and that other people let alone other animal species did not have a significant role in it. However, this impression is misleading. As has been pointed out by several scholars (e.g. Annas 1993), the contrast between egoism and altruism is not a fruitful conceptual tool in analysing ancient ethics. For the Aristotelians, in particular, it was an important supposition that human beings are in nature sociable and that genuinely human life is possible only within a human community. Further, the idea that one could be virtuous but not good to others is alien to ancient ethics. But how can we reconcile the claim we found in Aspasius and Simplicius that friends are *instrumental* for certain goals in life with the idea that other people have intrinsic value? Or, if Porphyry exhorts philosophers to turn to an ascetic form of life, where everything bodily is avoided, how is it possible to see this as anything but egoistic?

Let us begin with the Aristotelians. One of the questions dealt with in *Ethical Problems* (no. 24) is how virtues are choiceworthy for their own sake. An example treated in the context is whether community (*koinōnia*) is to be chosen for its own sake or for some external reasons, and the author strongly asserts that community is choiceworthy as such. The argument is based on the affirmation that the essence of a human being requires community: we need it to use our natural capacity for communicating our thoughts and feelings to our fellow human beings (*Ethical Problems* 24.147,25–30). However, it is not to attain some further or more abstract good (communication and expression of one's nature) that community is vital for us. Rather, it is stated that community is necessary for our very being. If isolated even for a very short time, a human being is not capable of living as a human being (i.e. to live a distinctly human life as opposed to the life of the beasts).

However, the claim that a community is necessary for our being does not say anything very specific about how one should act towards one's fellow human beings. Another very interesting formulation of human sociability that does contain such a reference is found in Aspasius' commentary on the *Nicomachean Ethics*. Aspasius formulates the content of the claim that human beings are by nature sociable as follows: human sociability means that we treat our partners well (*eu poiein … tous koinōnous*). In fact, Aspasius is not just saying that our natural sociability means that we, by nature, do good things to our fellow human beings: he adds that this, that is, our natural sociability, is also the reason why happiness requires a complete life. It is only in a complete life that one is able to exercise one's communal nature and "do the maximum amount of good" (*in EN* 19,3–12, trans. Konstan 2006). Therefore, for Aspasius, the claim about human sociability is not merely the claim that human nature involves doing good to other people. He also states that our happiness requires it in the sense that our happiness is increased when we do more good things to others. In order for us to maximize our own happiness, we need to maximize the amount of good we do to others.

Even though Aspasius points out that friends have instrumental value (e.g. I need friends to be able to overthrow a tyrant – this kind of undertaking could never succeed if I tried alone), there is no indication in him that friends should have *merely* instrumental value. The commentary contains a discussion on friendship (or however we translate the Greek *philia*; see trans. Konstan 2006: n. 416) extending up to almost thirty pages (*in EN* 158,4–186,29). Aspasius firmly asserts that the focal meaning of *philia*, from which other uses of the notion derive, is friendship between virtuous people because of their virtue (163,27–164,32). In this case, friendship consists of "good will that does not go unnoticed among those who feel it mutually, and good will is a wish for good for the own sake of the one for whom one wishes good things" (164,22–3, trans. Konstan 2006). Here the point is precisely to underline that, in good friendship, one needs to have good will (*eunoia*) towards the other person *for the sake of that very person*, that is, not for one's own sake. Therefore, as a social virtue, friendship is clearly directed towards the good of the other and not an instrument for egoistic happiness.

Within the Aristotelian framework, *philia* or fellowship belongs to the members of the same community. This means that communities are bound together by ties that are stronger than merely inhabiting the same city or state. In this case, *philia* refers to some reciprocal obligations rather than strong feelings of unity or togetherness. In any case, the idea that bonds of *philia* or fellowship exist within human communities serves to strengthen natural human sociability and the demands that it sets for how to act towards other people.

How about later Platonists, then? In Simplicius, we also found the notion of an instrument: civic virtues are instrumental for our detachment from the body. If this means that all human interaction must be subordinated to the intellectual improvement of the philosopher, it seems to entail that no genuine value is found in other people. Further, if such social relations as marriage and childrearing are merely something that can be chosen provided that one's moral improvement is already quite solid, what does this tell us about human relations within Simplicius' framework?

In the course of his commentary on how to employ external things, Simplicius praises Epictetus for saying that the person who does not compete about external things is unbeatable (D 56,30–31). If we consider this from the point of view of the distinction between egoism and altruism, the advice is not to stick to externals and compete about them with others. Therefore, the person who is making progress, according to the advice given by Epictetus and Simplicius, is not greedy and does not want things for himself at the expense of others. It seems that the case is quite the contrary: happiness is only obtained when we fully understand that external things cannot be ours, but only rational choice is. In addition, when Simplicius instructs one not to get involved when trying to console a grieving friend, this advice is not just to protect the person who gives the consolation. Rather, Simplicius emphasizes that it is no use for the grieving person if one takes the grief upon oneself as well. If one does this, the consolation will not be helpful at all (Hadot 1996: 292–3/D 54,27–38).

Further, even if human life in a community were valuable from an instrumental rather than from an intrinsic perspective, it would be misleading to understand this as an *egoistic* take on ethics. As has been pointed out above, for Simplicius, detachment from ordinary human life and the objective of returning to the Intellect is a programme of cosmic improvement and perfection. The individual's perspective is not primary here. Rather, the idea is that, through philosophical work and understanding of human nature, the whole material world can come to a more orderly state. Since human beings have the double bond to the material and to the intelligible, they have the unique possibility of promoting this perfection. Simplicius' ideal can in some sense be solitary, but it is not egoistic: cosmic improvement certainly involves the objective of *common* rather than individual good. "Common" in this context is not even restricted to human good, but extends to the whole material world.

We noted above that in Aspasius human sociability is formulated in rather altruistic terms. In fact, a similar formulation can be found in Porphyry's *Starting Points to the Intelligible* or *Sentences* § 32. However, the point is not exactly the same: whereas Aspasius understands sociability as doing good to others, Porphyry's formulation is that sociability consists in action that avoids doing harm to our neighbours (§ 32 23,4–12; trans. Sorabji in Sorabji 2004: vol. 1, 338). This is perhaps in line with his ideal of ascetic life, which we shall now discuss.

Porphyry: ascetic ideal and animal ethics

Porphyry's treatise *On Abstinence from Killing Animals* is addressed to a friend, Firmus Castricius, who, as Porphyry's informants had reported, had resumed his habit of consuming flesh (Porph. *On Abstinence* 1.1.1). Porphyry writes him an open letter to convince him that there are no sufficient rational grounds for eating meat. Even though Porphyry brings in animal cognitive capacities and their suffering (especially in Book 3; see e.g. 3.19.2), his argument is not restricted to animal ethics. Rather, it is concerned with a comprehensive ideal of ascetic life peculiar to true philosophers, who among philosophers are rare cases.

The viewpoint of purity and "true philosophy" is visible in some of the arguments, for example, the one where Porphyry argues that even though animals were sacrificed, it is not necessary or advisable to eat them (Book 2). This point, which might seem odd, can be understood in Porphyry's program of purification. The purity of a true philosopher is only achieved through detachment from everything bodily. This applies equally to one's own bodily desires, to other human bodies (sex) and to consuming animal flesh (see e.g. 2.43.1–5). Therefore, if an animal has been sacrificed, this will not be a reason for eating it, since the most important thing is to keep one's soul pure. The point about sacrifice is important for Porphyry in arguing that piety towards gods does not demand consuming animal flesh.

This said, it is significant that Porphyry presents his purificatory ideal within a framework where justice is interpreted as avoiding doing harm to others: "And we, even if all wolves and vultures approve of meat-eating, will not agree that what they say is just, so long as humans are naturally harmless and inclined to refrain from acquiring pleasure for themselves by harming others" (3.1.3, trans. Clark 2000). This is not the only occasion where Porphyry underlines that justice should be understood in this manner. He argues against the Stoics, who maintained that moral notions such as justice are acquired through a process called "appropriation" (*oikeiōsis*). In this process, one turns to what is in accordance with one's nature and learns that what is in accordance with nature in this way is also good. Appropriation does not belong only to human beings; it is common to all animals. It explains, for example, why animals do not eat poisonous food. However, since human nature is, for the Stoics, different from the nature of all other animals (because human beings are the only rational animals according to them), this means that what is just for human beings is defined with reference to the human nature. Porphyry's point seems to be that this limits the applications of justice to the human species: what is in accordance with the nature of a rational creature is not the same as what is in accordance with the nature of the creatures that do not have reason. According to Porphyry, this is a misinterpretation of justice as a kind of philanthropy. Rather, Porphyry points out, justice consists in "restraint and harmlessness towards everything that does not do harm" (3.26.6, trans. Clark 2000).

The qualification "towards everything that does not do harm" is important in another argument: against those who wish to justify consuming flesh on the basis of the fact that some animals are harmful to human beings. Porphyry argues that even though it might be necessary to destroy some animals because of their savagery, this does not entail that domesticated animals should be killed (see e.g. 2.4.2). Further, Porphyry is also rather optimistic when it comes to animal goodwill towards human beings. He claims that animals only aim at harming us to the extent that it is necessary for them to survive. If an animal has a sufficient amount of food, then it feels no compulsion to attack human beings (3.12.4). According to Porphyry, it is evident that when it comes to savagery, anger and aggression, many human beings far surpass even the most terrifying animals: "they murder their children and kill their fathers" (3.19.3; trans. Clark 2000).

There are some who claim that justice does not extend to animals because they lack reason or cannot make contracts with us. The most important representatives of the claim that animals do not have reason are the Stoics, and the Aristotelians are also included, even though Aristotle's own position clearly varies in his different works.[15] Porphyry ascribes the point about contracts to the Epicureans (1.12.6–7).[16] The third book of Porphyry's treatise concentrates on the former point, that is, on showing that animals are rational.[17]

Porphyry's main arguments for animal rationality consist of the commonly accepted points that they have perception and memory

(3.1.4). Against those who claim that perception and memory do not require reason Porphyry argues as follows. Even if we granted that perception is possible without reason, memory would not be. His idea is that, in the absence of perception, there must be an active cognitive principle by virtue of which the animal "remembers, is afraid of painful things, longs for beneficial things and devises ways to make absent things present … and also traps for prey and escape-routes from attackers" (3.22.1, trans. Clark 2000). His conclusion, implicit in this particular context, is that only reason can explain these functions.

According to Porphyry, senses alone would in fact be of no use without emotions such as expectation, hope or fear. If there were a creature endowed with a capacity to suffer but no means of repelling the sufferings, then the capacity to feel would be entirely useless and bad (3.21.7). This argument shows a very interesting version of cosmic providence: in order for suffering to serve a purpose, it needs to come together with means to repair the injustice done.

One central argument for animal rationality in Book 3 is that animals have language (see e.g. 3.3–4). Porphyry takes this to be an obvious truth. He argues against some other philosophers who deny animal language on the grounds that they do not understand it. According to Porphyry, the difference between animal language and human language is similar to the difference between a human language that one understands and a human language that one does not understand. Even if we do not understand a human language, we do not claim that its speakers are devoid of language. Porphyry even claims that the idea that human beings in general do not understand animal language is false: he says that Arabs can understand ravens and Etruscans eagles (see trans. Clark 2000 n.396 *ad* 3.4.1).

A curious additional point that is repeated a couple of times in the treatise is the observation that animals also go mad. Porphyry refers to a common conviction that this happens to cattle and foxes (3.24.4). However, he points out that these cases are not needed, since we all know about dogs getting rabies. According to Porphyry, this shows that animals have rationality (*logos*): in rabies and madness reason is disturbed and confused (*ibid.*), and this cannot happen if one does not have reason to begin with. In addition to the madness argument, Porphyry produces rather extensive lists of common illnesses that are intended to underline the similarities between human beings and other animals (e.g. 3.7.3–7).

For Porphyry, the difference between human and animal rationality is one of degree.[18] Porphyry maintains that those who deny animal rationality make the fallacy of understanding it as one in kind:

> It is no wonder that humans are so different from animals in ability to learn, quickness of thought and all that concerns justice and community. Many animals too surpass human beings, some in size and swiftness, others in strength of sight and keenness of hearing; but this does not mean that humans are deaf or blind or powerless … Similarly, let us not say that if beasts think more sluggishly and are worse at reflection, they do not reflect or think at all, or even have reason (*logos*); but let us say that they have weak and turbid reason, like blurred and disturbed vision.
>
> (3.23.7–8; trans. Clark 2000, modified; cf. also 3.8.7)

The allegedly Epicurean point about contracts is taken up again towards the end of Book 3 (3.26.6). Porphyry denies such a requirement and claims that justice is increased by abstinence, even though animals are not capable of making contracts with us. In addition, he supposes that abstaining from harming animals will increase one's willingness to abstain from harming those of one's own kind. According to Porphyry, "the friend of the genus will not hate the species" (*ibid.*, trans. Clark 2000). He does not bring in any further arguments, but we might consider the point in the wider framework of understanding justice as abstinence from doing harm. If we suppose that one is willing to abstain from killing animals, this can be a sign of a just character. A just character would no doubt manifest itself as justice towards human beings as well.

As has been indicated, the guiding refrain for Porphyry's ascetic programme is "get rid of all body". This means a total liberation and detachment from one's own body as much as abstaining from sex and consuming animals. All contact with body (one's own or another's) pulls the soul down and prevents it from attaining the ideal of calmness and detachment. Contact with body also increases bodily desires, and those desires are insatiable (1.44–5). Porphyry often borrows from Plato's *Phaedo* the phrase "practising for death" (67e) to describe his ideal, but he strongly discourages one from taking one's own life: "A base, irrational soul, which leaves the body because it has been violently seized from it, remains with it; so when people die by violence their souls too are kept close by the body (and this is an obstacle to taking oneself out by violence)" (2.47.1, trans. Clark 2000). Porphyry reports that an Egyptian theologian[19] had even tested this point through experience. However, no specific method for testing it is given. In any case, Porphyry's passage clearly makes a point: even though one should strive for detachment from the body, this objective should not be searched for through violent means. It is through much more peaceful forms of asceticism that the detachment is to be attained.

Accordingly, starving oneself to death is not recommended either. But if one is not supposed to eat ensouled beings, how can one eat plants? Porphyry shows no willingness to deny that plants have soul (in this he deviates from some Platonists, such as Galen, who only attributed nature but not soul to plants). However, it is here that the animal capacity to perceive and suffer comes into the picture. Because plants have no perception, nothing will be bad for them, and there is no injustice towards them (3.19.2). This distinction blocks the argument according to which it makes no difference if we eat meat because we are forced to eat plants anyway.

Finally, even though Porphyry preaches total abstinence, he does not present this as a universal human ideal. Athletes need meat and even among philosophers the ascetic life is for some especially devoted individuals. For those individuals, the goal is to become like God:

> We must feed everything in us, but endeavour to fatten that which is most important in us. Now the food of the rational soul is that which maintains its rationality; and that is intel-

lect. So it should be fed on intellect, and we should strive to fatten it on that, not to fatten our flesh on meat. For intellect sustains our everlasting life, but when the body is fattened it starves the soul of blessed life and enlarges the mortal part, distracting and obstructing the soul on its way to immortal life, and it stains the soul by incarnating it and dragging it down to that which is alien.   (4.20.11; trans. Clark 2000)

EIGHT
Conclusion

We have now followed the outline of the commentators' curriculum and proceeded from themes in epistemology, logic and natural philosophy to the questions concerning the nature and structure of reality and the content and conditions of a happy human life. We have seen that the ancient commentaries are a rich source of arguments and developments in, sometimes also revisions and criticism of, the Platonic–Aristotelian tradition. Let us now consider the most significant systematic outcomes of our discussion.

One important strand that runs through the Platonic–Aristotelian tradition as we encounter it in the commentators consists in the assumption that reality is intelligible and knowable for human beings. This idea has consequences for the analysis of both human cognitive capacities and reality, and also links these two in a specific manner. In general, there are two kinds of objects of cognition related to our basic cognitive capacities: we perceive what is perceptible and can intellectually grasp what is intelligible. These aspects of reality are in a hierarchical relation to each other such that the intelligible is higher than the perceptible. An influential assumption formulated by Aristotle (which he attributes to Plato as well) is that the human cognitive development proceeds in the reverse order. We first come to know what is perceptible and proceed towards the intelligible.

Philoponus and Themistius follow Plato and Aristotle in arguing for the existence of principles and against the possibility of infinite knowledge claims (Chapter 2). On the one hand, this means that we start acquiring knowledge by making perceptions and that there are some general logical principles that regulate all forms of arguments and inference. On the other hand, mere perceptions of qualities and logical principles do not take us very far. In order to begin systematic enquiry into the nature of things, we need to be acquainted with much more complex things than perceptible qualities (Chapter 3). Starting from basic knowledge of facts and of the meanings of terms involved, such as that eclipses of the moon occur or that void is a certain kind of emptiness, we can discover general regularities in nature that explain the facts such as eclipses and come to understand what being void really means and whether it exists, and even proceed to form more abstract theories about the metaphysical structure of reality. This means that knowledge in the proper sense is not a simple structure in which conclusions are drawn from self-evident principles; rather, it requires pre-existent knowledge from which further principles are established that are more general and explanatory of previously cognized facts. Knowledge in the proper sense of the word (*epistēmē*) proceeds from these primary principles that are discovered by enquiry.

Even though Philoponus accepts this rather Aristotelian conception of knowledge about nature, he occasionally points out that the principles in nature need to be subordinated to higher principles "up there". Therefore, he indicates that knowledge about nature conceived in Aristotelian terms requires higher principles grasped by a Plotinian metaphysical Intellect. Simplicius, for his part, emphasizes that ordinary reasoning in our soul is always restricted by language and hence does not grasp the principles in the purest form. This is possible only by "turning back" to our origin, the Intellect.

Alexander and Philoponus have illuminating things to say about a tension that has been central in recent scholarly literature on Aristotle's philosophy of science: syllogistic is not useful in research and dialectic cannot establish the truth because it is based on credible but not true premises (Chapter 3). However, rather than seeing this as a harmful contradiction, Alexander (who articulates it) and Philoponus tend to take it that dialectic and syllogistic are instances of the same kind of activity. Alexander is certainly too optimistic when it comes to this point about unity, but there is a reasonable point behind the idea. Both dialectic and syllogistic are concerned with what we consider the validity of arguments but the premises have different requirements. When it comes to syllogistic, it is typically not the logic of discovery, but this does not mean that it would be useless in research. Its significance lies in offering a structure for what we are looking for, how we organize the results of our enquiry (see Ch. 3, "Alexander" and "Philoponus" in § "Syllogistic scheme"), and sometimes also for establishing what we have found out (see Ch. 3, "From facts to reasons"). As regards dialectic, Alexander and Philoponus recognize that even though dialectical arguments can only establish credibility but not truth, they are important in research. According to Alexander, dialectic helps us distinguish between truth and falsity. Logic and methodology can only take us to a certain point in which our grasping the result is dependent on whether we see it or not. What a scientist or a philosopher understands is always dependent on what he or she grasps and sees in the material; it cannot be an automatic outcome of mechanically applying a particular method. Alexander is certainly not pointing out the role of individual interpretation here; rather, he supposes that human beings do find general truths about reality.

In natural philosophy, an important general discussion concerns the question of what kinds of explanations one should look for in nature (Chapter 4). Combining Plato and Aristotle, the commentators articulate a complex system of types of causes some of which are prior to others. The main point made by Philoponus and Simplicius on causes is that in natural things final causes are predominant and that material conditions are contributory causes. This means, for example, that the primary cause for our having a certain material constitution is that we have certain psychic capacities for the realization of which those material components are necessary (Chapters 4 and 5, articulated by Philoponus). When arguing for the primacy of final causation, Simplicius presents an interesting example. If we want to know what the word "drachma" means, it is not informative to account for what a false drachma is. In general, we need to explain what successful instances are. As we saw, this is not just an epistemological point or a point about how we grasp the meaning of words. Rather, it is based on the idea that there are ends and functions in nature and that there are objective standards according to which we can evaluate to what extent things realize their ends and perform their natural functions.

If, then, there is final causation in nature, does this require that a divine agent is guiding its course or has put it in motion? Alexander affirms the existence of final causation and its compatibility with mechanism but denies rational choice or design. According to Simplicius, he illustrates the point by reference to an analogy: nature nods towards the form as a model, not through choice, but more like a marionette. This seems to imply that, for Alexander, natural mechanisms, as it were automatically, function to realize the ends that their forms imply. Simplicius does not accept Alexander's view. For him, the crucial point is that the marionette device starts to move only when the operator initiates the movement. It is not just that the operator gives the dolls (i.e. nature) an initial push. Rather, Simplicius argues that the operator also gives the dolls an inner impulse to move. Therefore, for Simplicius, final causation in nature needs to be initiated by divine intervention, which also installs ends in natural things and a drive to attain these ends.

Philoponus develops the idea of impressed impulses in his dynamic and the inventive critique of Aristotle's remark on how projectile motion is transmitted from a mover (e.g. a hand) to that, which is moved (e.g. a javelin). Philoponus rejects the idea that, in order for a hand to move the javelin, it needs to have pressed the air, which then moves the javelin. Philoponus argues that the hand impresses a force to the javelin and that force moves it when it has been dispatched from the hand. Philoponus' analysis was ahead of its time and proved persistent: Galileo still uses the notion of impressed force in a narrower application. It is not just Aristotle's dynamics that comes to be challenged by Philoponus and Simplicius. They also abandon Aristotle's analysis of space as the limit of a thing's surroundings and argue that place should be conceived of as a three-dimensional extension. In doing so they have essentially transformed Aristotle's notion of place into something close to a modern notion of space.

Let us now return to the question of knowledge acquisition. Both the idea that we have an ability to distinguish the truth from falsity when suitably trained and the view that research starts from pre-existent knowledge or cognition are based on the conception that such cognition can be explained by the natural functions of human cognitive capacities, the most important of which are perception and intellect. As to the more specific question of how perceptions occur (Chapter 5), Themistius and particularly Philoponus steer clear from the pitfalls of both an overtly materialist and a completely immaterialist account. Philoponus makes it explicit that in essence our perceptions are psychic capacities. However, such capacities require a certain kind of material constitution and definite bodily changes. For Philoponus perception is not an entirely immaterial process detached from the body; nor does he state that our perceptions somehow emerge from or are primarily caused by purely material processes. Changes in the body are necessary for perceptions to occur, but similar changes without the right kind of psychic capacities would not result in perception but mere bodily change.

As for the intellect, we have seen that for Alexander it is the pure receptivity of the intellect that explains its accuracy. When we grasp something intellectually, the intelligible form of that thing comes to be actualized in our intellect exactly as it is in the object. Without education this simply entails the capacities of recognition and language use, and perhaps some additional general conceptions (e.g. that human beings are animals, or that white is a certain colour). However, with education and habituation naturally suited individuals can come to understand the complex theoretical structure of reality (e.g. how various animal species relate to each other and what their specific differences are). The idea that receptivity is crucial for human cognition is challenged in the later Platonic commentaries. This applies both to perception and to intellectual apprehension. As for the former, the focus changes from the accounts of how perceptible objects can affect us to analysing perceptual and reflexive awareness of perceptions. With this development, later commentators such as Pseudo-Simplicius and Pseudo-Philoponus follow an important thread in later Platonism: what is essential in perception is an act of reason through which we become aware that we perceive or by which we make a perceptual judgement. Both in the case of perception and intellect, projective or attentive activity of reason is required.

The metaphysical assumption according to which reality is intelligible is interpreted in different ways in the commentaries (Chapter 6). For Alexander it means that there are immanent forms, the existence of which is dependent on the individual instances in which they exist. In addition to being the structuring principles of and immanent in the enmattered things, the forms are also actualized in the human intellect when we grasp those things. After Alexander, this analysis gives way to a more Platonically oriented variant according to which forms are not dependent on their enmattered instances but prior to them in existence. By contrast to Plato, who is more sceptical when it comes to the stability of the perceptible world (and Plotinus follows him here), most of the later commentators accept the immanent forms in addition to the transcendent forms (Porphyry is a major figure in this development). They conceive the immanent forms as being subordinated or secondary to the transcendent ones. The immanent forms in perceptible things could not exist without there being transcendent forms that fully realize what it is for their instances to be the kinds of things they are.

There are two main interpretations of this further claim. One is the account (coming from Plato's *Timaeus*) according to which a divine artificer or a demiurge has moulded and structured chaotic material into an organized whole using transcendent forms as models or paradigms for this "creation". Another one is to understand the forms within a Plotinian emanation hierarchy. In this context, the intelligible forms are fully realized in the metaphysical Intellect that eternally grasps them. This activity produces as its external aspect the order in the perceptible world. Both these tendencies are found, for example, in Simplicius, who at times claims that the order of the world derives from the activity of the demiurge (and the alleged fact that the demiurge is good). On other occasions he rather points to an emanation hierarchy where no personal artificer is needed but in which several levels of reality are separated and the higher levels are reflected in the lower ones in a less perfect form.

A major problem that the commentators follow in their attempt to make this kind of metaphysics work with respect to their sources is the following. Employing the basic Platonic–Aristotelian machinery, they conceive forms as being what is most fully real: as substances. However, in the *Categories* Aristotle seems to deny the primary substantiality of general forms. A substance in a primary sense is an individual instance of a certain species (this human being, this horse), and species are conceived as merely secondary substances. This is the exact reverse of the order of priority found in the majority of the commentators. Again, an influential move to reconcile these conflicting tendencies is found in Porphyry. He rejects his teacher Plotinus' view according to which the *Categories* cannot be a satisfactory analysis of being because it does not give a classification of the intelligible realm. Porphyry argues that Aristotle's categories are not meant to pertain to the intelligible but they concern words in so far as they signify things. Porphyry has clearly noted, as many philosophers in our time have also done, that the *Categories* lays much stress on how we speak about things. Yet the work clearly is not just a treatise on language. Rather, it makes sense to say that what being is in being a quality (being white) is distinct from the being of substances (being a horse). Another formulation of the application of the categories that emphasizes the latter observation is found in Simplicius: the *Categories* concerns things in so far as they are signified by words.

Ancient ethics in general is dominated by the claim that human beings aim at being happy. What happiness consists in and how it is acquired are disputed. A central more specific question in this dispute is whether virtue is sufficient for happiness. Whereas Plato, in the *Republic*, claims that it is, Aristotle denies this. For Aspasius, virtue results in a state in which one can appropriately react to great strokes of both good and bad fortune. If the misfortunes are sufficiently great, even a virtuous person is dislodged from happiness. However, even in this case a virtuous person is calm, not because of insensibility but because of the greatness of soul. By contrast, for Porphyry and Simplicius, virtue must be understood within a framework of purification and cosmic improvement in which Porphyry distinguishes between several hierarchical kinds of virtues. According to Porphyry, social and political virtues are instrumental with respect to a higher end, purification of the body and soul and theoretical activity. The highest virtues are paradigmatic and exercising them consists of entirely self-sufficient reflective activity and merging to the higher levels of being. For Simplicius, our end is to return to our origin, the Intellect. To do so, we need to be clear not to identify ourselves with the body, since otherwise we shall start to conceive our bodily affections, needs and desires as our own. Only when we deeply and fully understand that we are not our body but that our soul uses it as an instrument, and when we act accordingly, can we prepare ourselves for ascending back to the Intellect. Within Simplicius' scheme, human action also functions in the emanation process. Since we have a unique role within reality, being bound to the intelligible as well as to the sensible, our actions improve the material world around us when they are in accordance with true principles about what is good.

In the ethics of the commentators, we also find a striking development not sufficiently highlighted in existing scholarly literature. This is that the commentators radically transform Aristotle's idea according to which human beings are naturally sociable. Whereas Aristotle concentrates on the point that human essence requires an organized community and that groups have a common good, Aspasius' and Porphyry's formulations have an entirely different focus. According to Aspasius human sociability means we do well to our fellow human beings. In addition, he indicates that our happiness requires that we do the maximum amount of good to others, and it is to do so that happiness can only be realized in a complete life. Porphyry does not explicitly formulate his point in terms of sociability, but he claims that human beings have a natural tendency to avoid doing harm to creatures that are not harmful to them. Even though this might seem to be weaker than Aspasius' formulation, Porphyry needs it for additional, radical purposes: he wants to include other animal species as well. According to Porphyry, justice understood as harmlessness to those that do not harm us, needs to be extended even to other animal species. Otherwise it is in danger of being weakened into mere philanthropy.

Notes

1. Introduction

1. For the ancient commentaries as commentaries see, for example, G. E. Most (ed.), *Commentaries – Kommentare* (Göttingen: Vandenhoeck & Ruprecht, 1999) and D. N. Sedley, "Plato's Auctoritas and the Rebirth of the Commentary Tradition", in *Philosophia Togata II: Essays on Philosophy and Roman Society*, M. Griffin & J. Barnes (eds), 110–29 (Oxford: Oxford University Press, 1997).

2. For the emergence of a linear commentary in the Platonic tradition, see also G. Karamanolis, "Porphyry: The First Platonist Commentator on Aristotle", in *Philosophy, Science, and Exegesis in Greek, Arabic and Latin Commentaries*, P. Adamson, H. Baltussen & M. W. F. Stone (eds), *Bulletin of the Institute of Classical Studies Supplement* **83**(1&2) (London: Institute of Classical Studies, 2004), vol. 1, 97–120.

3. For the section in *Protagoras* as a commentary, see H. Baltussen, "Plato *Protagoras* 340–8: Commentary in the Making?", in Adamson *et al.* (eds), *Philosophy, Science, and Exegesis*, vol. 1, 21–35. For the ancient commentators more generally, see P. Hoffman, "What Was Commentary in Late Antiquity? The Example of the Neoplatonic Commentators", in *A Companion to Ancient Philosophy*, M. L. Gill & P. Pellegrin (eds), 597–622 (Oxford: Blackwell, 2006); H. Baltussen, "From Polemic to Exegesis: The Ancient Philosophical Commentary", in *Genres in Philosophy I*, J. Lavery (ed.). *Poetics Today* **28**(2) (2007), 247–81; cf. also G. Betegh, "Exegesis in the Derveni Papyrus", in Adamson *et al.* (eds), *Philosophy, Science, and Exegesis*, vol. 1, 37–50.

4. A similar pejorative tone is involved if the ancient commentaries are described as secondary sources, as sometimes happens; see I. Sluiter, "The Dialectics of Genre: Some Aspects of Secondary Literature and Genre in Antiquity", in *Matrices of Genre: Authors, Canons and Society*, M. Depew & D. Obbink (eds), 183–203 (Cambridge, MA: Harvard University Press, 2000) discussed in Baltussen, "From Polemic to Exegesis", 248.

5. For this reason Baltussen includes these discussions in his history of the commentary tradition ("From Polemic to Exegesis", 259).
6. Aristotle himself uses this term, when he divides his works into the exoteric and the others; see e.g. *Ph.* 217b31; *Metaph.* 1076a28; *Pol.* 1254a33, 1278b31.
7. For more references on the commentators on the exoteric works, see W. D. Ross (ed. & trans.), *The Works of Aristotle Vol. 12: Selected Fragments* (Oxford: Clarendon Press, 1952).
8. See J. Dillon, *The Heirs of Plato: A Study of the Old Academy (347–274 BC)* (Oxford: Oxford University Press 2003) for the "old", non-sceptical Academy.
9. On the term "Hellenistic", see K. Algra, J. Barnes, J. Mansfeld & M. Schofield (eds), *The Cambridge History of Hellenistic Philosophy* (Cambridge: Cambridge University Press, 1999), xii.
10. For a discussion of what Platonism is, see e.g. L. P. Gerson, "What is Platonism?", *Journal of the History of Philosophy* **43**(3) (2005), 253–76.
11. Richard Sorabji also accepts this: *The Philosophy of the Commentators: A Sourcebook*, 3 vols (London: Duckworth, 2004), vol. 1, 14–19.
12. For the term *Neuplatonismus*, see F.-P. Hager, "Zur Geschichte, Problematik, und Bedeutung des Begriffes 'Neuplatonismus'", *Diotima* **11** (1983), 98–110.
13. For Xenocrates, see Dillon, *The Heirs of Plato*, esp. chs 2–3, on the "Neoplatonic" elements in the Old Academy.
14. For the commentaries on *On Generation and Corruption*, see J. M. M. H. Thijssen & H. A. G. Braakhuis (eds), *The Commentary Tradition on Aristotle's De Generatione et Corruptione: Ancient, Medieval and Early Modern* (Turnhout: Brepols, 1999).
15. For discussion, see C. Natali, "Aspasius on the *Nicomachean Ethics* 7: An Ancient Example of 'Higher Criticism'?", *Oxford Studies in Ancient Philosophy* **33** (2007), 347–67; cf. A. Kenny, "Aspasius and the *Nicomachean Ethics* of Aristotle", in *Proceedings of the World Congress on Aristotle I*, 172–4 (Athens: Publication of the Ministry of Culture and Sciences, 1981).
16. For Alexander on Stoic physics, see R. Todd, *Alexander of Aphrodisias on Stoic Physics* (Leiden: Brill, 1976).
17. See, for example, A. Smith, *Philosophy in Late Antiquity* (London: Routledge, 2004), which concentrates on Neoplatonism, and particularly on Plotinus.
18. For the role of Aristotle in the curriculum, see Ammon. *in Cat.* 7,15ff.; Simp. *in Cat.* 3,18–6,18; L. G. Westerink, "The Alexandrian Commentators and the Introductions to Their Commentaries", in *Aristotle Transformed: The Ancient Commentators and their Influence*, R. Sorabji (ed.), 325–48 (London: Duckworth, 1990), 341–7; I. Hadot, "The Role of the Commentaries on Aristotle in the Teaching of Philosophy according to the Prefaces of the Neoplatonic Commentaries on the *Categories*", in *Aristotle and the Later Tradition*, H. Blumenthal & H. Robinson (eds), 175–89 (Oxford: Clarendon Press, 1991).
19. For example, Syrianus instructed Proclus (Marin. *Procl.* 13) to read all of Aristotle's works in two years and to become familiar with Plato's metaphysics through those works; see also Hadot, "The Role of the Commentaries", 176–87.
20. For Boethus of Sidon and Nicolaus of Damascus see S. Fazzo, "Aristotelianism as a Commentary Tradition", in Adamson *et al.* (eds), *Philosophy, Science, and Exegesis*, vol. 1, 5 n.14, and H. J. Drossaart-Lulofs, *Aristotle's De generatione animalium*

(Oxford: Oxford University Press, 1965). For Alexander of Aegae and Sotion see M. Frede, "Epilogue", in Algra *et al.* (eds), *The Cambridge History of Hellenistic Philosophy*, 776.

21. It has recently been argued that Aristotle comes to a similar conclusion in *Metaphysics* VII; e.g. M. Frede & G. Patzig, *Aristoteles' "Metaphysik Z": Text, Übersetzung, Kommentar* (Munich: Beck, 1988).

22. For Aristotle on time, see U. Coope, *Time for Aristotle* (Oxford: Oxford University Press, 2005).

23. For the early commentaries on the *Categories* in general, see H. B. Gottschalk, "The Earliest Aristotelian Commentators", in Sorabji (ed.), *Aristotle Transformed*, 55–81, originally published in *Aufstieg und Niedergang der römischen Welt (ANRW)* II 36.2 (Berlin: de Gruyter, 1987).

24. The evidence is collected in I. Mariotti, *Aristone d'Alessandria* (Bologna: Riccardo Patron, 1966).

25. For discussion of Eudorus' work, see further K. Praechter, "Nikostratos der Platoniker", *Hermes* **57** (1922), 481–517, reprinted in his *Kleine Schriften*, H. Dörrie (ed.), 101–37 (Hildesheim: Georg Olms, 1973); P. Moraux, *Der Aristotelismus bei den Griechen von Andronikos bis Alexander von Aphrodisias 1: im I Jh v. Chr.* (Berlin: de Gruyter, 1973); J. Dillon, *The Middle Platonists: 80 BC to 220 AD*, 2nd edn (Ithaca, NY: Cornell University Press, 1996).

26. For Alexander's school, see R. W. Sharples, "The School of Alexander?", in Sorabji (ed.), *Aristotle Transformed*, 83–111.

27. For Nicostratus, see Gottschalk, "The Earliest Aristotelian Commentators", 80; Praechter, "Nikostratos der Platoniker".

28. For more information about Lucius' and Nicostratus' objections against Aristotle's *Categories*, see Strange's introduction to his translation of Porph. *on Cat.* (1992: 2 n.8).

29. A new English translation of the *Mantissa* is by R. W. Sharples, *Alexander of Aphyrodisias: Supplement to* On the Soul (Ithaca, NY: Cornell University Press, 2004). His "Alexander of Aphrodisias: What is a Mantissa?", in Adamson *et al.* (eds), *Philosophy, Science, and Exegesis*, **83**(1), 51–69, offers a longer introduction to the treatise.

30. More references concerning Alexander's life and works are found in R. W. Sharples, "Alexander of Aphrodisias: Scholasticism and Innovation", *Aufstieg und Niedergang der römischen Welt* **36**(2) (1987), 1176–243.

31. See I. Kupreeva's review of Robert B. Todd (trans.), *Themistius: On Aristotle's* On the soul (1996), in *Bryn Mawr Classical Review* 97.7.1 http://ccat.sas.upenn.edu/bmcr/1997/97.07.01.html (accessed January 2009).

32. For the earlier uses of *paraphrasis*, see H. J. Blumenthal, "Photius on Themistius (cod. 74): Did Themistius Write Commentaries on Aristotle?", *Hermes* **107**(2) (1979), 168–82; O. Ballériaux, "Thémistius et l'exégèse de la noétique aristotelicienne", *Revue de la philosophie ancienne* 7 (1989), 199–233.

33. As Todd notes in *Themistius on Aristotle on the Soul* (London: Duckworth, 1996), 4 n.25, Themistius' description of his method fits rather nicely with Quintilian's definition of *paraphrasis*.

34. Balleriaux ("Thémistius et l'exégèse") advocates a Neoplatonic reading; Todd (*Themistius on Aristotle on the Soul*) opposes him; cf. also H. J. Blumenthal, "Alexander

of Aphrodisias in the Later Greek Commentaries on Aristotle's *de Anima*", in *Aristoteles: Werk und Wirkung, Paul Moraux gewidmet*, J. Wiesner (ed.), vol. 2. 90–106 (Berlin: de Gruyter, 1987).

35. As to whether Themistius employs the principle of harmony between Plato and Aristotle, see J. Vanderspoel, *Themistius and the Imperial Court: Oratory, Civic Duty, and Paideia from Constantius to Theodosius* (Ann Arbor, MI: University of Michigan Press, 1995), 20 and ch. 2.

36. See also Simp. *in Ph.* 1249,12–13, where a contrast is made between a difference in words (*onomata*) and one concerning things (*pragmata*). As to the tasks of a commentator, Elias/David adds that he should strive for finding consistency rather than inconsistency within Plato and Aristotle separately (*in Cat.* 123,7–12).

37. See Dillon's introduction to the translation of Dexippus' commentary on the *Categories* (trans. Dillon, 1990: 7).

38. For a recent historical study of the schools, see E. Watts, *City and School in Late Antique Athens and Alexandria* (Berkeley, CA: University of California Press, 2006).

39. For these authors and their relation to Platonism and to Christianity, see Westerink, "The Alexandrian Commentators".

40. For the archaeological evidence concerning the location of the Neoplatonic school in Athens, see P. Hoffmann, "Damascius", in *Dictionnaire des philosophes antiques* (vol. 2), 541–93 (Paris: CNRS, 1994), 548–55.

41. The suggestion has been made by M. Tardieu, "Les calendriers en usage à Harran d'après les sources arabes et le commentaire de Simplicius à la *Physique* d'Aristote", in *Simplicius: sa vie, son oeuvre, sa survie*, I. Hadot (ed.), 40–57 (Berlin: de Gruyter, 1987) and *Les paysages reliques: Routes et haltes syriennes d'Isidore à Simplicius* (Louvain: Peeters, 1990). J. Lameer, "From Alexandria to Bagdad: Reflections on the Genesis of a Problematical Tradition", in *The Ancient Tradition in Christian and Islamic Hellenism*, G. Endress & R. Kruk (eds), 181–91 (Leiden: CNWS Publications, 1997) corrects some mistaken suppositions in Tardieu. Criticism of Tardieu is also found in P. Folkes, "Where Was Simplicius?", *Journal of Hellenic Studies* **112** (1992), 143, to whom Hadot replies in *Simplicius: Commentaire sur le Manuel d'Epictète* (Leiden: Brill, 1996). See also Sorabji, *The Philosophy of the Commentators*, 11 n.8 (in all three volumes) and Simp. *in Epict.*, trans. Brittain & Brennan (2002), 3–4.

42. Simplicius' commentary on Epictetus' *Handbook* was translated in two volumes, 1–26 and 27–53, in the *Ancient Commentators on Aristotle* series by T. Brennan & C. Brittain (2002). For a Greek text of Simplicius' commentary, the reader is recommended to use Hadot, *Simplicius*; in addition, references in the form D 71,48 refer to page and line numbers in the Schweighäuser (1800) edition, reprinted by Dübner (1840), and given by trans. Brennan & Brittain (2002).

43. For a discussion of the narratives, see D. Gutas, "The 'Alexandria to Bagdad' Complex of Narratives: A Contribution to the Study of Philosophical and Medical Historiography among the Arabs", *Documenti e studi sulla tradizione filosofica medievale* **10** (1999), 155–93.

44. This claim goes against Verrycken's thesis, but seems to correspond better to Philoponus' procedure.

45. For further reading on Byzantine philosophy, see K. Ierodiakonou (ed.), *Byzantine Philosophy and its Ancient Sources* (Oxford: Clarendon Press, 2002).

46. For the transmission, see, e.g., Gutas, "The 'Alexandria to Bagdad' Complex of Narratives".
47. For the commentaries that the Arabs consulted, see F. E. Peters, *Aristoteles Arabus: The Oriental Translations and Commentaries of the Aristotelian Corpus* (Leiden: Brill, 1968).

2. Epistemology

1. For the qualification "we think we know", see M. R. Johnson, *Aristotle on Teleology* (Oxford: Clarendon Press, 2005), 94–5.
2. For Philoponus, see *in APo*. 20,28–21,4, although he explicitly presents this as a view of Aristotle (20,28). For Themistius, see *in APo*. 5,8–13.
3. For further reading, see D. N. Sedley, "Alcinous' Epistemology", in *Polyhistor: Studies in the History and Historiography of Philosophy*, K. Algra, P. W. van der Horst & D. Runia (eds), 300–312 (Leiden: Brill, 1996), which provides a classification of cognitive faculties in that commentary, and his "A New Reading in the Anonymous *Theaetetus* Commentary (PBerol. 9782 fragment D)", in *Papiri filosofici: Miscellanea di studi I*, 139–44 (Florence: L. S. Olschki, 1997). As to the dating of the commentary, Harold Tarrant, *Scepticism or Platonism: The Philosophy of the Fourth Academy?* (Cambridge: Cambridge University Press, 1985) dates it back to the first century BCE. See also the edition by G. Bastiniani & D. Sedley, "Anonymous Commentarius in Platonis *Theaetetum*", in *Corpus dei papiri filosofici greci e latini,* vol. III, 227–562 (Florence: Olschki, 1995). More recently, Charles Brittain, *Philo of Larissa: The Last of the Academic Sceptics* (Oxford: Oxford University Press, 2001), has argued for a later dating in the first century CE.
4. A similar idea also occurs, for example, in Simp. *in Cat*. 17,18–20, and Porph. *in Cat*. 89,1–27.
5. For syllogistic figures, see Chapter 3; for Stoic indemonstrables, see M. Frede, *Die Stoische Logik* (Göttingen: Vandenhoek & Ruprecht, 1974); S. Bobzien, "Logic", in *The Cambridge Companion to the Stoics*, B. Inwood (ed.), 85–123 (Cambridge: Cambridge University Press, 2003); and my *Apprehension and Argument: Ancient Theories of Starting Points for Knowledge* (Dordrecht: Springer, 2007), 265–7.
6. The claim and scholarly reactions to it are discussed in my *Apprehension and Argument*, 228–33.
7. Simplicius also refers to this idea in his commentary on the *Categories* 8,3–8.
8. The fallacy is analysed in S. Schreiber, *Aristotle on False Reasoning: Language and the World in the Sophistical Refutations* (Albany, NY: SUNY Press, 2003), 132–3.
9. Alexander also uses the expression *ou mallon* (*in Metaph*. 301,9). The expression originated with Democritus, and Aristotle employs it when discussing him. It also had an important role in later scepticism.

3. Science and logic

1. The commentary published after Philoponus on book II in CAG XIII 3 is spurious.

2. For further reading on question (ii), see Sorabji, *The Philosophy of the Commentators*, vol. 3, 37–55.

3. For general introductions to Aristotle's dialectic, see R. Smith, *Aristotle: Topics, Books I and VIII with Excerpts from Related Texts* (Oxford: Clarendon Press, 1997); T. Wagner & C. Rapp (comments & trans.), *Aristoteles "Topik"* (Stuttgart: Reclam, 2004), 7–38.

4. Nicholas Rescher attributed this role to Galen in "New Light from Arabic Sources on Galen and the Fourth Figure of the Syllogism", *Journal of the History of Philosophy* 3 (1963), 27–41; for references and a discussion, see Sorabji, *The Philosophy of the Commentators*, vol. 3, 258–9.

5. See Ammon. *in APr.* 10,34–11,14; Sorabji, *The Philosophy of the Commentators*, vol. 3, 32–6. For Aristotle's statement, see *Top.* 163b9–12.

6. For the role of dialectic in philosophy, see also Simp. *in Ph.* 47,22, *in Cael.* 523,25–7; Alex.Aphr. *in Top.* 174,3; Ascl. *in Metaph.* 140,7.

7. For the medieval interpretation of the *Isagoge*, see also A. de Libera, *Isagoge: texte grec, translatio Boethii* (Paris: Vrin, 1998), cxxvii–cxxxv. For Porphyry's influence on Boethius, see also S. Ebbesen, *Greek–Latin Philosophical Interaction: Collected Essays of Sten Ebbesen*, vol. 1 (Aldershot: Ashgate, 2008), e.g. 109–13.

8. See the translation by Barnes (2003: 110) for a diagram of how this division can be made to look like a tree.

9. For example, I. Düring, *Aristotle in the Ancient Biographical Tradition* (Göteborg/Stockholm: Intitute of Classical Studies in the University of Göteborg, 1957); O. Ballériaux, "Thémistius et le Néoplatonisme: le *nous pathetikos* et l'immortalité de l'ame", *Revue de la philosophie ancienne* 12 (1994), 171–200; H. J. Blumenthal, "Themistius: The Last Peripatetic Commentator on Aristotle", in Sorabji (ed.), *Aristotle Transformed*, 113–24. Gerson ("What is Platonism?") claims that in the passages quoted by Düring, Themistius supposes Plato and Aristotle to be in harmony.

10. For Plotinus on Intellect, see E. K. Emilsson, *Plotinus on Intellect* (Oxford: Oxford University Press, 2007).

11. See e.g. Alcinous *Didaskalikos* 5.5, 157,22–36, discussed in Tuominen, *Apprehension and Argument*, 120–22.

12. Philoponus also presents the geometrical example from Plato's *Meno* in detail (*in APo.* 14,13–15,20).

13. For example, the proofs might have been given in collections mentioned in the ancient lists of Aristotle's works; D.L. 112–17, *Vita Hesychii* 53, 100–104, 160; see M. R. Johnson, "Aristotle the Natural Philosopher", unpublished manuscript.

14. The whole proof can be found in McKirahan's translation (2008).

15. The examples are from the commentaries of Themistius (*in APo. ad* II 8) and Philoponus (*in APo.* 42,22–6).

16. Cf. the objections by Proclus *in Metaph.* I 1, discussed in C. Helmig, "Proclus and other Neoplatonists on Universals and Predication", *Documenti e studi sulla tradizione filsofica medievale* 19 (2008), 31–52.

17. Themistius and Philoponus do not explain how we come to know this reason, unless we take *ankhinoia* to be an explanation of this; for the example, see Aristotle *APo.* II 8; Phlp *in APo.* 65,15–20. For Aristotle's view on how we come to know causes, see my *Apprehension and Argument*, 102–10, 181–4; C. H. Kahn, "The Role of *Nous* in the Cognition of First Principles in *Posterior Analytics* II 19", in *Proceedings of the*

Eighth Symposium Aristotelicum: Aristotle on Science: The "Posterior Analytics", E. Berti (ed.), 385–414 (Padua: Antenore, 1981); J. Lesher, "The Meaning of *Nous* in the *Posterior Analytics*", *Phronesis* **18**(1) (1973), 44–68.

18. For Philoponus' use of the examples, see Phlp. *in APr.* 481,10–25.
19. For a reference to signs in Themistius, see *in APo.* 6,20–26.
20. Philoponus' commentary is based on Ammonius' lectures. Ammonius himself also wrote a commentary on *Prior Analytics*, but for some reason his comments end after Chapter 26 of Book I. He does not explain why.
21. Aristotle speaks only of "procedure" (*hodos*) in this connection; he does not employ the word "method" (*methodos*).
22. In his translation of Alexander's *On Aristotle* Prior Analytics (2006), Ian Mueller translates this as "music theorist". It is, of course, possible that this is what Alexander is saying in the passage. However, the word as such does not necessitate such a technical reading.
23. On this problem, see J. Barnes, "Aristotle's Theory of Demonstration", *Phronesis* **14** (1969), 123–52, revised and reprinted in *Articles on Aristotle, Vol. 1: Science*, J. Barnes, M. Schofield & R. Sorabji (eds), 65–87 (London: Duckworth, 1975), and "Proof and the Syllogism", in Berti (ed.), *Proceedings of the Eighth Symposium*, 17–59; W. Wians, "Aristotle, Demonstration and Teaching", *Ancient Philosophy* **9** (1989), and "Commentary on Lloyd", *Proceedings of the Boston Area Colloquium in Ancient Philosophy* **VI** (1990), 402–12; R. Bolton, "Definition and Scientific Method in Aristotle's *Posterior Analytics* and *Generation of Animals*", in *Philosophical Issues in Aristotle's Biology*, A. Gotthelf & J. Lennox (eds), 120–66 (Cambridge: Cambridge University Press, 1987); A. Gotthelf, "First Principles in Aristotle's *Parts of Animals*", in Gotthelf & Lennox (eds), *Philosophical Issues in Aristotle's Biology*, 167–98; J. Lennox, "Divide and Explain: The Posterior Analytics in Practice", in Gotthelf & Lennox (eds), *Philosophical Issues in Aristotle's Biology*, 90–119, reprinted in his *Aristotle's Biology: Studies in the Origins of Life Sciences* (Cambridge: Cambridge University Press, 2001). G. E. R. Lloyd calls it "the hoary old chestnut indeed" in "The Theories and Practices of Demonstration in Aristotle", *Proceedings of the Boston Area Colloquium in Ancient Philosophy* **6** (1990), 371–401, esp. 371.
24. For a discussion, see my "Alexander and Philoponus on the *Prior Analytics* I 27–30: Is there Tension between Aristotle's Scientific Theory and Practice?", in *Interpretations of the* Posterior Analytics, F. A. J. de Haas, forthcoming, and "How Do We Know the Principles?", in *Erfahrung und Beweis: Die Wissenschaften von der Natur im 13. und 14. Jahrhundert*, A. Fidora & M. Lutz-Bachmann (eds), 11–22 (Berlin: Akademie).

4. Physics

1. For Simplicius, see *in Ph.* 10,25ff.; F. A. J. de Haas, "Modifications of the Method of Inquiry in Aristotle's *Physics* I.1: An Essay on the Dynamics of the Ancient Commentary Tradition", in *The Dynamics of Aristotelian Natural Philosophy from Antiquity to the Seventeenth Century*, C. H. Leijenhorst, C. Lüthy, J. M. Thijssen & C. Leijenhorst (eds), 31–56 (Leiden: Brill, 2002).

2. See Sorabji, *The Philosophy of the Commentators*, vol. 2, 44–5. For Porphyry, see Ch. 7. § "Porphyry: ascetic ideal and animal ethics". Cf. *To Gaurus [ad Gaurum]*, an extant tr, which G. Karamanolis, *Plato and Aristotle in Agreement? Platonists on Aristotle from Antiochus to Porphyry* (Oxford: Clarendon Press, 2006) treats as authentic.
3. See Philoponus, *On Aristotle* Physics 2, trans. Lacey (1993), n.342 *ad* 241,19. For immanent forms in Platonic tradition, see Karamanolis, *Plato and Aristotle in Agreement?*, 272ff.
4. More than seven centuries later in 1277, this view was banned in the Paris condemnations.
5. For example, Phlp. *in Ph*. 318,5–14; for the scribe example, see Arist. *Ph*. 199a33.
6. For references, see R. Sorabji, *Matter, Space and Motion: Theories in Antiquity and Their Sequel* (London: Duckworth, 1988), 228–9.
7. Galileo still uses the notion of impressed force to explain projectile motion, but his application of the notion is narrower than it is in Philoponus; see *ibid.*, 238.
8. Which of the three authors it was who introduced this idea, has been disputed; see e.g. R. S. Westfall, "Circular Motion in Seventeenth-Century Mechanics", *Isis* **63** (1972), 184–9.
9. It has been suggested that Proclus was the source of these developments, but this is not certain; see M. Wolff, "Philoponus and the Rise of Preclassical Dynamics", in Sorabji (ed.), *Philoponus and the Rejection*, 84–120.
10. See further Sorabji, *The Philosophy of the Commentators*, vol. 2, 234; D. N. Sedley, "Philoponus' Conception of Space", in Sorabji (ed.), *Philoponus and the Rejection*, 140–53. For Simplicius, see Sorabji, *The Philosophy of the Commentators*, vol. 2, 243.
11. See also Sorabji, *Philoponus and the Rejection*, 23–4.
12. At first sight, it seems paradoxical to claim that the Intellect could be above anything because it is not spatial at all. For an interpretation, see J. Wilberding, "Creeping Spatiality: 'The Location of *Nous* in Plotinus' Universe'", *Phronesis* **50**(4) (2005), 315–34.
13. For Alexander's position, see further I. M. Bodnár, "Alexander of Aphrodisias on Celestial Motion", *Phronesis* **42**(2) (1997), 190–205.
14. For references, see Wilberding, "Creeping Spatiality".
15. For internal tensions in Philoponus' work, see K. Verrycken, "The Development of Philoponus' Thought and its Chronology", in Sorabji (ed.), *Aristotle Transformed*, 233–74, and L. S. B. MacCoul, "A New Look at the Career of John Philoponus", *Journal of Early Christian Studies* **3**(1) (1995), 47–60.
16. For this methodological idea, see Philoponus *contra Proclum* 9,14ff.

5. Psychology: perception and intellect

1. For Plotinus on Intellect, see Emilsson, *Plotinus on Intellect*.
2. See further P. Moraux, *Alexandre d'Aphrodise: Exégète de la Noétique d'Aristote* (Liège: University of Liège, 1942) and "Aristoteles, der Lehrer Alexanders von Aphrodisias", *Archiv für Geschichte der Philosophie* **49**(2) (1967), 169–82; B. Bazán, "L'authenticité

du 'De Intellectu' attribué à Alexandre d'Aphrodise", *Révue Philosophique de Louvain* 71 (1973), 468–87; and F. W. Schroeder, "The Potential or Material Intellect and the Authorship of the *De Intellectu*: A Reply to B. C. Bazán", *Symbolae Osloenses* 57 (1982), 115–25.

3. The editor of the CAG edition, M. Hayduck, makes a brief but effective remark about its weaknesses in interpretation and its brevity (p. v) and he attributes the commentary to Stephanus. This identification is criticized by William Charlton in his translation of *On Aristotle* On the Intellect (1991), 4–12.

4. Charlton conjectures that the commentary that William of Moerbeke translates was originally in the place of the spurious commentary on Book III. He adds that how and why it came to be replaced by the spurious text is a mystery.

5. Their arguments are criticized by Hadot, *Simplicius* and "Simplicius or Priscianus? On the Author of the Commentary on Aristotle's *De anima* (CAG XI): A methodological study", *Mnemosyne* 55(2) (2002), 159–99.

6. A short list of the differences is found in Steel's introduction to his translation (1997: 112–16).

7. *Ibid.*: 116–20.

8. For the parts of soul, see *de An.* II 2, 413b11–14.

9. For a general discussion of animal minds in antiquity, see R. Sorabji, *Animal Minds and Human Morals: The Origins of the Western Debate* (Ithaca, NY: Cornell University Press, 1993). For the ethical implications of animal cognition, see Chapter 7, § "Porphyry: ascetic ideal and animal ethics".

10. For the discussion, see P. Lautner, "Plutarch of Athens on *koinê aisthêsis* and *phantasia*", *Ancient Philosophy* 20 (2000), 425–46.

11. For the discussion, see the texts in Sorabji, *The Philosophy of the Commentators*, vol. 1, 253–61.

12. For Plotinus on the relation between human souls and the world soul, see *ibid.*, vol. 1, 252–3.

13. The point of saying that a colour is a limit of the transparent seems to be that in order to be able to affect air that functions as the medium for sight, the colour needs to be contiguous with air.

14. For the argument, see e.g. Phlp. *in de An.* 329,24–30. See also the argument in 329,15–24: if the air were coloured, it could not transmit contrary colours at the same time.

15. The metaphor of the wax block was a common one; Plato does not seem to accept it in the *Theaetetus* (191c–d), whereas Aristotle uses it approvingly (*de An.* II 12, 424a19ff.); Plutarch also attributes a similar view to the Stoics (*tupōsis; Comm. not.* 1084f–1085a; also A. A. Long & D. N. Sedley, *The Hellenistic Philosophers*, vol. 1 (Cambridge: Cambridge University Press, 1987), 39F), whereas Chrysippus is reported to have rejected the wax block model (D.L. 7.50; also Long & Sedley, *The Hellenistic Philosophers,* 39A); cf. also Porphyry (*Harm.* 14,7–21.)

16. For the question in the commentaries, see R. Sorabji, "From Aristotle to Brentano: The Development of the Concept of Intentionality", in Blumenthal & Robinson (eds), *Aristotle and the Later Tradition*, 227–59.

17. The reader can access this discussion in Charlton's translation (2005; CAG XV 354,19–384,33).

18. In fact, Aristotle seems to accept sight streams or rays in Book III of the *Meteorology*, but the view is contradicted in the *De anima*.
19. According to Philoponus (*in de An.* 354,13–16), it comes from Theophrastus. Themistius attributes it to a vague group of "the commentators" (*exēgētai*; *in de An.* 62,31–2). Cf. *to diaphanes* "the transparent" in Aristotle.
20. Philoponus' claim that balls rebound from *soft* surfaces seems odd, since we would rather think that they do so from hard surfaces. What he means here, is not entirely clear.
21. Again, Philoponus has difficulty in directly contradicting Aristotle. When commenting on the passage where Aristotle denies that light moves, Philoponus follows him (*in de An.* 344,33–345,11).
22. Philoponus identifies the bodily mixture as a contributory cause (*sunaition*). The notion of a contributory cause is familiar to us in the Stoic analysis of causes. However, it is already used by Plato in the *Timaeus*, where he characterizes the material restrictions as contributory causes (*sunaitia*; 46c–d, 47e–48a, 68e–69a). They are contributory in the sense that they affect to what extent the forms as paradigms can be realized in our cosmos.
23. The evidence and the origins of the argument are discussed in Lautner, "Plutarch of Athens".
24. For Aristotle's discussion of in what sense psychic capacities are affected, see e.g. *de An.* II 5.
25. For mathematical imagination, see Proclus' commentary on Euclid's *Elements*.
26. None of these authors identified the vocal chords.
27. For animal language in the commentaries, see further Chapter 7, § "Porphyry: Ascetic ideal and animal ethics".
28. Aristotle's discussion is so unsystematic that it is slightly misleading to say that he took common sense to be a specific function of the perceptive soul. This often happens in the scholarly literature; for a recent study see P. Gregoric, *Aristotle on the Common Sense* (Oxford: Oxford University Press, 2007).
29. For a Neoplatonic account of *phantasia*, see A. Sheppard, "Phantasia and Inspiration in Neoplatonism", in *Studies in Plato and the Platonic Tradition*, M. Joyal (ed.), 201–10 (Aldershot: Ashgate, 1997); "The Mirror of Imagination: The Influence of *Timaeus* 55cff.", in *Ancient Approaches to Plato's Timaeus*, R. W. Sharples & A. Sheppard (eds), 203–12 (London: Institute of Classical Studies, 2003); A. Sheppard, "Porphyry's Views on Phantasia", in *Studies on Porphyry*, G. Karamanolis & A. Sheppard (eds), *Bulletin of the Institute of Classical Studies*, supplement 98 (London: Institute of Classical Studies, 2007). For *phantasia* in perception, see E. K. Emilsson, *Plotinus on Sense Perception: A Philosophical Study* (Cambridge: Cambridge University Press, 1988).
30. Aristotle is vague here. He just points out that the difference holds in the case of soul but does not specify whether he means within a specific kind of soul or between different kinds of souls. Cf. V. Caston, "Aristotle's Two Intellects: A Modest Proposal", *Phronesis* **44**(3) (1999), 199–227.
31. For a defence of Themistius' Neoplatonism, see Ballériaux, "Thémistius et l'exégèse".

6. Metaphysics

1. For problems related to the ancient edition, see J. Barnes, "Aristotle in Rome", in Griffin & Barnes (eds), *Philosophia Togata II*, 1–69; S. Menn, "The Editors of the *Metaphysics*", *Phronesis* **40**(2) (1995), 202–8.
2. Asclepius was a student of Ammonius.
3. Outside the *Categories* the full list of ten appears only once, in *Topics* I 9, which probably was written around the same time as the *Categories*.
4. These verbs are used as substantive participles, for example, in the *Theaetetus* 156a: "that which acts upon" (*to poioun*) and "that which is acted upon" (*to paskhon*)
5. For analyses of Plotinus' criticism, see R. Chiaradonna, *Sostanza, movimento, analogia: Plotino critico di Aristotele* (Naples: Bibliopolis, 2002), 117–46; A. C. Lloyd, *The Anatomy of Neoplatonism* (Oxford: Clarendon Press, 1990); S. K. Strange, "Plotinus, Porphyry, and the Neoplatonic Interpretation of the *Categories*", *Aufstieg und Niedergang der römischen Welt* (*ANRW*) II **36**(2) (1987), 955–74; cf. Karamanolis, *Plato and Aristotle in Agreement?*, 234–8.
6. For additional passages on the topic, see Sorabji, *The Philosophy of the Commentators*, vol. 3, 68–73.
7. For Aristotle on time, see further Coope, *Time for Aristotle*.
8. B. Morison, *On Location: Aristotle on the Concept of Place* (Oxford: Oxford University Press, 2002), 57, classifies being in a place in this sense as "receptive containing".
9. Cf. the Neoplatonic view of the cosmos as a living being in Chapter 4. Iamblichus supposes that the cosmos must have reason, not just a living soul.
10. Sorabji, for example, discusses the question of forms under the general heading "Universals", but presents some reservations; see Sorabji, *The Philosophy of the Commentators*, vol. 3, 133. For the commentators' discussions as the development of a theory of universals, see R. Sorabji, "Universals Transformed: The First Thousand Years After Plato", in *Universals, Concepts and Qualities: New Essays on the Meaning of Predicates*, P. F. Strawson & A. Chakrabarti (eds), 105–25 (Aldershot: Ashgate, 2006).
11. In his recent book on Alexander's metaphysics, Marwan Rashed talks about "auto-constitutive activity" of forms; see M. Rashed, *Essentialisme: Alexandre d'Aphrodise entre logique, physique et cosmologie* (Berlin: de Gruyter, 2007), 325.
12. For denials that form could be an accident, see texts in Sorabji, *The Philosophy of the Commentators*, vol. 3, 122–5.
13. For the relation between the universals in Alexander's *De anima* and the *Quaestiones*, see R. W. Sharples, "Alexander of Aphrodisias on Universals: Two Problematic Texts", *Phronesis* **50**(1) (1998), 43–55.
14. The non-individualist reading of Alexander's forms is the one dominant in recent scholarship. See Rashed, *Essentialisme*; Sorabji, *The Philosophy of the Commentators*, vol. 3, 149–56.
15. The evidence is discussed in Karamanolis, *Plato and Aristotle in Agreement?*, 315–16.
16. For Proclus' use of *husterogenēs*, see Helmig, "Proclus and other Neoplatonists".
17. For references and discussion, see Rashed, *Essentialisme*.

18. See the *Mantissa*, an appendix to Alexander's *De anima* originating from Alexander's school but not necessarily by Alexander himself (119,31–120,17, in Sorabji, *The Philosophy of the Commentators*, vol. 3, 122–3).
19. For this complex debate, see e.g. M. V. Wedin, "PARTisanship in *Metaphysics Z*", *Ancient Philosophy* 11 (1991), 361–85. For forms and individuation in Aristotle, see e.g. J. E. Whiting, "Form and Individuation in Aristotle", *History of Philosophy Quarterly* 3 (1986), 359–77.
20. See further texts in Sorabji, *The Philosophy of the Commentators*, vol. 3, 161–2, e.g. Proclus *in Parm.* 650,18–34.
21. For Platonic forms as causes, see also D. N. Sedley, "Platonic Causes", *Phronesis* 43(2) (1998), 114–32.
22. This need not mean that we should endorse Alexander's interpretation. It could well be that, for Aristotle, the essential properties are determined by the form but are not identical with it; the form can be a further, more abstract metaphysical component of a thing.
23. The whole passage Simp. *in Cat.* 95,10–35 is found in Sorabji, *The Philosophy of the Commentators*, vol. 3, 113–14.

7. Ethics

1. For a general introduction to Aspasius, see J. Barnes, "An Introduction to Aspasius", in *Aspasius: The Earliest Extant Commentary on Aristotle's Ethics*, A. Alberti & R. W. Sharples, 1–50 (Berlin: de Gruyter, 1999).
2. Simplicius' commentary on Epictetus' *Handbook* was translated in two volumes, 1–26 and 27–53, in the *Ancient Commentators on Aristotle* series by T. Brennan & C. Brittain (2002).
3. For Aristotle's analysis, see also *EN* II 1.
4. For the discussion, see e.g. J. M. Cooper, *Reason and Human Good in Aristotle* (Cambridge, MA: Harvard University Press, 1975) and "Contemplation and Happiness: A Reconsideration", *Synthese* 72 (1987), 187–216; R. Kraut, *Aristotle on the Human Good* (Princeton, NJ: Princeton University Press, 1989); G. Richardson Lear, *Happy Lives and the Highest Good: An Essay on Aristotle's* Nicomachean Ethics (Princeton, NJ: Princeton University Press, 2004).
5. For the Stoic ideal, see J. Sellars, *Stoicism* (Stocksfield: Acumen, 2006); for Epictetus, see A. A. Long, *Epictetus: A Stoic and Socratic Guide to Life* (Oxford: Oxford University Press, 2002).
6. This is the position of Eustratius, Albert the Great and Thomas Aquinas; see R. W. Sharples, "Aspasius on *Eudaimonia*", in Alberti & Sharples (eds), *Aspasius*, 85–95 (Berlin: de Gruyter, 1999), 88–9.
7. Much more recently, Martha Nussbaum has defended the truth of this claim: *The Fragility of Goodness*, rev. edn (Cambridge: Cambridge University Press, [1986] 2001).
8. For the role of action in Plotinus, see D. J. O'Meara, *Platonopolis: Platonic Political Philosophy in Late Antiquity* (Oxford: Clarendon Press, 2003).

9. For references and a discussion, see Karamanolis, *Plato and Aristotle in Agreement?*, 303–9.
10. The question of whether the soul descends in its entirety or whether a part of it remains undescended was disputed among Neoplatonists. Plotinus claimed that a part remains undescended, but later Neoplatonists denied this; for the discussion, see e.g. P. Remes, *Neoplatonism* (Stocksfield: Acumen, 2008), ch. 4.
11. See e.g. D. Konstan, *The Emotions of the Classical Greeks: Studies in Aristotle and Classical Literature* (Toronto: University of Toronto Press, 2006); S. Knuuttila, *Emotions in Ancient and Medieval Philosophy* (Oxford: Oxford University Press, 2004); and M. C. Nussbaum, *Therapy of Desire: Theory and Practice in Hellenistic Ethics* (Princeton, NJ: Princeton University Press, 1994).
12. See e.g. Knuuttila, *Emotions in Ancient and Medieval Philosophy*; R. Sorabji, *Emotions and Peace of Mind: From Stoic Agitation to Christian Temptation* (Oxford: Oxford University Press, 2000); Nussbaum, *Therapy of Desire*.
13. For Aspasius' classification, see R. Sorabji, "Aspasius in Emotion", in Alberti & Sharples (eds), *Aspasius*, 96ff.; Sorabji, *Emotions and Peace of Mind*, 134–6; Knuuttila, *Emotions in Ancient and Medieval Philosophy*, 90 n.219; Konstan, *The Emotions of the Classical Greeks*, 34 n.48.
14. For the debate between Aspasius and Andronicus, see also Sorabji, *Emotions and Peace of Mind*, 133–4, and "Aspasius in Emotion".
15. For cases where Aristotle attributes crafts or even prudence and wisdom to animals, see Johnson, *Aristotle on Teleology*, 205–6.
16. For Epicurus' formulations, see Epicurus *Key Doctrines* 32, 36; D.L. 10.151.
17. For this debate in antiquity and its relation to animal ethics, see Sorabji, *Animal Minds and Human Morals*.
18. For evidence that Aristotle would agree, see Johnson, *Aristotle on Teleology*, 205–6.
19. Identified as Hermes Trismegistus; see trans. Clark (2000: n.334) for further references.

Further reading

Important articles on general and more detailed topics in the commentaries are found in the following collections, which are frequently referred to in this book as well.

Sorabji, R. (ed.) 1990. *Aristotle Transformed: The Ancient Commentators and their Influence*. London: Duckworth.
Adamson, P., H. Baltussen & M. W. F. Stone (eds) 2004. *Philosophy, Science, and Exegesis in Greek, Arabic and Latin Commentaries. Bulletin of the Institute of Classical Studies Supplement* **83**(1&2). London: Institute of Classical Studies.

The former also includes an extensive bibliographical guide to research on the commentaries made before 1990. The latter contains an updated bibliography (J. Sellars, "The Aristotelian Commentators: A Bibliographical Guide", **83**(1), 239–68).

It is important to read the commentators in their own voice. The individual translations of commentaries and parts of commentaries published in the series *Ancient Commentators on Aristotle* edited by Richard Sorabji (London: Duckworth, 1989–) have introductions that are helpful when one is starting to do this (see § "Sources and translations" in the Bibliography).

Key excerpts collected in a thematic order with introductory remarks and bibliographical references are found in Richard Sorabji's sourcebook in three volumes: *The Philosophy of the Commentators: A Sourcebook* (London: Duckworth, 2004–2005). All three volumes also contain Sorabji's general introduction (the same in each volume) to the commentators' philosophy.

The following monographs offer important information concerning the historical and philosophical background of the commentaries.

Boys-Stones, G. R. 2001. *Post-Hellenistic Philosophy: A Study of its Development from the Stoics to Origen*. Oxford: Oxford University Press.
Gibson, R. K. & C. S. Kraus (eds) 2002. *The Classical Commentary: Histories, Practices, Theory*. Leiden: Brill.

Sharples, R. W. (ed.) 2001. *Whose Aristotle? Whose Aristotelianism?*. Aldershot: Ashgate.

Synder, H. G. 2000. *Teachers and Texts in the Ancient World*. London: Routledge.

Tempelis, E. 1998. *The School of Ammonius, Son of Hermias, on Knowledge of the Divine*. Athens: Parnassos Literary Society.

More information concerning Neoplatonic philosophy as well as key texts can be found in the following monographs and collections.

D'Ancona, C. (ed.) 2007. *The Libraries of the Neoplatonists*. Leiden: Brill.

Dillon, J. & L. P. Gerson 2004. *Neoplatonic Philosophy: Introductory Readings*. Indianapolis, IN: Hackett.

Remes, P. 2008. *Neoplatonism*. Stocksfield: Acumen.

Rappe, S. 2000. *Reading Neoplatonism: Non-Discursive Thinking in the Texts of Plotinus, Proclus and Damascius*. Cambridge: Cambridge University Press.

Wilberding. J. 2006. *Plotinus' Cosmology: A Study of Ennead II 1 (40). Text, Translation, and a Commentary*. Oxford: Oxford University Press.

Below more detailed articles and monographs are found on the commentators and their philosophy.

Ethics

Gill, C. (ed.) 2005. *Virtue, Norms, and Objectivity: Issues in Ancient and Modern Ethics*. Oxford: Oxford University Press.

Hadot, I. 1995. "Le *Commentaire de Simplicius sur le Manuel d'Épictète* comme exercice spirituel". In *Esegesi, Parafrasi e Compilazione in Età Tardoantica*, C. Moreschini (ed.), 175–85. Naples: M. D'Auria Editore.

Sharples, R. W. 2005. "An Aristotelian Commentator on the Naturalness of Justice". In Gill (ed.), *Virtue, Norms, and Objectivity*, 279–94.

Historical background

Athanassiadi, P. 1993 "Persecution and Response in Late Paganism: The Evidence of Damascius". *Journal of Hellenic Studies* **113**: 1–29.

Blumenthal, H. J. 1978. "529 and its Sequel: What Happened to the Academy?". *Byzantium* **48**: 369–85.

Castrén, P. (ed.) 1994. *Post-Herulian Athens*. Helsinki: Foundation of the Finnish Institute at Athens.

Hällström, G. 1994. "The Closing of the Neoplatonic School in AD 529: An Additional Aspect". In Castrén (ed.), *Post-Herulian Athens*, 141–60.

Fazzo, S. 2002. "Alexandre d'Aphrodise contre Galien: la naissance d'une légende". *Philosophie Antique: Problèmes, Renaissances, Usages* **2**: 109–44.

Praechter, K. 1910. "Richtungen und Schulen im Neuplatonismus". In *Genethliakon für Carl Robert*, 103–56. Berlin: Weidmann. Reprinted in *Kleine Schriften*, H. Dörrie (ed.), 165–216 (Hildesheim: Georg Olms, 1973).

Sandbach, F. H. 1985. *Proceedings of the Cambridge Philological Society, suppl. 10: Aristotle and the Stoics*. Cambridge: Cambridge Philological Society.

Tardieu, M. 1986. "Sabiens coraniques et 'Sabiens' de Harran". *Journal asiatique* **274**(1–2): 1–44.

Language
Gaskin, R. 1998. "Simplicius on the Meaning of Sentences: A Commentary on *In Cat.* 396, 30-397, 28". *Phronesis* **43**(1): 42–62.
Todd, R. 1976. "Alexander of Aphrodisias on *De interpretatione* 16a26–29". *Hermes* **104**: 140–46.

Logic, modalities, mathematics
Flannery, K. L. 1993. "Alexander of Aphrodisias and Others on a Controversial Demonstration in Aristotle's Modal Syllogistic". *History and Philosophy of Logic* **14**(2): 201–14.
Lloyd, A. C. 1955. "Neoplatonic Logic and Aristotelian Logic I". *Phronesis* **1**: 58–72.
Mignucci, M. 1996. "Ammonius on Future Contingent Propositions". In *Rationality in Greek Thought*, M. Frede & G. Striker (eds), 279–310. Oxford: Clarendon Press.
Mignucci, M. 1998. "Ammonius' Sea Battle". In *Ammonius, On Aristotle On Interpretation 9 with Boethius, On Aristotle On Interpretation 9*, D. Blank & N. Kretzmann (trans.) (*Ancient Commentators on Aristotle*), 53–86 (London: Duckworth, 1998).
Mueller, I. 1956. "Aristotle and Simplicius on Mathematical Infinity". In *Proceedings of the World Congress on Aristotle I*, 179–82. Athens: Publication of the Ministry of Culture and Sciences.
Mueller, I. 1990. "Aristotle's Doctrine of Abstractionism in the Commentators". In Sorabji (ed.), *Aristotle Transformed*, 463–80.
Seel, G. (ed.) 2001. *Ammonius and the Seabattle: Texts, Commentary, Essays*. Berlin: de Gruyter.
Sorabji, R. 1998. "The Three Deterministic Arguments Opposed by Ammonius". In *Ammonius, On Aristotle On Interpretation 9 with Boethius, On Aristotle On Interpretation 9*, D. Blank & N. Kretzmann (trans.) (*Ancient Commentators on Aristotle*), 3–15 (London: Duckworth, 1998).

Metaphysics
Berryman, S. 2002. "Sweetness of Honey: Philoponus against the Doctors on Supervening Qualities". In *The Dynamics of Aristotelian Natural Philosophy from Antiquity to the Seventeenth Century*, C. Leijenhorst, C. Lüthy & J. M. Thiksen (eds), 65–79. Leiden: Brill.
Chiaradonna, R. 1996. "L'interpretazione della sostanza aristotelica in Porfirio". *Elenchos* **17**: 55–94.
Ellis, J. 1994. "Alexander's Defence of Aristotle's Categories". *Phronesis* **39**: 69–89.
Hadot, I. (ed.) 1990. *Simplicius, Commentaire sur les Catégories*, Fasc. 1–3. Leiden: Brill.
Hoffmann, P. 2000. "Les categories aristotéliciennes *pote* et *pou* d'après le commentaire de Simplicius: Méthode d'exégèse et aspects doctrinaux". In *Le commentaire: entre tradition et innovation*, M.-O. Goulet-Cazé (ed.), 355–76. Paris: Vrin.
Kupreeva, I. 2003. "Qualities and Bodies: Alexander Against the Stoics". *Oxford Studies in Ancient Philosophy* **25**: 297–344.
Madigan, A. 1986. "Syrianus and Asclepius on Forms and Intermediates in Plato and Aristotle". *Journal of the History of Philosophy* **24**(2): 149–71.

Methodological issues

Dillon, J. 1999. "A Case-Study in Commentary: The Neoplatonic Exegesis of the *Prooimia* of Plato's Dialogues". In *Commentaries – Kommentare*, G. W. Most, (ed.), 206–22. Göttingen: Vandenhoeck & Ruprecht.

Mansfeld, J. 1994. *Prolegomena: Questions to be Settled Before the Study of an Author, or a Text*. Leiden: Brill.

Natural philosophy and cosmology

Berryman, S. 2005. "Necessitation and Explanation in Philoponus' Aristotelian Physics". In Salles (ed.), *Metaphysics, Soul, and Ethics*, 65–79.

Blumenthal, H. J. 1996. "*Dunamis* in Simplicius". In Romano & Loredana Cardullo (eds), *Dunamis nel Neoplatonismo*.

Croese, I. 1998. *Simplicius on Continuous and Instantaneous Change: Neoplatonic Elements in Simplicius' Interpretation of Aristotelian Physics*. Utrecht: Zeno.

Feldman, S. 1988. "Philoponus on the Metaphysics of Creation". In Link-Salinger *et al.* (eds), *A Straight Path*, 74–85.

Haas, F. A. J. de 1999. "Mixture in Philoponus: An Encounter with a Third Kind of Potentiality". In *The Commentary Tradition on Aristotle's De Generatione et Corruptione. Ancient, Medieval and Early Modern*, J. M. M. H. Thijssen & H.A.G. Braakhuis (eds), 21–46. Turnhout: Brepols.

Henry, D. 2003. "Themistius on Spontaneous Generation in Aristotle's *Metaphysics*". *Oxford Studies in Ancient Philosophy* 24: 183–208.

Lang, H. S. 2001. "Philoponus' Aristotle: The Extension of Place". In *Whose Aristotle? Whose Aristotelianism?*, R. W. Sharples (ed.), 11–27. Aldershot: Ashgate.

Link-Salinger R., J. Hackett, M. S. Hyman, R. J. Long & C. H. Manekin (eds) 1988. *A Straight Path: Studies in Medieval Philosophy and Culture*. Washington, DC: Catholic University of America Press.

Osborne, C. 1989. "Philoponus on the Origins of the Universe and other Issues". *Studies in History and Philosophy of Science* 20: 389–95.

Romano, F. & R. Loredana Cardullo (eds) 1996. *Dunamis nel Neoplatonismo*. Florence: La Nuova Italia Editrice.

Wilberding, J. 2005. "Aristotle, Plotinus, and Simplicius on the Relation of the Changer to the Changed". *Classical Quarterly* 55(2): 447–54.

Wildberg, C. 1988. *John Philoponus' Criticism of Aristotle's Theory of Aether*. Berlin: de Gruyter.

Psychology

Blumenthal, H. J. 1996. *Aristotle and Neoplatonism in Late Antiquity: Interpretations of the De anima*. Ithaca, NY: Cornell University Press.

Blumenthal, H. J. 1997. "Some Notes on the Text of Pseudo-Simplicius' Commentary on Aristotle's *De Anima*, III.1–5". In *Studies in Plato and the Platonic Tradition*, M. Joyal (ed.), 213–29. Aldershot: Ashgate.

Ellis, J. 1990. "The Trouble with Fragrance". *Phronesis* 35(3): 290–302.

Emilsson, E .K. 1996. "Cognition and Its Object". In *The Cambridge Companion to Plotinus*, L. P. Gerson (ed.), 217–49. Cambridge: Cambridge University Press.

Frede, M. 1996. "La théorie aristotélicienne de l'intellect agent". In *Corps et âme: Sur le De anima d'Aristote*, G. Romeyer-Dherbey (dir.), C. Viano (ed.), 377–90. Paris: Vrin.

Frede, M. & D. Charles (eds) 2000. *Aristotle's Metaphysics Lambda*. Oxford: Clarendon Press.

Haas, F. A. J. de 2000. "Recollection and Potentiality in Philoponus". In *The Winged Chariot*, M. Kardaun & J. Spruyt (eds), 165–84. Leiden: Brill.

Kosman, L. A. 1992. "What Does the Maker Mind Make?". In *Essays on Aristotle's De Anima*, M. C. Nussbaum & A. O. Rorty (eds), 343–58. Oxford: Clarendon Press.

Laks, A. 2000. "Metaphysics Λ 7". In Frede & Charles (eds), *Aristotle's Metaphysics Lambda*, 207–43.

Lautner, P. 1992. "Philoponus, *In De Anima III*: Quest for an Author". *Classical Quarterly* **42**(2): 510–22.

Lautner, P. 1993. "Philoponean Accounts of *Phantasia*". *Acta Antiqua Academiae Scientiarum Hungaricae* **34**: 159–70.

Menn, S. 1992. "Aristotle and Plato on God as *Nous* and as the Good". *Review of Metaphysics* **45**(3): 543–73.

Merlan, P. 1963. *Monopsychism, Mysticism, Metaconsciousness: Problems of the Soul in the Neo-Aristotelian and Neo-Platonic Tradition*. The Hague: Martinus Nijhoff.

Schroeder, F. W. & R. B. Todd 1990. *Two Greek Aristotelian Commentators on the Intellect: The* De Intellectu *Attributed to Alexander of Aphrodisias and Themistius' Paraphrase of Aristotle* De Anima *3.4–8*. Toronto: Pontifical Institute of Mediaeval Studies.

Sharples, R. W. 2005. "Alexander of Aphrodisias on the Nature and Location of Vision". See Salles (ed.) (2005), 345–62.

Steel, C. 1978. *The Changing Self: A Study on the Soul in Later Neoplatonism – Iamblichus, Damascius and Priscianus*. Brussels: Paleis der Academien.

Bibliography

Sources and translations

Full editions of the commentaries in Greek are published as part of *Commentaria in Aristotelem Graeca* (CAG) of the Berlin Academy. Olympiodorus' commentary on Plato's *Gorgias* is *In Platonis Gorgiam commentaria* (Bibliotheca scriptorum Graecorum et Romanorum Teubneriana) (Hildesheim: G. Olms 1966). Porphyry's *On Abstinence from Killing Animals* is in the Budé editions: Book I: *De l'abstinence* 1, J. Bouffartigue (ed.) (Paris: Les belles lettres, 1977); Books II–III: *De l'abstinence* 2, J. Bouffartigue & M. Patillon (eds) (Paris: Les belles lettres, 1979); Book IV: *De l'abstinence* 3, A. Segonds (ed.) (Paris: Les belles lettres, 1995). Simplicius' *On Epictetus' Handbook* has been edited by I. Hadot, *Simplicius: Commentaire sur le Manuel d'Epictète* (Leiden: Brill, 1996). Anonymous commentaries on Plato's *Theaetetus* are in G. Bastiniani & D. Sedley (eds), "Anonymous Commentarius in Platonis Theaetetum", in *Corpus dei papiri filosofici greci e latini,* vol. III, 227–562 (Florence: Olschki, 1995). Porphyry's commentary on Ptolemy's *Harmonics* has been edited by I. Düring, *Porphyrios, Kommentar zur Harmonielehre de Ptolemaios* (Götebog: Elanders, 1932). Galen's *De usu partium* was edited in two volumes by G. Helmreich (Leipzig: Teubner 1907–9). Fragments from Porphyry have been edited as *Porphyrius: Fragmenta*, A. Smith (ed.) (Stuttgart: Teubner, 1993). Boethius's commentary on Aristotle's *Categories* is in *Anicii Manlii Severini Boethii in Categorias Aristotelis commentaria,* J.-P. Migne (ed.), in *Patrologia Latina,* vol. 64 (1891), cols 159–264. Proclus' commentary on Plato's *Parmenides* is in *Proclii philosophi Platonici opera inedita,* 2nd edn, V. Cousin (ed.) (Paris: Les belles lettres, 1864).

For the texts of Plato and Aristotle, the reader is advised to consult the editions in the series *Oxford Classical Texts* (OCT) or the French Budé editions published by Les belles lettres (Paris). For the Hellenistic material in general, editions of important passages are found in A. A. Long & D. N. Sedley, *The Hellenistic Philosophers,* vol. 1 (Cambridge: Cambridge University Press, 1987). For Plotinus' texts, the edition of Henry and Schwyzer *Plotini opera* (in OCT) is recommended.

Translations: Ancient Commentators on Aristotle

These translations are from the series *Ancient Commentators on Aristotle*, R. Sorabji (ed.) (London/Ithaca, NY: Duckworth/Cornell University Press, 1989–).

Alexander of Aphrodisias
On Aristotle On Coming-to-Be and Perishing *2.2–5*, E. Gannagé (trans.) (2005).
On Aristotle Metaphysics *1*, W. E. Dooley (trans.) (1989).
On Aristotle Metaphysics *2–3*, W. E. Dooley & A. Madigan (trans.) (1992).
On Aristotle Metaphysics *4*, A. Madigan (trans.) (1993).
On Aristotle Metaphysics *5*, W. E. Dooley (trans.) (1993).
On Aristotle Meteorology *4*, E. Lewi (trans.) (1996).
On Aristotle On Sense Perception, A. Towey (trans.) (2000).
On Aristotle Prior Analytics *1.1–7*, J. Barnes, S. Bobzien, K. Flannery & K. Ierodiakonou (trans.) (1991).
On Aristotle Prior Analytics *1.8–13*, I. Mueller (trans.) (1998).
On Aristotle Prior Analytics *1.14–22*, I. Mueller (trans.) (1998).
On Aristotle Prior Analytics *1.23–31*, I. Mueller (trans.) (2006).
On Aristotle Prior Analytics *1.32–46*, I. Mueller (trans.) (2006).
On Aristotle Topics *1*, J. M. Van Ophuijsen (trans.) (2001).

Alexander?
Alexander of Aphrodisias: Supplement to On the Soul, R.W. Sharples (trans.) (2004).
Ethical Problems, R. W. Sharples (trans.) (1990).
Quaestiones 1.1–2.15, R. W. Sharples (trans.) (1992).
Quaestiones 2.16–3.15, R. W. Sharples (trans.) (1994).

Ammonius
On Aristotle Categories, S. M. Cohen & G. B. Matthews (trans.) (1991).
On Aristotle On Interpretation *1–8*, D. Blank (trans.) (1996).
On Aristotle On Interpretation 9, D. Blank (trans.), with Boethius, *On Aristotle* On Interpretation *9*, N. Kretzmann (trans.) (1998).

Aspasius
On Aristotle's Nicomachean Ethics *1–4, 7–8*, D. Konstan (trans.) (2006).
On Aristotle Nicomachean Ethics 8; Michael of Ephesus, *On Aristotle* Nicomachean Ethics 9; Anonymous, *On Aristotle* Nicomachean Ethics *8–9*, D. Konstan (trans.) (2001).

Dexippus
On Aristotle Categories, J. Dillon (trans.) (1990).

Philoponus
Against Aristotle on the Eternity of the World, C. Wildberg (trans.) (1987).
Against Proclus on the Eternity of the World 1–5, M. Share (trans.) (2005).
Against Proclus on the Eternity of the World 6–8, M. Share (trans.) (2005).

Against Proclus on the Eternity of the World 12–18, J. Wilberding (trans.) (2006).
On Aristotle On Coming-to-Be and Perishing *1.1–5*, C. J. F. Williams (trans.) (1999).
On Aristotle On Coming-to-Be and Perishing *1.6–2.4*, C. J. F. Williams (trans.) (1999).
On Aristotle On Coming-to-Be and Perishing *2.5–11*, I. Kupreeva (trans.) (2005).
Corollaries on Place and Void, D. Furley (trans.), with Simplicius, *Against Philoponus on the Eternity of the World*, C. Wildberg (trans.) (1991).
On Aristotle On the Soul *1.1–2*, P. van der Eijk (trans.) (2005).
On Aristotle On the Soul *1.3–5*, P. van der Eijk (trans.) (2006).
On Aristotle On the Soul *2.1–6*, W. Charlton (trans.) (2005).
On Aristotle On the Soul *2.7–12*, W. Charlton (trans.) (2005).
On Aristotle Physics *1.1–3*, C. Osborne (trans.) (2006).
On Aristotle Physics *2*, A. R. Lacey (trans.) (1993).
On Aristotle Physics *3*, M. Edwards (trans.) (1994).
On Aristotle Physics *5–8*, P. Lettinck (trans.), with Simplicius, *On Aristotle on the Void*, J. O. Urmson (trans.) (1994).
On Aristotle Posterior Analytics *1.1–8*, McKirahan (trans.) (2008).

Latin Philoponus
On Aristotle On the Intellect, W. Charlton (trans.) (1991).

Pseudo-Philoponus
On Aristotle On the Soul *3.1–8*, W. Charlton (trans.) (2000).
On Aristotle On the Soul *3.9–13*, with Stephanus, *On Interpretation*, W. Charlton (trans.) (2000).

Porphyry
On Abstinence from Killing Animals, G. Clark (trans.) (2000).
On Aristotle Categories, S. Strange (trans.) (1992).

Proclus
On Providence, C. Steel (trans.) (2007).

Simplicius
On Aristotle Categories *1–4*, M. Chase (trans.) (2003).
On Aristotle Categories *5–6*, F. A. J. de Haas & B. Fleet (trans.) (2001).
On Aristotle Categories *7–8*, B. Fleet (trans.) (2002).
On Aristotle Categories *9–15*, R. Gaskin (trans.) (2000).
On Aristotle Physics *2*, B. Fleet (trans.) (1997).
On Aristotle Physics *3*, J. O. Urmson (trans.) (2002).
On Aristotle Physics *4.1–5 & 4.10–14*, J. O. Urmson (trans.) (1992).
On Aristotle Physics *4.6–9*: see Philoponus, *On Aristotle* Physics *5–8*, P. Lettinck (trans.), with Simplicius, *On Aristotle on the Void*, J. O. Urmson (trans.) (1994).
On Aristotle Physics *5*, J. O. Urmson (trans.) (1997).
On Aristotle Physics *6*, D. Konstan (trans.) (1989).
On Aristotle Physics *7*, C. Hagen (trans.) (1994).
On Aristotle Physics *8.6–10*, R. McKirahan (trans.) (2001).

On Aristotle On the Heavens *1.1–4*, R. J. Hankinson (trans.) (2002).
On Aristotle On the Heavens *1.5–9*, R. J. Hankinson (trans.) (2004).
On Aristotle On the Heavens *1.10–12*, R. J. Hankinson (trans.) (2006).
On Aristotle On the Heavens *2.1–9*, I. Mueller (trans.) (2004).
On Aristotle On the Heavens *2.10–14*, I. Mueller (trans.) (2005).
Corollaries on Time and Place, J. O. Urmson (trans.) (1992).
On Epictetus Handbook *1–26*, T. Brennan & C. Brittain (trans.) (2002).
On Epictetus Handbook *27–53*, T. Brennan & C. Brittain (trans.) (2002).

Pseudo-Simplicius
On Aristotle On the Soul *1.1–2.4*, J. O. Urmson (trans.) (1995). (Published under the name Simplicius.)
On Aristotle On the Soul *2.5–12*, C. Steel (trans.), with Priscian, *On Theophrastus* On Sense Perception, P. Huby (trans.) (1997). (Published under the name "Simplicius".)
On Aristotle On the Soul *3.1–5*, H. J. Blumenthal (trans.) (2000) (Published under the name "Simplicius".)

Syrianus
On Aristotle Metaphysics *3–4*, D. O'Meara (trans.) (2008).
On Aristotle Metaphysics *13–14*, J. Dillon & D. O'Meara (trans.) (2006).

Themistius
On Aristotle On the Soul, R. B. Todd (trans.) (1996).
On Aristotle Physics *4*, R. B. Todd (trans.) (2003).

Translations: other English translations of the commentators' works

Alexander
De fato: Alexander of Aphrodisias On Fate, text, translation and commentary by R. W. Sharples (London: Duckworth, 1983).
De mixtione: Alexander of Aphrodisias on Stoic Physics: a study of the De mixtione *with preliminary essay*, text, translation and commentary by R. B. Todd (Leiden: Brill, 1976)

Porphyry
Introduction, J. Barnes (trans.), with introduction and commentary (Oxford: Clarendon Press, 2003).

Proclus
Proclus' Commentary on Plato's Parmenides, G. R. Morrow & J. Dillon (trans.) (Princeton, NJ: Princeton University Press, 1987).
Proclus: A Commentary on the First Book of Euclid's Elements, G. R. Morrow (trans.), with introduction and notes (Princeton, NJ: Princeton University Press, 1970).

Translations: other cited works

For translations of Plato's works, the recommended collection is *Plato: Complete Works*, J. M. Cooper (ed.), D. S. Hutchinson (associate ed.) (Indianapolis, IN: Hackett, 1997). Aristotle's works can be found in translation in *The Complete Works of Aristotle: The Revised Oxford Translation* (2 vols), J. Barnes (ed.) (Princeton, NJ: Princeton University Press, 1984). The cited translation by Pickard-Cambridge is in *Works of Aristotle*, W. D. Ross (ed.) (Oxford: Clarendon Press, 1937). Hellenistic philosophy is found in translation in A. Long & D. N. Sedley, *The Hellenistic Philosophers*, vol. 1 (Cambridge: Cambridge University Press, 1987).

Translations for Plotinus can be found in *Plotinus* (7 vols), Greek text with English translation, A. H. Armstrong (trans.) (Cambridge, MA: Loeb Classical Library, 1968–88) and *Plotinus: The Enneads*, S. MacKenna (trans.), J. Dillon (abridged and ed.) (Harmondsworth: Penguin, 1991). Galen's *De usupartium* has been translated in two volumes as *On the Usefulness of the Parts of the Body*, M. T. May (trans.) (Ithaca, NY: Cornell University Press, 1968).

References

Ackrill, J. 1963. *Aristotle's Categories and De interpretatione*, trans. with notes. Oxford: Clarendon Press.
Adamson, P. 2002. *Arabic Plotinus: A Philosophical Study of the "Theology of Aristotle"*. London: Duckworth.
Adamson, P., H. Baltussen & M. W. F. Stone (eds) 2004. *Philosophy, Science, and Exegesis in Greek, Arabic and Latin Commentaries. Bulletin of the Institute of Classical Studies Supplement* 83(1&2). London: Institute of Classical Studies.
Alberti, A. & R. Sharples 1999. *Aspasius: The Earliest Extant Commentary on Aristotle's Ethics*. Berlin: de Gruyter
Algra, K., P. W. van der Horst & D. Runia (eds) 1996. *Polyhistor: Studies in the History and Historiography of Philosophy*. Leiden: Brill.
Algra, K., J. Barnes, J. Mansfeld & M. Schofield (eds) 1999. *The Cambridge History of Hellenistic Philosophy*. Cambridge: Cambridge University Press.
Alföldi, A. A. 1952. *A Conflict of Ideas in the Late Roman Empire: The Clash between the Senate and Valentinian I*. Oxford: Clarendon Press.
Allen, J. 2001. *Inference from Signs: Ancient Debates about the Nature of Evidence*. Oxford: Oxford University Press.
Annas, J. 1993. *The Morality of Happiness*. Oxford: Oxford University Press.
Ballériaux, O. 1989. "Thémistius et l'exégèse de la noétique aristotelicienne". *Revue de la philosophie ancienne* 7: 199–233.
Ballériaux, O. 1994. "Thémistius et le Néoplatonisme: le *nous pathetikos* et l'immortalité de l'ame". *Revue de la philosophie ancienne* 12: 171–200.
Baltussen, H. 2003. "Early Reactions to Plato's *Timaeus*: Polemic and Exegesis in Theophrastus and Epicurus". In *Ancient Approaches to the "Timaeus"*, R. W. Sharples & A. Sheppard (eds), 49–71. *Bulletin of the Institute of Classical Studies*, supplement 78. London: Institute of Classical Studies.

Baltussen, H. 2004. "Plato *Protagoras* 340-8: Commentary in the Making?". See Adamson *et al.* (eds) (2004), vol. 1, 21–35.

Baltussen H. 2007. "From Polemic to Exegesis: The Ancient Philosophical Commentary". In *Genres in Philosophy I*, J. Lavery (ed.). *Poetics Today* **28**(2): 247–81.

Barnes, J. 1969. "Aristotle's Theory of Demonstration". *Phronesis* **14**: 123–52. Revised and reprinted in J. Barnes, M. Schofield & R. Sorabji (eds), *Articles on Aristotle, Vol. 1: Science*, 65–87 (London: Duckworth, 1975).

Barnes, J. 1981. "Proof and the Syllogism". See Berti (ed.) (1981), 17–59.

Barnes, J. 1992. "Metacommentary". *Oxford Studies in Ancient Philosophy* **10**: 267–81.

Barnes, J. 1997. "Aristotle in Rome". See Griffin & Barnes (eds) (1997), 1–69.

Barnes, J. 1999. "An Introduction to Aspasius". See Alberti & Sharples (eds) (1999), 1–50.

Bazán, B. C. 1973. "L'authenticité du 'De Intellectu' attribué à Alexandre d'Aphrodise". *Révue Philosophique de Louvain* **71**: 468–87.

Berti, E. (ed.) 1981. *Proceedings of the Eighth Symposium Aristotelicum: Aristotle on Science: The "Posterior Analytics"*. Padua: Antenore.

Betegh, G. 2004. "Exegesis in the Derveni Papyrus". See Adamson *et al.* (eds) (2004), vol. 1, 37–50.

Blumenthal, H. J. 1979. "Photius on Themistius (cod. 74): Did Themistius Write Commentaries on Aristotle?". *Hermes* **107**(2): 168–82.

Blumenthal, H. J. 1982. "The Psychology of (?) Simplicius' Commentary on the *De anima*". In *Soul and Structure of Being in Late Neoplatonism*, H. J. Blumenthal & A. C. Lloyd (eds), 73–93. Liverpool: Liverpool University Press.

Blumenthal, H. J. 1987. "Alexander of Aphrodisias in the Later Greek Commentaries on Aristotle's *de Anima*". See Wiesner (ed.) (1987), 90–106.

Blumenthal, H. J. 1990. "Themistius: The Last Peripatetic Commentator on Aristotle". See Sorabji (ed.) (1990), 113–24.

Blumenthal, H. & H. Robinson (eds) 1991. *Aristotle and the Later Tradition*. Oxford: Clarendon Press.

Bobzien, S. 2003. "Logic". In *The Cambridge Companion to the Stoics*, B. Inwood (ed.), 85–123. Cambridge: Cambridge University Press.

Bodnár, I. M. 1997. "Alexander of Aphrodisias on Celestial Motion". *Phronesis* **42**(2): 190–205.

Bolton, R. 1987. "Definition and Scientific Method in Aristotle's *Posterior Analytics* and *Generation of Animals*". See Gotthelf & Lennox (eds) (1987), 120–66.

Bossier, F. & C. Steel 1972. "Priscianus Lydus en de 'In de anima' van Pseudo(?)-Simplicius". *Tijdschrift voor Filosofie* **34**: 761–822.

Brittain, C. 2001. *Philo of Larissa: The Last of the Academic Sceptics*. Oxford: Oxford University Press.

Burnyeat, M. 1992. "Is an Aristotelian Philosophy of Mind Still Credible?". See Nussbaum & Rorty (eds), *Essays on Aristotle's De Anima*, 15–26.

Burnyeat, M. 2001. *A Map of Metaphysics Zeta*. Pittsburgh, PA: Mathesis.

Cameron, A. 1969. "The Last Days of the Academy at Athens". *Proceedings of the Cambridge Philological Society* **195**: 7–29.

Caston, V. 1999. "Aristotle's Two Intellects: A Modest Proposal". *Phronesis* **44**(3): 199–227.

Caston, V. 2005. "The Spirit and the Letter: Aristotle on Perception". See Salles (ed.) (2005), 245–320.

Chaniotis, A. 2004. "Epigraphic Evidence for the Philosopher Alexander of Aphrodisias". *Bulletin of the Institute of Classical Studies* **47**: 79–81.

Chiaradonna, R. 2002. *Sostanza, movimento, analogia: Plotino critico di Aristotele.* Naples: Bibliopolis.

Coope, U. 2005. *Time for Aristotle*. Oxford: Oxford University Press.

Cooper, J. M. 1975. *Reason and Human Good in Aristotle*. Cambridge, MA: Harvard University Press.

Cooper, J. M. 1987. "Contemplation and Happiness: A Reconsideration". *Synthese* **72**: 187–216.

de Libera, A. 1998. *Isagoge: texte grec, translatio Boethii*. Paris: Vrin.

de Libera, A. 2004. *La Philosophie médiévale*. Paris: Presses universitaires de France.

Dillon, J. 1996. *The Middle Platonists: 80 BC to 220 AD*, 2nd edn. Ithaca, NY: Cornell University Press.

Dillon J. 1997. "Iamblichus' Noera Theoria of Aristotle's *Categorie*". *Syllecta Classica* **8**: 65–77.

Dillon, J. 2003. *The Heirs of Plato*: *A Study of the Old Academy (347–274 BC)*. Oxford: Oxford University Press.

Drossaart-Lulofs, H. J. 1965. *Aristotle's* De generatione animalium. Oxford: Oxford University Press.

Düring, I. 1957. *Aristotle in the Ancient Biographical Tradition*. Göteborg/Stockholm: Intitute of Classical Studies in the University of Göteborg.

Ebbesen, S. 1981. *Commentators and Commentaries on Aristotle's* Sophistici Elenchi: *A Study of Post-Aristotelian Ancient and Medieval Writings on Fallacies*. Leiden: Brill.

Ebbesen, S. 1990. "Boethius as an Aristotelian Commentator". See Sorabji (ed.) (1990), 373–92.

Ebbesen, S. 2008. *Greek–Latin Philosophical Interaction: Collected Essays of Sten Ebbesen*, vol. 1. Aldershot: Ashgate.

Edmonds, J. M. 1961. *The Fragments of Attic Comedy*, 3 vols. Leiden: Brill.

Emilsson, E. K. 1988. *Plotinus on Sense Perception: A Philosophical Study*. Cambridge: Cambridge University Press.

Emilsson, E. K. 2007. *Plotinus on Intellect*. Oxford: Oxford University Press.

Fazzo, S. 2004. "Aristotelianism as a Commentary Tradition". See Adamson *et al.* (eds) (2004), vol. 1, 1–19.

Festugière, A.-J. 1963. "Modes de composition des commentaires de Proclus". *Museum Helveticum* **20**: 77–100. Reprinted in his *Etudes de philosophie grecque* (Paris: Vrin, 1971).

Fine, G. 1993. *On Ideas: Aristotle's Criticism of Plato's Theory of Forms*. Oxford: Clarendon Press.

Folkes, P. 1992. "Where Was Simplicius?". *Journal of Hellenic Studies* **112**: 143.

Frede, M. 1974. *Die Stoische Logik*. Göttingen: Vandenhoeck & Ruprecht.

Frede, M. 1987. "Categories in Aristotle". In his *Essays in Ancient Philosophy*, 29–48 (Minneapolis, MN: University of Minnesota Press).

Frede, M. 1999. "Epilogue". In *The Cambridge History of Hellenistic Philosophy*, K. Algra,

J. Barnes, J. Mansfeld & M. Schofield (eds), 771–97. Cambridge: Cambridge University Press.

Frede, M. & G. Patzig 1988. *Aristoteles' "Metaphysik Z": Text, Übersetzung, Kommentar*. Munich: Beck.

Furley, D. 1966. "Lucretius and the Stoics". *Bulletin of the Institute of Classical Studies* **13**: 13–33. Reprinted in his *Cosmic Problems*, 183–205 (Cambridge: Cambridge University Press, 1989).

Gerson, L. P. 2005a. *Aristotle and Other Platonists*. Ithaca, NY: Cornell University Press.

Gerson, L. P. 2005b. "What is Platonism?". *Journal of the History of Philosophy* **43**(3): 253–76.

Glucker, J. 1978. *Antiochus and the Late Academy*. Göttingen: Vandenhoeck & Ruprecht.

Gotthelf, A. 1987. "First Principles in Aristotle's *Parts of Animals*". See Gotthelf & Lennox (eds) (1987), 167–98.

Gotthelf, A. & J. Lennox (eds) 1987. *Philosophical Issues in Aristotle's Biology*. Cambridge: Cambridge University Press.

Gottschalk, H. B. 1990. "The Earliest Aristotelian Commentators". Reprinted in Sorabji (ed.) (1990), 55–81. Originally published in *Aufstieg und Niedergang der römischen Welt* (*ANRW*) II 36.2. (Berlin: de Gruyter, 1987).

Goulet-Cazé, M.-O. (ed.) 2000. *Le commentaire: entre tradition et innovation*. Paris: Vrin.

Gregoric, P. 2007. *Aristotle on the Common Sense*. Oxford: Oxford University Press.

Griffin, M. & J. Barnes (eds) 1997. *Philosophia Togata II. Essays on Philosophy and Roman Society*. Oxford: Oxford University Press.

Gutas, D. 1999. "The 'Alexandria to Bagdad' Complex of Narratives: A Contribution to the Study of Philosophical and Medical Historiography among the Arabs". *Documenti e studi sulla tradizione filosofica medievale* **10**: 155–93.

Haas, F. A. J. de 1997. *John Philoponus' New Definition of Prime Matter: Aspects of its Background in Neoplatonism and the Ancient Commentary Tradition*. Leiden: Brill.

Haas, F. A. J. de 2001. "Did Plotinus and Porphyry Disagree on Aristotle's Categories?". *Phronesis* **44**(4): 492–526.

Haas, F. A. J. de 2002. "Modifications of the Method of Inquiry in Aristotle's *Physics* I.1: An Essay on the Dynamics of the Ancient Commentary Tradition". In *The Dynamics of Aristotelian Natural Philosophy from Antiquity to the Seventeenth Century*, C. H. Leijenhorst, C. Lüthy, J. M. Thijssen & C. Leijenhorst (eds), 31–56. Leiden: Brill.

Haas, F. A. J. de forthcoming. *Interpretations of the* Posterior Analytics.

Hadot, I. 1978. "La tradition manuscrite du commentaire de Simplicius sur le *Manuel* d'Épictète". *Revue d'histoire des textes* **8**: 1–108.

Hadot, I. (ed.) 1987a. *Simplicius: sa vie, son oeuvre, sa survie*. Berlin: de Gruyter.

Hadot, I. 1987b. "La vie at oeuvre de Simplicius d'après des sources grecques et arabes". See Hadot (ed.) (1987a), 3–39. [Translated and updated as Hadot (1990a).]

Hadot, I. 1990. "The Life and Work of Simplicius in Greek and Arabic Sources", V. Caston (trans.). See Sorabji (ed.) (1990), 275–303. [Translated and updated from Hadot (1987b).]

Hadot, I. 1991. "The Role of the Commentaries on Aristotle in the Teaching of Philosophy according to the Prefaces of the Neoplatonic Commentaries on the *Categories*". See Blumenthal & Robinson (eds) (1991), 175–89.

Hadot, I. 1996. *Simplicius: Commentaire sur le Manuel d'Epictète*. Leiden: Brill.

Hadot, I. 1997. "Aspects de la théorie de la perception chez les néoplatoniciens: sensation (*aisthêsis*), sensation commune (*koinê aisthêsis*) at de conscience de soi (*sunaisthêsis*)". *Documenti e studi sulla tradizione filosofica medievale* 8: 33–87.

Hadot, I. 2002. "Simplicius or Priscianus? On the Author of the Commentary on Aristotle's *De anima* (CAG XI): A methodological study". *Mnemosyne* 55(2): 159–99.

Hager, F.-P. 1983. "Zur Geschichte, Problematik, und Bedeutung des Begriffes 'Neuplatonismus'". *Diotima* 11: 98–110.

Helmig. C. 2008. "Proclus and other Neoplatonists on Universals and Predication". *Documenti e studi sulla tradizione filsofica medievale* 19: 31–52.

Hoffmann, P. 1994. "Damascius". In *Dictionnaire des philosophes antiques* (vol. 2), 541–93. Paris: CNRS.

Hoffman, P. 2006. "What Was Commentary in Late Antiquity? The Example of the Neoplatonic Commentators". In *A Companion to Ancient Philosophy*, M. L. Gill & P. Pellegrin (eds), 597–622. Oxford: Blackwell.

Hursthouse, R. 1999. *On Virtue Ethics*. Oxford: Oxford University Press.

Hutchinson, D. S. & M. R. Johnson 2005. "Authenticating Aristotle's *Protrepticus*". *Oxford Studies in Ancient Philosophy* 29: 193–294.

Hutchinson, D. S. & M. R. Johnson forthcoming. *Aristotle: Protrepticus*. Cambridge: Cambridge University Press.

Ierodiakonou, K. (ed.) 2002. *Byzantine Philosophy and its Ancient Sources*. Oxford: Clarendon Press.

Inwood, B. 2003. *The Cambridge Companion to the Stoics*. Cambridge: Cambridge University Press.

Johansen, T. 1998. *Aristotle on the Sense-Organs*. Cambridge: Cambridge University Press.

Johnson, M. R. 2005. *Aristotle on Teleology*. Oxford: Clarendon Press.

Johnson, M. R. 2007. "Aristotle's Teleology: What it is and What it is Not". Paper presented at Aristotelianism and the Critique of Modernity conference, 23–5 November 2007, Helsinki.

Johnson, M. R. n.d. "Aristotle the Natural Philosopher". Unpublished manuscript.

Kahn, C. H. 1981. "The Role of *Nous* in the Cognition of First Principles in *Posterior Analytics* II 19". See Berti (ed.) (1981), 385–414.

Kakkuri-Knuuttila, M.-L. 2005. "The Relevance of Dialectical Skills to Philosophical Inquiry in Aristotle". *Rhizai: A Journal for Ancient Philosophy and Science* 2(1): 31–74.

Karamanolis, G. 2004. "Porphyry: The First Platonist Commentator on Aristotle". See Adamson *et al.* (eds) (2004), vol. 1, 97–120.

Karamanolis, G. 2006. *Plato and Aristotle in Agreement? Platonists on Aristotle from Antiochus to Porphyry*. Oxford: Clarendon Press.

Kenny, A. 1981. "Aspasius and the *Nicomachean Ethics* of Aristotle". In *Proceedings of the World Congress on Aristotle I*, 172–4. Athens: Publication of the Ministry of Culture and Sciences.

Knuuttila, S. 2004. *Emotions in Ancient and Medieval Philosophy*. Oxford: Oxford University Press.

Konstan, D. 2006. *The Emotions of the Classical Greeks: Studies in Aristotle and Classical Literature*. Toronto: University of Toronto Press.

Kraut, R. 1989. *Aristotle on the Human Good*. Princeton, NJ: Princeton University Press.

Kupreeva, I. 1997. Review of Robert B. Todd (trans.), *Themistius: On Aristotle's On the soul* (1996). *Bryn Mawr Classical Review* 97.7.1 http://ccat.sas.upenn.edu/bmcr/1997/97.07.01.html (accessed January 2009).

Lameer, J. 1997. "From Alexandria to Bagdad: Reflections on the Genesis of a Problematical Tradition". In *The Ancient Tradition in Christian and Islamic Hellenism*, G. Endress & R. Kruk (eds), 181–91. Leiden: CNWS Publications.

Lautner, P. 2000. "Plutarch of Athens on *koinê aisthêsis* and *phantasia*". *Ancient Philosophy* **20**: 425–46.

Lautner, P. 2004. "The *Koinê aisthêsis* in Proclus and Ps.-Simplicius". See Adamson *et al.* (eds) (2004) **83**(1): 163–73.

Lennox, J. 1987. "Divide and Explain: The Posterior Analytics in Practice". See Gotthelf & Lennox (eds) (1987), 90–119. Reprinted in his *Aristotle's Biology: Studies in the Origins of Life Sciences* (Cambridge: Cambridge University Press, 2001).

Lesher, J. 1973. "The Meaning of *Nous* in the *Posterior Analytics*". *Phronesis* **18**(1): 44–68.

Lloyd, A. C. 1990. *The Anatomy of Neoplatonism*. Oxford: Clarendon Press.

Lloyd, G. E. R. 1990. "The Theories and Practices of Demonstration in Aristotle". *Proceedings of the Boston Area Colloquium in Ancient Philosophy* **6**: 371–401.

Long, A. A. 2002. *Epictetus: A Stoic and Socratic Guide to Life*. Oxford: Oxford University Press.

MacCoul, L. S. B. 1995. "A New Look at the Career of John Philoponus". *Journal of Early Christian Studies* **3**(1): 47–60.

Macierowski, E. M. & R. F. Hassing 1988. "John Philoponus on Aristotle's Definition of Nature". *Ancient Philosophy* **8**(1): 73–100.

MacIntyre, A. [1981] 2007. *After Virtue: A Study in Moral Theory*, 3rd edn. Notre Dame, IN: University of Notre Dame Press.

Marenbon, J. 2003. *Boethius*. Oxford: Oxford University Press.

Marenbon, J. 2007. *Medieval Philosophy: An Historical and Philosophical Introduction*. London: Routledge.

Mariotti, I. 1966. *Aristone d'Alessandria*. Bologna: Riccardo Patron.

Menn, S. 1995. "The Editors of the *Metaphysics*". *Phronesis* **40**(2): 202–8.

Moraux, P. 1942. *Alexandre d'Aphrodise: Exégète de la Noétique d'Aristote*. Liège: University of Liège.

Moraux, P. 1967. "Aristoteles, der Lehrer Alexanders von Aphrodisias". *Archiv für Geschichte der Philosophie* **49**(2): 169–82.

Moraux, P. 1973. *Der Aristotelismus bei den Griechen von Andronikos bis Alexander von Aphrodisias 1: im I Jh v. Chr.* Berlin: de Gruyter.

Moraux, P. 1979. *Le commentaire d'Alexandre d'Aphrodise aux "Seconds analytiques" d'Aristote*. Berlin: de Gruyter.

Moraux, P. 1984. *Der Aristotelismus bei den Griechen von Andronikos bis Alexander von Aphrodisias 2: im I und II Jh n. Chr.* Berlin: de Gruyter.

Moraux, P. 2001. *Der Aristotelismus bei den Griechen 3 von Andronikos bis Alexander von Aphrodisias 3: Alexander von Aphrodisias*. Berlin: de Gruyter.

Morison, B. 2002. *On Location: Aristotle on the Concept of Place*. Oxford: Oxford University Press.

Morrison, D. 1997. "Philoponus and Simplicius on Tekmeriodic Proof". In *Method and Order in Renaissance Philosophy of Nature: The Aristotle Commentary Tradition*, D. A. Di Liscia, E. Kessler & C. Metthuen (eds), 1–22. Aldershot: Ashgate.

Most, G. W. (ed.) 1999. *Commentaries – Kommentare*. Göttingen: Vandenhoeck & Ruprecht.

Natali, C. 2007. "Aspasius on the Nicomachean Ethics 7: An Ancient Example of 'Higher Criticism'?". *Oxford Studies in Ancient Philosophy* **33**: 347–67.

Nussbaum, M. C. 1994. *Therapy of Desire: Theory and Practice in Hellenistic Ethics*. Princeton, NJ: Princeton University Press.

Nussbaum, M. C. [1986] 2001. *The Fragility of Goodness*, rev. edn. Cambridge: Cambridge University Press.

Nussbaum, M. C. & A. O. Rorty (eds.) 1992. *Essays on Aristotle's De Anima*. Oxford: Clarendon Press.

O'Meara, D. J. 1989. *Pythagoras Revived: Mathematics and Philosophy in Late Antiquity*. Oxford: Clarendon Press.

O'Meara, D. J. 2003. *Platonopolis: Platonic Political Philosophy in Late Antiquity*. Oxford: Clarendon Press.

Peters, F. E. 1968. *Aristoteles Arabus: The Oriental Translations and Commentaries of the Aristotelian Corpus*. Leiden: Brill.

Pinès, S. 1987. "Some Distinctive Metaphysical Conceptions in Themistius' Commentary on Book Lambda and Their Place in the History of Philosophy". See Wiesner (ed.) (1987), 177–204.

Praechter, K. 1906. "Hierax der Platoniker". *Hermes* **41**(4): 593–618.

Praechter, K. 1922. "Nikostratos der Platoniker". *Hermes* **57**: 481–517. Reprinted in his *Kleine Schriften*, H. Dörrie (ed.), 101–37 (Hildesheim: Georg Olms, 1973).

Praechter, K. 1926. *Die Philosophie des Altertums*, 12th edn. Berlin: E. S. Mittler und Sohn.

Quarantotto, D. 2005. *Causa finale, sostanza, essenza in Aristotele*. Naples: Bibliopolis.

Rashed, M. 2007. *Essentialisme: Alexandre d'Aphrodise entre logique, physique et cosmologie*. Berlin: de Gruyter.

Remes, P. 2008. *Neoplatonism*. Stocksfield: Acumen.

Rescher, N. 1963. "New Light from Arabic Souces on Galen and the Fourth Figure of the Syllogism", *Journal of the History of Philosophy* **3** (1963), 27–41.

Richardson Lear, G. 2004. *Happy Lives and the Highest Good: An Essay on Aristotle's Nicomachean Ethics*. Princeton, NJ: Princeton University Press.

Ross, W. D. (ed. & trans.) 1952. *The Works of Aristotle Vol. 12: Selected Fragments*. Oxford: Clarendon Press.

Sabra, A. I. 1969. "Simplicius' Proof of Euclid's Parallel Postulate". *Journal of Warburg and Courtauld Institutes* **32**: 1–24.

Salles, R. (ed.) 2005. *Metaphysics, Soul, and Ethics: Themes from the Work of Richard Sorabji*. Oxford: Oxford University Press.

Schreiber, S. 2003. *Aristotle on False Reasoning: Language and the World in the Sophistical Refutations*. Albany, NY: SUNY Press.

Schroeder, F. W. 1982. "The Potential or Material Intellect and the Authorship of the De Intellectu: A Reply to B. C. Bazán". *Symbolae Osloenses* **57**: 115–25.

Sedley, D. N. 1987. "Philoponus' Conception of Space". See Sorabji (ed.) (1987), 140–53.

Sedley, D. N. 1996. "Alcinous' Epistemology". In *Polyhistor: Studies in the History and Historiography of Philosophy*, K. Algra, P. W. van der Horst & D. Runia (eds), 300–312. Leiden: Brill.

Sedley, D. N. 1997a. "A New Reading in the Anonymous *Theaetetus* Commentary (PBerol. 9782 fragment D)". In *Papiri filosofici: Miscellanea di studi I*, 139–44. Florence: L. S. Olschki.

Sedley, D. N. 1997b. "Plato's Auctoritas and the Rebirth of the Commentary Tradition". See Griffin & Barnes (eds) (1997), 110–29.

Sedley, D. N. 1998a. *Lucretius and the Transformation of Greek Wisdom*. Cambridge: Cambridge University Press.

Sedley, D. N. 1998b. "Platonic Causes". *Phronesis* **43**(2): 114–32.

Sellars, J. 2006. *Stoicism*. Stocksfield: Acumen.

Sharples, R. W. 1987. "Alexander of Aphrodisias: Scholasticism and Innovation". *Aufstieg und Niedergang der römischen Welt* **36**(2): 1176–243.

Sharples, R. W. 1990. "The School of Alexander?". See Sorabji (ed.) (1990), 83–111.

Sharples, R. W. 1998. "Alexander of Aphrodisias on Universals: Two Problematic Texts". *Phronesis* **50**(1): 43–55.

Sharples, R. W. 1999. "Aspasius on *Eudaimonia*". See Alberti & Sharples (eds) (1999), 85–95.

Sharples, R. W. 2004a. "Alexander of Aphrodisias: What is a Mantissa?". See Adamson *et al.* (eds) (2004) **83**(1), 51–69.

Sharples, R. W. 2004b. *Alexander of Aphrodisias: Supplement to* On the Soul. Ithaca. NY: Cornell University Press.

Sheppard, A. 1997. "Phantasia and Inspiration in Neoplatonism". In *Studies in Plato and the Platonic Tradition*, M. Joyal (ed.), 201–10. Aldershot: Ashgate.

Sheppard, A. 2003. "The Mirror of Imagination: The Influence of *Timaeus* 55cff.". In *Ancient Approaches to Plato's* Timaeus, R. W. Sharples & A. Sheppard (eds), 203–12. London: Institute of Classical Studies.

Sheppard, A. 2007. "Porphyry's Views on Phantasia". In *Studies on Porphyry*, G. Karamanolis & A. Sheppard (eds), *Bulletin of the Institute of Classical Studies*, supplement 98. London: Institute of Classical Studies.

Shiel, J. [1954] 1990. "Boethius' Commentaries on Aristotle". See Sorabji (ed.) (1990), 349–72.

Sluiter, I. 2000. "The Dialectics of Genre: Some Aspects of Secondary Literature and Genre in Antiquity". In *Matrices of Genre: Authors, Canons and Society*, M. Depew & D. Obbink (eds), 183–203. Cambridge, MA: Harvard University Press.

Smith, A. 2004. *Philosophy in Late Antiquity*. London: Routledge.

Smith, R. 1997. *Aristotle: Topics, Books I and VIII with Excerpts from Related Texts*. Oxford: Clarendon Press.

Sorabji, R. 1974. "Body and Soul in Aristotle". *Philosophy* **49**: 63–89.

Sorabji, R. (ed.) 1987. *Philoponus and the Rejection of Aristotelian Science*. London: Duckworth.

Sorabji, R. 1988. *Matter, Space and Motion: Theories in Antiquity and Their Sequel*. London: Duckworth.

Sorabji, R. (ed.) 1990. *Aristotle Transformed: The Ancient Commentators and their Influence*. London: Duckworth.

Sorabji, R. 1991. "From Aristotle to Brentano: The Development of the Concept of Intentionality". See Blumenthal & Robinson (eds) (1991), 227–59.

Sorabji, R. 1993. *Animal Minds and Human Morals: The Origins of the Western Debate*. Ithaca, NY: Cornell University Press.

Sorabji, R. 1999. "Aspasius on Emotion". See Alberti & Sharples (eds) (1999), 96–106.

Sorabji, R. 2000. *Emotions and Peace of Mind: From Stoic Agitation to Christian Temptation*. Oxford: Oxford University Press.

Sorabji, R. 2004. *The Philosophy of the Commentators 200–600 AD: A Sourcebook. Volume 2: Physics*. London: Duckworth.

Sorabji, R. 2005. *The Philosophy of the Commentators 200–600 AD: A Sourcebook. Volume 1: Psychology (with Ethics and Religion)*. London: Duckworth.

Sorabji, R. 2005. *The Philosophy of the Commentators 200–600 AD: A Sourcebook. Volume 3: Logic and Metaphysics*. London: Duckworth.

Sorabji, R. 2006. "Universals Transformed: The First Thousand Years After Plato". In *Universals, Concepts and Qualities: New Essays on the Meaning of Predicates*, P. F. Strawson & A. Chakrabarti (eds), 105–25. Aldershot: Ashgate.

Strange, S. K. 1987. "Plotinus, Porphyry, and the Neoplatonic Interpretation of the *Categories*". *Aufstieg und Niedergang der römischen Welt* (*ANRW*) II **36**(2): 955–74.

Stump, E. 1978. *Boethius's De topicis differentiis*, trans. with notes and essay. Ithaca, NY: Cornell University Press.

Tardieu, M. 1987. "Les calendriers en usage à Harran d'après les sources arabes et le commentaire de Simplicius à la *Physique* d'Aristote". See Hadot (ed.) (1987a), 40–57.

Tardieu, M. 1990. *Les paysages reliques: Routes et haltes syriennes d'Isidore à Simplicius*. Louvain: Peeters.

Tarrant, H. 1985. *Scepticism or Platonism: The Philosophy of the Fourth Academy?* Cambridge: Cambridge University Press.

Thiel, R. 1999. *Simplikios und das Ende der neuplatonischen Schule in Athen*. Stuttgart: Steiner.

Thijssen, J. M. M. H. & H. A. G. Braakhuis (eds) 1999. *The Commentary Tradition on Aristotle's De Generatione et Corruptione: Ancient, Medieval and Early Modern*. Turnhout: Brepols.

Todd, R. 1976. *Alexander of Aphrodisias on Stoic Physics*. Leiden: Brill.

Todd, R. 1996. *Themistius on Aristotle on the Soul*. London: Duckworth.

Tuominen, M. 2007a. *Apprehension and Argument: Ancient Theories of Starting Points for Knowledge*. Dordrecht: Springer.

Tuominen, M. 2007b. "How Do We Know the Principles?". In *Erfahrung und Beweis: Die Wissenschaften von der Natur im 13. und 14. Jahrhundert*, A. Fidora & M. Lutz-Bachmann (eds), 11–22. Berlin: Akademie.

Tuominen, M. (forthcoming). "Alexander and Philoponus on the *Prior Analytics* I 27–30: Is there Tension between Aristotle's Scientific Theory and Practice?". In *Interpretations of the* Posterior Analytics, F. A. J. de Haas, forthcoming.

Vanderspoel, J. 1995. *Themistius and the Imperial Court: Oratory, Civic Duty, and Paideia from Constantius to Theodosius*. Ann Arbor, MI: University of Michigan Press.

Verrycken, K. 1990. "The Development of Philoponus' Thought and its Chronology". See Sorabji (ed.) (1990), 233–74.

Wagner, T. & C. Rapp (comments & trans.) 2004. *Aristoteles "Topik"*. Stuttgart: Reclam.

Watts, E. 2006. *City and School in Late Antique Athens and Alexandria*. Berkeley, CA: University of California Press.

Wedin, M. V. 1991. "PARTisanship in *Metaphysics Z*". *Ancient Philosophy* **11**: 361–85.

Westerink, L. G. 1990. "The Alexandrian Commentators and the Introductions to Their Commentaries". See Sorabji (ed.) (1990), 325–48.

Westfall, R. S. 1972. "Circular Motion in Seventeenth-Century Mechanics", *Isis* **63**: 184–9.

Whiting, J. E. 1986. "Form and Individuation in Aristotle". *History of Philosophy Quarterly* **3**: 359–77.

Wiesner, J. (ed.) 1987. *Aristoteles: Werk und Wirkung, Paul Moraux gewidmet*, vol. 2. Berlin: de Gruyter.

Wians, W. 1989. "Aristotle, Demonstration and Teaching". *Ancient Philosophy* **9**: 245–53.

Wians, W. 1990. "Commentary on Lloyd". *Proceedings of the Boston Area Colloquium in Ancient Philosophy* **VI**: 402–12.

Wilberding, J. 2005. "Creeping Spatiality: 'The Location of *Nous* in Plotinus' Universe'". *Phronesis* **50**(4): 315–34.

Wildberg, C. 1990. "Three Neoplatonic Introductions to Philosophy: Ammonius, David and Elias". *Hermathena* **149**: 33–51.

Wolff, M. 1987. "Philoponus and the Rise of Preclassical Dynamics". See Sorabji (ed.) (1987), 84–120.

Zeller, E. 1903. *Die Philosophie der Griechen in ihrer geschichtliche Entwiklung*, 4th edn, part 3, volume 1, E. Wellmann (ed.). Hildesheim: Georg Olms.

Index

on sociability 271–2
attention 163, 182–4
axioms 51–2, 85–6, 88–101

Baltussen, H. 2, 4, 288 n.3
Barnes, J. 5, 14, 18, 82–3, 110, 237–8,
        293 n.8, 294 n.23, 298 n.1, 299 n.1
Blumenthal, H. J. 35–6
Boethius 30, 39, 82, 202, 214
Bossier, F. 35–6, 160
Burnyeat, M. 165

Cantor, G. 157
Carneades 54, 248
categories
    application 204–7
    notion of 203–4
    Plotinus' criticism of 204, 210–12
    spatiotemporal 212–16
causes
    natural *versus* artificial 119, 123–4,
        126–7, 132–3, 144–6
    final causation 136–44
    the existence of ends in nature 137–9
    in relation to cosmic design 142–4
    in relation to mechanism 139–41
    four Aristotelian causes 127–9
        combined with Platonic causes
        129–32
    as principles of knowledge 81, 86–7,
        90–93
    soul as a natural cause 133–6, 150–55
celestial motion 150–55
Cicero 5–6
concepts 98–9, 162, 187–8, 192–7, 208,
        221, 223
    conceptual priority 89–90
    conceptual reasoning 158–9, 206
creation *see* universe, eternal *versus*
        created

Damascius 34
David 33, 291 n.36 (Elias?)
de Libera, A. 30, 39–40, 202, 293 n.7
detachment from the body 253–5,
        258–65, 269, 273–4, 277–9

dialectic in enquiry 115–17

Ebbesen, S. 24, 39, 293 n.7
Elias 33, 201, 222, 291 n.36 (David?)
Emilsson, E. K. 84, 168, 293 n.10
emotions
    cognitivist interpretation and its
        critique 265–70
    see also happiness and emotions
Epictetus 35, 239–40, 252–3, 255, 264,
        268–9, 272, 291 n.42, 299 n.2,
        299 n.5
epistemological foundationalism
        68–9
eternity *see* universe

Fazzo, S. 5–6, 289 n.20
forms 45, 83–4, 88, 101, 120–22,
        128–9, 131–2, 137, 140–43, 148–
        50, 161, 165, 171–2, 176–7, 180,
        187–91, 198, 201, 205–6, 227–36
    argument forms and logical forms
        see logic
    forms as substances 209–12
    forms and universals 217–26
function argument 241–2
Frede, M. 5, 18, 229, 290 n.21
friendship (*philia*) 249–50, 270–73

Galen 21, 23, 123–4, 174, 278, 293 n.4
Gerson, L. P. 10, 12, 289 n.10, 293 n.9

Haas, F. A. J. de 148–50, 206–7
Hadot, I. 4, 15, 32, 35–6, 239, 289
        n.18
happiness (*eudaimonia*) 111, 114,
        240–41
    and emotions 255–65
    and virtue 241–4, 247–55
Hermeias 32–4

Iamblichus 10, 27, 30–31, 36, 179,
        207–8, 215–16, 222, 226, 235,
        298 n.9
identity of intellect to its object
        161–2, 189